MEXICAN SOCIETY
DURING THE REVOLUTION

Mexican Society during the Revolution

A LITERARY APPROACH

JOHN RUTHERFORD

CLARENDON PRESS · OXFORD

1971

Oxford University Press, Ely House, London W.1

GLASGOW NEW YORK TORONTO MELBOURNE WELLINGTON
CAPE TOWN IBADAN NAIROBI DAR ES SALAAM LUSAKA ADDIS ABABA
DELHI BOMBAY CALCUTTA MADRAS KARACHI LAHORE DACCA
KUALA LUMPUR SINGAPORE HONG KONG TOKYO

PRINTED IN GREAT BRITAIN
BY THE CAMELOT PRESS, LTD.,
LONDON AND SOUTHAMPTON

FOR MY PARENTS

PREFACE

MEXICANS now spell the Revolution which started in their country in 1910 with a capital 'R'. It is, for them, not just another revolution, one more of the many civil wars for which Latin America, and Mexico in particular, has become notorious in the western world: it is the Revolution. Since its conclusion, Mexican society has gradually evolved a stability and a relative prosperity unique in Latin America—the notion that still persists in European folk-lore that Mexico is the country of revolutions is at least fifty years out of date. Furthermore, the society that emerged at the end of the Mexican Revolution was quite different from the society of pre-revolutionary times. Unlike the succession of nineteenth-century uprisings which gained Mexico her notoriety, the 1910 Revolution can be said to have made significant and lasting changes in Mexican society: so much so that it is normally considered a cross-roads in Mexican history, a decisive event by which vital and irrevocable decisions were taken regarding Mexico's development and after which nothing could ever be the same again.

Although the social sense of the Mexican Revolution is what gives it its special importance, the history of what exactly happened to Mexican society during it has hardly been touched upon. Several sound and scholarly books analysing the political events of the Revolution have been published, principally by American writers, but its social history has been little more than alluded to. The main reason for this gap is, perhaps, the difficulty of obtaining the documentary data upon which to base a satisfactory study. The written material that could throw light on this aspect of the Revolution (both personal accounts, like diaries and letters, and statistical evidence, like municipal records) is scant and elusive. Newspapers, heavily censored during most of the Revolution, are insufficient by themselves as a basis for a social study.

In spite of all the scholarly work that has been done on the subject of the Mexican Revolution, then, the central problem of what is meant in human and social terms to the Mexicans who lived through it has not been tackled at all. The exact nature and mechanism of the rapid social changes that took place during this period

of intensive turmoil; the process of the creation of new classes and
the annihilation or reshaping of old ones; the rearrangement of the
complex and delicately balanced network of relationships between
the various component parts of society; the emergence of certain
temporary revolutionary classes, formed in response to the particular needs of a military situation, and dispersed into the new social
order once the Revolution was over: all of these and many other
social movements which give the Revolution its special significance
in Mexican history, and out of which modern Mexico has sprung,
remain uncharted. They are vital changes, but hard to follow
because they occur under the surface of events. They are the sub-
marine currents whose hidden flow helps to create the visible
swell and waves above—the struggle for power, the manifestos, the
battles, the political documents.

A social study of the Mexican Revolution seems, in short, to be
called for. In view of the lack of other data for such a study, this is
a suitable field in which to try out an approach to social history
which has hardly ever been essayed in any detail: the use of the
novel as a principal source of information. Very many novels—
nearly 150—have been written about the Mexican Revolution,
most of them serious attempts to portray imaginatively, but realistically and accurately, the human events that are the concern of the
social historian. It has often been remarked that the novels of the
Mexican Revolution have considerable documentary value; yet no
worthwhile attempt has yet been made to follow this observation
up and to use them as sources for the social history of the period
they refer to. There is a great store of otherwise inaccessible
information here, if a satisfactory method of extracting and
evaluating it can be evolved.

The purpose of this book is, then, to put to the test of practice,
in a particularly suitable field, the literary approach to historical
sociology: to see whether the idea of using novels as sources can be
made to yield reliable results. To do this, it will be necessary to
compile an outline social history of the Mexican Revolution, based
principally on the novels.

Because of considerations of length, marginal or peripheral sectors of the Revolution—like the special happenings in, for example,
Lower California and Yucatán—can only be dealt with incidentally. The Zapatista revolution in the south, too, was in so many
respects a separate movement that it can hardly be considered in

the same terms as the rest of the Revolution. In many ways it was a completely different and independent revolution which happened to occur at the same time as the movements led by Madero, Villa, and Carranza. Furthermore, the novelists of the Revolution do not have much to say about it. Many of the general points made in this study do not, therefore, apply to Zapatismo. The phenomenon cannot be totally neglected in a general study of this sort; but where it is considered here, we shall principally be concerned to evaluate its social significance within the national struggle as a whole, and to indicate how the rest of revolutionary Mexico saw the Zapatistas. To tell the 'inside story' of Zapatismo demands a separate book altogether. Such a book has recently been written by John Womack (*Zapata and the Mexican Revolution*, New York, 1969).

The Mexican Revolution was a vastly complex phenomenon, spanning a huge area of territory and many years in time: there is room in a general study of this nature only for the consideration of what seem to be the central elements of overall importance in it. For the inhabitants of each different village, town, and city in Mexico the Revolution was a different experience, and a general treatment can only aspire to bring together most of the common factors in this multiple process.

The book has three introductory chapters. Chapter 1 examines the crucial question of methodology, and evolves the technique which it is proposed to apply to the project of using the novels as principal sources for the study of the social history of the Mexican Revolution. Chapter 2 gives a concise survey of the political history of the Mexican Revolution. It is not the purpose of this book to study this side of the problem in any detail; this chapter is merely meant to be a summary guide for the purpose of reference. Chapter 3 seeks to describe in overall terms the novels that we are concerned with. It is a discussion of the manner of their writing, their general nature, the chronology of their production, the influences at work on them, and so on.

After this general introduction in three chapters to the method, subject, and sources of this study, an analytical social history follows in four chapters. It is convenient to separate the society of a country in revolution into two camps: the revolutionaries and the anti-revolutionaries. Three chapters are devoted to the revolutionaries, one to each of the principal components of any revolutionary movement: the intellectuals, who guide, plan, and co-ordinate it; the leaders, who provide it with its symbolic figureheads and its mythology; and the fighting masses, who do its physical work. One chapter is then concerned with the Revolution's various enemies: the old ruling élites, foreign interests, the Church, the Army, the bureaucracy.

The desired result of this combination of the disciplines of literary criticism, historiography, and sociology is to illustrate what the Mexican Revolution meant in concrete, human terms to those who lived through it and, in one way or another, more or less actively, participated in it; to chart the social currents flowing through it; and hence to demonstrate that the novel can indeed provide valid documentation of social history, and that it can profitably be used, together with other sources, for historiographical and sociological purposes.

So many people have contributed directly or indirectly to this book that I can only mention a few of them. I owe an immense debt of gratitude, above all, to two men: to Professor P. E. Russell, who drew my attention to the possibilities of the subject, who supervised my work in its earliest stages, and who has generously given his wise advice at crucial points in its subsequent progress; and to Mr. A. R. M. Carr, the Warden of St. Antony's College, Oxford, who supervised most of my work for the D.Phil. thesis on which this book is based, with unfailing patience, sagacity, and good humour.

I am also indebted to the Astor Foundation, for a generous grant which paid for my research in Mexico City, in 1964–5; to St. Antony's College, Oxford, for supporting me during most of the subsequent period of preparation of this book; and to my present college, The Queen's College, Oxford, for financing the preparation of the final typescript.

Among other individuals who have given their kind help in various ways I should like specially to mention Professor Dámaso Alonso, Señor Héctor Mendoza, Señor Luis Miravalles, Dr. Alastair Hennessy and the late Miss Irene Nicholson.

CONTENTS

'You can, if you please, turn
[history] into literature—a collection
of stories and legends about the past
without meaning or significance.'

E. H. CARR, *What is History?*, 2nd
edition, Harmondsworth, 1967,
p. 132.

I

NOVELS AS HISTORICAL SOURCES

NOVELS are the principal sources of information for this study of the social history of the Mexican Revolution. There are several obvious and fundamental objections that might be raised against this unorthodox way of approaching social history, and they must be answered. Is not the novel one thing and history something wholly different? Is there any possible justification for using fiction as a source of factual evidence? Does not this whole approach pre-suppose an intolerable relaxation of the careful and rigorous criteria vital to proper historiography? The methodology of the subject clearly demands close theoretical examination before any progress can be made.

We may begin by observing that there is a much closer connection between literature and life than is often allowed. Literature is not a ghostly disembodied element, living in an isolated world of its own and feeding solely on itself: a discipline solely to be considered in its own terms. On the contrary, like all art and all products of human endeavour, it occurs in a social context, in a certain milieu, and it is necessarily shaped and moulded by that milieu. It is a product of social man, indissolubly tied to his life and environment. A novelist can ultimately only reproduce his own experience in his novels, for however much he employs his individual imagination and sentiment in their creation, these in themselves are two of so many elements moulded and formed by the novelist's experience of life in his particular environment. In literature and in all art the common style of an epoch is a social phenomenon, to be interpreted in the light of its historical context; and the individual variations of this common style add further to our full knowledge and understanding of it, in so far as the complete social complex at any given place and time is the product of the common elements and the individual divergences from them. The whole body of literature of an age is a historical occurrence; and literary history is fully meaningful only if its links with social, economic and political history are examined and defined, and the reciprocal relations and influences between literature and other spheres of human activity properly explored.

This social view of literature is not even now, of course, universally accepted. It has been most notably challenged in the recent past by the New Humanists of the United States and, more recently still, by the New Critics of France. The former held that the peculiar domain of literature is all that which is most typically and essentially human, freed from the restricting confines of particular historical ambiences; only thus could literature fulfil its functions of illustrating eternal ethical problems to man, who—since his moral struggle is an inner one—can only confront them on an individual basis. The New Critics consider a work of literature to be a structure of words, possessing an autonomous identity as such, and to be studied for its own sake; in this structure, only the inner patterns which make it a structure are relevant, not any hypothetical connections with life as a whole. Both schools of criticism, while asserting important points about the nature of literature, seem to make the error of taking up an unnecessarily exclusive attitude. If there are such things as eternal truths about human nature, literature is no doubt an excellent medium for charting and exploring them; but this view of literature is in no way irreconcilable with the view that it is also a medium for the documentation of specific historical and social situations. This is particularly true of the novel, for however much the novelist may be concerned with revealing general truths about humanity, the tradition of the genre which he has decided to cultivate press him to attempt to do so by means of the description of specific, historically-defined human situations within which these general truths may be examined. And the New Critics' important theory that a work of literature is a total structure with its own inner workings and principles controlling them, is perfectly compatible with the assertion that these individual structures have close, though complex relationships with all the other structures and systems into which we can divide existence (the economic and social structures of the group; the physiological and psychological structures of the individual).

We may come to the conclusion that all literature, like all human activity, is influenced by its material environment: the influence merely varies in degree. Some writers consistently strive to free their art from the immediate, specific, and transient; and some writers seek only to portray man within his immediate, specific and transient surroundings. There is—to take examples from the field of poetry in Spanish—the approach of the Góngora, the Saint John of the Cross, the Rubén Darío; and there is the approach of the Antonio Machado and the Pablo Neruda. The former sort of writer, however hard he tries to dissociate his art from his surroundings in his search for absolute truth and beauty, can never wholly succeed in doing so; the latter sort sees the only possible way of approaching truth and beauty as via the specific and concrete. The modern realistic novel clearly adopts the second approach to the problem of artistic creation; it is, then, the novel, because of its detailed realistic human content, whose connections with history are the most transparently obvious, if not the strongest and closest.

And this last observation is even more relevant to the twentieth-century Latin-American novel than to the modern European novel. It is a consistent feature of the modern novel in Latin America, with few exceptions (mainly to be found among Argentinian writers), that it is not only realistic but also basically sociological; in other words that it is primarily concerned with the problems of a specific society: its aim is to record and analyse these problems and possibly suggest a solution for them. The sociological novel can thus be distinguished from the psychological novel, mainly concerned with the examination of the mental processes and development of interesting or unusual human beings, or of people in interesting or unusual situations: social observation will inevitably be important in the realistic psychological novel, but it is not the main thing, as it is in the realistic sociological novel. The hero of a psychological novel is often created as an illustration of a general theme, and thought of as being to a large degree representative of common humanity—a figure who could occur, with slight variations, in any society. Galdós's *Fortunata y Jacinta* shows, amongst other things, the predicament of a poor girl in love with a rich, married man. It happens to be set in the Madrid of the late nineteenth century, but Fortunata's problem is not presented as particularly characteristic of this society. Galdós's principal object in this novel is not to make an analysis of class struggles in the Spain of his epoch, even though elements of these class struggles play an important role in his story—a more important role, perhaps, than Galdós himself is likely to have realized. As an example of a sociological novel the same author's earlier work *Doña Perfecta* will serve very well. Here, Galdós is not concerned so much with individual man and his problems as with the conflicts besetting late nineteenth-century Spanish society. The characters of this novel are conceived, live, move and have their being as functions of these problems, and could not exist without them. Doña Perfecta herself represents the reactionary intransigence to the liberal reforming effort for which Pepe Rey stands; and Orbajosa, as a whole, is a microcosm of Spanish society of the period. We turn to *Doña Perfecta*, then, as an illustration not of individual human psychology but of the struggle in nineteenth-century Spanish society between progressive and conservative forces.

Most modern Latin-American novels are sociological rather than psychological. They are concerned not so much with the psychological examination of interesting human types as with the specific sociological problems facing the peoples of various parts of Latin America; they tend to show individual characters as the children of their particular conditions, closely defined by the time and place within which their lives develop.

The novels of the Mexican Revolution have, as common characteristics, not only this sociological intent, but also a distinctly documentary nature and often a very strong autobiographical content[1] [ch. 3, esp. pp. 43–4]. They contain a greater proportion than do most novels of straightforward reporting of events seen and heard, and a smaller part than usual of the author's inner world, of imagined happenings. They seem to be more outward-looking than most: novels in which the element of pure observation is stronger than that of imagination or reorganization. It is this aspect of the novels of the Mexican Revolution that has given rise to an opinion about them which has been so often repeated that it has become a critical commonplace: that they are of more interest as reflections of the social problems that they deal with than for their strictly literary, aesthetic qualities[2] (an opinion often, indeed,

---

[1] Cross-references in this book are given in the text, inside square brackets.

[2] For example, Manuel Pedro González, *Trayectoria de la novela en México* (Mexico, 1951), pp. 97–8:
  By limiting his inventive powers to merely giving a faithful copy of the events and the protagonists of the Revolution, the novelist reduces the imaginative scope of his work and turns it into little more than a document, a more or less faithful portrait of an instant in the history of Mexico; and so its aesthetic worth is diminished.
The widespread idea that literature which seeks accurately to portray a particular

expressed about the whole body of Latin-American literature). It might seem, then, that the links between literature and society, always anyway strong and undeniable, are, in the case of the Mexican Revolution and the novels that describe its various facets, clear, direct, and uncomplicated. This, at least, is what many previous students of the subject have unquestioningly assumed. Like many a critics' cliché, however, this one is of more apparent than real validity. The early novels of the Revolution are often composed, as will be seen [pp. 72–4], from a very strongly biased or committed viewpoint, and present a picture of events which is coloured by the author's political opinions. The novels of the most important single author for this study, Mariano Azuela, are of a smaller propagandist importance than most of the other early ones, and they certainly appear to have great autobiographical and documentary content. *Los de abajo*, particularly, could well seem to be the account of Azuela's personal experiences in the Revolution, scarcely veiled by its fictional form.[3] Azuela himself has, however, attempted to refute this suggestion, and to show that his novel is, like any other, based on his personal experiences and on experiences that others have related to him, all reworked and reorganized to form a united, balanced and artistically pleasing whole.[4] None of the characters in *Los de abajo* are simply portrayals of real people, he claims, in spite of the alleged identifications of this sort that have been made; rather, each one is a combination of the various traits of character of several different people whom Azuela met during the Revolution: 'Most of the events I relate were not witnessed by me: they were constructed, or reconstructed, out of various partial visions of people and events. Those who call *Los de abajo* a reportage are only revealing their ignorance, if by

society at a given historical moment is necessarily inferior to literature which deals with other aspects of life is based on some very questionable unspoken assumptions. (Translations are my own throughout.)

[3] Azuela served with the guerrilla band of Julián Medina in the state of Jalisco in 1914 and 1915. He performed the duties of camp doctor (Cervantes's medical knowledge is strongly stressed in *Los de abajo*). As a city-bred, educated man, he must have come up against the same sort of class alienation among the peasant guerrillas of Medina as does Cervantes among those of Macías. Medina's band, like that of Macías, only emerges from obscurity into the mainstream of the Revolution on two occasions: the assault on Zacatecas and the Convention at Aguascalientes. Azuela, like Cervantes, fled into exile and took up residence in El Paso, Texas.

[4] 'El novelista y su ambiente', in *Obras completas de Mariano Azuela* (Mexico, 1958–60), Vol. III, pp. 1079–86.

BM

that they mean that I wrote it in the manner of a chronicler or journalist . . . Many events are recounted quite differently from how I witnessed them.'[5] However much extra-literary motivation there might have been behind these retrospective statements of Azuela (the professional pride of the artist, wounded by the common critical opinion that his work is no more than a mere copy of events and consequently, by implication, lacking in aesthetic values; or simply the conscience of the man, anxious that unflattering portraits should not be interpreted as referring to previous companions in arms—or, of course, to himself) they are enough to call attention to the danger of accepting uncritically what appear at first sight to be unquestionable characteristics of these novels.

In spite of Azuela's protestations reproduced above, however, it is worth noting that he still affirmed that his motive for writing his novels of the Revolution was a socio-historical one: 'I can be accused of everything except of having distorted truth . . . One of the principal intentions of most of my novels has been to give a transcription of the medium and the moment which I have lived: that the reader might find in a couple of hundred pages what he could otherwise only get by drowning himself in a sea of printed papers.'[6] His implied point seems to be that in order to recapture in literary form the feeling and atmosphere of the Revolution he was not content just to reproduce slavishly what he saw and experienced, but that he made a genuine artistic effort: that he worked creatively, not just imitatively. He is, nevertheless, far from denying that his novels are of the type we have called 'sociological'.

The central and—for the present purposes—inconvenient fact to which we inevitably have to return is that art is never, and cannot ever be, simply a mirror of life, however much the artist may try to make it into one, however much he may even think he is succeeding in doing so (or, to put it differently and perhaps more accurately, life is not an external series of phenomena to be impassively reflected in a 'mirror'). As Percy Lubbock puts it, a novel is life which 'has passed through an imagination'[7]—as also, one might add, is any statement about life. At the very most, then, a novel can only be a 'distorting mirror', for there is unavoidably every kind of hidden influence working on even the most apparently

[5] *Obras completas de Mariano Azuela*, Vol. III, pp. 1082 and 1086.
[6] Ibid., p. 1098.   [7] *The Craft of Fiction* (London, 1966), p. 19.

unprejudiced author: he cannot be 'objective', for the simple reason that he is a human being, is a part of what he is describing. Political, class, religious, psychological factors, probably largely unknown to the novelist himself, make him see and report things in a certain special light. Even the cinema documentary, surely the most objective form of art imaginable, is a personal and therefore biased account of the subject it deals with; for the movie camera has to be controlled by someone, who will obviously point it at the scenes he is personally interested in showing. And, as far as literature is concerned, even the most 'realistic' novels, like those of the Mexican Revolution, are careful selections from life rearranged according to various personal criteria. Each novel is a view of reality through one pair of eyes, with all their defects and blind spots; it is impossible for it to be otherwise, for no man can eradicate his subjective attitude towards the behaviour of his fellow men, however hard he tries. Even a coldly dispassionate view of events reflects in itself a subjective, individual attitude, and represents the artist's personal outlook on life.

Every work of art is, then, a synthesis of the artist and his world, a fusion of the individual and society. The novel may, perhaps, usually have a greater proportion of social content than other forms of art, but the definitive importance of the individual viewpoint from which the social is portrayed is as undeniable in the novel as in any other genre. The basic problem of the use of novels as historical sources is, then, that of establishing the exact relationship in them between the individual and the social, the subjective and the objective, of identifying each factor and distinguishing one from the other. The terms 'objective' and 'subjective' are misleading, but the ensuing theoretical discussion would be impossible without recourse to them. They imply the false dichotomy of, on the one hand, a world existing outside and independent of the individual and his perception of it; and on the other a personal imagination arbitrarily imposed on this world. The 'pure' objectivity of certain scientists is as much a myth as the 'pure' subjectivity of some artists: for the 'objective' world is only perceived through the senses of the individual; and the individual's 'subjective' attitudes are really no more than a special permutation —determined, above all, by his social experience—of many separate social attitudes. Only by attempting a breakdown of this extremely complex interaction, however, is it possible to investigate the relationship between literature and society, and discover exactly how far and in what ways art does reproduce life. All analysis is artificial; this fact does not invalidate the idea of analysis.

There are, then, two kinds of information to be acquired and carefully distinguished between: information which we can conveniently categorize respectively as personal or subjective (information about the author himself and his artistic method) and social or objective (information about the world the novelist lives in and writes about). This knowledge, assembled from the novels themselves and from outside the novels, is indispensable for the accurate analysis of the texts.

We must first consider the particular artistic method of the novelist under consideration. A prime distinction can be made between two sorts of novelist: those who have been styled 'ethical' and those who have been styled 'aesthetic'.[8] The former are concerned to point out the differences between society as it is and as they think it ought to be; the main *raison d'être* of their work is social criticism. The ethical novelist can be expected to tend towards satire and caricature in those parts of his novels which refer to social phenomena of which he disapproves; and, conversely, towards romantic idealization and sentimentalism when writing about characters or events representing real or utopian social phenomena which enjoy his sympathy. The ethical novelist also tends to create certain characters whose sole function in the novel is to give explicit voice to the novelist's own opinions (many of the characters of, for example, D. H. Lawrence are of this sort). These personal mouthpieces are usually endowed with extraordinary dignity, authority, wisdom, and foresight. They must clearly be handled with care by the critic who attempts a social interpretation of the novel; they do not belong to the same plane of creation as the other characters in a novel: as embodiments of the novelist's wisdom after the event they come from outside the world on to which they are grafted (Azuela makes frequent use of this device of idealized self-projection [pp. 87–92]). The aesthetic novelist, on the other hand, seeks to describe society simply as it is,

---

[8] Ernst Kohn-Bramstedt, *Aristocracy and the Middle Classes* (London, 1937), introduction, 'The Sociological Approach to Literature'. Kohn-Bramstedt is the only scholar who has recognized and faced up to the complexities of the approach to literature that seeks to extract social information from it directly as well as indirectly. The ensuing discussion of methodology is based upon a development of his ideas.

showing indiscriminately, and without explicit or implicit comment, just as much the good as the evil in it, its beauty and its ugliness. His works are much less liable to distortion. One might call Dickens an outstanding example of an ethical novelist: his strong feelings about social injustice lead him frequently to sentimentalize the suffering poor and to caricature those who make them suffer. Balzac could be cited among the many examples of primarily aesthetic novelists, whose principal concern is to understand and, as far as possible, to sympathize with all types of people, however apparently unattractive or unpleasant or immoral, in order to give a rounded, credible, and realistic portrait of them.

The 'aesthetic' novelist is, of course, a wholly abstract and hypothetical proposition. The completely 'aesthetic' or 'objective' writer cannot exist, as we have already shown. This does not invalidate the distinction so long as it is remembered that it is a purely theoretical one, useful as a convenient way of identifying the various grades of 'distortion' one can expect to find in novels; and that it should not lead one into accepting that any given novelist, because of the apparent 'realism' of his work, is of the 'aesthetic' sort and consequently an unambiguous and straightforward source of information for the social historian. The 'aesthetic' novel is simply an imaginary desideratum, to which certain works may approximate more than others.

There are several other influences at work on any novelist to make his portrayal of life vary from 'objective' historical truth. It is important to establish, for example, the class position of the novelist under consideration: not so much the class he was born into, for writers, like all intellectuals, very often put themselves in the service of another class; but rather the class he represents. This is a particularly important consideration in the socio-historical study of novels of revolution, because of the weighty role that political or religious propaganda inevitably plays in many of them.

Another influence of great importance is that of previous literary tradition. Although literature does not feed solely on itself, as the formal, aesthetic school of literary criticism appears to assume, neither does it feed only on society, as some crude Marxist criticism presupposes. It does, indeed, feed on itself to the extent that any author must of necessity have been brought up in a certain cultural atmosphere, the product of past achievements and discoveries. The weight of this vast body of tradition bears heavily upon even the most revolutionary novelist, and it makes him think and write about things in a certain light. Indeed, the very fact that he has to use language—a system of communication forged and developed not by him, according to his own special needs, but developed by successive generations of his ancestors on the basis of theirs—means in itself that he is subjected, like it or not, to certain very considerable formal limitations imposed by the past.[9] As for strictly literary influences, there are two important kinds to be discerned in the early novels of the Mexican Revolution, both heritages of the nineteenth century. They are realism and naturalism on the one hand (particularly in Azuela), and sentimentalism and romanticism on the other. They display in these novels the continuous influence of the past on the present. Such a literary influence is not, however—and this fact is most convenient for our purposes—as strong in the novels of the Mexican Revolution as in other literature. Precisely because they are revolutionary novels, the works under study tend on the whole to have only relatively slight literary affiliations. The Revolution produced a whole new literary élite, the members of which attempted as far as they could to free themselves from tradition; and to some extent they succeeded [ch. 3]. We may further observe that the very tradition of literary realism, which exerted a conscious or unconscious influence on all our novelists, encouraged them to write precisely as the social historian who seeks to use their novels as documents would wish them to write.

A further factor of possible importance to make a novelist distort reality in his writing is the psychological one. A man passing through a period of spiritual or mental crisis is less likely to view what goes on around him with equanimity and impassiveness than one who is tranquil and at peace with the world. In a period of civil war the national crisis affects individual psychology in a radical way; so the former state of mind is very much more common than the latter, in the non-belligerent as well as the fighting population. This is not altogether a disadvantage from our point of

---

[9] Blake uses the English language; and to say that he uses it is not to say that it is for him a mere instrument. His individuality has developed in terms of the language, with the ways of experiencing, as well as of handling experience, that it involves. The mind and sensibility that he has to express are of the language.
F. R. Leavis, *The Common Pursuit* (Harmondsworth 1966), pp. 186–7. (See also Stephen Ullman, *Language and Style* (Oxford, 1964), pp. 205–62.)

view, however: a witness's emotional involvement in events can also strengthen his observation and subsequent memory of them. Although it can give rise to distortion, psychological disturbance can also, in a compensatory way, make for a considerably heightened perception.

The literary approach to social history depends first of all, then, on a careful, exhaustive, and detailed examination of all those influences—literary, class, political, religious, psychological, or whatever—at work on the author under consideration, in order to make it possible subsequently to locate those parts of the picture he paints of reality which are most likely to be subject to distortion, and to know what kind of distortion to expect. If it consists of straightforward misrepresentation, the evidence thus affected can be of little direct sociological value; if, however (as more often occurs) it is the result of a more subtle variation—change of emphasis, concentration on certain aspects of reality to the exclusion of others, or exaggeration, for example—it will perhaps be possible to correct it for historiographical purposes, by careful reinterpretation leading back to the factual basis of the distortion.

Let us pass on to the sound part of the preliminary knowledge that it is necessary to acquire before subjecting a novel to sociohistorical examination. This is as complete an acquaintance with the structure of society to which the novel refers and with the general history of its period as can be obtained from other sources. The critic thus complements his knowledge of the novelist's particular artistic methods with knowledge of the world he lived in and wrote about; and so the foundation is laid for the work of comparing the two on which, in turn, must be based any definition of the relationship between the novel and the social reality it seeks to reproduce. Into the firm framework of general sociological information constructed from orthodox sources of history one can then fit the extra data to be gleaned from the novels, with their different approach to reality: the general sociological base acts as the solid point of continual reference against which to check the validity of the observations derived from the novels, a further and indispensable safeguard against the element of distortion which is inevitable in all imaginative writing. It serves, one might say, as the essential skeleton on which must hang the more alive and moving, yet by itself less substantial flesh and blood of the information taken from novels.

There is, finally, another sort of comparison which can act as an extremely useful way of confirming evidence and ensuring that the distinction between historical fact and personal interpretation of it is kept clear in the analysis of the novels. This is the correlation of the novels themselves. If a certain social phenomenon appears similarly reflected in several different works by separate and unrelated authors of diverse artistic procedures, class positions, and so on, the testimony can be considered valid even if not directly confirmed in 'factual' sources. Once all other possible explanations for the coincidence have been discounted, it is perfectly reasonable to assume that the recurrent appearance in novels of a stereotype is the consequence of independent and spontaneous observation by the various novelists of the same social phenomenon: that such a fictional stock figure is the representation of a social type with real existence in the life of the period. It is, indeed, precisely this kind of comparison which offers the most exciting possibilities of discovering new and original information unavailable elsewhere.

The method we are to adopt consists of an inductive-deductive process. From a preliminary study of the novelists, their art and their world, one acquires a basic framework of knowledge about both the subjective and the objective elements which, fused together, give the novels; and then one can use this framework, in turn, as a basis for the detailed analysis of the chosen texts, to glean from them the extra information that they contain. It is a demanding and complicated method, admittedly—in part, because it requires the equipment not only of the historian and sociologist but also of the literary critic. F. R. Leavis stresses this important point:

Literature will yield to the sociologist, or anyone else, what it has to give only if it is approached as literature . . . no attempt to relate literary studies with sociological will yield much profit unless informed and controlled by a real and intelligent interest—a first hand critical interest —in literature. That is, no use of literature is of any use unless it is a real use; literature isn't so much material lying there to be turned over from the outside, and drawn on, for reference and exemplification, by the critically inert . . . the sociologist here will be a literary critic or nothing . . . The possible uses of literature to the historian and the sociologist are many in kind, and all the important ones demand that the user shall be able, in the fullest sense, to read. If, for instance, we want to go further than the mere constatation that a century and a half ago the family counted for much more than it does now, if we want some notion of the difference involved in day-to-day living—in the sense of life and its dimensions and in its emotional and moral accenting—for the ordinary cultivated person, we may profitably start trying to form it from the novels of Jane Austen. But only if we are capable of appreciating shade, tone, implication and essential structure—as (it is necessary to add) none of the academically, or fashionably, accredited authorities seems to be.[10]

In spite of the difficulties and the pitfalls of this literary approach to social history, it is worth attempting to put it into practice. The novel is unique in its approach to the description of social reality; one must at least try to tap this hitherto almost unexploited source of social history. The novel, especially the 'realistic' novel, and above all the 'sociological' novel, sets out to capture living, moving reality, as exemplified in individual, concrete cases. It attempts to get beneath the surface of social life. Its subject is the inner struggles of a society or of an individual, precisely those conflicts which are normally carefully hidden and, consequently, difficult to uncover. One can often therefore find better illustration in the novel than elsewhere of such complex social problems as class struggles, race relations, religious attitudes, personal loyalties, and so on. The novel reveals, then, things which the orthodox sources of history cannot reveal, in their tendency to portray humanity *en masse* and on the surface. From the novelist's description of society one can glean and piece together into a complete picture those little details of conduct that can reveal so much. The realistic novel is animated social history; it is precisely the animation which makes it as a source both dangerous if not handled properly and uniquely revealing if used with care.

The sociological interpretation of the novel can well be compared with the role of field work for the student of modern sociology or anthropology. The sociologist goes to live in the society he is studying, interviewing members of that society and generally doing everything possible to get to grips with its hidden motivations. He takes information from various sources within the group under observation, and then he sifts and interprets that information, always making allowances for the various biases and prejudices that might have influenced his informants. For the sociological survey of a past epoch, the nearest we can get to such a

[10] Leavis, pp. 193, 198, 200, and 203.

procedure is in the study of contemporary testimonies of the life of the society we are concerned with—the novels of the period.[11] The novelists are the informants—unusually willing and eloquent informants—and the sifting and interpreting of the information they provide is a very similar process to the one the field sociologist or anthropologist must go through.

The comparisons with normal sociological method can be pursued in more detail. The historian and the sociologist are often primarily concerned with statistically verifiable evidence. Perhaps it is not stretching a point too far to suggest that the sociological novelist provides evidence of this sort, too, even though he does not furnish any figures. Since it is his aim to give an accurate and representative portrayal of a given society, he will naturally strive to make his novel a microcosm of it; and so he includes characters and situations that he regards as typical of the society portrayed, not as idiosyncratic or unusual. He will depend, in his characterization, very heavily upon the stereotype, the figure who, though he may possess certain individual qualities, is representative of a whole class or group within the society portrayed—in other words, he attempts to make a typical case-study. Each character in a sociological novel is, then, the synthesis of all those of this sort that the novelist has known or known about in life. We cannot know, for example, how many revolutionary intellectuals of Mariano Azuela's acquaintance were fused together to make Luis Cervantes [pp. 96–100], or how many were combined to give other similar fictional portrayals of members of this social group in other novels; but the accumulative factor is nonetheless important in their creation. Considered as a group with many common characteristics, these stereotyped revolutionary intellectuals do provide statistically valid evidence, of the sort that the historian and the sociologist demand. Each stands for many—even though we are not told *how* many—and, taken altogether, they can fairly be said to stand for the whole social group.

The method laid out above for the sociological approach to the novel is not, then, so foreign to normal historiographical discipline after all. 'Orthodox' historical sources have, in fact, to be treated

[11] Even for the student of a comparatively recent event such as the Mexican Revolution, personal interviews provide very little valid sociological information. During the fifty years that have elapsed direct memories of the event have not only deteriorated but also been materially altered—usually embittered—by subsequent developments.

with as much circumspection as prose fiction, for exactly the same fundamental reason: all men necessarily have a prejudiced view of reality and tend, consciously or unconsciously, to twist the account they render of events to suit their particular bias or interests. No objective account of a system can be given from within that system. The writer of allegedly factual accounts of human affairs is just as liable to be prejudiced (that is, he is just as human) as the novelist, and in some ways his report of events can be even more dangerously misleading: for his account is arbitrarily and unquestioningly categorized as 'fact' and the novelist's as 'fiction', as if the two were absolute opposites. In reality the difference is simply one of degree; and nowhere is this fact better illustrated than in the novels of the Mexican Revolution [pp. 40–5].

The method outlined above starts from two bases, knowledge about the novelist and knowledge about his world: the new information it is designed to uncover can be similarly categorized. There is the new information about the 'objective' world, derived from those parts of the novels in which life is quite closely 'mirrored', where we can find out about problems of class, race, religion, and so on, with all the above-mentioned advantages of studying them in prose fiction. And there is the new information about the novelist's exact relationship with this objective world. The authors of novels written about a society from within that society are, of course, themselves part of the social processes they describe. Therefore those very 'distortions', biases, prejudices, exaggerations, and idiosyncrasies which we find in their accounts of society are in themselves of interest in reflecting social attitudes, particularly those of the intellectual group and of the other groups that each member of it can be seen to represent. The theory of causation governing each novel, its structure, style, characterization, and general artistic method, are all reflections of the sociology of the artist and intellectual, and of the society that produced him. It is particularly useful to find the answers to such questions as: what is missing in the novels that one would expect to find? What is given more prominence than it appears to merit? And what particular class interests was the novelist serving, what particular class attitudes was he voicing, in thus 'misrepresenting' reality?

The distinction between these two kinds of information is, to some extent, a false one. The subjective and the objective in a work of art form, as remarked above, a fusion or synthesis, and they cannot be precisely separated and placed in isolated compartments: there is no absolutely clear division between the two in literature (any more than there is in life), for the novelist (the 'subjective') is a part of the world he lives in (the 'objective'). But any attempt at serious literary criticism necessarily involves the critic in the exercise of analytically compartmentalizing the diverse elements that, welded together in intricate patterns, make up the work of art. The fact that a watertight division is ultimately impossible, because of the very nature of art and of life, in no way invalidates, however, the attempt to analyse, so long as the analyst always bears humbly in mind the fluidity and intricacy of the subject of his attention.

This, then, is the method for the literary approach to social history which it is proposed to follow in this study. It differs from regular historiographical and sociological approaches not, in fact, so much in method itself, as in the nature of the goal which the method is designed to enable us to reach. The expression 'objective historical truth' has been used during the above discussion: indeed, the discussion has necessarily turned about this concept. What the literary approach to history proposes is that an area of meaning which the term does cover, but which historians sometimes neglect, be made the subject of more careful and methodical study.

It has often been observed that there are two different approaches to reality, and there has been much argument about their relative validity. The 'quantitative' or 'scientific' approach claims to concern itself with empirically verifiable facts: for the scientist the spade is a long, shaped piece of wood—of a certain molecular structure—with a flat piece of metal—of a certain chemical composition—attached to one end. The 'qualitative' or 'artistic' approach is concerned with the invisible affective connotations of objects and the relationships between them: the artist sees the spade as a symbol of the dignity of manual work, or of the charms of the suburban garden, or of the unpleasantness of mindless drudgery. The literary approach to social history simply stresses that in the studies of past societies the connotations are at least as relevant as the phenomena, and indeed are an inseparable part of them: that connotations as well as phenomena enter into the meaning of the expression 'objective historical truth'. Historians do, in fact, pay attention to the connotations—it would be impossible for them to avoid doing so—but often in a rather haphazard way. This approach sets out to be a methodical study of the connotations. In this study the expression 'objective historical truth' does not, then, refer only to a series of measurable phenomena, but also to the affective and invisible relationships between them and to their qualitative properties. Such relationships and properties exist only so far as men can apprehend them—as also, of course, do the measurable phenomena and the instruments with which they are measured. If the adjective 'objective' can be applied to the one (where it is, of course, very loosely applied [pp. 6–7]) it can be equally well applied to the other, so long as these affective properties and relationships are ones about whose existence there can be shown to have been a sufficiently broad consensus among observers for them to be socially relevant. It follows from this that the word 'distortion' when used in this work (it has been used several times already) refers simply to significant individual variation from this consensus, with regard to both quantitative and qualitative data.

The aim of this study is to open new perspectives of social history. It is not proposed to find mere illustrations of facts already known about the Mexican Revolution, nor to record the processes more or less common to all civil wars—the anarchy, economic collapse, hunger, slaughter, moral decline, and so on—which enter into the general picture but are not in themselves (viewed from a comfortable distance) the main thing. We are concerned to define the particular characteristics of the Mexican Revolution and to trace the movements during it of the various groups that comprised Mexican society.

Nor are we concerned simply with the explicit opinions of the novelists about the Revolution, although this is certainly a part of the study. What matters in a work of art is not what the artist wants to express or even thinks he is expressing, but what he does express. Novelists often say their best things in spite of their conscious opinions; for fictional characters are properly guided by their own inner mechanisms which might lead them to develop in a way which directly contradicts their creator's expressly-held views. Lukacs has given a detailed analysis of this process at work in Balzac and Tolstoy, showing that their conservative political opinions are in practice by no means illustrated or confirmed in their novels. His studies of these two novelists seek to prove the theory that:

A great realist such as Balzac, if the intrinsic artistic development of situations and characters he has created comes into conflict with his most cherished prejudices or even his most sacred convictions, will, without an instant's hesitation, set aside these his own prejudices and convictions and describe what he really sees, not what he would prefer to see. The ruthlessness towards their own subjective world-picture is the hall-mark of all great realists, in sharp contrast to the second-raters, who nearly always succeed in bringing their own *Weltanschauung* into 'harmony' with reality, that is forcing a falsified or distorted picture of reality into the shape of their own world-view. This difference in the ethical attitude of the greater and lesser writers is closely linked with the difference between genuine and spurious creation. The characters created by the great realists, once conceived in the vision of their creator, live an independent life of their own: their comings and goings, their development, their destiny is dictated by the inner dialectic of their social and individual existence. No writer is a true realist—or even a truly good writer, if he can direct the evolution of his own characters at will.[12]

This study of some much less important realists than Balzac and Tolstoy will show that the same process, by which objective reality imposes itself upon subjective opinion, is not restricted to 'great' novelists, but that it can also be seen at work in lesser writers. This fact is, indeed, one of the bases upon which this literary approach to sociology rests.

The body of socio-literary theory which has been elaborated in this chapter is now ready to be put to the test of practice, in the examination of the various groups that formed Mexican society during the Revolution, and their relationships and movements, as shown principally in novels. But first it will be necessary to make brief preparatory examinations of the history of the Revolution and of the large body of novels that came to be written about it, and which provide the basis of this study.

[12] *Studies in European Realism* (London, 1950), p. 11.

2

THE MEXICAN REVOLUTION, 1910–1917: A BRIEF SURVEY

IN September 1910 Mexico City was the scene of lavish and extravagant celebrations which, officially, were supposed to commemorate the centenary of the Republic's independence, but in reality were also intended to celebrate the culmination of thirty-four years of effective rule by the dictator Porfirio Díaz (1830–1915).[1] As in most of Spanish America, the independence which had been gained in the early part of the nineteenth century had been followed by fifty years of political instability and economic stagnation; but Díaz, after coming to power in 1876 as a result of yet another one of those *pronunciamientos* which had characterized the previous half-century in Mexico,[2] succeeded in keeping peace and fostering economic growth in the country. By 1910 his regime had attracted praise from all parts of the world, and Díaz himself was acclaimed as 'El héroe de la paz'. Mexico, it was believed, had put behind herself the years of almost continuous revolution that had made her notorious in the nineteenth century, and was at last a respectable country in the eyes of the world.

In spite of the liberal constitution of 1857 by which Mexico was theoretically ruled, Porfirio Díaz succeeded in governing effectively for such a long time precisely by ignoring that constitution and imposing a personal dictatorship on his country. The period of the *Reforma* (1855–67) had appeared to bring the long struggle between liberals and conservatives to an end, with the triumph of the former,[3]

---

[1] General Manuel González (1833–93), a personal friend of Porfirio Díaz, was president from 1880 to 1884. Díaz occupied the presidency from 1876 to 1910, with the exception of this four-year period.

[2] Each *pronunciamiento*, or military uprising, was inevitably accompanied by its *plan*, or written justification and programme for the future. Porfirio Díaz came to power under the Plan de Tuxtepec, which declared its signatories' adherence to the 1857 Constitution and to the principle of *no-reelección* of the president.

[3] The 1857 Constitution was designed to make Mexico a liberal, democratic republic. Two of its most important measures were to establish secular education and to prohibit the ownership of land by corporations (which not only meant that the Church could not own land in Mexico but also that the age-old right of

but Díaz was, in many respects, to reverse this process. His government's policies were dominated by the need to attract capital investment to Mexico and encourage industrialization at all costs, for this was believed to be the only way to make the country solvent. Political activity was, it was decided, an irrelevant hindrance to material advance; so the old Spanish saying 'poca política, mucha administración' became one of the Porfirian mottoes. The country was thrown open to foreign and Mexican capitalists—and especially to the former—on terms that were extremely favourable to them: labour was kept cheap and unprotected, systematized corruption favoured the rich and powerful in every possible way, the press was muzzled, all able men were either bought or oppressed (the policy known succinctly at the time as 'pan o palo'), and any sign of social unease was ruthlessly repressed. One result was that industrialization did get under way and that Mexico did become solvent. The new, primitive capitalism, which flourished particularly in mining, in the manufacturing industries, in oil, and —above all—in the construction and operation of railways, ushered industrial change into Mexico. Inevitably, however, the social ills which normally accompany the early stages of industrialization were also introduced into the country. The life of the poor became even harder and more insecure than before. A group of over-privileged monopoly capitalists developed, who were known loosely as 'los científicos', who obtained excessive influence in the government, and who were generally hated (so much so that the word *científico* was semantically extended into an emotional term of abuse constantly on the lips of Díaz's liberal opponents).

At the same time as all this was happening in the industrial sector, however, the basic structure of rural Mexico continued to be the traditional one established during the colonial period, which had certain affinities with a feudal system. Indeed, with Díaz's neglect of agrarian problems in favour of industrial progress, the traditional rural system tended, free from outside influences, to become even more entrenched. Agricultural production was, for the most part, in the hands of *hacendados*, whose main interest in their *haciendas* was the aristocratic pride they felt in the possession

the Indians to their common lands was removed). The War of the Reform (1858–61) was won by the liberals under Benito Juárez (1806–72); the conservatives' subsequent attempt to regain power with the imposition, with French help, of the Emperor Maximilian (1864) was foiled by the later withdrawal of the French and another triumph for Juárez (1867). Juárez died, however, in 1872.

of vast lands and numerous peons. Left largely to their own devices under Porfirio Díaz, they—or, more often, their administrators— concentrated their efforts on evading taxation, reducing costs and expanding their possessions at the expense of the more productive but defenceless smallholders. Profitable and expanding production was, in a real pre-capitalist sense, something that worried them very little; for their vast possessions, however inefficiently farmed, always produced a steady and large enough income to finance their lives of luxury in Mexico City or Paris. Their peons, meanwhile, tied to their masters by debt-slavery[4] and kept in ignorance and degradation—and hence unrebellious—were now even worse off than ever, not only because of the government's general policy of favouring the rich and powerful but also because of the rapid rise in prices, especially after 1900, when real wages seem to have fallen dramatically.[5] Mexico, in spite of her industrial advances, was still very far from being able to feed herself at the end of Díaz's rule.

There was in Porfirian Mexico, then, a clash between the traditional agrarian structure and the new capitalism. Throughout the Porfirian period each had dug itself into a strong position, yet it was difficult for two such opposing economic and social systems to continue to coexist in one society. The contradiction was reflected in many ways: for example, the new ideas and opportunities brought to agricultural workers by the beginnings of industrialism seem to have been making cracks in the closed and hierarchical system of the haciendas, and there are, indeed, signs that the whole hacienda system was in danger of being undermined by the *científicos'* arguments in favour of a modern, capitalist attitude towards farming;[6] and at the same time, continued industrial

[4] Wages were very low, and the hacienda store (*tienda de raya*) charged high prices for inferior products. An hacendado could keep his peons tied to him by allowing them to run up huge debts which they would never be able to repay, and which were inheritable. Hacendados were, therefore, willing occasionally to make splendid loans to their peons for special celebrations, like christenings, marriages, saints' days, and so on [pp. 184–7].

[5] This rise in prices was mainly due to the imposition by the Díaz government of high tariff walls to protect the Mexican producer and make industrial advance possible. At the same time, the wages of the rural workers did not increase.

[6] F. Chevalier, 'Un facteur décisif de la révolution agraire au Mexique: le soulèvement de Zapata, 1911–19' in *Annales*, 1961, pp. 66–82: It is Chevalier's thesis that the vitality of the Morelos revolution under Zapata was a direct result of special circumstances there: the intensive capitalist exploitation of the land (for the profitable sugar crop). Against this capitalism the rural poor had no protection, and conditions were consequently even worse for them in Morelos than elsewhere. See also Womack, pp. 42ff.

CM

expansion on a large scale was difficult as long as the greater part of Mexico's population continued to live the wretched hand-to-mouth existence of the peasant and so to have virtually no purchasing power.[7] Those who did have money to spend scorned Mexican products and bought foreign goods whenever it was possible to do so [pp. 241–54]. It could be argued that one of the two had to give way: that the incompatibility, in all fields—social, economic and ideological—between rural traditionalism and industrial capitalism made it impossible for them to continue to coexist in Mexico. It does, however, seem possible that the conversion of Mexico from a country based on a traditional rural and colonial economy into a modern capitalist one, which was under way by 1910, could have been carried through to its conclusion without a revolution.

It is, indeed, difficult in the case of the Mexican Revolution to find either the precondition (that which creates a potentially explosive situation) or the precipitant (that which triggers the explosion) to explain it. Modern economic and sociological studies[8] have shown that revolutions occur in societies which are in a transitional stage between rural traditionalism and advanced industrialization and which are undergoing rapid economic growth. This growth can produce severe dislocation of established social patterns and this gives rise to a dangerously unstable situation. In particular, it can create a widening gap between, on the one hand, men's social, economic and political expectations and, on the other, the realities of their lives.[9] When such a situation occurs and the ruling élite is

[7] Andrés Molina Enríquez commented on this contradiction in 1909 in *Los grandes problemas nacionales* (Mexico, 1964, p. 229): Azuela examines another aspect of the incompatibility between traditionalism and capitalism in his novel *Los caciques* [p. 254n.].
   The term 'peasant' is used in this study in the wide sense of 'a member of the rural poor'.

[8] This outline theory of the causes of the revolutions is derived from the following: Chalmers Johnson, *Revolution and the Social System* (Stanford, 1964); Harry Eckstein, 'On the Etiology of Internal Wars', *History and Theory*, IV. 2 (1965), pp. 133–63; M. Olson, 'Rapid Growth as a Destabilizing Force', *Journal of Economic History*, XXIII (1963), pp. 529–52; James C. Davies, 'Toward a Theory of Revolution', *American Sociological Review*, XXVII (1962), pp. 5–19; and Lawrence Stone, 'Theories of Revolution', *World Politics*, XVIII. 2 (1966), pp. 159–76, which is a concise summary and critique of the work of the above and other scholars.

[9] Davies, op. cit., advances the theory of the 'J-curve'. Sometime, he says, in any period of economic growth there is bound to come a period of stagnation. At such a time men's expectations continue to soar, far ahead of the satisfaction of their needs. 'The crucial factor is the vague or specific fear that ground gained over a long period of time will be quickly lost.'

incapable of dealing with it by the various means at its disposal—effective repression, diversionary techniques, well-calculated concessions—then there is a state of 'multiple dysfunction' within society. Society polarizes into two opposing groups and the preconditions which make a revolution possible are in existence. Then the precipitant can do its work. The three most common precipitants are the emergence of an inspired leader, the formation of a secret revolutionary organization, and the crushing defeat of the national army in a foreign war. In Mexico in 1910 some of the above elements could be found. Mexico at that time certainly falls into the category of a society neither wholly pre-industrial and rural nor highly industrialized, but caught somewhere between the two. It was undergoing rapid economic growth, which had exacerbated social injustice and inequality by making the rich still richer and more powerful and the poor still poorer and more repressed. It is also true that the Porfirian élite was showing signs of weakness. But it cannot be said that a state of 'multiple dysfunction' had been reached by 1910. In spite of the aggravating circumstances there seems not to have been any widespread feeling of deprivation and frustration [pp. 25, 184–6, 189–97, and 235–9]. Society had not been polarized. Neither was there any identifiable precipitant; Madero can scarcely be considered an 'inspired leader'—certainly Mexican society on the outbreak of his rebellion was far from recognizing him as one [pp. 25–6, 137–8, 144–7, and 236–7]. The various conditions which modern sociologists and historians consider necessary for the outbreak of revolution do not seem to have existed in Mexico until 1913; Madero's revolt created a situation of 'multiple dysfunction' rather than being caused by one.[10]

Mexico was faced with serious problems, then, in 1910, but not necessarily ones which made a revolution inevitable. The ultimate explanation for the Mexican Revolution—the factor, in other words, which changed a merely awkward situation into a revolutionary one—may well lie in the gross ineffectiveness of the forces of law and order, and particularly the Army. Throughout the long period of Porfirian peace it had had little to do, and such sustained inactivity had led to stagnation and loss of efficiency [pp. 292–3].

[10] It must be stressed that the above comments refer to Mexico as a whole in 1910; in Morelos, Zapata's territory, there were special and exceptional circumstances creating a much more genuinely revolutionary situation [pp. 21n. and 196 n.].

It is arguable that a moderately competent army would have had no difficulty in crushing the Revolution in its weak Maderista early stages, thus obviating the risk of further disturbance.

From 1900 onwards the Revolution was foreshadowed in the formation of several opposition groups, ranging from the anarchist —and strangely named—*Partido Liberal* of the Flores Magón brothers, based in Lower California,[11] to the gentle, purely political liberalism of Francisco I. Madero (1873–1913); and in a few strikes which were brutally repressed (in particular, those of Cananea, Sonora, 1906, and Río Blanco, Veracruz, 1907).[12] Towards the end of the period of *Pax porfiriana*, Díaz, now a frail old man, showed signs of losing his iron grip: in 1908 he granted a famous interview to the American journalist Creelman, in which he declared that it was his intention to resign the presidency, in the belief that Mexico was now ready for democracy. He furthermore allowed the interview to be reproduced in the Mexican press.[13] Press censorship was slackened considerably in the final months of Díaz's rule. Another grave factor was the growing coldness of the United States to Díaz, which was caused by the increasing preference he was showing to English interests in Mexico in an attempt to correct United States dominance of Mexican business.[14] The

---

[11] The *Partido Liberal*, under Enrique (1887–1954) and Ricardo (1873–1922) Flores Magón, published two important documents, the *Plan del Partido Liberal* of 1906 and the *Manifiesto del Partido Liberal Mexicano* of Sept. 1911. The former is a precursor of the 1917 Constitution [pp. 37–8]: it demands the suppression of Church schools, the nationalization of Church wealth, the prohibition of Church interference in politics, the establishment of far-reaching labour laws, strong measures against unproductive haciendas, and the adoption of nationalistic criteria in the resolution of Mexican problems. From this radical reformist position the party turned anarchist during the next five years: its manifesto of 1911 attacks the concept of private property and with it all institutions which restrict the freedom of the individual—authority, capital, and the Church.

[12] At Cananea the Mexican employees of the Cananea Consolidated Copper Company went on strike in protest against the bad treatment their American overseers subjected them to, and the inferiority of their wages as compared with the wages of American employees doing the same work. They were fired upon, some two dozen being killed and their leaders taken to the dreaded dungeons of San Juan de Ulúa, Veracruz. At Río Blanco a strike of textile workers, organized by the Partido Liberal, turned into a riot which culminated in a clash between the Army and the workers, armed with sticks and stones. When, after a day's fighting (7 Jan.), the strikers were finally subdued, their leaders were executed.

[13] See José Yves Limantour, *Apuntes sobre mi vida política* (Mexico, 1965), pp. 153–66, where the interview and its consequences are discussed at some length. The same book also describes Díaz's personal decline in 1910 and 1911 (especially pp. 257–9, 264–5, and 296–7).

[14] See Peter Calvert, *The Mexican Revolution, 1910–1914: the Diplomacy of*

foreign preponderance in financial matters was also, of course, a source of unrest among Mexican businessmen.

At the same time as all this was happening under the surface, however, the fifteen million inhabitants of Mexico had never seemed more at peace with themselves and the world. In 1909 a Spaniard who had lived in Mexico for ten years (and who a few years later was to write his own novel of the Revolution [p. 48]) expressed the feeling of most: 'There is no menace for Mexico's future. Stability, the result of economic progress and of the passive attitude of the people, is a guarantee of peace in that country—a peace which, in my opinion, will be eternal, because that nation, but yesterday a child, is now a mature man.'[15] The habit of obedience to his personal authority, which Díaz had established over the years in the Mexican people, seemed far from being broken.

1910 was the year for new presidential elections. The opposition to Porfirio Díaz's re-election finally crystallized around don Francisco I. Madero.[16] Madero, the youngest member of a very rich hacendado family, was to show himself in subsequent events as a kind, trusting, and honest man, full of good intentions but naïve and stubborn in constantly preferring his own excessively optimistic view of things to reality. In spite of a history of some six years of mild opposition to Díaz, and the publication of his now famous book *La sucesión presidencial en 1910* (Coahuila, 1908)—a weak, inaccurate examination of the evils of dictatorship in Mexico's history—Madero was little known at the start of the election campaign. He toured the country on the old liberal platform of 'Sufragio efectivo: no reelección', proposing purely political reforms; yet he achieved such renown as the first person ever to dare to seriously oppose Díaz's re-election that the government took fright and imprisoned him in June 1910. His family used its influence to have Madero released on bail—only to see Díaz re-elected in the clearly fraudulent elections of July. Madero took the only alternative course left to him if he was to continue pursuing his political ambitions. He fled to the United States and published

Anglo-American Conflict (Cambridge, 1968), pp. 15–84 and 285–7; and Limantour, pp. 196–205.

[15] Julio Sesto, *El México de Porfirio Díaz* (Mexico, 1909), p. 260.

[16] General Bernardo Reyes (1850–1913) had been a serious opposition candidate for a period in 1909, but he finally declined to accept candidacy. Much of his support passed on to Madero.

there his *Plan de San Luis Potosí*, calling the Mexican nation to rebellion on 20 November.[17]

Madero's revolution had a very slow start. On 18 November the police of Puebla, having seized arms during the previous week from several Maderistas in the city, were surprised in their raid on the home of the Serdán family by armed resistance. A handful of men and women held out—in the vain hope of support from the people of Puebla—against a seige by the massed forces of police and army for several hours until their ammunition was exhausted; the Mexico City press reported the incident under the front-page headline 'Government forces in scenes of nobility and heroism'.[18] The campaign of remarkably clumsy and unsophisticated bluff continued in the press—immediately re-subjected to strict control —throughout the Maderista revolution. The Revolution had begun, then, significantly enough, on a note of gross Army inefficiency, made to look even worse by the government's unskilful attempts to cover it up.

Nothing much seemed to happen during the next few months; and yet this was the most important period of the whole Revolution in the sense that it was, above all, the government's failure to suppress Madero at this time that opened the way for later events. Very gradually the revolt gathered a certain momentum on the northern border of Mexico, especially in the state of Chihuahua. The revolutionaries won no important battles, yet the Federal Army was incapable of defeating them decisively; and public opinion, observing Díaz's unexpected weakness, began to favour Madero. Madero himself stayed in the United States until February 1911. As the Revolution dragged indecisively on, small isolated bands sprang up in rebellion all over Mexico, but Maderismo itself continued to fight its battles on the northern border. It was there that Madero finally won his first victory of any importance at all, taking Cuidad Juárez on 9 May. It was a significant defeat for Porfirio Díaz, for the capture of this border town enormously facilitated the supply of arms to the rebels; but it could not in any sense be called a disastrous or decisive loss, and Maderismo

---

[17] It denies recognition to the 1910 presidential elections, reaffirming the principle of *no reelección*, and makes provisions for the election of another president on the victory of the Maderista revolution. It is purely political, except for some vague promises to restore unfairly confiscated lands to their proper owners.

[18] *El Diario*, 19 Nov. 1910.

would still have had to win many more formidable battles to claim real victory. But both sides seemed anxious for an end to the fighting (peace negotiations had, in fact, been in progress almost from the beginning of Madero's revolt); Madero, because of strong family pressure, because of a genuine humanitarian dislike of bloodshed and suffering, and because a simple political solution— the deposition of Díaz—was all he sought; and Díaz, because old age and disillusionment had deprived him of the will to continue the struggle to keep himself in power.[19] On 21 May the treaty of Ciudad Juárez was signed: Díaz was to go into exile (he went on the 25th) and a provisional government was to take control in preparation for fresh elections.

Madero's victory was one of public opinion rather than force of arms. Maderismo was never a national revolution; it was a rather minor revolt made into a successful revolution by the particular moment in history at which it happened to occur. Its success was due not to its own strength but to its opponents' weaknesses: the senility of Díaz and his government, and the inadequacy of the Army.

The inexorable process of the decline of Maderismo began at the very moment of victory, as, indeed, it was almost bound to. It had been united only by opposition to Díaz; with Díaz went the only central idea of the movement, for otherwise the ideals of the Maderistas were disparate. Madero himself was interested only in political reform; many of his supporters were solely concerned with ridding Mexico of the *científicos*; the poor attributed to Madero intentions of social and economic reform which he never possessed yet never publicly disowned until his revolution had triumphed.

Furthermore, Madero's all too easy victory was more apparent than real. The peace treaty was a transaction by which, although Porfirio Díaz disappeared, the old order of Porfirismo was left intact: the legislature, the judiciary, the army, the police, all were left untouched; Madero himself seemed to his supporters to be acting as if it had all been a game of tennis in which he was the magnanimous victor with a ready smile and a pat on the back for the loser. Given the situation that, as a result of the treaty of Ciudad Juárez, he found himself in, Madero was, in fact, left with

[19] He was also, at the time, in great pain from a septic jaw. It should also be remembered that the Zapatista revolution in Morelos [pp. 28–9] had started and was considered, because of its proximity to the capital, to pose a disturbing threat.

little choice but to try to placate and win over his former enemies, for power remained in their hands, and without their support he was lost. He went about trying to gain it, however, without the skill and tact that such a delicate mission required, so that he both failed fully to gain the Porfiristas' confidence and alienated many of his own followers by his actions. Many of the latter soon began to think that Madero's sympathy for the loser was alarmingly strong, and that he was showing disloyalty and ingratitude in insistently rejecting Maderistas in favour of his old enemies.[20] The highly aristocratic tone of Madero's triumphal entry into Mexico City in June 1911, in a luxurious coach complete with liveried, bewigged, and bepowdered footmen, was also seen by some as an ominous sign.[21] And such declarations as the following, contained in the extraordinary manifesto to working men of 25 June, seemed to augur ill for his radical supporters: 'You must know that you will only find happiness within yourselves, in the domination of your passions and the repression of your vices; and that you will only succeed in achieving wealth and prosperity by saving your money and developing your will-power, in order always to act according to the dictates of your conscience and of your patriotism, not those of your passions.'[22]

Meanwhile, the provisional government of the conservative Francisco León de la Barra (1863–1939) was doing still more to lose Madero his only weapon, public opinion. Throughout the period of his interim presidency de la Barra prevented all effective radical action, and Madero received the blame. The case of Emiliano Zapata (1879–1919) was perhaps the most damaging. Zapata, a peon from the state of Morelos (to the south of Mexico City), had been in arms since March 1911, fighting at the head of a peasant army in Morelos for agrarian reform. On seeing the lack of reforming purpose in the de la Barra government, the Zapatistas continued in arms, determined at any cost to achieve their aims, as

[20] For example, in discharging the revolutionary army and leaving the federal one intact; in dissolving the revolutionary party, the *Partido Antirreeleccionista*, and forming in its place the *Partido Constitucional Progresista*; and in making public declarations of sympathy for hacendados in the losses they suffered in the course of the revolution (*El Tiempo*, 20 June 1911) [p. 142].

[21] *El Diario del Hogar*, 8 June 1911.

[22] Ibid., 25 June 1911. Madero's failure to grasp the reality of the situation was also noted in his fondness for an expression he repeated several times in his victory speeches: 'The people don't want bread, they want freedom.' (Silva Herzog, I, pp. 123–5).

they were later to be set forth in the *Plan de Ayala*.[23] Madero, by
personal intervention with Zapata, achieved a peaceful agreement,
and the demobilization of the Zapatistas began; upon which de la
Barra and the federal general Victoriano Huerta (1845–1916)
ignored Madero's recommendations and, in the hope of crushing
Zapatismo, marched in and attacked. So Zapata continued fighting
and Madero was universally condemned for breaking his word.[24]

Madero was, in spite of everything, duly elected president by a
large majority, but he had lost much ground already. His government took office on 6 November 1911. It proved to be incompetent
and ineffective, and lost the support of both conservatives and
radicals. It was at the huge disadvantage of any government which
comes to power under a radical banner and then, for whatever
reason, appears to move to the right and adopt conservative
policies: it is very difficult for any such government to make the
conservatives entirely forget its radical label, and at the same time
to retain its original radical support. Such sophisticated sleight of
hand was certainly beyond the Madero administration. Furthermore Madero, ever true to his principles, insisted on guaranteeing
absolute freedom of expression in Mexico; and as his popularity
declined the press grew more and more wildly, indeed hysterically,
opposed to him. The concerted press campaign against Madero
did much to hasten his fall [pp. 143ff.].

Armed resistance to Madero's regime was not long in appearing.
Zapata continued in arms. In December 1911 General Bernardo
Reyes led a rebellion in the north. It failed completely, and Reyes
surrendered to the government forces. In March 1912 Pascual
Orozco (1882–1915), a Maderista military leader, led a rebellion
which, despite a reformist direction of intent,[25] was financed by
large landowners of the north; Victoriano Huerta defeated him,

[23] The *Plan de Ayala* (25 Nov. 1911) accuses Madero of having betrayed the
Revolution, calls for his downfall, and proposes an extensive programme of
agrarian reform.

[24] For the full account, of which this is a simplification, see Womack, pp. 108–
24. Madero was not, in fact, altogether free of blame.

[25] Orozco's *plan* was the *Pacto de la Empacadora*, dated 25 Mar. 1912. It
makes detailed accusations that Madero is a puppet of United States interests
[p. 270] and demands his deposition. It proposes the nationalization of Mexican
railways and the *mexicanización* of its personnel; labour laws, including the
abolition of plantation stores, a ten-hour day, and vague and carefully-hedged
proposals regarding wage-rises; agrarian reform, including the restoration of
illegally confiscated land and the confiscation of inefficiently farmed hacienda
lands; and absolute freedom of expression.

and Orozco fled to the United States, yet his rebellion continued on a smaller scale. And in October 1912 Félix Díaz (1868–1945), the nephew of Porfirio, led a barracks uprising in Veracruz, which was put down easily. Madero refused to have Díaz and Reyes executed, and imprisoned them both in Mexico City. By January 1913 it was common knowledge that they, together with other Federal Army officers, were planning a *coup*. Madero was repeatedly warned of it by his friends and advisers, but he refused to take any notice of them. He seemed by now completely isolated in his own dream-like view of events.

The expected revolt broke out on 8 February 1913. Díaz and Reyes were released by the rebelling Army; in the opening skirmishes with the loyalist forces Reyes was killed and General Lauro Villar (1849–1923), the commander of that part of the army which remained loyal, was wounded. Madero committed his last, crowning blunder by appointing Huerta in Villar's place. The stage was now set for the *decena trágica* (8–18 February), the tragic ten days of cynically-planned slaughter and desolation in Mexico City, during which Díaz, beseiged in the Ciudadela barracks, and Huerta, having come to a secret agreement to oust Madero, daily fought mock battles in which no one was killed except innocent civilians and loyal Maderistas whom Huerta criminally sent into suicidal attacks. The bloody farce came to an end when the terrified population of Mexico City was ready to accept anything to bring their suffering to a finish, even Huerta's scarcely-disguised admission of his own treachery: 'The intolerable and anguished situation through which the capital city of the Republic has passed has obliged the Army, represented by the undersigned, to unite in brotherly sentiment in order to achieve the country's salvation.'[26] On 18 February a pact between Díaz and Huerta was signed. This act took place, fittingly enough, in the American Embassy; the ambassador, Henry Lane Wilson, had been an element of some importance in Madero's fall, having for some months conducted a personal vendetta against him. Wilson's reports to his government only too often stated as facts the malicious rumours and exaggerations started by Madero's enemies;[27] and during the decena

[26] *The Mexican Herald*, 19 Feb. 1913. The signatories were Huerta and Díaz.

[27] These reports, in which the gradual hardening of his attitude can be traced, are printed in *Papers Relating to the Foreign Relations of the United States* (henceforth referred to as *Foreign Relations*), 1912 (Washington, 1919), pp. 706–986, and *Foreign Relations*, 1913 (Washington, 1920), pp. 692–724, 770 and 775–6. See

trágica, acting on his own initiative, he did all he could to help Díaz and Huerta.

Within a few days of the signing of the pact it was, to most people's surprise, Huerta, and not Díaz, who emerged as the new figure of power. Huerta had made his reputation as a ruthless and unscrupulous soldier. In a very short time he now established himself as the melodramatic villain of the Revolution: absolutely treacherous and cynical, yet an extraordinarily incompetent statesman, who tried very clumsily to impose a rule of terror and to return Mexico to Porfirian times. The well-known fact that he kept himself in a state of almost continuous drunkenness did much to increase both his personal disrepute and the inefficiency of his government. Nevertheless, all the traditionally right-wing sectors —the wealthy, the Church,[28] the Army—immediately hailed him as the saviour of Mexico. Ambassador Wilson supported him tenaciously from the beginning, repeatedly pressing his government to recognize Huerta. Pascual Orozco halted his rebellion in the north and recognized him.

Opposition to the Huerta regime soon appeared. Madero, having been captured at gunpoint in the National Palace on 18 February and persuaded to resign his presidency on the following day, was murdered—'shot while attempting to escape'[29]—together with his vice-president, Pino Suárez (1869–1913), on 22 February. He immediately became as popular as he had ever been; and the movement against Huerta was provided with a martyr whom its leaders were not slow to exploit. The *Casa del Obrero Mundial*, a trade union organization started during Madero's presidency [p. 235n.], openly and valiantly opposed Huerta in Mexico City itself. Zapata continued fighting in Morelos and revised his *Plan de Ayala* to meet the new situation.[30] Congress soon showed signs

also Stanley R. Ross, *Francisco I. Madero, Apostle of Mexican Democracy* (New York, 1955), pp. 236–40, 279–80, and 293–311.

[28] The Church had broadly been in favour of Porfirio Díaz, for although he had failed to revoke the anti-clerical provisions of the 1857 Constitution, he had avoided enforcing them. It had never been certain what to think about Madero, and it now welcomed the return of what appeared to be a straightforward, strong right-wing dictator [pp. 286–9].

[29] The *ley fuga* (law of flight) was a traditional method, much used during the Porfirian period, of executing prisoners without recourse to legal methods.

[30] The reformed *Plan de Ayala*, dated 30 May 1913, declares that Huerta is even worse than Madero and that it is even more necessary to depose him. It adds that Orozco, whom it had originally recognized as the formal head of the

of opposition; it was forcibly dissolved on 11 October 1913, and all deputies but the members of the Catholic Party (refounded under Madero) imprisoned. But the main revolutionary opposition came, once again, from the north. Venustiano Carranza (1859–1920), fighting under the banner of the *Plan de Guadalupe*,[31] soon had a full-scale military force under his civilian command, composed of the Army of the North-West under Álvaro Obregón (1880–1928), the Army of the North-East under Pablo González (1879–1950), and the Division of the North under Francisco Villa (1878–1923). And once again the United States' influence was decisive. The new president, Woodrow Wilson (who had taken office a week after Madero's death), made it his personal mission to re-establish democracy in Mexico. Furthermore, English interests supported Huerta and England recognized his government almost immediately, so United States interests tended generally to oppose him.[32] From October 1913 onwards, Wilson openly pressed for Huerta's resignation.

The Revolution under Carranza slowly but inexorably gained ground against Huerta's disorganized government. Carranza himself was a rich hacendado who had been a senator under Díaz without ever suggesting reform. He was loquacious, complacent, and aloof; he thought and spoke in platitudes and surrounded himself with a court of adulatory admirers. It only seems to have been personal ambition which made him into a revolutionary.

The campaign followed the railway network of north Mexico, as the three principal revolutionary forces pressed down these vital lines of communication towards Mexico City. By the early months of 1914 the rebels were winning victory after victory, Huerta's press-gangs were rounding up more and more unfortunate civilians, and his propagandists were inventing more and more atrocious lies in their desperate attempt to keep the truth from Mexicans. On 26 March 1914 Villa triumphantly captured the vitally important rail centre of Torreón (Coahuila); the newspapers

Revolution, has forfeited his position by coming to terms with Huerta, and that Zapata now takes his place.

[31] The *Plan de Guadalupe* was signed on 26 Mar. 1913. In its original form it is a brief and purely political document, rejecting Huerta and those who recognize him, naming Carranza the 'First Chief of the Constitutionalist Army', and prescribing general elections on the triumph of the Revolution (Carranza or his successor to act as Interim President). It was modified in late 1914 [p. 35n.].

[32] See Calvert, especially pp. 150ff., where the story of Huerta's recognition by England and non-recognition by the United States is told in great detail.

denied for two weeks that such a thing had happened, and then stated that the Federal Army had cunningly evacuated the town so that Villa, bottled up inside it, would be easy prey. They continued to report daily for another two weeks that his situation was desperate, that he was trapped and bound to succumb at any moment.

In April 1914 President Wilson's personal crusade to rid Mexico of Huerta took the form of definite action. Using, as it appears, a minor incident as an excuse,[33] he ordered the occupation of the Veracruz customs house by the United States Marines on 20 April. Unexpected civilian resistance obliged the invaders to take the whole town. The immediate effect of this ill-conceived action was to arouse the patriotic fury of all Mexicans and so to tend to unite them behind Huerta, who, in his inexpert way, made the best of the situation. He announced that the United States army was marching on Mexico City and that war had been declared between the two countries, and he presented himself as the heroic protector of Mexico's territorial integrity. Carranza, too, took every opportunity to express patriotic hostility to the invasion. Wilson thus found that his move had had the opposite effect to that intended, and that he had blundered into an unexpectedly complicated situation, from which he was to have great trouble in extricating himself. The conference of the 'ABC powers' (Argentina, Brazil, and Chile) which met at Niagara Falls to mediate the dispute was ineffective, chiefly because of Carranza's refusal to co-operate. Not until 23 November was Wilson able finally to withdraw without losing too much face.

In spite of the aid Wilson unwittingly offered Huerta, the latter was too far advanced down the path of decline for any real recovery to be possible. Defeat was now inevitable; the invasion of Veracruz possibly delayed that defeat a little.

It is difficult to weigh the advantage to Huerta of the rise of patriotism against the disadvantage of the loss of Mexico's principal gulf coast port. Carranza carefully maintained a position of hostility to the invasion; but Villa did not make any effort to hide his pleasure, and Villistas added new verses to the revolutionary song, *La cucaracha*:

[33] Robert E. Quirk, *An Affair of Honor: Woodrow Wilson and the Occupation of Veracruz* (University of Kentucky Press, 1962), is a detailed account of the whole complicated affair.

> 'Ora sí que se cai Huerta
> con toditos sus pelones
> porque ya no tiene puerta
> pa' que le entren municiones.
>
> Ya se le cerró la puerta,
> ya se va la cucaracha:
> ese Victoriano Huerta,
> con narices de tlacuacha.[34]

Whatever the effect of the invasion of Veracruz, the Battle of Zacatecas of 24 June 1914, won by the revolutionaries under Villa's command, was decisive. The federal garrison of 12,000 men, including the best of the remains of Huerta's army, was routed by 22,000 revolutionaries. Huerta, protesting until the very end that he would die rather than resign, and even holding farcical presidential elections at the very last moment (5 July)—about which the Mexican public first heard when the election of Huerta was announced the next day—finally renounced the presidency and fled into exile (15 July). The last words of his formal renunciation, most characteristic of the man with their overtones of jaunty and irresponsible buffoonery, acquired some brief notoriety: 'Dios les bendiga a Vds. y a mí también' ('God bless you all, and me as well').[35]

The worst was yet to come. Ever since the Battle of Torreón a growing split had been apparent in the ranks of the revolutionaries between Carranza and his most successful general, Pancho Villa. The common need to defeat Huerta had preserved a precarious unity but now, with victory, the enmity between the two men came into the open. Carranza and Villa were repulsive to each other. Pancho Villa was a working-class outlaw and rebel: impulsive, ignorant, and brutal—indeed perhaps psychopathic—but cunning and brave. To Carranza, with his middle-class preoccupation with legalism and respectability, he was intolerable. Furthermore

---

[34] Now Huerta's really going to fall,
Him and all his men,
Because he's got no doorway
For munitions to come in.

The door is shut fast,
The cockroach is leaving,
Old Victoriano Huerta,
Old opossum-nose.

'Pelón' was a common nickname for a soldier in the Federal Army.

[35] *El Independiente*, 16 July 1914.

Carranza, a resolutely non-military leader, always insisted upon civilian government after triumph, a proposition which was unacceptable to the military caudillo, Villa. On Huerta's withdrawal, Carranza used the last vestige of his authority over Villa to delay him as much as possible and to ensure that Obregón, who had remained faithful to Carranza, reached Mexico City first. Obregón took possession on 5 August 1914; demobilization of the defeated Federal Army started immediately.

As a last attempt to reunite Villa and Carranza, a convention of generals was held at Aguascalientes in October. Little was achieved but the election of a provisional president of Mexico, Eulalio Gutiérrez (1881–1939). Carranza did not recognize the validity of the convention's decisions, and refused to hand over power; Villa, too, refused to budge and acquired control of the convention and of Gutiérrez, making them both his own. The Convention of Aguascalientes, then, only confirmed the irreparable split between Carranza's followers—the *constitucionalistas*—under the command of Obregón, and the *convencionistas* of Villa and his new ally, Zapata. Zapata had continued his isolated Morelos revolution throughout Huerta's period of office and, more intransigent than ever in his demands for agrarian reform, had soon restarted hostilities against the latest occupant of the National Palace in Mexico City, Carranza. Now, for the first time, he was formally allied with a larger national revolutionary movement.

The Convencionistas took control of the centre of the country, and Carranza withdrew his government to Veracruz in order to reorganize his forces. Villa failed to press home his advantage by attacking Veracruz, and Carranza was thus granted precious time to gather strength. He produced additions to his *Plan de Guadalupe* (12 December 1914)[36] and the law of 6 January 1915,[37] which together promised sweeping agrarian and industrial reform; both effective pieces of window-dressing to attract working-class support. Meanwhile, Villa and his men indulged in high living in

---

[36] After accusing Villa of disrupting revolutionary unity and leading a reactionary counter-revolution, the document goes on to promise a sweeping, but vaguely-worded series of radical reforms: agrarian reforms, fiscal laws, laws for the protection of the proletariat, both urban and rural, and so on.

[37] This was the first tangible result of the general proposals contained in the additions to the *Plan de Guadalupe*. It declares that all lands illegally confiscated by local authorities are to be restored to their rightful owners. The practical difficulties of implementing such a law are obvious.

Mexico City. In January 1915 Gutiérrez fled from Villa's grasp and Obregón took advantage of the ensuing confusion by taking Mexico City, enlisting several workers' battalions, and moving out again before Villa could cut him off from his Veracruz base. For three months Villistas and Carrancistas fought without either side being able to obtain a decisive advantage. Zapata soon proved a weak ally for Villa, for he and his men were only really interested in victory in their own region, and fought with small conviction in the national struggle. Nevertheless the scales were evenly balanced until the battles of Celaya in April 1915, when Villa and Obregón brought their respective military strategies to a conclusive trial of strength. Obregón's army, using canals and ditches, barbed wire and machine-guns—methods their leader had learnt from reports of the European war—repelled wave after wave of massed Villista charges. There was something symbolic about this confrontation between modern tactics and primitive fury which formed the climax of the Mexican Revolution. When Obregón and modern tactics eventually won it was as if the old order had irrevocably succumbed to the new.

The rest of 1915 saw the rapid consolidation of Carranza's power and the decline of Villa in a bankrupt, hungry, exhausted Mexico. Villa retreated to his home state of Chihuahua. By the end of 1915 he and Zapata were confined to marauding in their own territories and all the major world powers had recognized the Carranza government.

The United States, having strongly supported Villa throughout the fight against Huerta, had come out in favour of Carranza after the split in the revolutionary ranks. Villa now, in January 1916, thought he must punish the Americans for their treachery. The worst of his subsequent atrocities was his raid across the border on the town of Columbus (New Mexico) in the early hours of 9 March. His band, comprising about 400 men, descended on the town and galloped whooping through its streets, shooting passers-by (seven Americans and twenty-three Villistas were killed) and burning buildings; in retaliation, the United States government sent an expedition under General John J. Pershing into Mexican territory, without waiting for Carranza to give or deny his consent. The Punitive Expedition crossed the border on 15 March in pursuit of Villa, but, to great joy throughout Mexico, it returned empty-handed to the United States on 6 February 1917. It had, however, achieved one of its objectives, which was to dissuade Villa from making further attacks on United States citizens. The pacification of Mexico continued during 1916. Carranza started behaving in a way that boded ill for the future of many of his supporters, passing drastic legislation against strikes. He seemed already to be turning against the workers whose support he had courted so carefully less than two years earlier. In December 1916 he summoned in Querétaro a convention of his most loyal supporters to effect the necessary changes in the Constitution. The changes he proposed, and expected to be passively accepted, were mild and unimportant, and clearly showed his intention of not fulfilling the promises he had made at Veracruz. He was surprised, however, by the refusal of many of his followers, led by Obregón himself, to accept his proposals, and by their advancement of other, less innocuous ones. These he was obliged to accept as the basis of the Constitution of 1917.

The new Constitution, promulgated on 5 February 1917, represented a success on paper for the radical and reformist sectors of the revolutionary movement. It declares that the ownership of Mexican land and natural resources is vested originally in the nation, which has the right to impose on private property such limitation as the public interest may demand (Article 27); the way is thus prepared for agrarian reform and nationalization. It attacks the power of the Church, imposing compulsory secular education to the age of 15 (Articles 3 and 31), making places of public worship the property of the nation (Article 27), and forbidding ministers of religion to interfere in any way in political affairs—they are even deprived of the vote (Article 130). It includes a complete series of labour laws in Article 123, a combination of all the methods then known for protecting workers from excessive exploitation (and an implicit acceptance, therefore, that Mexico was to remain a capitalist country): Article 123 establishes an eight-hour working day, at least one full day's rest in every week, compulsory paid leave for pregnant and nursing women, guarantees of an adequate minimum wage, the employers' responsibility for proper hygiene and safety, the right to strike, and so on. And finally, the Constitution is uniformly nationalistic in tone and spirit.

Many of the Constitution's provisions were utterly impracticable in 1917, and indeed remain so over fifty years later. The document is, however, important as the formal assertion that post-revolutionary

Mexico was to be a managed, industrialized state, with a capitalist structure tempered by certain limited socialist leanings.

It is convenient to consider the year 1917 as the end of the military phase of the Mexican Revolution.[38] There were still several loose ends to tie up before a firmly established post-revolutionary dynasty of rulers could emerge; among other things, most of the serious competitors for power had yet to be eliminated—Zapata was murdered in 1919, Carranza in 1920, Villa in 1923, Obregón in 1928. But it was the Constitution, the formal recognition of the triumph of a certain system of ideas, which marks the conclusion of this stage of the Revolution. The process that Madero had unwittingly started in 1910 had finally come to an end.

It had been a disorganized, patchwork revolution, with some farcical and grotesque elements; a long, painful, energy-sapping process without much apparent meaning or direction. The seemingly senseless fighting had gone on and on until a state of exhaustion had been reached and it could go on no more: seven years, as it were, of blind groping in the dark. Few of those who took part in the Revolution even suspected what they were groping for. The Revolution did nothing to establish liberty or restore justice, or even to bring democracy to Mexico. What it did do was to deal a death-blow to the economic and social system inherited from colonial times, and thus to clear the way for the social, economic and political modernization which has made it possible for Mexico to enjoy rapid economic expansion since 1940.

But whether this important change could not have been effected more efficiently, more painlessly, and perhaps more rapidly by peaceful evolution, is quite another question. Mexico's rapid growth dates, after all, from fully thirty years after the outbreak of the Revolution, and many factors apart from the Revolution contributed to it (the Second World War, general world economic development, etc.). Furthermore, some of the changes directly brought about by the Revolution have demonstrably held back economic advance rather than facilitating it. For example, the break-up of the hacienda system and the creation of small *ejidos*, which has often been considered the most radical achievement of the Revolution, has in fact created serious obstacles to modernization. Modern mechanized farming depends on the existence of

---

[38] A possible alternative date is that of Carranza's deposition and murder, 1920. But 1917 has been preferred for the reasons stated [pp. 45-6].

large units of land; the division of large estates into small parcels has therefore checked agricultural productivity (the Mexican rural population remains extremely poor). Economic development was already, of course, under way before the Revolution; and the Revolution was in part, at least, fought against precisely the men and the ideas—científicos and cientificismo—that had engineered that development. It could be argued, then, that the Revolution was retrograde in its destruction of this economically active and productive sector of Mexican society, a substitute for which had to be created completely afresh after 1917 from the ranks of the triumphant revolutionaries [pp. 210–16]; and that the twenty years between the end of the Revolution and the beginnings of expansion were occupied by the re-establishment of this *entrepreneur* sector which the Revolution destroyed. There are signs, however, that the dynamic capitalist spirit of cientificismo was fast giving way at the end of the Porfirian era to a parasitical pseudo-aristocratic attitude among the wealthy bourgeoisie [pp. 254–68]; and consequently that the destruction of this élite—and of the landowning oligarchy it aped—and its replacement by a new, more vital one was a necessary step. One clear result of the Revolution has been the growth of Mexican nationalism [pp. 268–79]; but here, again, it can be objected that it does not necessarily take a revolution to produce patriotic fervour.

One positive result of the Revolution about which there can certainly be no doubt was the important literary movement which grew out of it. It is time now to turn to the novels of the Mexican Revolution themselves, with, first of all, a general summary of their production, to prepare the way for the subsequent analysis of those which illuminate various facets of the social history of the Revolution.

3

THE NOVEL OF THE MEXICAN REVOLUTION

THERE has been little agreement among critics about precisely which works of literature are rightly included within the category 'the novel of the Mexican Revolution'. The problem of definition is made particularly acute by the fact that opinions vary considerably about both concepts involved. When the possible meanings of 'novel' are permuted with the possible meanings of 'the Mexican Revolution', a bewildering number of assorted definitions is produced; so that when critics talk about 'the novel of the Mexican Revolution', each one is usually referring to something significantly different from what each of the others is. It would be a good idea to try to discover how to define and delimit the subject in a way which could be generally accepted and recognized.

A representative dictionary definition of the novel is provided by the *Shorter Oxford English Dictionary*: 'A fictitious prose narrative or tale of considerable length in which characters and actions representative of the real life of past or present times are portrayed in a plot of more or less complexity.' The difficult word here is 'fictitious', with its main meaning of 'existing only in the imagination of an individual'. Novelists often take their subjects from actual events and from their own personal experience, and their works are frequently imbued with an air of factual reality: the above quotation goes on to recognize this in 'representative of the *real* life . . .', which appears to bring an element of self-contradiction to the definition. It hardly, then, seems accurate, for example, to label a painstaking reconstruction in novel form of a certain historical event 'fiction'; or, conversely, to say that the work of a historian—who may be guilty of greatly distorting his account to suit his prejudices, and who can never, in any case, be 'objective'— is necessarily, just because it is the work of a historian, the precise opposite, 'factual writing'. Indeed the good historian shares many qualities with the novelist, one of which is a powerful but disciplined imagination. The genuinely fictitious genres are, of course, not the novel and the short story but the fantasy and the romance.

The word 'fictitious', in short, suggests detachment from the exterior world of phenomena; and the novel is much concerned precisely with this world. We cannot distinguish between the novel and other types of narrative (such as historical writing) by saying that one is not concerned with what is called 'objective reality' and the other is. Where, perhaps, some kind of distinction can be found, however, is in the special way reality is perceived and recorded in each. One could say in general terms—the distinction cannot be an absolute one, of course—that the novel, like other sorts of artistic literature, tends to approach reality in a qualitative rather than a quantitative way [p. 16]; and that the reverse applies to other narrative writing of the kind often misleadingly called 'factual'. This is to say that while the historian, for example, is concerned to report precisely, unambiguously, referentially, and thus give an accurate quantitative account of the period of history he has chosen as his subject, the novelist—while not necessarily ignoring this side of things—is more interested in the symbolic values (using the word 'symbolic' in a wide sense) of phenomena, in the invisible associations and connotations they acquire in men's minds: in reality's qualitative aspect. Furthermore, whereas the historian's methods, and his language, are essentially analytical, the novel is concerned with reality as experienced, and its language is consequently a plurivalent language of synthesis. The writings of both the novelist and the historian (or the sociologist, or the psychologist, for example) are, then, factual, but each in a different way. Each concentrates on a different aspect of external reality: one sees and describes it 'artistically' (with techniques based on qualitative synthesis), and the other sees and describes it 'scientifically' (with techniques based on quantitative analysis). Even novelists like Zola, who thought of themselves as 'scientific', could not in practice prevent themselves (simply because they were creating novels and not anything else) from writing 'artistically'. The words 'factual' and 'fictitious', as they are commonly used to refer to the written word, are actually no more than misleading synonyms for 'scientific' and 'artistic'.

The novel cannot, though, be precisely defined: it is a genre much more recently developed than others, and it has not had time to be fossilized into fixed forms. This is what has led some critics to formulate deliberately loose definitions of the term 'novel': for example E. M. Forster, who quotes Chevalley with strong approval:

'a fiction in prose of a certain extent' . . . That is quite good enough for us, and we may perhaps go so far as to add that the extent should not be less than 50,000 words. Any fictitious prose work over 50,000 words will be a novel for the purposes of these lectures, and if this seems to you unphilosophic will you think of an alternative definition, which will include *The Pilgrim's Progress, Marius the Epicurean, The Adventures of a Younger Son, The Magic Flute, The Journal of the Plague, Zuleika Dobson, Rasselas, Ulysses,* and *Green Mansions,* or else will you give reasons for their exclusion? Parts of our spongy tract seem more fictitious than other parts, it is true . . . but no intelligent remark known to me will define the tract as a whole. All we can say of it is that it is bounded by two chains of mountains neither of which rises very abruptly—the opposing ranges of Poetry and of History.[1]

And even such an inclusive definition as this is open to qualification: the term 'fiction', as suggested above, and as Forster himself acknowledges ('parts . . . seem more fictitious than other parts') is not very helpful to us, and the specification that the novel must have 50,000 words at least is an artificial one which would unreasonably exclude many works normally regarded as novels: *Lazarillo de Tormes,* for example, and many of the novels of Unamuno. The novels of the Revolution tend to be brief, and many of them are of less than 50,000 words. It seems wise to avoid the crude arithmetical implications of a definition in terms of length; the difference between a novel and a short story is surely more fundamentally one of range and scope than of numbers of words employed. A tentative definition of the novel might, then, read thus: 'A prose narrative which is wide in range and scope, concerned with the qualitative aspects of external reality as experienced, and thus written in evocative rather than expositive language.' It would be dangerous, not to say pedantic, to attempt to delimit the novel any more than this; for it is, above all else, the essentially free, open and fluid form of the novel which distinguishes it from all other literary genres. The most important thing about the novel is that it cannot ultimately be defined, that the literary artist who chooses to cultivate the novel has a much freer

[1] *Aspects of the Novel* (Harmondsworth, 1966), pp. 13–14.

hand and is much less inhibited by formal considerations than writers who work in other genres. The fact that the novel cannot be defined must prominently be written into any definition of the novel. Whether or not this definition is acceptable generally, there is no doubt that when dealing with the novels of the Mexican Revolution any meaningful and practical definition must be thus based on wide criteria. Nearly all these works have even more documentary and autobiographical content than is usual in novels, and a smaller proportion of imagination, invention and artistic reorganization. One of the most important of all the novels of the Mexican Revolution—Martín Luis Guzmán's *El águila y la serpiente* (Madrid, 1928²)—would hardly be considered a novel outside Mexico, for it is simply a collection of well-written traveller's tales referring to the years 1913–15. José Rubén Romero's *Apuntes de un lugareño* (Barcelona, 1932) are the author's memoirs of his early life before and during the Revolution, as dictated to his secretary; and the same author's *Desbandada* (Mexico, 1934), though somewhat more carefully composed, is equally autobiographical. José Vasconcelos's *Ulises criollo* (Mexico, 1935) is similarly, in the normal terminology of literary criticism, without any possible doubt an autobiography, not a novel. Nellie Campobello's *Cartucho* (Mexico, 1931), and *Las manos de mamá* (Mexico, 1937), are both anecdotal memoirs of a childhood spent during the Revolution, recalled in isolated, disconnected scenes (which are not set out in chronological order). Gregorio López y Fuentes's *Campamento* (Madrid, 1931) is simply a description—without any plot or individual characters—of a night in a camp of revolutionary soldiers. Not a single one of these works is a novel, as the term is normally understood; yet all of them are now classed as novels by all critics of Mexican literature. They all find a place, together with other works that more closely resemble the traditional novel, in the important anthology of novels of the Mexican Revolution compiled by Antonio Castro Leal.³ And there are many other less extreme and less well-known examples.

It is clear, then, that it would be misguided and pedantic to impose the normal definition—such as it is—of the term 'novel' on

---

² For more details of the novels of the Revolution mentioned during the course of this and subsequent chapters, see John Rutherford, *An Annotated Bibliography of the Novels of the Mexican Revolution of 1910–1917* (New York, 1971).

³ *La novela de la Revolución mexicana* (Madrid-Mexico-Buenos Aires, 1960).

the works of prose narrative dealing with the Mexican Revolution, thereby creating unnatural divisions within a group of writers and books that manifestly belong together. All these works have performed the literary and social functions of novels and all were considered by their authors and readers as novels: therefore, for all practical purposes, they all are novels. Consequently we must include, under the heading 'novels of the Mexican Revolution', all those prose narratives—whether autobiographies, memoirs, collections of short stories, of sketches or of descriptions around a common theme, novelized biographies, or more orthodox novels—which concern themselves with the Revolution in a largely artistic way. The novel's connection with all these other narrative forms is a very close one: one of direct descent, according to Warren and Wellek—'the novel develops from the lineage of non-fictitious narrative forms—the letter, the journal, the memoir or biography, the chronicle or history; it develops, so to speak, out of documents'.[4] If one thinks of the Novel of the Mexican Revolution as the first stage in the development of a Mexican novel tradition [pp. 47–8 and 66ff.], then it provides a fine illustration of Warren and Wellek's point: it represents the stage in the history of Mexican literature at which the novel starts to grow out of various non-fictional narrative forms. It is natural, then, that its affinity with these other forms should be marked and obvious; and imperative, consequently, that any definition of the Novel of the Revolution should take account of this affinity. Warren and Wellek's observation also provides, incidentally, another objection to the use of the word 'fictitious' in the definition of the novel. The novel, not only in its intrinsic nature but also in its literary pedigree, is basically non-fictitious.

When dealing with a sub-genre which is so heterogeneous as far as artistic form is concerned, it is clearly wise to run the risk of being excessively inclusive in definition rather than excessively exclusive. It would be quite nonsensical to separate the works of Guzmán, López y Fuentes, Vasconcelos and Romero from those of Azuela, Ancona, Muñoz, and Ferretis, for example, just because the normal (non-Mexican) definitions of the novel happen to be applicable to the writings of the latter but not to those of the former. Since all, in practice and in fact, belong firmly together as

[4] René Wellek and Austin Warren, *Theory of Literature* (Harmondsworth, 1966), p. 216.

members of the same literary movement, and since the works of all of them are and always have been called 'novels', we must if necessary, be ready to change the definition to include them all. For our present purposes, then, a novel is simply a prose narrative which takes a basically artistic approach to reality.

Most definitions of the term 'revolution' consider that the period of actual civil war is merely one stage of the whole revolutionary process, and not even the most important stage at that. The theories of the only Mexican who has made a serious study of the sociology of revolutions, Lucio Mendieta y Núñez,[5] are particularly apposite here. He states that any revolution has four distinct stages: the incubatory, when revolutionary unrest and tension is gradually built up; the destructive, when fighting breaks out and continues until one side emerges as the definitive victor; the consolidatory, when the triumphant party establishes itself in power, a dangerous stage because of the possibilities of counter-revolution during it; and 'la etapa verdaderamente revolucionaria' when the revolutionary regime, now firmly settled, makes the basic legal changes in social and economic structure that really revolutionalize the country. In the case of Mexico it would be possible to identify, in broad terms, the decade 1900–10 as the first stage; the years 1910–17 as the second; the period from 1917 to approximately 1940 as the third; and from 1940 to 1950 (the decade of intensive industrialization and economic expansion) or even later, as the fourth. Within this scheme of things, it is very difficult to say when the fourth stage of any revolution has finished, and quite impossible for the power élite established by any given revolution to admit that it has, thus appearing to declare that it is betraying revolutionary ideals. Indeed the most important and influential myth of modern Mexico is the one that states that the Revolution still continues as radically as ever, in its 'institutionalized' phase. The party which governs Mexico calls itself the *Partido Revolucionario Institucional*; stage four of Lucio Mendieta y Núñez's scheme will continue for ever (according to official Mexican government doctrine) and so no fresh revolution will ever be necessary.

Because various different possible definitions of the Mexican Revolution exist, there has been confusion among critics about the

---

[5] In *Teoría de la revolución* (Mexico, 1959), pp. 51–66. Mendieta y Núñez writes about revolutions in general, but he clearly has one eye firmly fixed upon the Mexican Revolution as he formulates his theories.

meaning of the term 'the novel of the Revolution' not only, as seen in the preceding pages, as regards form, but also as regards content. The principal difficulty is the tendency of some of them to call 'novels of the Revolution' works referring to all four stages of Mendieta y Núñez's scheme, so long as they are written in what one of them, Antonio Magaña Esquivel, calls 'a spirit of revindication'.[6] All novels written between 1900 and the present day which portray Mexican society in a critical and realistic way are, according to this reasoning, novels of the Revolution. Such a wide definition makes the term virtually meaningless; if it is to have any meaning at all it must be a strictly and specifically chronological one. The Mexican Revolution is, then, for present purposes, whatever the Mexican government and government-influenced writers may say, the period corresponding to the second stage of Mendieta y Núñez's scheme, the military or destructive phrase, which started in Mexico in late 1910 and can conveniently be considered to have finally come to an end in 1917 with the compilation of the new revolutionary constitution.[7]

We have now reached, it is hoped, a convenient, meaningful, precise, and manageable definition of the novels of the Mexican Revolution: 'those basically artistic wide-ranging prose narratives written by Mexicans which deal in their entirety or in a part of considerable importance with events which took place in Mexico between November 1910 and February 1917'. It will be noticed that although the definition specifies that these novels have to be concerned with the military phase of the Revolution, as explained above, to be included in the category, it does not state that they must necessarily deal with military actions. To do so would be to curtail the list drastically, and to exclude many works which have always been considered to belong to it: for many of the novelists of the Revolution quite rightly considered that the radical changes it caused during 1910–17 to civilian society were at least as important as its military campaigns. The most important novelist of the Revolution, Mariano Azuela, wrote seven revolutionary novels: only one of them is concerned with the actual fighting.

Objections could no doubt be raised about the above definition;

[6] Antonio Magaña Esquivel, *La novela de la Revolución mexicana* (Mexico, 1964) Vol. I, p. 15.

[7] I have taken the Constitution as a more convenient milestone than Carranza's fall and death: by 1917 the Revolution had triumphed and most of Mexico was pacified.

but at least it is based on careful examination of the subject—one which badly needs careful defining—and on logical reasoning. The group of works thus set apart do form a coherent sub-genre, and it is sensible and rewarding to consider them all together as a group: and the differences between these novels and all the other modern Mexican novels that are excluded from the group by this definition are real and important differences.

Novels of the Revolution started to be written in the earliest months of the armed conflict. The first two to be written were both published in 1911: one a mere curiosity, the other a novel of real importance. The curiosity was *La majestad caída* (Mexico-Buenos Aires, 1911: the title refers to Porfirio Díaz) by the octogenarian Juan A. Mateos (1831–1913), written in the cloying sentimental style for which he had enjoyed a certain popularity throughout the second half of the nineteenth century, with a lengthy series of light romantic historical novels. *La majestad caída* shows the decline of Mateos's limited powers as a writer; it is a thoroughly unfortunate caricature of all the clichés of character and situation of the sentimental historical novel.

The work of importance was *Andrés Pérez, maderista* (Mexico, 1911) by Mariano Azuela (1879–1950), a doctor who wrote novels in his spare time[8] without achieving any critical recognition or popular success. *Andrés Pérez, maderista* is a realistic and convincing study of an apathetic and listless journalist who, as a result of some strange but credible coincidences, gets caught up in the Maderista revolution and becomes gradually and ironically converted into a popular hero. Azuela was to write and publish five more novels about the Revolution during the next seven years,[9] mostly concerned, like his first one, with various aspects of middle-class life of the time; although one, *Los de abajo*, is principally about peasant revolutionaries, and another, *Las tribulaciones de una familia decente*, describes the effects of the Revolution on an upper-class family of hacendados. All of these novels of Azuela are of considerable literary interest in their own right; but they are perhaps of

[8] *Andrés Pérez, maderista* was his fifth novel. His previous novels were *María Luisa* (Lagos de Moreno, Jalisco, 1907); *Los fracasados* (Mexico, 1908); *Mala yerba* (Guadalajara, Jalisco, 1909); and *Sin amor* (Mexico, 1912—but written earlier) [p. 83n.].

[9] *Los de abajo* (El Paso, Texas, 1915); *Los caciques* (Mexico, 1917); *Las moscas* (Mexico, 1918); *Domitilo quiere ser diputado* (Mexico, 1918); and *Las tribulaciones de una familia decente* (Tampico, Tamaulipas, 1918).

even greater importance as one of the first serious and sustained attempts by a Spanish-American novelist to break away from the slavish imitation of European styles—which had doomed the Spanish-American novel, with very few exceptions, to inferiority throughout the nineteenth century—and to describe the reality around him in a fresh, original, direct way. At the time of their first publication, however, none of them attracted any attention at all, and by 1920, in view of his continued lack of success, Azuela had brought his cycle of novels of the Revolution to an earlier end than he had originally intended.

Various other authors were also writing novels of the Revolution while the Revolution was still being fought. In 1913 the right-wing journalist Alfonso López Ituarte published—under the pseudonym 'Héctor Ribot'—the third one to appear: an extremely crude and incompetent piece of pro-Huerta propaganda entitled *El Atila del sur* (Mexico, 1913): the title refers to Emiliano Zapata, who was dubbed 'the Attila of the South' by the Mexico City press [pp. 148–9]. He followed it in 1914 with an equally bad novelized account of the United States invasion of Veracruz, called *Satanás* (Mexico, 1914). In 1914, too, the old liberal journalist and politician Ireneo Paz (1836–1924) started to print, on his own press, his novelized biography of Madero (*Madero*: Mexico, 1914), but was unable to finish the task. 1915 saw not only the first, unnoticed, publication of *Los de abajo* but also the appearance of *La tórtola del Ajusco* (Barcelona–Mexico, 1915) by the Spanish professor of literature now established in Mexico, Julio Sesto (1879–1960). It is a sentimental love story, set against the shadowy and remote background of the Revolution; and it was a best-seller in Mexico City—the only one of these early novels of the Revolution to enjoy any popular success on first publication—clearly fulfilling the need of the suffering city populace [pp. 265–8] for a literary escape from their terrible problems. The *Animal Farm* of the Mexican Revolution, Jerónimo Sanz's *La revolución en el reino animal* (Mexico, 1915), was also published in 1915, under the pseudonym 'Fierabrás'. In the following year the feeble blood-and-thunder novel by Manuel Mateos, *La venganza del caporal*, which reaches its climax during the Maderista revolt, appeared, published, like *Los de abajo* and several other early novels of the Revolution, in Texas.[10] In 1917

[10] San Antonio and El Paso became the homes of large numbers of Mexican exiles. The following novels of the Revolution were published in San Antonio:

the memoirs of Huerta, almost certainly apocryphal but written in a convincing imitation of Huerta's style, were published (Fort Bliss, 1917) as well as Azuela's *Los caciques* (most of which was, however, written three years earlier).[11] The years 1910–17, which we have described as the military phase of the Revolution, saw the publication, then, of a small handful of novels whose action takes place during this period. With the exception of those of Azuela, none hold much interest for the reader who is solely concerned with literary values; and with the exception of Sesto's novel, and to a lesser degree, the memoirs of Huerta, none enjoyed any success or popularity. They are, on the whole, a miscellaneous bunch of literary oddities. There is certainly no question yet of the emergence of any coherent movement or school of novelists of the Revolution.[12]

After 1917 things continued in much the same vein for a few more years. The slow and unnoticed[13] trickle of novels dealing with aspects of the Revolution persisted, and grew gradually. In 1918 Azuela published his three final novels of the Revolution [p. 47n.]. In 1919 two novels appeared that were exceptional in that their authors were both well-educated and well-read men of letters: *Fuertes y débiles* (Mexico, 1919), by José López-Portillo y Rojas (1850–1923), and *La fuga de la quimera* (Mexico, 1919) by Carlos González Peña (1885–1955). The former is the only novel of this early period to attempt a realistic portrayal of the relationships

Arce, *Ladrona!* (1925) and *Sólo tú* (1928); Espinosa, *Cadena eterna* (1926); González, *Carranza* (1928); Maqueo Castellanos, *La ruina de la casona* (1921?); Mateos, *La venganza del caporal* (1916 and 1926); Reyes, *El automóvil gris* (1922, 1924, and 1929); and Torres, *Pancho Villa* (1924, 1925, and 1929) and *Como perros y gatos* (1924). *Los de abajo* was first published in El Paso, and Huerta's *Memorias* in Fort Bliss.

[11] Azuela, 'El novelista y su ambiente', *Obras completas*, III, pp. 1074–6.

[12] It was, somewhat surprisingly perhaps, the theatre rather than the novel that was cultivated widely during the years of the Revolution. Many plays and light operas about various aspects of the Revolution were written and performed with considerable popular success, though their appeal was ephemeral and none have lasted. See Acevedo Escobedo, 'Alusiones a la literatura de la Revolución mexicana', *El Nacional* (Mexico), 17 Nov. 1935; and Armando de María y Campos, *El teatro de género chico en la Revolución mexicana* (Mexico, 1957) and *El teatro de género dramático en la Revolución mexicana* (Mexico, 1957) (pp. 83–209 and 93–193, respectively, refer to the production of the years 1910–17).

[13] So unnoticed, indeed, that some critics have still not spotted them. Magaña Esquivel asserts (op. cit., I, p. 16) that 'the only novels published between 1910 and 1920 on the subject of the Revolution are three by Mariano Azuela—*Los de abajo*, *Los caciques* and *Las moscas*' (!!—he even misses three by Azuela himself).

between an hacendado and his peons (it is, however, very badly researched); the latter is a much more lyrical and personal novel, though it does incidentally—as does *Fuertes y débiles*—present interesting scenes from the life of the Mexico City bourgeoisie. In 1920 Antonio Ancona Albertos (1883–1954) published the two volumes of his penetrating and well-written novel of the life of a revolutionary journalist and intellectual, *En el sendero de las mandrágoras* (Mérida, Yucatán, 1920) but it, like the other novels, was ignored by critics and public. The same year saw the appearance of three other works of interest to us: K. Lepino's *Sangre y humo* (Mexico, 1918, i.e. 1920)[14] a long and tedious indictment of the whole Revolution from an extreme right-wing viewpoint, hung on a fragile cloak-and-dagger plot; Alberto A. Rodríguez's *Don Pascual* (Paris–Mexico, 1920), a hysterically xenophobic account, in novel form, of the United States invasion and occupation of Veracruz; and Lino Matamoros's *¡El terror!* (Mexico, 1920), which deals, in the manner of a third-rate romantic historical novel, with the events of the decena trágica of February 1913 in Mexico City. In 1921 two long and ambitious attempts to novelize the whole Revolution appeared: Esteban Maqueo Castellanos's *La ruina de la casona* (Mexico, 1921), and *En tierra de sangre y broma* (Mexico, 1921) by Salvador Quevedo y Zubieta (1859–1936), one of the first conscious attempts to analyse in fiction the national psychology of Mexico. In 1922 José Asunción Reyes's unpleasantly sanctimonious *El automóvil gris* (San Antonio, Texas, 1922) expressed its devout author's distaste for the Revolution and revolutionaries. The newly awakened interest in and sympathy for the indigenous population of Mexico [p. 234] was reflected in two novels published in 1923: Eduardo Luquín's *El indio* (Mexico, 1923), in which the only *indigenista* feature is, however, the title, for the novel itself is a trite little sentimental story set during the Revolution; and the rather more significant *Yórem Tamegua* (Guatemala, 1923) by Juan de Dios Bojórquez (b. 1892; pseudonym 'Djed Bórquez'), an attempt to portray the much-feared *yaqui* indians of northern Mexico as a noble and admirable, but misunderstood people. The *indigenista* novel did not become fashionable in Mexico, however, until over a

---

[14] 'K. Lepino' is probably a pseudonym for a writer who has not been traced. Some of the other writers under consideration here are, for all intents and purposes, anonymous, for their obscurity is such that their names are all that is known of them. Those novelists mentioned in the course of this chapter whose dates are not given are mostly of this type.

decade later, with López y Fuentes's *El indio*; so *Yórem Tamegua* is notable from a chronological point of view, if not from an aesthetic one. In 1923, also, Alfonso Teja Zabre (1888–1962) published his whimsical story of a university student's life in the Revolution and his involvement with a Spanish music-hall star and a mysterious Japanese spy: *La Esperanza y Hatí-Ke* (Mexico, 1923).[15] In the following year there appeared a Zapatista's account of his experiences during a campaign in 1915 (Dr. Miguel Galindo [1883–1942], *A través de la sierra* [Colima, 1924]), an extreme right-wing satire of the Revolution (Teodoro Torres, jr. [1891–1944], *Como perros y gatos* [San Antonio, Texas, 1924]) and, by the same author (now in a non-satirical mood) a romantic novelized biography of the recently murdered Pancho Villa (*Pancho Villa* [San Antonio, Texas, 1924]). Torres's biography is one of several that appeared soon after the murder of Villa [p. 165n.].

By 1925, then, a small but significant number of assorted novels of the Revolution had been written, most of them by unknown authors. The most important of these novels have been mentioned above. Only two of them had enjoyed an ephemeral popularity, and none had made any permanent mark at all. There was still, fifteen years after Madero's uprising, no coherent school or movement of Mexican novelists of the Revolution. Neither the taste of the reading public nor the style of the established literary figures had changed in the slightest; literate Mexicans continued to prefer sentimental novels and *modernista* poetry and short stories [p. 83n.] of the sort that had become popular in the tranquil, lethargic atmosphere of the Porfirian world, and Mexican writers continued to provide them. It seemed that, as far as literature was concerned, the Revolution might never have happened.

The reason was not difficult to find, as Mariano Azuela had shown in a long-since forgotten article which he published shortly after *Los de abajo*. The established literary figures could hardly be expected to write novels of the Revolution, for they had been trained to write for the very society that the Revolution sought to destroy.

---

[15] The presence of the Japanese in the novel is not as arbitrary as it might seem. There were strong rumours, at the end of the Porfirian period and during the years following, of a secret alliance between Japan and Mexico. The United States was much afraid of such a possibility. No such alliance, in fact, existed, but Japan was, at this time, taking a great interest in Mexico because of the latter's proximity to the United States. See Calvert, pp. 3, 27, 29, 50–1, 115–16, and 286.

The Novel of the Revolution could only be written by new writers representing the classes of Mexican society that emerged triumphant from the Revolution. Until a group of such writers formed up, and until they had a receptive and numerous public—a process which naturally enough took time to get under way—the dominant literary fashions were bound to continue being the old, pre-revolutionary ones. Azuela reasoned as follows in his perceptive, if highly rhetorical, article of 1917:

As far as the future of the Mexican novel is concerned, little can be expected of our professional men of letters. What do they know of those palpitations of the nation's soul which are, at these very moments, agitating our race? Is it not in these moments of supreme anguish, when the people's soul is soaked with tears and still pouring with blood, that the leading lights of our letters write books entitled *Senderos ocultos, La hora del Ticiano*, and *El libro del loco amor?*

... From the bedrock of Mexican society will rise, as we hope and expect, one who will rend our ears with his cry, swollen with all the anguish, all the hope, all the happiness of our race. And then, only then, will we have the book we have awaited so avidly, the book which we will snatch from each others' hands in order to experience its overwhelming bludgeoning of our senses, the scalpel which pitilessly cuts into our flesh, the cautery which burns it: the book which will reach the most hidden regions of our subsoil like the novels of Emile Zola in France and those of Leo Tolstoy in Russia. And it will be our book: flesh of our flesh and blood of our blood.[16]

It was not until the beginning of 1925 that this important turning-point was reached. Spokesmen for Mexican revolutionary governments had long, however, been preparing the way for this moment with appeals for a genuinely revolutionary literature. Although these appeals appeared at the time to fall on deaf

---

[16] Reprinted in *El Universal Ilustrado* (Mexico), 22 Jan. 1925. The place and exact date of publication of the original article are not given. It looks rather like an attempt to draw attention to *Los de abajo*, which had been published in 1915 and 1916 in Texas and was to be published in 1917 in Tampico—and which clearly strives to attain the qualities enumerated by Azuela in this article. He does not actually name or refer directly to *Los de abajo* in his article, however (as we have it in the *Universal Ilustrado* version, at least). Azuela's belief that the revolution in literature would have to be made by writers 'from the bedrock of Mexican society' was not, of course, verified: the other novelists of the Revolution were no more lower-class than he was. The three books to which Azuela refers are collections of lyric poetry by, respectively, Enrique González Martínez, José de Jesús Núñez y Domínguez and Efrén Rebolledo, published in 1911, 1917, and 1916.

ears, their cumulative effect must, in the long term, have been significant.

As early as 1915, with Carranza scarcely yet securely in control, the prominent Carrancista Félix F. Palavicini (1881–1952) wrote an article, 'La literatura revolucionaria' (published as the prologue to Marcelino Dávalos, *Carne de cañón* [Mexico, 1915]) calling for a school of writers of an imaginative literature which would adequately reflect the spirit of the Revolution. The literature which he envisaged would be a social and political tool; its function would be to consolidate the triumph of the Revolution: to serve as constant witness to the evils and injustices which the Revolution was fought to suppress, and so to prevent Mexican society from slipping back into its old ways:

The vigorous impulse which has been stirring our country for five years cannot be understood nor will it ever be substantialized unless it is accorded literary consecration. . . . Modification, change, complete renovation are not understood, perceived or sensed until they have been profoundly impressed on people by literature. . . . It is necessary for the indignant protest to parade daily before our eyes: for our ears to hear, each hour, the anthem of liberty; and for page after page to repeat in every tone and to paint in all colours the wickedness of a society censured by progress and condemned by morality. . . . Just as a country is only known and only becomes prestigious through the merits and glory of its writers, so a revolution does not gain distinction and consecration except through the worth and the importance of its literature.

The propagandist literature that Palavicini was demanding failed, however, to appear in significant quantities during the period of Carranza's rule. It was not until the next administration, that of Alvaro Obregón (1920–4), that a positive attempt to revive Mexican cultural life was made. The Secretary of Education during most of this period was José Vasconcelos (1881–1959), and he devoted himself single-mindedly to the task of educating Mexicans in the fullest sense, in order to give them an awareness of their own human capabilities. Although his educational campaign was not designed to produce a rebirth in Mexican imaginative literature, but rather to bring all Mexicans into active awareness of all the arts, it can only have had the general effect of stimulating such a rebirth. It is no coincidence that the rediscovery of Azuela, which in turn provoked the vast literary production of the 1930s in Mexico, occurred immediately after the end of Vasconcelos's period of office: Vasconcelos's admirable work as Secretary of Education had, indirectly, been preparing Mexico for this decisive moment. The importance of Vasconcelos in the creation of the modern Mexican novel has not been sufficiently noticed. His ambitious educational programme covered a wide field. He did much to stimulate the popular appreciation of music[17] and painting. His initiation of the important modern school of Mexican muralists is of particular interest to us here, for a close connection has been claimed between their paintings and the novels of the Revolution. He originated the policy of commissioning Mexican artists to paint on the walls of public buildings; the most usual subjects came to be the glories of the pre-conquest Mexican civilizations, the Reforma and the Revolution, all presented in a frankly propagandist light. The Revolution came to be commonly represented, particularly by Diego Rivera (1887–1957), as a co-ordinated socialist movement for the redemption of the working classes, particularly the Indians, and the suppression of capitalists, especially American ones, together with their ally, the Church.[18] In view of the enormous difference between the fundamental concept of the Revolution of the muralists and the novelists [p. 67], M. P. González's thesis that the former exerted a strong influence upon the latter seems difficult to uphold.[19] Although dealing with the same subject, they were two different art forms directed at different audiences. The murals give a simplified—and manifestly untrue— picture of a great popular struggle; they interpret the Revolution optimistically for the largely illiterate masses at which they were aimed. Whether Rivera unscrupulously intended it or not (if he did not, if his communism was sincere, he was remarkably naïve), the murals' effect on those masses can only have been to content

---

[17] Vasconcelos sponsored the reorganization, under the composer Julián Carrillo, of orchestras in the Republic. He gave the folklorist Joaquín Beristaín the job of encouraging popular dance and song. The latter initiative met with great success, and the vigorous flourishing of Mexican folk-music in modern times is a direct result: to Vasconcelos's displeasure, ironically enough, for he had intended the encouragement of popular interest in folk music as a purely temporary expedient, leading the people on to an appreciation of classical music. See *El desastre* (*Obras completas de José Vasconcelos*, Mexico, 1957), Vol. I, pp. 1271–2, and 1373–4, and *Boletín de la Secretaría de Educación Pública*, Vol. I (1922), p. 349, and Vol. II (1923), pp. 212–22.

[18] See L. E. Schmeckebier, *Modern Mexican Art* (Minneapolis, 1939); L. Cardoza y Aragón, *Orozco* (Mexico, 1959); and B. D. Wolfe, *Diego Rivera* (London, 1959).

[19] Op. cit., pp. 99–102.

and restrain them: to inhibit them from taking further revolutionary action in the belief that the events of 1910–17 were going to be to their great advantage (that is, to further the myth of the 'permanent' Mexican Revolution [p. 45]). The novels of the Revolution were totally different: addressed to a more sophisticated public, their message is pessimistic and closer to the truth, and their interpretation of revolutionary processes dissimilar in almost every way possible.

Vasconcelos's chief efforts, however, were concentrated on the literary education of the Mexican people. He greatly encouraged elementary education, believing it was of the first importance that all Mexicans should be able to read and write in order that the world of books should not be closed to them. He took an unprecedented step in persuading the President to allow him the use of the government presses—the *Talleres Gráficos de la Nación*—in order to print on them a series of world classics in cheap editions, as well as many text books and manuals of geography, agriculture, and national history. He initiated an ambitious programme of construction of public libraries, and founded in 1922 the government-financed periodical *El Libro y el Pueblo,* designed to foster the love of books in those classes of Mexican society which, before the Revolution, had had no access to culture or education of any sort.

In his final year of office Vasconcelos summarized his aims and ideals as educator in an open letter to the French novelist Romain Rolland. Art, he said, was Mexico's only salvation. In these tumultuous revolutionary moments, what was palpably lacking in Mexico was any social ideal, any general sense of direction. Society was disintegrating as each individual member of it unscrupulously followed his own selfish ambitions; the only hope of salvation from this widespread decay, the only way of converting the Revolution from a negative, destructive movement into a positive and constructive one, lay in an appeal to the Mexican people's inbred aesthetic instincts: the establishment, by art, of a new scale of social values, a new concept of life. It was necessary that literature, like all art, should contribute to revolutionary progress in a considerably more subtle and sophisticated way than that envisaged earlier by Palavicini:

Mexico . . . must transform her destructive fury into a fury of material and moral construction. She must construct an ideal. We are an atheistic nation, in the worst sense of the term: atheistic not so much because we deny dogmas but rather because we lack ideals, because when we are not mocking ideals, we are treading them underfoot and ignoring them. . . . Maybe this is a consequence—I sometimes think so—not of a lack of religious inclinations, but rather of the fact that we are forging, together with a new race, a new concept of life. In any case, we are living without any sense of purpose in the midst of the most despicable ambitions and the most unrestrained appetites. You affirm that we possess a living and passionate sense of beauty, and it is doubtless there where we must try to find the stimulus for our regeneration.[20]

Vasconcelos resigned as Secretary of Education in late July 1924. Several months later, however, in November, a most significant event, long planned-for under his secretaryship, finally took place. This was the first *Feria del libro* to be organized in Mexico City for many years; and it was, to judge from contemporary newspaper reports, a great success. It was a general exhibition of Mexican books, both old and new, intended to 'promote awareness of book production and to display, with moderate pride, Mexico's typographical and publishing activity'.[21] It had a clear nationalistic bias, and it featured a history of book-production in Mexico, illustrated by rare and precious examples of the past production of Mexican printers and binders. In the section devoted to modern books the booksellers and publishers who exhibited were strongly encouraged to allow the public to browse at will; for one of the declared aims of the *Feria* was to alter the attitude of Mexican booksellers, who never allowed customers access to their stocks, being interested only in certain, uncomplicated sales. Altogether, the *Feria del libro* both stimulated the Mexican public's interest in books, particularly Mexican books, and encouraged publishers to make new books more readily available. Mexican publishers had, in fact, been very inactive throughout the post-revolutionary period, producing very few new books and selling them at relatively high prices. Not only the *Feria del libro* but also, for example, the printing on the government's presses of cheap books—to which the commercial publishers violently objected—were intended, partly at least, to remedy this state of affairs. In fact, however, the resultant improvement in Mexican commercial publishing seems

[20] *El Libro y el Pueblo*, Vol. III (1924), p. 5. For a more detailed and specific exposition of Vasconcelos's intention, plans and policies as Secretary of Education, see *La educación pública en México* (Secretaría de Educación Pública: Mexico, 1922), and *De Róbinson a Odiseo* (*Obras completas*, II, pp. 1495–1719).
[21] *El libro y el pueblo*, III (1924), p. 141.

to have been only a relative one and not to have noticeably affected the novels of the Revolution until about 1932, by which time the movement was already well under way. Of the five novelists of the Revolution who came to prominence before 1932 (Azuela, Guzmán, Campobello, López y Fuentes and Muñoz), only Campobello did so with novels published in Mexico. The success of *Los de abajo*, on which the school of novelists of the Revolution was founded, was only assured by its publication in Madrid in 1927 [pp. 60–1]: its first Mexican edition by a leading company was not until 1938. Of the novelists writing after 1932, however, only two first published abroad (Romero and Ferretis). The fame and fortune of the novel of the Mexican Revolution was, then, made in Madrid; the Mexican publishers only began to take a real interest once the movement was firmly established, and cannot be said to have given it any initial impetus, rather helping to sustain it once it had started. It could well be argued, indeed, that the Novel of the Revolution invigorated Mexican publishing houses at least as much as the publishers animated the production of the novel; they certainly remained true to their tradition of timorous conservatism in only publishing novels of the Revolution once the literary movement was well under way and already fashionable—that is, precisely when these novels were ceasing to be new or revolutionary.

The *Feria del libro* was, nevertheless, the climax of the laudable efforts of Vasconcelos to foment a cultural and literary revival in Mexico—the efforts which were ultimately to bring the Novel of the Revolution into existence as a fashionable, flourishing, and influential literary movement.

In December 1924 the new president, Calles, was sworn into office. With him came a new Secretary of Education, José Manuel Puig Casauranc (1888–1939). In his inaugural speech he declared that Obregón's educational policies—Vasconcelos, now out of favour (he never made any secret of his hatred for Calles) was not mentioned—were excellent and would be continued. As far as the Secretariat's particular policy on literature was concerned, Puig Casauranc made a firm promise which was of considerable interest to young Mexicans with literary aspirations (Puig himself gained some passing renown as a novelist and short-story writer):

The Secretariat of Education will publish and will assist the divulgation of any Mexican work in which the mannered decoration of a false understanding of life is replaced by the other kind of decoration, rough and severe and often gloomy, but always truthful, taken from life itself. A literary work which, depicting suffering—not that suffering which is often feigned by poets of perpetual melancholy, but rather the suffering of others—and which, searching out its origins, coming face to face with desperation, the fruit of the grossly unsatisfactory organization of our society, and pulling apart the curtains which cover the life of those who are condemned to humiliation and woe by our brutal egoism, attempts to make us more human, to refine our understanding, and to make us experience, not the syrupy sweetness of an idyll nor the grief of a disappointment in romantic love, but rather Comprehension, with its wholesome rebelliousness and its soft tenderness which lead us to search for real reform; literary works whose authors' whole hope and aim is to jolt the minds of even those who are most lacking in awareness, and whose aspiration is not to cause wonderment among the members of our tiny 'élite' or fainting fits among romantic young ladies, but to produce in all readers a frown which signifies meditation, responsibility, comprehension and analysis.

To those who could cope with the jumbled pseudo-socialist rhetoric—typical of the Mexico of the 1920s—of the speech of Puig Casauranc, the message was clear: the government was prepared actively to encourage, and even to publish, the works of any author who wrote in a realistic, socially orientated and popular—rather than a lyrical, sentimental, or exquisite—style. Literature with a vigorous and critical social content was now officially approved, and the conventional and still popular *novela rosa* officially frowned upon. The views about the novel which Azuela had expressed some seven years previously—and which were, naturally enough, reflected in practice in *Los de abajo* and his other novels of the Revolution—had been publicly incorporated into government policy. Although there is little evidence to suggest that Puig Casauranc was very careful to keep his generous promise, his inaugural speech helped to create the climate of opinion in literary circles towards the end of 1924 which made it possible for *Los de abajo* to come to sudden and fruitful prominence.

Evidence of a growth of interest—largely government-directed, as has been seen—at the end of 1924 in the problem of a truly national literature, with special reference to the novel, can be found in the pages of newspapers and periodicals of the time. *El Libro y el Pueblo* reprinted from the Buenos Aires periodical *Nosotros* an article, 'La novela en America' by Alfredo S. Clulow, which discussed 'el americanismo literario', and asked when the genuinely

Latin-American novel would finally appear. It did not, of course, mention Azuela. *El Libro y el Pueblo* also printed a list of 'the best books published in Mexico in 1924'; it mentioned scarcely any novels, and none at all dealing with the Revolution. In the last month of the year, too, the national press published various summaries of the literary scene in Mexico, reporting the achievements of the year and discussing the future possibilities of Mexican literature. It was from a polemic developing out of these articles that Azuela and his *Los de abajo* sprang suddenly to fame.

In their reappraisals the majority of the critics reached the conclusion that Mexican literature, in spite of the Revolution, was still disappointingly feeble, gutless, and even effeminate. In the nineteenth century the combination of the dearth of good Mexican novelists and the educated classes' preference for French culture had led to the formulation of a complaint so common that it became a critical byword: 'There is no Mexican novel'.[22] Now, at the end of 1924, this expression was resuscitated, and most critics were wholly in agreement with all that it implied. Articles came to be written about the question 'Does a modern Mexican literature exist?', and in January 1925 a polemic grew up around the subject. The principal protagonists of the literary argument were Julio Jiménez Rueda and the Marxist Victoriano Salado Álvarez (both of whom answered the question negatively), and Francisco Monterde García Icazbalceta, the editor of *El Libro y el Pueblo* (who, in the pages of the national daily *El Universal*, defended contemporary Mexican literature against their attacks). Monterde, in his defence, rested most of his case on the hitherto unknown author Mariano Azuela, and underlined the literary values of *Los de abajo*. Azuela had, indeed, been mentioned in two slightly earlier articles, which may have attracted Monterde's attention: in one, the poet Rafael López, in an interview with Azuela's friend Gregorio Ortega, had

---

[22] The calls for Mexican authors to write in a genuinely and originally Mexican way at the end of 1924 were, in fact, nothing new, but a continuation of a nineteenth-century tradition, whether the critics of 1924 knew it or not. Nineteenth-century men of letters like Guillermo Prieto (1818–97), Ignacio Manuel Altamirano (1834–93) and José María Vigil (1829–1909) had repeatedly stressed Mexico's lack of a real literary tradition and called attention to the need to create one: and the *Liceo Hidalgo* was founded in 1850 with the principal aim of encouraging an authentically national literature. Under Porfirio Díaz, however, this preoccupation disappeared; the *Liceo Hidalgo* closed down in 1893. (See María Rosa Uría Santos, 'El Ateneo de la Juventud: su influencia en la vida intelectual de México' [Ph. D. Thesis, 1965, University of Florida], pp. 97–101.)

declared that *Los de abajo* was the best Mexican novel that had come out in the past ten years,[23] and in the other Ortega, under the pseudonym José Corral Rigan, had said that Azuela would be a great novelist when he finally produced 'the novel of the Revolution', meaning by that a panoramic, all-embracing portrayal of the Revolution as a whole in a work of prose fiction[24]—something, perhaps, like Gironella's later treatment of the Spanish civil war in *Un millón de muertos* (in fact none of the important novelists of the Revolution have attempted to do this at all, though Mexican literary critics have incessantly called out for them to do so).[25] But it was Monterde's article, not the others, which attracted widespread attention and succeeded in bringing Azuela and *Los de abajo* into the limelight. He became famous almost overnight. In the literary reviews published at the end of 1924 he had hardly been mentioned; less than a month later he had become the author of the day. Interviews with him appeared in most of the serious national newspapers, and *Los de abajo* was republished in serial form by *El Universal Ilustrado*, the first instalment appearing on 29 January. Articles in the Spanish press by prominent critics attracted attention to the novel in the peninsula, and a Madrid edition followed.

According to Azuela, however, his friend the journalist Gregorio Ortega must take most of the credit for the success of *Los de abajo* (its triumph is normally presented as the virtually single-handed achievement of the more eminent Monterde). Ortega not only was the author of the first articles in 1924 containing laudatory references to *Los de abajo*, but also was directly responsible for the publication of Azuela's novel by *El Universal Illustrado* and the spate of subsequent interviews.[26]

His remarkable efforts did not stop even here, however. Azuela holds him responsible for *Los de abajo*'s decisive success in Spain, too:

I don't know what would have come of all this if Ortega had not taken with him to Spain thirty of the fifty copies with which *El Universal*

[23] Azuela, 'El novelista y su ambiente': *Obras completas*, III, pp. 1117 and 1174. Azuela does not mention the newspaper in which the interview was published or its exact date of publication.
[24] 'La influencia de la Revolución en nuestra literatura', in *El Universal Ilustrado*, 20 Nov. 1924, p. 43.
[25] See Azuela's characteristically forthright comments in 'Algo sobre novela mexicana contemporánea': *Obras completas*, III, pp. 699-700.
[26] 'El novelista y su ambiente': *Obras completas*, III, p. 1174.

Ilustrado paid me. The fact is that when I thought that my name was well-known and that people were interested in my books, I took five copies of my *Mala yerba* to Botas bookshop. I returned a month later, sure that they would buy up the whole edition. But instead of that they returned three copies that they had been unable to sell.

An article by Enrique Díez-Canedo made a Spanish edition of *Los de abajo* inevitable, and another article by Giménez Caballero put the seal on its success. From that moment *Los de abajo* could walk alone.[27]

Ortega wrote the prologue to the 1927 Madrid edition. With it, Azuela's fame, based rather arbitrarily on *Los de abajo*, was assured. Here was a further, vital stimulus for the composition of other novels of the Revolution. Young novelists now had proof that the Revolution could provide the subject matter for a commercially and artistically successful novel, and they had a master whose example to follow. This practical demonstration of the possibilities of the Revolution as a literary subject was undoubtedly more influential than all the exhortation of Secretaries of Education and literary critics together; but, of course, the demonstration was only made possible in the first place by the activities and declarations of the politicians and of the critics.[28]

The government-inspired birth of interest in revolutionary literature soon had its practical, desired result: the growth of a homogeneous school of novelists of the Revolution. A large group of new, young novelists came into being, all of whom went back to the Revolution of 1910–17 for their subject matter and for their inspiration. They came to form a new literary élite in place of the old Porfirian one, replacing the lyrical sentimentalism that the latter had stood for by a new Mexican social realism after the style and manner of Azuela, and writing for a different public, the developing post-revolutionary middle-classes which were fast becoming a vigorous and powerful sector of society throughout the period in

[27] Ibid., pp. 1174–5.

[28] The first number of *El Libro y el Pueblo* for 1925 contained three articles reflecting the continued interest in the possibilities of a national literary revival: 'Los libros útiles para México' by Dr. Manuel Gamio, the new Subsecretary of Education (p. 14): 'Dejemos nuestra torre de marfil para ir a la tierra baja' by Guillermo de Luzuriaga (p. 94); and 'Notas sobre la novela en México' by Gilberto Loyo (p. 118). They all continue the call for realistic and relevant writing. Loyo's article, dated Mar. 1925 (two months after the rise to prominence of *Los de abajo*), makes no mention of Azuela and indeed specifically comments on the lack of novels about the Revolution—interesting confirmation of Azuela's suspicion that the Mexican success of *Los de abajo* would not have lasted had it not been for its subsequent success in Spain.

question. The change in style and taste that literary critics and government spokesmen had been calling for ever since 1915— Azuela himself, Palavicini, Puig Casauranc, Gamio, Loyo, and Luzuriaga have been mentioned here as notable representatives of a movement in Mexican criticism that came to its climax in the mid 1920s—was finally realized. The genuine Mexican novel was, together with the Mexican bourgeoisie, about to be born: or rather, having been born slightly prematurely with Azuela's works, it was ready to emerge from the incubator as a healthy and powerful infant.

The first important work of this new movement to be published (in 1928) was by Martín Luis Guzmán y Franco (b. 1887), *El águila y la serpiente*, memoirs of the Revolution in the north of Mexico between 1913 and 1915. Its lack of a plot and its autobiographical nature are characteristic of the novels of the Revolution; but the consciously elegant, almost aristocratic style in which it is written—and for which it is widely admired—is not at all typical of the movement as a whole. Guzmán, almost alone among the novelists of the Revolution, came from a family that was quite well-placed in the Porfirian hierarchy (his father was a colonel in the federal army). The strange fascination that the figure of Pancho Villa exercised over Guzmán led him, a decade later, to embark on the ambitious scheme of writing, in ten extensive volumes (of which only five have appeared), the *Memorias de Pancho Villa* (Mexico, 1938, 1938, 1939, 1940 and 1964), in the first person and in imitation of Villa's highly personal and colourful style of speech.

After Guzmán's start with *El águila y la serpiente* the movement gained impetus quickly and flourished spectacularly throughout the 1930s, when an average of five new novels of the Revolution were published each year. In 1931 three novels were published that brought the names of three new novelists of the Revolution to the attention of the reading public: *Campamento*, by Gregorio López y Fuentes (b. 1897) *¡Vámonos con Pancho Villa!* (Madrid, 1931), by Rafael Muñoz (b. 1894), and *Cartucho* by Nellie Campobello (b. 1912).

Both López y Fuentes and Muñoz were journalists by profession, as were Guzmán and many of the other members of the movement that was beginning to flourish—and which had itself been conceived in the pages of a newspaper. This was no mere coincidence; on the contrary, several factors combined to make it almost inevitable that journalism should exert a strong influence upon Mexican prose fiction of the 1930s. The Revolution had shattered the calm of the Porfirian world and caused a violent upheaval in Mexican society; so that a fluid, unstable situation had been created, in which important and exciting events occurred with frequency. As a result, journalism was relevant again, and the journalist became a vital and respected figure in society. Vigorous and energetic social groups tend to expand their field of activity, and the journalists turned towards prose fiction. They were, indeed, the only people in post-revolutionary Mexico with regular practice in the art of writing—the only social group, therefore, which was equipped to fill the gap left by the fall of the Porfirian men of letters and form the new literary élite. What was more, the new straightforward, concrete, realistic, narrative style practised by Azuela and advocated by critics is precisely the style of the newspaperman.

Journalism, then, helped to mould the style in which the majority of the novels of the Revolution were written; even those novelists who were not journalists could not help being influenced by the general tendency. The influence was not altogether beneficial. The modern journalist by nature tends not, perhaps, to have the qualities of a good novelist. The work he does leads him to concern himself with immediate first impressions of people and events, rather than with deep or sustained analysis of them. He will tend to discern the sensational rather than the deeply relevant; his writing is, and indeed ought to be, ephemeral rather than lasting. The finest artistic possibilities which the novel as a literary genre offers to the writer who cultivates it—the scope it offers for the portrayal in depth of the complexities of human personality and of human relationships—are precisely those which the journalist is least well-equipped to realize. Many of the shortcomings of the Mexican novelists of the 1930s can be traced to this fundamental discrepancy between the approach and attitudes of the journalist and of the novelist.

Gregorio López y Fuentes is a good example. He was employed by one of the important Mexican daily newspapers (*El Gráfico*) for several years during the 1920s writing a daily column, *La novela diaria de la vida real*, which consisted of one of the more sensational or sordid pieces of news of each day dressed up in short-story form. Such was López y Fuentes's literary training. *Campamento*, his first novel, is a documentary account of a typical night in an imaginary revolutionary camp. It is completely journalistic in style and approach; a photographic record of various of the activities of the soldiers, with no attempt to understand, explain, evaluate, or penetrate surface appearances in any way. In the following year he published *Tierra* (Mexico, 1933), a year-by-year account of Zapatismo, and in 1934 *¡Mi general!*. He is most renowned, however, for a novel which deals not with the Revolution but with the life of the oppressed and exploited Indians of Mexico, *El indio* (Mexico, 1935). All three novels suffer from the defects that make *Campamento* a minor work: defects which are directly attributable to López y Fuentes's journalistic training.

The case of Rafael Muñoz is similar. He was a reporter with *El Universal Gráfico* when Villa was killed in 1923, and was sent to Chihuahua to cover the story. At the same time he wrote a popularized account of Villa's last years, which was published in serial form in *El Universal Gráfico*. From here he went on to establish a modest reputation for himself during the late 1920s as a writer of short stories, many of them describing sensational events in the extravagant life of Pancho Villa.[29] In *¡Vámonos con Pancho Villa!* his love of sensationalism reaches its peak. The careers of both Muñoz and López y Fuentes as newspaper reporters gave them fluid and easy narrative styles but also left them with serious disabilities as novelists.

The third important novel of the Revolution published in 1931 was Nellie Campobello's *Cartucho*, a child's impressions of Villa's movement. Free of direct journalistic influence, it is a more interesting and disturbing novel than either of the other two published in the same year that have been mentioned above. As an innocent, uncomprehending child watches and impassively reports the terrible scenes that constitute for her no more than a great, exciting game, so the unconscious cruelty of her cold, detached, almost clinical attitude throws into relief the sheer brutality and inhumanity of fighting and slaughter much more forcibly than all the sensationalism of Muñoz. Nellie Campobello's other novel of the

---

[29] There are four books of his short stories of the Revolution, two of them first published before 1931: *El feroz cabecilla* (Mexico, 1928); *El hombre malo* (Mexico, n.d.—2nd ed., Mexico, 1930); *Si me han de matar mañana* (Mexico, 1934); and *Fuego en el norte* (Mexico, 1960)—a selection of various stories already published in the three earlier collections.

Revolution, *Las manos de mamá*, is very similar but lays more stress upon the child's relationship with her mother than upon the Revolution itself.

Another important novelist of the Revolution emerged in 1932, with the publication of his first novel, *Apuntes de un lugareño*: José Rubén Romero (1890–1952). Although he spent a short period as a newspaperman, journalism was of secondary importance in the literary formation of Romero, who was by profession a civil servant and diplomat. His novels (*Apuntes de un lugareño*; *Desbandada* (Mexico, 1934); *Mi caballo, mi perro y mi rifle* (Barcelona, 1936); and *Rosenda* (Mexico, 1946)) give the impression of only being concerned with the Revolution because the Revolution was, during the years he was writing, such a fashionable and popular subject that it was almost impossible for any novelist to ignore it. In all his work it is the quietly picturesque charm of the traditional life of the Mexican provinces, not the Revolution, which occupies the central place; the Revolution is merely a malign alien force which from time to time shatters the idyllic calm of small-town life. Indeed his best and most successful novel, *La vida inútil de Pito Pérez* (Mexico, 1938), is also the only novel of Romero's which is not concerned with the Revolution at all.

In 1935 the man who, more than any other, had brought about the revival of prose fiction in Mexico—José Vasconcelos—made another contribution to the now flourishing movement by writing one of the most important novels of the Revolution, *Ulises criollo* (Mexico, 1935). It was the first volume of a four-volume autobiography, of which the second volume, *La tormenta* (Mexico, 1936), also deals with Vasconcelos's life during the Revolution. The two together give a highly personal and polemical view of the events of the period, presented in a fluent, racy, vigorous style.

During the late 1930s and early 1940s there appeared on Mexico's literary scene three more novelists of the Revolution, who had much in common. Not only were they all, like Muñoz, Guzmán and López y Fuentes, journalists; they were also all politically conscious and approached the Revolution from a radical standpoint. The last important development in the literary movement we have been discussing was, then, the appearance during its latter stages of the socialist novels of the Revolution written by Jorge Ferretis (1905–62), Mauricio Magdaleno (b. 1906) and José Mancisidor (1894–1956). Ferretis was more interested in post-revolutionary political corruption, but he wrote one novel of the Revolution in which he analyses the inadequacies of Zapatismo, particularly those of the intellectuals in the movement: *Tierra Caliente* (Madrid, 1935). Magdaleno wrote two novels which deprecate the Revolution's failure to do anything to improve the miserable lot of Mexico's indigenous population: *El resplandor* (Mexico, 1937) and *La Tierra Grande* (Mexico, 1949). Mancisidor was the only one of these three left-wing novelists to defend and extol the Revolution, to consider it as a progressive movement rather than one which betrayed the faith of the masses; he reveals his optimistic vision of it in two novels, *En la rosa de los vientos* (Mexico, 1941) and *Frontera junto al mar* (Mexico, 1953).

And so the literary movement which revitalized Mexican letters and initiated the flourishing modern Mexican novel tradition came to its end. By about 1940 most Mexican novelists seem to have felt —a little tardily, perhaps—that the Revolution was exhausted as a source of inspiration,[30] and since then they have increasingly directed their attention to the more up-to-date and urgent problems of post-revolutionary society: the plight of the indio, the struggle for the control of Mexican oil, the political corruption which accompanied the reorganization of public life and the establishment of a new ruling élite, and, finally and most recently, the problems of life in the big industrial cities. Novels of the Revolution have appeared less and less frequently, and by now the school is virtually extinct.

Mexican governments fostered and supported the movement which had, in the first place, come into being largely as a result of governmental action, as we have seen above. The vital importance of governmental initiative in both generating and nurturing the Novel of the Revolution is a feature of this literary movement which has not been sufficiently noted. During the 1930s and later the government provided many of the novelists of the Revolution with employment to ensure their financial security and to provide

[30] Urquizo's *Tropa vieja* (1943) is, perhaps, the most significant novel of the Revolution to have appeared after 1940—not, certainly, for any literary qualities, but because of the considerable popular success it has enjoyed. This success is probably due in part to the original approach of Urquizo in describing the Revolution from the standpoint of a soldier in the Federal Army fighting against the revolutionaries (only Muñoz had done this before, in some of his short stories). He thus acquired the flattering title 'el novelista del soldado'. This is the only originality in the novel, however; for the rest it is a dreary recapitulation of all the tired clichés of situation, character and language of the movement.

them with enough spare time to continue writing.[31] At the same time, and perhaps rather remarkably, it sought to exercise no direct censorship or control over what they wrote. Indeed the almost unanimous conclusion reached in their novels by all these writers of the 1930s was a pessimistic one: that the Revolution had not made any important changes and that Mexican society was, after so much suffering and bloodshed, as corrupt and unjust as ever. Following Azuela, they saw the revolutionary process as a basically meaningless struggle between an old ruling class and a group that aspired to take its place, both of which cynically used as mere munitions the working classes in whose name the Revolution was hypocritically fought but who emerged at the end of it all weaker and more deprived than ever. There is a good deal of truth, of course, in the novelists' interpretation. But their judgment of the Revolution tended to be based rather on moral than on social or political precepts [pp. 70-1 and 123-6]—here, too, they took their cue from Azuela—and in their condemnation of the iniquities of civil war they largely overlooked the importance of the real changes that did occur. Expecting the wrong sort of change, envisaging the ideal revolution as some sort of process of national moral purification, they failed to take due account of the radical alterations in Mexico's social structure brought about by the Revolution, or to realize that these alterations might possibly be advantageous ones. The disappointment of their hopes for a moral crusade tended to lead the novelists of the Revolution into an indiscriminate condemnation of the whole affair. Francisco Rojas González, who was later to write his own novel of the Revolution (*La negra Angustias*: Mexico, 1944), published an article when the movement was at its height, accusing the novelists of gross ingratitude: 'many of them live at the expense of a government which, according to their stories, was put in power by rogues and murderers'.[32]

In fact, however, these writers were fulfilling their mission well. Simply by writing in such quantity about the Revolution, they did

[31] Some, like Campobello, Mancisidor and Magdaleno, were employed as teachers in state-run educational establishments. Muñoz occupied the position of chief of the Press Department in the Ministry of Education. Urquizo, a general in the Mexican army, occupied important positions in the administration. Romero was, between 1930 and 1945 (when he wrote his novels of the Revolution), successively Mexican Consul in Barcelona, Ambassador in Brazil and Ambassador in Cuba.

[32] 'Sobre la literatura de la post-revolución' in *Crisol*, May 1934.

much to stimulate a widespread interest in and awareness of its history, and to turn its leaders into legendary national heroes. Thus they helped—in conjunction with muralists, film-makers, and writers of popular songs—to foment the fierce nationalism which has been a central factor in Mexico's subsequent political stability and economic growth. Even the novelists who show the greatest disenchantment with the Revolution have contributed towards its establishment as a firm, unforgettable milestone in the collective memory of Mexico.

The novels of the Revolution divide, as we have seen, into two very distinct groups. Before 1925 they are more or less contemporary accounts of the Revolution, written by authors who had no contact with each other, who achieved at this stage no fame or success, who had no specific public to write for, and who had virtually no native precedents to follow. They are the novels that one can expect to present a comparatively fresh and direct picture of the events they describe.

After 1925, and particularly after 1930, the novelists of the Revolution form a clear literary movement. Their work is generally much more significant, as regards both quantity and—with the exception of Azuela and Ancona—quality. They were writing a sub-genre which was by now popular and fashionable; so they were very conscious of the public they were writing for. They had a universally recognized master—Azuela—whose lead to follow in questions of style, form, content, even attitude. And so the novels of this period tend to fall into certain well-proved moulds of plot and character; just like the Western or the detective or the sentimental novel, the Novel of the Revolution, on acquiring popular appeal, tended to become stereotyped and standardized; and certain commonplace characters and situations were evolved and appeared repeatedly.[33] By following well-trodden paths the authors could be sure of retaining the selling power of their stories.

[33] Some of the stock characters of the novels of the Revolution are: the rebel peasant (ignorant and undisciplined but immoderately brave), the hypocritical priest (fat, lascivious, caricatured), the cynical opportunist, the tyrannical hacendado and his cruel administrator, the long-suffering and ill-treated indio and the hard-working and miserly Spanish storekeeper. Some stock situations : scenes on the crowded military trains; sacking and booty-hunting; bodies hanging from telegraph poles; the forced conscription of unsubmissive peons; the confrontation between hacendado and peon, caused by the former's amorous approaches to a female relative or intimate of the latter (this is a particularly favoured situation). Urquizo's *Tropa vieja* and Vera's *La revancha* are perhaps the two novels of the Revolution which bring together most such commonplaces.

Another result of the popularity and commercialization of the Novel of the Revolution was a certain tendency towards sensationalism, to which the influence of journalism, as we have seen, also probably contributed. Rafael Muñoz is the outstanding example of a novelist of the Revolution who suffers from this defect, but it is present in most of the novelists of the 1930s to some extent at least. Daniel de Guzmán, in the course of his analysis of Muñoz's sensationalism, suggests that the temptation to exaggerate and over-emphasize was made stronger by the large amounts of money novelists could make by selling plots to the directors of the rising Mexican film industry.[34] Many of the novels certainly read rather like film-scripts. One author who fought in the Revolution himself has stated that the popular demand for novels of the Revolution led some authors even as far as to resurrect and introduce into their tales episodes taken from other wars 'and even ideals which did not exist in the first place have been subsequently invented'.[35] The Marxist critic Arturo Turrent Rozas interpreted the sensationalism of the novelists as one aspect of their flight from contemporary reality, a taking refuge from the pressing problems of real life in the superficially exciting but essentially insignificant and incidental aspects of the Revolution. They preferred, he said, recounting morbid and macabre anecdotes to undertaking serious and responsible analysis of society. His indictment is a telling and perceptive one, and a further warning against accepting the novels of the 1930s at face value as historical documents:

The proletarian spirit could have been brilliantly displayed in the novel of the Mexican Revolution. But our revolutionary novel is as bourgeois as avant-garde literature itself. In the first place we should note its complete lack of bearings and ideology. And then, this literary movement has fled cravenly from the present-day reality which an honest work would analyse and study. It has fled from reality and taken refuge in anecdotes about the revolutionary struggle. The spectacle afforded by

---

[34] *México épico* (Mexico, 1962), p. 86; see also González, pp. 278–9. Muñoz and Magdaleno wrote many film scripts.

[35] Francisco L. Urquizo, *Recuerdo que . . .* (Mexico, 1934), quoted by Daniel de Guzmán, p. 41. One strange and ridiculous example of the transposition of episodes from other wars is to be found in Vera's *La revancha*, where the peasant guerrilla leader, el cojo Timoteo—Azuela's Demetrio Macías renamed—has his amputated leg buried with full military honours, an incident lifted straight from the life of the nineteenth-century caudillo Santa-Anna (Castro Leal, *La novela de la Revolución mexicana*, I, p. 790).

FM

hangings. The natural excesses of a people in the process of shaking itself free of the yoke of dictatorship. Pancho Villa exhibited to the joy of all reactionaries. . . . Everything which appeals to the hysteria of the bourgeoisie of this country and of the world.[36]

It was, of course, most convenient for the Mexican governments of the difficult and depressing decade of 1930–40 that the novelists should choose as their subject an earlier period, and thus divert some attention (the attention both of the novelists themselves and of their public) away from the problems of their own times. This sophisticated form of literary escapism—which successfully disguised itself as precisely the opposite—was of considerable aid to the governments of the period in their attempts to minimize discontent and preserve stability.

Post-revolutionary developments in Mexico tended to isolate the novels of the Revolution even further from their historical source. The time-lag between the events of 1910–17 and the novels of 1930–40 which deal with them was crucial, not only in dimming and blurring the memories of the novelists. During those twenty years Mexico could show very few signs of advance. There was little apparent economic expansion or implementation of social justice. The succeeding presidents had won a reputation for unparalleled corruption and venality, which seemed to culminate in the regimes of Calles and his puppet presidents[37] through whom he continued to exercise executive power. The Revolution, it seemed, had been miserably betrayed by its leaders. Not until the late 1930s, when in general the effects of the honest radical rule of Lázaro Cárdenas (1934–40) began to be seen and felt, and in particular with the traumatic repercussions on national morale of his overnight nationalization of the largely American-owned oil industry (18 March 1938), did the climate in Mexico start to become one of hopefulness and optimism; then the great economic growth of the 1940s confirmed and accentuated the new vitality and buoyancy. The majority of the novels of the Revolution were, however, written during the period of gloom and despondency, and consequently give a retrospectively pessimistic version of what happened during the Revolution; the political immorality of the times furthermore inclined the novelists to react into the narrowly

[36] *Hacia una literatura proletaria* (Jalapa, 1932), prologue.
[37] Plutarco Elías Calles, 1924–8; Emilio Portes Gil, 1928–30; Pascual Ortiz Rubio, 1930–2; Abelardo Rodríguez, 1932–4.

moral stance which, as we have seen above, characterizes their works.

For all these reasons it is evident that the novels written after 1925 are extremely unreliable as documentary sources of the social history of the Mexican Revolution, in spite of the carefully-contrived appearance of factual accuracy of many of them.[38] Their documentary form and presentation is itself simply a literary style, as much as any other, and it by no means guarantees that their pages contain a true account of the Revolution. The strong impression that many of them give of social realism is a carefully contrived effect: successfully contrived, certainly, to judge from the list of critics that it has led astray. The novelists of the 1930s give, after all, not a description but a reconstruction of the Revolution. Too many other influences were at work on them. Most of their novels were written a good fifteen years—during which many important events occurred—after the events they describe and, in general, they reflect rather the atmosphere of the period during which they were written than that of the Revolution itself.

Only the contemporary accounts are even moderately trustworthy. Therefore we are left for the purpose of this study with nearly thirty novels written and published before 1925, together with one or two others, listed here in approximate order of sociological interest and usefulness:

Mariano Azuela, *Los de abajo* (1915)
   Los caciques (1917)
   Andrés Pérez, maderista (1911)
   Domitilo quiere ser diputado (1918)
   Las moscas (1918)
   Las tribulaciones de una familia decente (1918)
Antonio Ancona Albertos, *En el sendero de las mandrágoras* (1920)
Esteban Maqueo Castellanos, *La ruina de la casona* (1921)
José López-Portillo y Rojas, *Fuertes y débiles* (1919)
Alfonso Teja Zabre, *La Esperanza y Hatí-Ke* (1923)
Alberto A. Rodríguez, *Don Pascual* (1920)

---

[38] There are one or two exceptions. Those few that were published between 1925 and, say, 1928—before the movement had started to prosper—were less subject to outside influences of the sort discussed in this chapter,—and more likely to be acceptable as evidence. Such a novel is Quevedo y Zubieta's *México manicomio* (Mexico, 1927). Among the later novels, the straightforward autobiographies or memoirs—like *El águila y la serpiente*, *Apuntes de un lugareño* or *Ulises criollo*—can yield valid information if used carefully.

José Vasconcelos, *Ulises criollo* (1935)
La tormenta (1936)
Carlos González Peña, *La fuga de la quimera* (1919)
Martín Luis Guzmán, *El águila y la serpiente* (1928)
Salvador Quevedo y Zubieta, *En tierra de sangre y broma* (1921)
México manicomio (1927)
K. Lepino, *Sangre y humo* (1920)
Alfonso López Ituarte, *El Atila del sur* (1913)
Satanás (1914)
Miguel Galindo, *A través de la sierra* (1924)
Teodoro Torres (jr.), *Como perros y gatos* (1924)
José Ugarte, *Undécimo* (c. 1918)
Juan A. Mateos, *La majestad caída* (1911)
Lino Matamoros, *¡El terror!* (1920)
José Asunción Reyes, *El automóvil gris* (1922)
Jerónimo Sanz, *La revolución en el reino animal* (1915)

There are several broad observations that can finally be made about this selection of novels (most of which are, in fact, 'novels' in the traditional sense of the term as well as in the special sense suggested at the beginning of this chapter).

They are much more ethical than aesthetic [pp. 8ff]. In a period of revolution people rarely, if ever, remain neutral, but rather become passionately committed one way or the other. The novels of such a period can be expected to reflect this polarization of opinions. Azuela describes this process of commitment as it happened to him and affected his writing, and as it surely must also have happened to the other novelists of the Mexican Revolution who wrote during the Revolution itself or soon after:

From that moment—whether I was fully conscious of what I was doing or not—I ceased to be the serene, impartial observer that I had set out to be in my first four novels. Sometimes as a witness, sometimes as a participator in the events which were to be a basis for my writings, I had to be, and in fact I was, a partial and impassioned narrator. By my own independent decision I had chosen my position in the great movement of renovation, and I intended to, and did, maintain it right to the end.[39]

Azuela insists, however, that this commitment did not in any

[39] 'El novelista y su ambiente', *Obras completas*, III, p. 1072. If Azuela really had intended to write with serene impartiality in his pre-revolutionary novels, he had hardly succeeded. In *Los fracasados*, for example, he makes a vigorous protest against Porfirian corruption. It is true to say, however, that his social commitment becomes stronger and more insistent in his novels of the Revolution.

way prevent him from writing truthfully, that his intense involvement with the subject of his novels did not lead to any misrepresentation of it: 'I wrote passionately, but I kept strictly to the truth'.[40] The sympathies of the early group of novelists of the Revolution are indeed nearly always very marked in their works—a fact which, though it tends to make for a moderately high element of conscious or unconscious distortion, renders that distortion itself all the easier to identify. Azuela himself tends to colour his account in two separate ways, each corresponding to one of his two coexisting but conflicting attitudes to the Revolution [pp. 87–92 and 122–3]: his positivist belief that revolutions can achieve nothing leads him to cast a pall of gloom over what he describes and to stress the ineffectiveness of individual action; while his emotional sympathy for the poor, oppressed, and suffering leads him to the insistent caricature, in all his novels of the Revolution, of their rich and powerful exploiters. More common, however, amongst these novelists is a straightforward right-wing hostility towards the Revolution and all the revolutionaries, who are consequently dismissed as wicked hordes of thieves and murderers: this is the attitude of the Huertista propagandist López Ituarte, the hysterically Roman Catholic Reyes, the deeply embittered Vasconcelos; and Quevedo y Zubieta, López-Portillo y Rojas, Sanz, Torres, Maqueo Castellanos, Rodríguez, and Lepino. The latter can perhaps speak for each one of them when he defines the aim of his novel as being to

draw . . . a more or less exact picture of the terrible harm caused by the revolution and to engender in people's hearts, by evoking the memory of the past, the conviction that revolutions are, without any doubt, the most agonizing whip with which a nation's back can be beaten; and, in this way, to persuade the masses to search for collective betterment through other channels, slow ones undoubtedly, but at the same time much more effective ones as regards their positive, beneficial results: channels such as the diffusion of culture and the love of order and of work.[41]

It will be clear that any evidence provided by the above authors about revolutionary fighters or leaders will have to be treated with the greatest caution. Among all the early novelists of the Mexican Revolution there are only three exceptions to the rule that the ethical approach, with its tendency to distortion, predominates

[40] Ibid., p. 1074.   [41] *Sangre y humo: prólogo.*

over the aesthetic. One of these, Guzmán, is not very valuable for our purposes as his novel is of much greater political and personal than sociological interest. Another, López-Portillo y Rojas, makes clear his firm hostility to the Revolution, and is not a reliable witness to the characteristics and activities of revolutionaries. His portrayal of the Mexican rich, both urban and rural, is, nevertheless, a generally impartial and aesthetic one: he neither praises nor condemns them, but tries to show them as they are. Since, in addition to this, he indulges in the most minute, exhaustive and detailed descriptions of the everyday and ordinary in his characters' lives, he is most useful to us as a chronicler of the upper classes. The other principally aesthetic novelist is Ancona Albertos. He, like Azuela, has both a general sympathy for the aims of the Revolution and an overall pessimism about its possibilities of success; but, unlike Azuela, he is able to restrain these feelings at least enough to prevent them from impairing his sympathetic understanding of human nature in all its various individual manifestations. He consequently gives a uniquely rounded, convincing, and perspicacious depiction of important revolutionary types, especially the irresolute intellectual [pp. 103–11] and the opportunist soldier [pp. 213–15]. He tells us much about the social history of the Mexican Revolution that no other writer is capable of telling us.

The novels chosen for study here are, on the whole, poor works of literature. Trotsky observed that all things, including literature, that are born of revolution are bound to show a certain roughness and imperfection, because the search for new ways to express new circumstances and ideas—a search made, it might be added, by new and inexperienced writers—necessitates the adoption of a technique of trial and error.[42] The novels of the Mexican Revolution show such characteristics very markedly. In view of this the novels of Azuela and Ancona are remarkable for having been written with considerable technical assurance; and so the novels of these two men must necessarily form the substance of the present study. The others, though with few exceptions bad novels, are still useful sources of knowledge; but the more accomplished works of Azuela and Ancona are perforce more complete and deep portrayals of those complex networks of conflicts and relationships in the illustration of which novels are uniquely rich.

[42] *Literature and Revolution* (Michigan, 1960), p. 78.

The influence of previous literary tradition on these novelists tends, as has already been indicated, not to be very strong. The only novelist among those listed above who relies heavily on literary sources is González Peña. The literary affiliations of the others vary in degree but never become sufficiently marked to influence their accounts in any basic or sustained way. As most of these novelists were not established literary figures they tended to employ a style of direct, fresh reporting to write about the Revolution. Not all went to the extreme of Lepino, López Ituarte, and Rodríguez, all of whose novels are built upon 'the methodical, annotated and collated compilation of official and private documents, and of press reports'.[43] But the documentary note is insistent in most of them; and many were clearly written with the main aim of presenting a history of the Revolution in novelized form, with the result that imaginative elements are subordinate to, and only work in function of, historiographical ones. The most notable examples of novelized histories of this kind are the works of Lepino, López Ituarte, Rodríguez, Quevedo y Zubieta, Maqueo Castellanos, Torres, Ugarte, Mateos, Matamoros, Reyes, Sanz, and Ancona (in the second part of his novel). On these and the other novelists discernible and intrusive literary influences are limited. The sentimentalism of the Porfirian style reveals itself in the importance of conventionally romantic love affairs in many of the novels; and the works of Mateos, Matamoros and Rodríguez fall wholly within the romantic historical-novel tradition,[44] and accordingly present the Revolution in a special light. The nineteenth-century French novel tradition has its inevitable effect on some of our novelists: Azuela and Galindo interpret the Revolution in terms of positivistic theories of human behaviour as expounded in naturalist novels, and Quevedo y Zubieta and Maqueo Castellanos occasionally dabble in the techniques of Zola and Balzac.[45] Other influences are

---

[43] Alberto A. Rodríguez, *Don Pascual* (Paris and Mexico, 1920), title page. It is perhaps worth noting that José María Gironella employed a similar method in writing his novel of the Spanish Civil War, *Un millón de muertos* (Barcelona, 1961): see his 'Aclaración indispensable', especially pp. 10-11.

[44] Rodríguez even goes so far as to make his characters address each other with the archaic pronoun *vos*, which had long been lost from Mexican usage by the time of the Revolution. The influence of the romantic historical-novel tradition can also be discerned in the feeble cloak-and-dagger stories on which the novels of Lepino and López Ituarte hang.

[45] The opening of *La ruina de la casona* is a straightforward imitation of the beginning of a Balzac novel, and some of Maqueo Castellanos's characters—notably the ambitious, astute, middle-aged, mildly promiscuous Tacha—have

more sporadic: Lepino and Quevedo y Zubieta have some *costumbrista* set pieces;[46] Azuela's ironic portrayal of upper-class life in *Las tribulaciones de una familia decente* possibly owes something to Eça de Queiroz; Ancona Albertos displays great admiration for Anatole France without showing any discernible literary dependence on him. This relative lack of strong literary influences on our novelists makes their works easier for the social historian to handle; it is one possible source of distortion, at least, that we do not have to worry very much about in the present study.

Between them these novelists cover the whole range of Mexican society in the Revolution, though some social groups are better documented than others. The lower classes that formed the masses of the revolutionary soldiery are the section that the novels tell us least about. The only serious attempts to portray peasants in the novels were made by Azuela and López-Portillo y Rojas; the former was only partially successful [pp. 125–6] and the latter wholly unsuccessful [pp. 101–2, 218, 227, 251–2 and 288n.]. For the middle classes of the cities (to which social group most of the novelists belonged) we turn to the pages of Ancona, Maqueo Castellanos, Azuela, Teja Zabre, Rodríguez and González Peña; between them these six give a complete panorama of the Mexican bourgeoisie, both that element which joined the revolutionary ranks and those who remained neutral. The anti-revolutionary upper-middle and upper classes (rich businessmen and politicians, and hacendados) are well delineated by López-Portillo y Rojas, and violently caricatured by Azuela.

The novels which form this select group vary greatly in literary interest and in documentary value. They do all, however, have in common the fresh, immediate interpretation of the hugely complex social process that was the Mexican Revolution. The stage has now finally been reached at which an attempt can be made to extract

more of a French than a Mexican ring about them. Quevedo y Zubieta similarly shows occasional signs of strong dependence on Balzac. But fortunately for the purpose of this study neither novelist is consistent enough to sustain this French note for very long, and both lapse into direct, 'unliterary' reporting for most of the length of their novels.

[46] *Sangre y humo*'s first two chapters—the only part of the novel with any possible claim to literary significance—contain a pleasant description of a *fiesta* in the *huasteca potosina* of West Central Mexico. Quevedo y Zubieta provides a few brief sketches of Indian customs. Juan de Dios Bojórquez's *Yórem Tamegua* (1923) [pp. 229–30] is a much idealized portrayal of the customs of the northern Mexican *yaqui* Indians.

from them the information they hold. Dividing our survey of Mexican revolutionary society into two main categories—revolutionaries and anti-revolutionaries—we will begin with a consideration of a vital group among the former: the organizers or, using the word in its widest sense, intellectuals of the Revolution.

4

REVOLUTIONARIES I: THE
INTELLECTUALS

F o r the purposes of this study it seems advisable to follow the lead
of the Italian Marxist, Antonio Gramsci, and give the term 'intellectual' a broad and inclusive meaning. Gramsci is one of the few
writers to have devoted careful attention to the subject of the
revolutionary intellectual. He pointed out that in a sense all men
are intellectuals, in so far as all men have the capacity for thinking;
the only valid way of distinguishing the intellectual, in the more
specific meaning of the word, from the rest of society is in terms of
his function within the whole social context:

Can a unitary criterion be found for characterizing equally all the
many varied intellectual activities and for distinguishing these at the
same time and in an essential way from the activities of other social
groupings? The most widespread methodological error seems to be that
of looking for this distinguishing criterion within the sphere of intellectual activities, rather than examining the whole general complex of
social relations within which these activities (and hence the groups
which personify them) are to be found. Indeed the worker or the proletarian, for example, are not specifically characterized by their manual
or skilled work, but by this work performed in certain conditions and in
certain social relationships. . . . All men are intellectuals, one could
therefore say; but all men do not have the function of intellectuals in
society. When we distinguish between intellectuals and non-intellectuals
we are in fact referring only to the immediate social function of the
intellectuals as a professional category, that is to say we are taking
account of the direction in which the particular professional activity
largely bears: whether in intellectual elaboration or in muscular-
nervous effort.[1]

Intellectuals are, then, those who have a directive function—in

---

[1] *Gli intellettuali e l'organizzazione della cultura* (Turin, 1948), pp. 5–6. I
follow the translation of Louis Marks (Gramsci, *The Modern Prince and Other
Writings* (London, 1957), pp. 120–1); except in the last sentence, where I correct
a serious error of translation.

the broadest sense—in society; the word refers to more than just a privileged élite of great thinkers:

> This statement of the problem has the effect of greatly broadening the concept of intellectuals, but only in this way is it possible to reach a concrete approximation to reality. This way of presenting the question strikes a blow against preconceptions of caste: it is true [however] that the very function of organizing social hegemony gives rise to a certain division of labour and so to a certain gradation of qualifications, in some of which no leading or organizing attribute any longer appears. . . . In fact intellectual activity must be divided into levels from an intrinsic point of view as well, levels which in moments of extreme opposition offer a true qualitative difference: in the highest grade will have to be placed the creators of the various sciences, of philosophy, of art, etc.; in the lowest, the most humble 'administrators' and propagators of already existing traditional and accumulated intellectual riches.[2]

By transferring Gramsci's ideas to a more specifically revolutionary context we can define the revolutionary intellectuals not merely as 'the exclusive group of enlightened and progressive thinkers who provide the mental stimulus for the revolution' but rather as 'all those who take their place on the revolutionary side and whose contribution to the revolutionary effort, whose primary revolutionary function, is rather mental or intellectual than physical—whatever the quality of their thought or the importance of their position in the hierarchy of revolutionary society'. Revolutionary intellectuals —as opposed to intelligentsia—are, according to this definition, to be found at all levels; they are both the advisers of the national leaders and the organizers and ralliers of support and enthusiasm on a purely local scale. Both the top intellectuals and the humbler rank-and-file intellectuals form part of the same phenomenon, and it is reasonable to consider them as making up a single social grouping, as Gramsci has demonstrated. Qualitative distinctions can be made within the grouping, but it would be arbitrary and unhelpful to use them as grounds for excluding certain sectors— the more modest ones—from the grouping. The rank-and-file intellectuals, indeed, provide the very foundations from which the top intellectuals spring and upon which they ultimately depend; they all form part of the same edifice.

It is a fact generally recognized by students of the sociology of revolutions that the role of the intellectual in a revolution is an

---

[2] Ibid., pp. 9–10: translated by Marks, pp. 124–5.

extremely important one.[3] From the ranks of the disaffected intellectuals—educated people who, for one reason or another, have not been taken into the ruling establishment and who remain outside the power system—typically those who have obtained an education in spite of a humble family background and precarious economic circumstances, would usually be expected to come strong opposition to a repressive government and, if revolution breaks out, firm support for the revolution. Any serious revolutionary movement will have intellectuals in vital and prominent positions from its very beginning.

The intellectual élite's indispensable role in a revolution is that of co-ordinating the movement. Without the guiding control of the intellectual group a revolution degenerates into isolated revolts and sporadic, disorganized violence or, rather, is unlikely in the first place to gain enough momentum to make any serious threat against the social order it seeks to overthrow. The revolutionary intellectual acts to hold together a movement all of whose innate tendencies are towards division and disunity; it is his job to harness the energy generated by the blind fury which leads oppressed men to take up arms against their masters, and direct it consciously and efficiently towards the common goal, the removal from power of the anti-revolutionary ruling class. When the revolution is being planned, it is the intellectual who must not only guide the military leaders in the formulation of their public statements of intent and their support-seeking promises of future political action, but also stir up as much popular discontent as possible; while the revolution is being fought, it is the intellectual's task to keep the fighting men, both the leaders and the rest, informed about the purposes, ideals, and progress of the movement, and so to maintain their revolutionary enthusiasm and their faith in an ultimate triumph; on the victory of the revolution, the intellectual plays a vital part in the official confirmation of victory—the establishment in power of the successful forces, the drawing up of new legislation, and so on.

Throughout a revolution the intellectuals are its keystones, and have a function which only men with their training and mental perspectives can fulfil. If they are to do so satisfactorily, they must

[3] See, for example, Gramsci, op. cit.; Lyford P. Edwards, *The Natural History of Revolution* (Chicago, 1927), pp. 38–66, 69, 91; George Sawyer Pettee, *The Process of Revolution* (New York, 1938), p. 89; Crane Brinton, *The Anatomy of Revolution* (London, 1953), pp. 42–53, 89–93, 119, 130–1; Mendieta y Núñez, pp. 83–8.

permeate revolutionary society, organizing, encouraging, co-ordinating and informing at all levels, the unrelenting and ubiqui-tous agents for the hope-filled future, equally active at the side of the famous military hero and amongst the humble members of the anonymous guerrilla band. The revolution, then, makes special demands on those intellectuals who join its ranks and urgently requires certain personal qualities of them. The intellectual who is to be of any use to the revolution he seeks to serve will need to be well endowed above all with certain practical attributes—decisive-ness, organizing ability, resilience, political awareness, and social flexibility.

The intellectual climate of the period immediately preceding the Mexican Revolution was not of the sort to encourage such qualities. The Díaz system was fundamentally anti-intellectual, in that it was based on the belief that society should be run not by dreaming idealists, whose abstract theories and moral preoccupations incap-acitate them from taking effective direct action, but by an élite of hard-headed businesslike technocrats. As a consequence, education was neglected by Díaz; and the intellectual was given no respon-sible place in the Porfirian scheme of things. Furthermore, the 'pan o palo' policy of Porfirio Díaz [p. 20] was employed as much with regard to intellectuals as any other section of society, so that independence of political and social thought was stifled. Intellec-tuals, particularly those who were active and ambitious, were attracted into comfortable, but relatively unimportant, positions within the system, where they could be controlled and kept out of mischief.

This integrated section of the Mexican intelligentsia was that which was largely responsible for the attempt to justify Porfirian materialism and social injustice by recourse to the doctrines of positivism—particularly by stressing the need for peace at all costs and the concept of life as a struggle between individuals, in which only the strong have the right to prosper. Positivism had been the official philosophy of Mexico since 1867, when Juárez had invited the positivist and educationalist Gabino Barreda to collaborate with him in the attempt to institute a genuinely liberal and secular system of education. It also answered the need to try to impose order on the anarchical situation that Mexico found herself in. Mexican positivism soon degenerated under Díaz into a convenient excuse for anomalies within the Porfirian system which would have been indefensible from a Christian moral standpoint. The only widespread intellectual endeavour which had any social relevance in the Porfirian period was, then, a work of assimilation and imitation at the best, and at the worst one of debasing and denaturing; it was anyway wholly anti-revolutionary.[4]

Opposition to Porfirian positivism was reflected in the founding in 1909 of the *Ateneo de la Juventud*, a club of young intellectuals. Its principal concern was to remedy the lack of humanism in the intellectual atmosphere of the times, and to undermine the influence of positivism—by now an outdated and sterile routine of conventional thought in Mexico—by encouraging serious interests in metaphysical and literary questions, which official Porfirian thought dismissed as unimportant. Although it helped, then, to pull away the ideological supports from under Porfirismo, its contribution was mainly a negative one, and it remained, until after Madero came to power, disdainfully aloof from all political matters: of the thirty-one founder members, only one—Vasconcelos—had anything to do with the Maderista revolt. Its importance as an ideological precursor to the Revolution is extremely limited; and its significance for its members in 1913 and 1914 (when it was disbanded) was precisely as an escape from revolutionary affairs. Although in 1912, when Vasconcelos became its president, it came nearer to politics and took an active part in the mission of the *Universidad Popular Mexicana* (founded in December 1912) to spread culture among the people, it always maintained its original aloofness from the Revolution itself. It did not feel any need, for example, either to attack or to defend Huerta. Here, then, were many of the brains the Revolution needed, busy discussing the problems of art and philosophy [p. 121].[5]

The colonial period had established the tradition of a native intellectual group divorced from all political power. The slogan 'poca política, mucha administración' [p. 20] when put into practice under Porfirio Díaz meant the active discouragement of political awareness and hence a return to the colonial predicament of a lack of public responsibility in precisely those Mexicans who would

---

[4] See Octavio Paz, *El laberinto de la soledad* (4th edition, Mexico, 1964), pp. 108–11; Leopoldo Zea, *El positivismo en Mexico* (Mexico, 1942); Uría-Santos, chap. 2.

[5] See Uría-Santos, op. cit.; María del Carmen Millán, 'La generación del Ateneo y el ensayo mexicano', in *Nueva Revista de Filología Hispánica*, 1961, pp. 625–36; Paz, pp. 116–17.

have to lead the country in the future. Because of Díaz's insistence on reserving important political office for men of his own generation, the young intellectuals, especially, were left out in the cold. Creative minds tend, in such circumstances, to turn their attentions elsewhere; and the complacent and sedate salon society of the capital [pp. 254–68] provided the atmosphere in which intellectual aspirations were easily channelled away from the outside world and its problems and towards complete involvement in a purely personal world. Pure aestheticism and romantic sentimentalism flourished. Many intellectuals devoted themselves to literature and kept well clear in their writings, on the whole, of social reality and hence of any possible criticism of contemporary Mexican life; the most popular and successful forms of literature were the frivolous sentimental novel and the *modernista* poem and short story.[6] In spite of a few isolated novels which attempt a description of contemporary social realities and imply adverse criticism of them[7] and the *Ateneo de la Juventud*'s attack on Porfirian positivism it is, in general terms, true to say that the Mexican Revolution differed from other important modern revolutions in its lack of significant ideological precursors in its national literature.[8]

[6] *Modernismo*, the late nineteenth- and early twentieth-century Latin-American movement of literary renovation in reaction against the stale traditions of Hispanic literature of the time, had its centre in Mexico City in the first decade of the twentieth century. A Mexican, Manuel Gutiérrez Nájera, was one of the movement's most important early writers, and a large group of Mexican modernistas flourished in the later period. One of the basic attitudes of modernismo was an aesthetic, poetic rejection of 'materialist' values and thinking— positivist philosophy, scientific advance, sociological enquiry, literary realism and naturalism. See Max Henríquez Ureña, *Breve historia del modernismo* (Mexico, Buenos Aires, 1954), pp. 64–87, 465–500.

[7] For example, Azuela's pre-revolutionary novels *Los fracasados* (written 1906, published 1908: the corrupt system of power and privileges in a provincial town), *Mala yerba* (1909: the lack of justice in rural Mexico which allows hacendados criminally to abuse their power), and *Sin amor* (published 1912, but written before the outbreak of the Revolution: the absurd aristocratic pretensions of the small-town bourgeoisie): *Obras completas*, I, pp. 3–319. But these early novels of Azuela attracted no attention in their time; nor did those of the few other novelists who attempted, with scant artistic success, to write in a realistic and critical way about Mexican society, like Emilio Rabasa (*La bola*: 4 parts, 1887–8: political intrigue in Mexico City and the provinces), Rafael Delgado (*La calandria*, 1891, and *Los parientes ricos*, 1903: satire of the wealthy classes of Mexican society), and Heriberto Frías (*Tomóchic*, 1892: sympathetic description of an Indio revolt). See Joaquina Navarro, *La novela realista mexicana* (Mexico, 1955).

[8] Eckstein (p. 150) considers the alienation of the intellectuals to be an important precondition for a revolution. John J. Johnson (*Political Change in*

The revolutionary intellectuals of 1910 and later had two very different traditions to look back upon as precedents in the history of their sort in Mexico. One, heroic and legendary, but somewhat remote, was that of the great Independence and Reform leaders: Morelos, Hidalgo, Juárez. The other was the tradition in which they themselves had grown up, and which was perhaps more firmly rooted after over thirty years of Díaz rule: that of the intellectual who either sells himself for a comfortable position in society or takes refuge from social reality in an exclusively private and personal world; or who expediently combines the former course of action with the latter.

In the novels written between 1910 and 1925 about the Mexican Revolution the most constantly-recurring social type is the rank-and-file intellectual. He appears with such frequency in these works, indeed, and with such remarkably consistent characteristics on each appearance, that he comes to be a stock type in these novels. In view of the importance of the intellectual in all revolutions, this is in no way surprising; the novels, in the prominence they give to the intellectual, are faithfully reproducing the reality of the revolutionary situation. It is one important difference between the early novels of the Revolution and those of the 1930s that the latter give very much less prominence to the revolutionary intellectual, and tend to dwell instead on those more picturesque, sensational, spectacular or romantic—and also, of course, more obvious and superficial—aspects of the revolutionary struggle such as the horrific suffering it caused, the amazing feats of arms it provoked, or the swashbuckling lives of its protagonists. This is a confirmation of the assertion made above, in Chapter 3, that only those novels written contemporarily or very nearly contemporarily with the Revolution can be trusted as sources of information about it, and that the later ones—in spite of all their appearances of documentary veracity—paint an unreliable picture. With regard to the intellectual in the Mexican Revolution, the early novels provide a hoard of information which is all the more valuable for its uniqueness.

Latin-America: the Emergence of the Middle Sectors (Stanford, 1958), pp. 128–30) considers that Díaz, by the anti-intellectual policies here described, did alienate intellectuals. It would be more correct to say that he tamed and disarmed them: there is no evidence of any real alienation of intellectuals on a significant scale in the Mexico of 1910.

The strongest reason for accepting the portrayal of the intellectual in these novels as historically accurate is that he does play such a central role in many of them, and possesses so many recurring characteristics. Novelists who display very different attitudes to the Revolution and who show widely varying political and personal prejudices, all coincide in the importance they ascribe to the intellectual and in the characteristics they attribute to him. The intellectual is presented in a highly sympathetic light in one novel, in a harshly critical one in the next; and yet his essential personal qualities are the same in both, and he is praised for precisely the same things in one that he is attacked for in the other. So personal bias and prejudice seem to count for little in the novelistic presentation of the revolutionary intellectuals, and not to change the picture of them in any important way. The great similarities between the characterizations of the intellectual in several very different novels written by men who had no contact at all with each other can only be explained by supposing that all the authors drew independently upon the same social reality for such characterization [p. 12].

This conclusion, which is convenient for the scholar who seeks to use these novels as sources for social history, is strengthened by the fact that in the literary traditions our novelists came into contact with and followed to a greater or lesser extent—in general terms, nineteenth-century realism and naturalism of France and Spain—there is no exactly-equivalent type of revolutionary intellectual; so it seems reasonable to discount any remote possibility that a common literary source, rather than a common source in social reality, is the explanation for the repeated appearance of a characteristic type of intellectual in a prominent position in many different novels. The frustrated revolutionary intellectuals of some of Galdós's novels (for example, *La Fontana de Oro*, *El audaz*, and *Angel Guerra*) are the characters in the nineteenth-century novel tradition that most nearly approximate to the intellectuals of the early novels of the Mexican Revolution; but the difference between even the Galdosian intellectuals and the Mexican ones are great enough to exclude the small possibility of any significant source-influence. The intellectual figure in the Mexican novels is unique and immediately distinguishable. Certainly he is, like those of Galdós, a failure as a revolutionary intellectual. Galdós's intellectuals fail as such, however, because their hot-headed idealism

GM

and high-mindedness are not matched by practical common sense and careful calculation: their emotional and highly personal radicalism is hopelessly unrealistic. As romantic radicals, they cannot distinguish between utopian and practicable courses of action, between illusion and reality; so they fall an easy prey to their more astute and pragmatic opponents.

The intellectuals of the Mexican Revolution are portrayed in the novels as failing for a different reason, the result of specifically Mexican conditions. They follow in the Porfirian tradition of the isolated, indifferent intellectual, which we have examined above, and they are consequently weak and spineless. Their revolutionary ardour and idealism is feeble from the very beginning, and they soon relinquish the struggle to change society or, at least, waver indecisively between periods of revolutionary activity and of defeatist lethargy. None of them shows signs of any real understanding of the situation or any sound political sense. Most of them seek regular refuge from the unpleasantness of the Revolution in the embraces of romantic love affairs, to which they tend to devote considerably more attention and energy than to any other activity. This cannot be explained in terms of the influence of the literary convention that demands that the heroes of novels be involved in romantic relationships, because of certain special features that recur in each individual case: above all the unhealthily obsessive nature of the sentimental eroticism and the idea of the love interest as an alternative, but never as a complement, to other action—as an escape from the overwhelming problems of society. There are common features, then, in the intellectuals of Galdós and those of many of the novelists of the Mexican Revolution. Both, above all, are highly romantic figures. The stresses are, however, quite different, and the Mexican intellectuals clearly form a unique and highly individual body of men, standing on their own and quite distinct from intellectuals of other sorts.

All the evidence is, then, in favour of accepting the portrayal of the intellectual group to be found in the early novels of the Revolution as, in essence, historically factual. Above all, the close affinity between the various novels themselves in their depiction of a specific type of intellectual, and the lack of any literary precedent for him point convincingly towards a common grounding in the social realities that the novelists claim to reflect. There is no other possible explanation for the recurrence in the novels of the same unprecedented stereotype. Furthermore, various other pieces of historical evidence add conviction to the picture: we have the fact, already noted, that the previous traditions of Mexican intellectual life would lead one to have expected precisely this sort of development. There are several other corroborating details which will be mentioned in due course in this chapter.

Let us move on to examine, in rather more detail, some of the intellectuals who appear in the chosen novels. The evidence they provide is particularly valuable in that it concerns the obscure, rank-and-file intellectuals about whom it is impossible to find much information elsewhere. The activities of leading intellectuals in the national revolutionary movement can best be studied from other sources; but the novels can tell us most about their humbler colleagues, whose importance should not be underestimated: for upon the shoulders of the latter rests the task of bringing unity and enthusiasm to all sections of the revolutionary movement, and from their ranks must come the leading intellectuals themselves, who are bound, therefore, to share many of their characteristics. The running of a revolution depends ultimately, it could be argued, upon the large but unrenowned group of modest intellectuals who are the principal subject of study in this chapter.

In the revolutionary novels of Mariano Azuela intellectuals play prominent parts; and it is obvious, from the considerable variety of types that he portrays, and the sympathy with which he deals with many of them, that he devoted his careful attention to this part of revolutionary society. He was, after all, like many of the other novelists, himself a member of the intellectual group and, consequently, he was in a splendid position to understand its problems intimately. This would seem, then, to be the ideal starting point for our enquiry.

The intellectual figure as presented by Azuela is not a straightforward depiction of reality, however. Azuela is, in his presentation of many of these figures, an interesting—and for the social historian, dangerous—exception to the general principle just established that the intellectuals that appear in the early novels of the Revolution are realistic reproductions of a social type. Let us take as an example the first novel of the Revolution, *Andrés Pérez, maderista*,[9]

[9] *Obras completas*, II, pp. 764–800. (Only the page numbers will be given in subsequent references to this work.)

and the opinions about the Maderista revolution ascribed in it to the intellectual who is its protagonist. They give a good illustration of the extreme care with which a study of this sort must be conducted.

These opinions are made explicit in a conversation Andrés has with don Octavio, who is described as a well-read, mature man and a careful, objective thinker. The latter believes that although the rule of Porfirio Díaz has been a good thing for Mexico, it has reached the end of its useful life and must be replaced by a more active government of younger men. Andrés, however, professes only scorn and contempt for Madero, for he believes that all revolutions are a senseless waste of effort and life: nothing, he thinks, can ever change the predetermined destiny of all mankind to be divided into exploiters and exploited. His peculiarly pessimistic and reactionary social Darwinism is given clear exposition in the course of the conversation, when he declares:

All this stuff about revolutions is only, and only can be, a lie, an enormous lie. The people have always shed their blood in order to tear out of their flesh the vampires that destroy them, but all they have ever achieved has been to substitute one set of vampires for another. Emperors, popes, kings, presidents, their title is irrelevant: they are, and always have been, exactly the same. It is a law of life that the strong devour the weak and feed on them.[10]

Don Octavio's interpretation of the Revolution is equally deterministic but it leads him to different, slightly more optimistic conclusions. A revolution, says he in his reply to this speech, is the atavistic call of the race on the individual, and the individual would be unforgiveably selfish to resist such a call; for

the weight of the species is enormously more powerful than the weight of the individual, of the feeble, ridiculous and fatuous individual creature, who is uncovered in all his insignificance and impotence in these supreme moments of life by atavism, race, species, etc.[11]

Azuela presents, then, a clash between two different interpretations of determinism. One leads to a qualified belief in progress, and in revolution as a possible means of progress; and the other to a despairing disbelief in the ability of man to do anything at all to improve his position, individually or collectively [pp. 122–3].

[10] p. 792.
[11] p. 792. See Galindo's similarly deterministic thought, below, pp. 117–18. Both men were doctors.

In the examination of this conflict of opinions *Andrés Pérez, maderista* anticipates Azuela's other novels of the Revolution, especially *Los de abajo*. The conflict is clearly one which much troubled Azuela, to judge by the insistence with which he returns to the consideration of it in other novels, always treating it in very similar terms. In *Andrés Pérez, maderista* and *Los de abajo*, and in all his other novels to a lesser extent, the question Azuela seems constantly—and unsuccessfully—to be trying to answer for himself is: how can I reconcile my deep sympathy for the professed aim of the Revolution to better the lot of the poor with my basic conviction that the fight is a hopeless one and a thorough waste? It is a contradiction he can never resolve. Its consequence in the novels is that often, as in the passage under consideration in *Andrés Pérez, maderista*, certain characters, particularly intellectuals, stop speaking at certain moments with their own voices and start speaking with that of Azuela; the author intrudes to externalize his own preoccupations in the guise of conversations between his characters. Thus, in the above conversation, don Octavio (introduced solely for this function, for he has no active role in the development of the plot) seems to represent the optimistic side of Azuela's thoughts on the problem of revolutions, the side that made Azuela write with some understanding about revolutionaries of all sorts, and led him to play an active role himself in the Revolution.[12] Andrés Pérez is the mouthpiece for the pessimistic side, the side which makes Azuela, in the conclusions of most of his novels, throw bitter doubt on the practical usefulness of the Revolution, and which presumably led him to leave for the United States before it ended. Already, in the conclusion of *Andrés Pérez, maderista*, the pessimistic interpretation is made to triumph, as the social situation returns to exactly what it was before Madero's

[12] Azuela was an active propagandist for Madero and on the triumph of Maderismo in 1911 he was made *jefe político* [pp. 241–2] of Lagos de Moreno (his home town), in the state of Jalisco. He resigned shortly afterwards in protest at the Maderista State Governor's dismissal by the Provisional President of Mexico, Francisco León de la Barra [pp. 28–9]. When Huerta overthrew Madero and became President in February 1913, Azuela went into hiding; in October 1914 he joined the guerrilla band of the Villista Julian Medina. He served Medina's guerrillas as camp doctor until, with Villismo clearly in irreversible decline, he went into exile in the United States in 1915. He returned and went in search of work to Mexico City in early 1917, and there he and his family suffered hardship for several months before he was able to establish a doctor's practice in a poor quarter of the city. (See Azuela, 'El novelista y su ambiente': *Obras completas*, III, pp. 1066–99.)

rising. Andrés, who is the narrator, reports: 'I made a point of looking at don Octavio; I wanted my eyes to convey to him my brutal, crushing triumph.'[13] This can be seen to indicate that Azuela thinks he has solved his inner conflict, and can resign himself to a pessimistic interpretation of determinism. The fact that precisely the same conflict runs throughout *Los de abajo* would seem to suggest that Azuela had not really reached any such final decision.

In all of Azuela's novels of the Revolution, with the exception of *Domitilo quiere ser diputado* and *Las tribulaciones de una familia decente*, intellectual figures talk with voices that are not always their own. In the speech of Andrés Pérez quoted above, not only are the sentiments expressed demonstrably Azuela's own: the crudely violent style, too, is clearly not that of the complacent and indifferent Pérez but of his very deeply and personally involved creator [other examples, pp. 93, 101 and 101n.]. Azuela sometimes uses intellectual figures, then, as mouthpieces through which to unburden himself of the ideas that worry him most.

In *Las moscas* and *Los caciques* there are examples of another sort of intrusion by the author into his characters. Here he uses them as mouthpieces to comment directly upon the action. This is particularly well illustrated by the treatment of Rodríguez in *Los caciques*. Azuela makes it evident in this novel that he feels particularly strong hatred for the sort of corruption practised by the *caciques*—defined in this novel as the rich, unscrupulous families in virtual control of small provincial towns [pp. 193–4]—for it is effected at the expense of the hard-working and thrifty, but vulnerable, lower-middle-class 'little people' for whom he shows his greatest sympathy [pp. 301–2]. Thus he seems to have felt obliged to use a character, the said Rodríguez, exclusively for the purpose of giving lengthy and recurrent expression to his own distaste for this sort of conduct and of making general observations about the action. Since Rodríguez is a mouthpiece for the author's opinions he is built up into as highly sympathetic a character as possible, in order to make these opinions the more acceptable; such a lather of admirable qualities, indeed, does Azuela work up on Rodríguez that he loses all semblance of reality. He is idealistically inflated to such an extent that he becomes only laughable and tiresome. The result of the use of the intellectual figure as a receptacle for the novelist's

[13] p. 800.

personal ideas and opinions is, in *Los caciques*, that he is rendered totally unreliable from the social historian's point of view: he is only on the outside the representation of a revolutionary intellectual, for really he is no more than a highly idealized projection and personification of some of his creator's own opinions. We should not, then, base any ideas about the intellectual group in the Mexican Revolution on Rodríguez; he has next to nothing to do with the sort of person he is purported to be. Luckily Azuela goes to such an extreme only in this one case. In *Las moscas* the major and the doctor are introduced into the tale to fulfil mainly the same function: that of expressing the author's judgement of the other characters and of the action, from a superior, almost omniscient, position. They are also, then, projections of Azuela himself and must be omitted from our survey of depictions in novels of revolutionary intellectuals, but at least they are given less prominence in their novel than Rodríguez is in his. In *Los de abajo* Solís is another such spokesman for the novelist, who voices on his behalf exactly the same sort of opinions as do Andrés Pérez, the major and the doctor. We are left in this novel with Luis Cervantes, a very different character indeed.

Azuela's personal intrusion has distorted many of his depictions of intellectuals; it is also a serious artistic flaw and detracts from the literary effectiveness of the novels. One must disregard the following characters as having been created to serve Azuela's personal moralizing aims and, therefore, as being wholly unreliable: Rodríguez, Solís, the major, and the doctor. Great care is necessary in the handling of others: Andrés Pérez, Luis Cervantes, and the minor figures, Neftalí of *Las moscas*, and the anonymous government candidate of *Los caciques*.

Finally, Azuela created two other intellectual figures in his revolutionary novels which it seems wise to leave out of the reckoning. Toño Reyes in *Andrés Pérez, maderista*, the wealthy and educated landowner Andrés goes to stay with, is an elated, fearless, and heroic fighter for Madero. Yet Azuela is at great pains to show that this is by no means a typical case: Toño is highly impulsive, is dying of tuberculosis, and it is frequently hinted that he is not completely sane. If Azuela is trying to make any social point with this character, it is that only if possessed by an unnatural, feverish, and irrational energy such as that of the last stages of consumption can an intellectual participate fully in the Revolution. Valderrama, who appears in the third part of *Los de abajo*, is similarly—though he is no hero and does nothing effective—set aside by the author: he is extravagant, romantic, and bohemian to the point of insanity (though Azuela uses him at times, in the absence of any more suitable character, as his mouthpiece [pp. 122–3]).

In short, the type of the good, far-seeing, competent intellectual in Azuela's novels is not to be taken at face value. It is not a representation of a social reality, but simply the novelist himself in disguise: a massive injection of the subjective factor into the depiction of objective reality [p. 8]. For the reliable portrayal of the 'good' intellectual we will have to look elsewhere; meanwhile Azuela is only useful as a source of information about the intellectual who behaves dishonestly or cynically. All these idealized self-projections are, on the other hand, most useful when it comes to analysing the attitudes and position of Azuela himself [pp. 122–5].

In *Andrés Pérez, maderista*, an inadequate revolutionary intellectual is the protagonist of the tale.[14] We have noted already that Pérez's opinions are not always his own; it is, however, safe to study his behaviour (as opposed to his ideas) as a more objective representation of a real social phenomenon, as there is no evidence to suggest that Azuela has inserted any extraneous factors here. Pérez is by no means just a vehicle for Azuela's opinions. It is simply that the novelist occasionally superimposes his own ideas on this character, who has his own separate existence and functional role in the novel; he is not treated specifically and solely as a mouthpiece for Azuela's ideas, as is, for example, Rodríguez in *Los caciques*.

Andrés Pérez is a young journalist living a comfortable, lethargic, shallow life in Mexico City. He does not usually encounter much difficulty in suppressing any inconveniently independent ideas that might find their way into his head, or in writing for his newspaper in the conventional, complacent, and deferential

---

[14] Azuela had already portrayed the intellectual in pre-revolutionary society, with Reséndez in *Los fracasados*. This precursor of the figures we are studying in this chapter shares very many of their features: he is disgusted by the Porfirian world of widespread injustice and corruption in which he is forced to live and work, and sets out to try and reform it; but his romantic feelings towards an attractive young woman are a rival claim on his attention, and when the task of making the world a better place proves extremely difficult, he transfers his idealism piecemeal from society to her. (*Obras completas*, I, pp. 3–112.)

manner that is expected of him.[15] He earns enough to keep a beautiful mistress, Luz. He is, in short, one of the many 'bought' intellectuals who have happily taken their place on the lower, but nevertheless comfortable, levels of the Porfirian establishment. The capital city of Mexico was inevitably the hot-bed for such parasitic intellectuals, and it consequently acquired a bad reputation. His friend Toño tells Andrés, using the language of great violence Azuela reserves to direct at people he disapproves of intensely:

I thought you were just one more abject intellectual from Mexico City: a herd of pen-wielding helots, swollen with venality; eunuchs forever moaning about peace, incapable of giving one drop of blood for their brothers, for their country, or for their own species; dolts who spend their whole lives burning incense to whoever fills their bellies, and who are quite pleased for their names to appear as so many more ciphers among the list of despicable, corrupt slaves, hardly worthy even to sing to their masters' concubines.[16]

Pérez is not, clearly, the sort of intellectual to be expected to take up the revolutionary banner—and, indeed, when he does so it is purely by accident. In a moment of general ennui, Andrés gives vent to some uncharacteristically hostile opinions about the government of Mexico and sympathetic ones about the incipient Maderista rebellion, in the presence of the editor of his newspaper. When, the next day, Andrés leaves almost without warning to spend a short time in the country with Toño, and to get away from the city atmosphere which has oppressed him sufficiently to lead to his outburst, the editor is so outraged that he denounces Andrés to the authorities as a Maderista agent. Andrés becomes a marked man; but by now, of course, the restful country life has restored him to normal, and he has abandoned his momentary radicalism. His opinions about the rebellion are as scornful as those of the most loyal Porfirista. By an increasingly ironic chain of events, however, Andrés Pérez becomes more and more of a hero in the eyes of the

[15] Several of the revolutionary intellectuals in the novels are journalists. One of the ways in which intellectuals can best perform the task of spreading the revolutionary gospel is through the press: it follows that one useful guide to the effectiveness of revolutionary intellectuals is the extent to which they manage to inform the country at large about the revolution, using all forms of communication possible, and particularly newspapers. Mexico's national press at this period was remarkable for its servility and inferiority with only very few exceptions, such as Filomeno Mata's radical daily *El Diario del Hogar* [p. 134n.].

[16] p. 786-7.

rebels, at the same time as his real convictions turn progressively more hostile to them. At the end of the short novel Andrés is momentarily shamed by Toño's heroic death into feeling considerable sympathy for the cause: but then follows the final, brutal disillusion when Andrés sees that all the former Porfiristas are already on the Maderista bandwaggon and firmly in control of it.

Andrés Pérez is an unrepresentative revolutionary intellectual because of his basic lack of sympathy with the movement in which he becomes involved in spite of himself (there seem to have been many like him in this respect, however [pp. 96, 118, and 128]), because his story refers only to the Maderista stage of the Revolution, and because the opinions he expresses are often, as we have already seen, merely those of the author. It is interesting, though, to note that even in this special and early example some of the standard characteristics of the Mexican revolutionary intellectual are prominent. The realization that society needs changing is present in Andrés, even if it comes to the surface only very rarely and in special circumstances: when the tedium of the frivolous existence of Mexico City overwhelms him and when the death of a friend shames him. But life is so much easier if one detaches oneself from its serious problems and retreats into a purely personal world, and particularly into the world of romantic love. Given that society is ugly and unjust, it is simpler to run away from it than to change it. So Andrés Pérez's reformist feelings give way very readily, particularly when there are attractive women within his reach. The problems of his fellow men cannot retain Andrés's errant attention for long against the competition provided by the attractions of first Luz, and then Toño's wife María. During a conversation with Toño and María, about the situation in Mexico City, Andrés's behaviour is characteristic: 'In the presence of a pretty woman, my tender years were becoming incompatible with the arduous problems of politics. I resolutely switched the conversation, and we turned to the subject of hobble skirts, the latest novelty from Mexico City.'[17]

Andrés's constant and conscious evasion of political matters, always associated with his flirting with María, is a minor theme of the novel. A little later, when a political discussion is about to take place in Toño's house, Andrés makes plans to escape, for 'I am unquestionably better suited to the company of silken skirts than to that of the prickly and smelly beards of virile patriots'.[18] When

[17] p. 770.   [18] p. 777.

asked what is his ideal in life, Andrés's reply is: 'it is said that Théophile Gautier offered his civic rights to see Giulia Grisi in her bath';[19] and Andrés's very last action in the novel, in the face of the final Maderista débâcle, is to get away from it all: 'as I passed by the entrance of María's home I stopped, hesitated a moment, and went in.'[20]

So one of the recurring characteristics of the intellectual in the novels of the Mexican Revolution is already shown on his first appearance: the conflict in him between the calls of revolutionary duty and of romantic love affairs, between his feeling that the world needs to be changed and the temptation to take the easy way out, of escape into the oblivion that eroticism provides. Andrés Pérez also displays—although his is, of course, a special case—that general uncertainty of purpose and wavering lack of resolution which will be seen to be common to all the intellectuals as portrayed in the novels. The tendency to lapse readily into selfish apathy appears over and over again as a part of their make-up, and cripples them in so far as the fulfilment of their revolutionary function is concerned.

We need spend less time with Neftalí Sancho Peredo, comparable with Andrés Pérez in that he is also an anti-revolutionary from Mexico City who finds himself by force of circumstances on the revolutionary side. He is a minor character, and what is more, like most of the protagonists of *Las moscas*, he is heavily caricatured. We must bear in mind in the case of Neftalí, then, that the most conspicuous and laughable qualities of his type, the aesthete from the city, have been exaggerated for comic effect and ethical purpose. It is justifiable, nevertheless, to throw a brief glimpse in his direction in order to discern the sort of real-life figure behind these exaggerations.

Neftalí Sancho Peredo belongs to one of the flocks of bureaucrats who follow in the wake of the Villista forces in the hope of obtaining employment upon a Villista victory (the novel is set in mid-1915). He is, then, even more than Andrés Pérez, a parasite and wholly passive, interested only in the Revolution in so far as it can be turned to his personal advantage. He is a law student, with poetic pretensions, and he is an effeminate aesthete. Even in the midst of the Revolution, he keeps himself, as far as circumstances permit, meticulously aloof from it all: 'you well know that I live

[19] p. 793.   [20] p. 800. María is now a widow.

shut away in my ivory tower, that my spirit soars over mountain peaks with their eternal snows of serenity, and that it will have nothing to do with all this wretchedness they call revolution'.[21]

Azuela makes his own opinion of this sort of intellectual quite clear to us by insisting gleefully on Neftalí's discomforts, particularly the deterioration of the clothes he takes such pride in keeping spotless, until finally the novelist has resort to slapstick to press his point fully home: ' "Carrancistas!. . . . Carrancistas!" Moralitos gives high-pitched little shouts and everyone runs and hides among the pillars which support the tanks of pitch. In his mad flight Neftalí Sancho Pereda de la Garza trips over his own feet and imprints his noble figure in the mud.'[22]

Through the exaggerations we can see that Azuela is, in this case as in that of Andrés Pérez, depicting a common type of intellectual in the revolutionary forces—the aloof, introverted snob from Mexico City, the creation of the rarified atmosphere of the capital in the last years of the Porfirian period. He is not only useless for the Revolution but a hindrance to it. These two are only revolutionaries, however, in the limited sense that they happen to find themselves involved, in spite of all their inclinations, on the revolutionary side. Luis Cervantes, of *Los de abajo*, is at once a more representative and more involved revolutionary intellectual, and is depicted more fully than either of them.

Luis Cervantes arrives one night in late 1913 at the temporary camp of the small group of nomadic guerrillas led by Demetrio Macías and active in and around the state of Jalisco. Luis has been a student of medicine and a journalist in the provinces. He tells the peasant fighters that he had been press-ganged into the Federal Army and thus forced to fight for Huerta, but that he deserted at the first opportunity in order to join the rebels, with whom his sympathies really lie. He is given rough treatment by the wary peasants who suspect him of being a Federal spy, particularly in view of his upper-class speech habits. In fact they are not far wrong in their suspicions. Luis, as a newspaperman, had wholeheartedly scourged the revolutionaries in his articles, and, far from being press-ganged, had rashly volunteered to join the

---

[21] *Obras completas*, I, p. 914.
[22] p. 916: Azuela has momentarily transferred the action from the trains to an irrigated piece of land, conveniently situated near a station, in order to provide the mud for Neftalí to fall into.

Federal Army. Only when actually under fire had he realized that he was no soldier; and he had fled in blind panic. He had soon been picked up, however, and brought back, to be ridiculed for his cowardice and demoted to the humble position of kitchen boy. This degradation, we are told, caused a change in his ideas, and he started to feel acute sympathy for the poor and the oppressed. What is more, he had also begun to believe that in the revolutionary struggle they were going to be the victors. At this point he deserted to the band of Demetrio.

Macías tests him by telling him he is going to be shot and staging a fake confession with one of his men dressed as a priest, the negative results of which convince him he was wrong in his suspicions. From this point on, Cervantes gradually gains the confidence of the guerrillas. The greatest barrier to this is the fact, impossible to forget for a moment, that he is, in their terminology, a *curro* (a Mexican colloquialism roughly translatable as 'young gentleman' with slight derogatory overtones). This class barrier is breached only as the peasants gradually become accustomed to Luis's superior attitudes and ways of expressing himself and are impressed by his ability both as camp doctor and as glib speaker: he certainly makes no concessions himself to bridge the gap in understanding between them. Luis enters the confidence especially of Camila, an innocent girl of the village where they have billeted themselves, and of Demetrio himself, to whom he eventually becomes secretary and personal adviser, the usual position—both in Mexico and in the wide Latin-American context—for an intellectual in a small band such as this. This remains his status until he leaves the band at the end of 1914, when it becomes apparent that its fortunes are declining fast, and goes to the United States.

It is not immediately clear to what extent Cervantes is, at the beginning, a sincere revolutionary and to what extent a cynical opportunist. At the start of his stay with Demetrio there appears to be a mixture of both attitudes in him: he has a belief in the rightness of the cause which is dependent upon a trust in its ultimate and inevitable triumph. In his speeches in the early stages the reader is aware that though Luis, viewed charitably, might just be sincere, such sincerity, if indeed it exists, is firmly buttressed by solid self-interest.[23] Even if genuine idealism ever had a place in Cervantes's make-up, opportunism soon takes over completely. In

[23] See *Obras completas*, I, pp. 336-7.

the crucial scene in which he persuades Macías that they should join the mass rebel attack that has been planned against the Federal stronghold of Zacatecas [p. 34], the only function of idealism is as an agent of self-interest. Demetrio is unwilling to submit himself to higher command for fear of losing his independence. Luis, however, points out that it is convenient to Demetrio to come out of the backwaters and join the mainstream of the revolutionary movement (it is, of course, to Luis as well, but he does not say so): there is more chance of acquiring wealth and power if he can make himself well-known as a prominent revolutionary. Luis clinches his argument by recourse to the most lofty and high-sounding clichés of revolutionary idealism, which he uses to disguise and make more acceptable his appeal to Demetrio's greed:

So many lives cut short; so many widows and orphans; so much blood spilt! And all to what purpose? Just for a few crooks to get rich and for everything to remain the same as before, or worse. You are an honest man, and you say 'I have no ambition save to return to my village.' But is it just to deprive your wife and children of the fortune which Divine Providence is placing in your hands? Would it be just to abandon the cause of the Motherland in these solemn moments when she is going to need all the abnegation of her children, the humble, who must save her and not allow her to fall once again into the hands of her eternal executioners and pillagers, the *caciques*? . . . Don't forget those two things which are most sacred to a man in this world: his family and his country![24]

After this confused, but in the circumstances, effective piece of sophistry (Azuela's guerrillas are remarkably gullible), Luis's reputation as an intellectual is established among the leaders of the band. Mocking suspicion of the man who can read and write turns into envious admiration.

Cervantes's cynicism grows apace. He advises Camila, who loves him, to accept the advances of Demetrio, on the grounds that the latter is on the way to becoming a rich and important general. Later he acts as a go-between for Macías and procures the girl for financial reward. Idealism is, for him, no more than a suitable ingredient for florid speeches: his toast on the meeting of the revolutionary general Pánfilo Natera and Macías is an anthology of the empty platitudes and clichés of revolutionary rhetoric, to which

[24] p. 348.

is added a suitable dash of lightly-veiled opportunism: 'To the triumph of our cause, which is the sublime triumph of Justice; to the rapid realization of all the ideals we share for the redemption of our long-suffering and noble people; and may the same men who have fertilized the soil with their own blood now reap the fruits that legitimately belong to them.'[25] And as he becomes infected with the widespread booty-fever of the triumphant revolutionary armies, 'la santa causa' becomes more and more a hollow, meaningless concept for him. By the end of his revolutionary career he is completely corrupt and indulges in the shadiest activities with more relish and thoroughness than anyone else. It is not, however, the story of a rapid moral decline under the influence of the ugly atmosphere of the Revolution: Cervantes was never, at the best of times, a righteous man.

But unworthiness of motivation does not in itself necessarily make a revolutionary intellectual ineffective. Indeed, although such radical ideas as Cervantes does seem to grasp are absurdly vague, as the passages just quoted indicate, he does at least perform a part of his function in giving his leader a wider vision of the Revolution, counteracting the parochial attitudes of the peasant guerrilla with his persuasive talk of the need for concerted action. The reasons he gives for joining the Revolution's mainstream are, however, the wrong ones. Cervantes also attempts to impress on Macías the need for a little strategic thought before an attack on a Federal garrison, but this comes up against the code of *machismo* which dismisses such considerations as unworthy of the full-blooded male [p. 153].[26] Against such few points as can be brought out in Cervantes's favour stands the fact that at no time does he show any sound grasp of the situation in political terms, for his selfishness blinds him to any considerations beyond those which immediately affect his material well-being. Furthermore, from the adviser of Macías, Cervantes soon degenerates into his fawning sycophant and pander. His only real talent is his persuasive tongue and his eye for a situation which can be turned to personal advantage. As soon as the going becomes hard he gets out.

Cervantes is different from Andrés Pérez and Neftalí in his lack of aesthetic or romantic concerns. Indeed he is brutally unromantic, cynically exploiting the feelings of the girl Camila towards him. He is similar to the other two intellectuals, however, in his gross

[25] p. 360.   [26] pp. 354–5.

inadequacy as a revolutionary. Each one of the three is, in one way or another, so completely bound up with himself that he is incapable of participating usefully in a social process such as a revolution; this selfishness is expressed in Andrés Pérez as eroticism, in Neftalí as narcissism and aestheticism, and in Luis Cervantes as straightforward materialistic self-interest. In the fourth intellectual that Azuela portrays, whom we are about to discuss—the government candidate in *Los caciques*—a similar selfishness is found embodied in his pompous self-importance.

During the government candidate's brief appearance in the novel Azuela makes his personal opinion of the whole breed he represents abundantly clear. When, in 1912, the population of the unnamed provincial town of *Los caciques* are required to elect a deputy to the State Congress (which was to replace the congress elected under Díaz), the government candidate—not a local man, but one sent from Mexico City—makes a short speech to the local Maderista Club. In it Azuela caricatures the intellectual who works in the higher levels of the administration:

The candidate, recommended to the Club by the government itself, was a chap with a waxed moustache with upturned points, who stood straight as a bolt and who thought a great deal of himself; he was full of aristocratic pretensions. When he came to the rostrum he looked irritable and, after spitting through his teeth, he said without much interest: 'You shouldn't worry your heads with high politics. Politics are beyond your reach. I'll make a comparison which you will be able to understand: whey is made one day for use the next. Well, politicians aren't like whey: they aren't made in a day. Do you really want a candidate selected from among yourselves? You would only make everyone laugh; you'd make fools of yourselves. Be content to choose your local councillors, which is all people in small towns should worry about. We State Deputies have to be whole men, hardened to political fray through the written word and the press. I am a man of letters and a journalist. . . . I have letters of recommendation from press VIPs, and from high-up people in the government. That's all you need to know. Give me your vote, then, for the sake of form, and you will have fulfilled your duty as honest citizens.' And, as puffed-up as when he had mounted it, he climbed down from the rostrum.[27]

But even all this is not enough for Azuela, whose violent feelings about this type oblige him to use his mouthpiece, Rodríguez, to

[27] *Obras completas*, II, p. 843. (Only volume and page numbers will be given in subsequent references to this novel.)

damn the pompous city intellectual even more explicitly and directly:

> The most shameful ignominy which the revolution of 1910 has revealed is the abjectness of our intellectuals, who drag their bellies over the mud, eternally licking the boots of all those in high positions ... intellectuals saturate the pages of the national press with their loathsome pimps' spittle ... eggheads make us cover our noses with our handkerchiefs.[28]

This particular piece of self-revelation by Azuela shows to what extent his views of the intellectuals is biased by personal feelings. It is, of course, possible that these personal feelings are the outcome of an adequate assessment of the situation: this possibility will have to be judged with the aid of the evidence provided by other novelist-witnesses. Nevertheless, all this is, after all, but one man's views; the views, furthermore, of a man who professed a vehement hostility towards most intellectuals and a deeply pessimistic and deterministic concept of the Revolution and of life itself. In *Los de abajo*, for example, the Revolution is presented as a process of inexorable decline, in which men, with no more control of their actions than marionettes, are dragged down to the level of animals. A rose-coloured portrait of Luis Cervantes is hardly to be expected in the circumstances. The same sort of consideration applies to the other intellectuals of Azuela that we have discussed.

In López-Portillo y Rojas's *Fuertes y débiles* there is another hostile portrait of a revolutionary intellectual. This is the schoolmaster Severiano Alcocer, who joins the ranks of Zapatismo and performs the task of stirring up revolutionary zeal in the southern part of Mexico State. Since he does so with considerable success, it might be claimed that he undermines the thesis of this chapter, which is that the intellectuals failed lamentably to carry out the duties that the Revolution demanded of them. There is every reason, however, to discount all of López-Portillo y Rojas's

---

[28] p. 844. Azuela's feelings run even higher than this! He has already prepared the government candidate's appearance by making Rodríguez give his harsh judgement on this sort of person in a distinctively Azuelesque outpouring of a chain of words evoking physical repulsion:

> intellectuals and politicians, faithful reflections of the cultured upper classes. What a loathsome crowd! They smell of muck, because they were born in it, they breathe it, they feed on it and they procreate in it. Whether in the newspapers or upon the rostrum they remind me of toads escaped from their ponds, lifting up their repugnant heads and their myopic eyes to a sun which blinds them (p. 836).

evidence about revolutionaries, whether leaders, or of the masses, or intellectuals. He is quite incapable of understanding them, and displays towards them only the uncomprehending hostility of the conventional conservative Porfirista; and his picture of them is totally unconvincing from beginning to end. He believes that the peasants were perfectly happy under Porfirio Díaz, and that the Revolution only happened because of the machinations of a few wicked plotters who played upon the fickleness of the simpleminded, ignorant and naïve masses. He creates Alcocer, then, as an example of the evil manipulators of the peasants; and he attacks him not for any failings as a revolutionary intellectual but, basically, for his success (of course he gives him an unpleasant personality and sordid motivation). Alcocer is a false and unreal character, the result not of the observation of social reality but of his creator's need to find a scapegoat upon whom to cast the entire blame for a revolution which he cannot otherwise explain away [pp. 218 and 251–2].[29]

We must look to other novelists for corroboration or refutation of Azuela's unflattering portraits, to see whether his hostile attitude is based on fact or is a result of purely personal idiosyncrasies—or, indeed, as the reader might sometimes suspect, of sour grapes.[30] We need, particularly, if we are to balance the scales, a novelist who is able to give a sympathetic likeness of a sincere intellectual, without identifying with him in the way Azuela does with all his 'good' intellectuals, rendering them unacceptable as sociological evidence.

Fortunately we have seven such novelists among the group we are examining. In the novels *La ruina de la casona* by Maqueo

---

[29] This conspiratorial interpretation of revolutions is, of course, a standard conservative recourse. One of the curious features of the Mexican Revolution is precisely that it does not give very strong support to Eckstein's dictum that 'one undoubtedly finds conspiratorial organizations in every internal war of any consequence' [p. 141].

[30] Azuela's experience of the Revolution was not, on the whole, a happy one [p. 89n.]. Each of his novels of the Revolution was, furthermore, written in difficult personal circumstances: *Andrés Pérez, maderista* in 1911 immediately after his resignation as *jefe político* of Lagos de Moreno ('El novelista y su ambiente' *Obras completas*, III, pp. 1066–72); *Los caciques* in 1914 while in hiding from Huerta's police (ibid., pp. 1072–5); *Los de abajo* in 1915 when he was exiled in Texas (ibid., pp. 1075–89); and *Las moscas, Domitilo quiere ser diputado*, and *Las tribulaciones de una familia decente* in 1917–18 when he was poor and out of work in Mexico City—and at the same time being made painfully aware of the rapid and spectacular rise to positions of wealth and power of the hated new Carrancista élite (ibid., pp. 1089–99).

Castellanos, *En tierra de sangre y broma* by Quevedo y Zubieta, *La Esperanza y Hatí-Ke* by Teja Zabre, and, above all, *En el sendero de las mandrágoras* by Ancona Albertos, intellectuals are portrayed with sympathy as essentially good men; and in the autobiographical pieces *A través de la sierra* by Galindo, *El águila y la serpiente* by Guzmán, and *Ulises criollo* and *La tormenta* by Vasconcelos, the authors present themselves as revolutionary intellectuals with, understandably, similar sympathy. To offset Azuela's vision, let us examine some of these other intellectuals, who can be expected to be given flattering, rather than hostile, treatment.

The most complete and penetrating study of the revolutionary intellectual in all the novels, including those of Azuela, is that made by Ancona Albertos in the two volumes of his undeservedly ignored work. It is worth paying considerable attention to the protagonist of *En el sendero de las mandrágoras*, Juan Ampudia. There are probably autobiographical elements in Ancona's picture of Ampudia; but, unlike Azuela, this novelist appears to have been honest enough—and artist enough—to be able to avoid the temptation to falsify the account he gives by idealistic self-inflation and by the artificial inclusion of judgements based on retrospective knowledge. As well as being the most subtle study of them all, Ancona's is also the most convincing: it seems much less distorted than any of the others. Although his view of the Revolution is ultimately, like Azuela's, pessimistic, he is, unlike Azuela, able to detach himself sufficiently from events to portray with equal sympathy both the characters who act nobly and those who act despicably—and, indeed, to realize that nobody falls completely into one category or the other.

Juan Ampudia lives in the city of Mérida, Yucatán [p. 228n.]; so he is free of the contaminating influence of Mexico City. He has a more promising revolutionary background than Azuela's intellectuals, also, in that he has not been absorbed into the Porfirian system, and is, indeed, highly critical of it. The novel tells the story of his physical and moral decline during the Revolution, and concludes with his death. The plot itself is simple and episodic, if not shapeless; what is important and significant in the novel is its detailed description of Ampudia's psychological development. A highly unstable character, he fluctuates between several different standpoints with regard to the Revolution, and it is the exposition of the relationship between these attitudes that gives Ancona's work special interest as a study of the behaviour and psychology of a Mexican revolutionary intellectual.

Most of these different attitudes are present in him at the beginning of the novel, where Ampudia's character in the immediate pre-revolutionary years is established. Juan is a radical journalist. His social awareness makes him react violently against the hypocrisy of the Porfirian way of life. The novel starts with a champagne party thrown to celebrate the completion of an operetta which all present, in spite of privately considering it to be an extremely bad one, praise in the most exaggerated terms; Juan, unable to restrain his anger, shocks everyone by making a speech attacking both the operetta and the insincerity of the other speakers. His greatest wish at this stage is to found a really independent newspaper, a worthy vehicle for radical opinion. His friend and confidant, Pérez, considers Juan is stupid to make problems for himself by insisting on being the black sheep in society, and advises him to follow his example and that of almost everyone else, and opt quietly for an easy life. Ancona contrasts notably with Azuela in his presentation of the 'bought' intellectual and his attitudes and, by avoiding exaggeration and outright moral condemnation, he is able to show convincingly how very difficult it is for an intellectual in a society like that of Porfirian Mexico to resist the constant temptation to give in and abdicate, publicly at least, his critical faculties. Juan is, indeed, strongly tempted, but he resists, for the moment at least. Pérez believes that

Ampudia should try to bring about a radical change in his character and live a life of indifference, the best life, unhampered by exertion, love or hate. Just looking after number one. All 'gestures' (as they say), all hopes and fears were ridiculous. Armed with calm and with indifference, anyone can triumph over impatient theorizers, over useless dreamers and over excessive passions.[31]

This, then, is the first constant in the character of Juan Ampudia: a radical, idealistic criticism of society and public life, together with the ever-present thought that it would be so much more comfortable to succumb to the temptations of opportunism.

Ampudia is, however, also a romantic poet, who writes love poetry. He carefully cultivates his appearance to fit this role. To

[31] Mérida, Yucatan, 1920, Vol. I, p. 24.

the gay, outspoken, and thoroughly unromantic Rosario, later to become his mistress, he

> seemed the ultimate in useless bohemians; a provincial poet, full of sighs and quite intolerable, with that enormous black tie, that looked like an ominous moth, and with that hairy wig and that little brown moustache which made him resemble some sort of sentimental musketeer.[32]

Her opinion of his poetry is similarly uncomplimentary:

> She was going to have to read his poems, full of nostalgia, of twilight scenes, of swallows and of clichés. How odious was this eternal romanticism of long-haired poets, clinging on to their woe, sighing and stupid, like an oyster to its shell. The sigh is the most ridiculous of all romantic anachronisms.[33]

This, then, is the second constant: aestheticism and the retreat into the world of personal lyricism. It is a factor which, though important at the beginning, loses its importance in the course of the novel, after the outbreak of the Revolution.

Juan's lyricism is connected with his relationship with women, towards whom he takes the exclusively romantic-erotic attitude of the lyric poem or the sentimental novel (another novelist of the time interestingly comments 'the practice of poetry goes hand in hand with the inclination towards eroticism'[34]). As the novel develops, his relations with a succession of mistresses become a major theme. This eroticism is the third constant in his life. We have already seen it in the case of Andrés Pérez and suggested that it was a characteristic obsession in the sectors of society to which the intellectuals belonged, and that because of its exclusive and obsessive nature it seems somehow to have been incompatible with forceful public activity. The impression Azuela's novels give of a conflict between one and the other in the Mexican intellectual is firmly substantiated by Ancona's work.

And, finally, there is a factor more peculiar to Ampudia. The loss of Malvina, his fiancée, has accentuated his tendency to drink too much (he lost her in the first place by getting drunk and making a disturbance outside her house). As the novel progresses, particularly in its second part, Ampudia moves by stages more and more deeply into the hell of alcoholic degeneration. This is the fourth constant.

[32] I, p. 42. [33] I, p. 50.
[34] González Peña, *La fuga de la quimera* (Mexico, 1919), p. 128.

The story of the bohemian Juan Ampudia's revolutionary life is, then, the story of his fluctuations between social involvement, both idealistic and opportunistic, and escape from social involvement into the transient paradises of Eros and Bacchus. He rings the changes on these different behaviour patterns through the series of personal crises which, seen in their relationship with the events of the Revolution, constitute the plot of the novel.

The first crisis occurs when Juan determines to renounce his present vegetative existence, spent largely in the bar and the brothel, and to go to Mexico City in order to do something positive with his life. On the boat, however, he meets Rosario, who becomes his mistress. He is immediately aware of the choice he must take: he must either sell himself to the government of Porfirio Díaz, acquiring an undemanding job with the national press which it controls, and being well paid for offering incessant and unconditional praise to the country's leaders; or he must persevere with his original proposition of fighting for his beliefs, with no prospect of material reward or—and this is the point—of being able adequately to support his mistress. The clash between public duty and private pleasure presents itself from the very start.

His decision to resist 'the national sin of cowardliness'[35] is followed only, however, by several months of further vegetation. Rosario's mother owns a boarding-house in Mexico City and Juan gives himself over to an increasingly inactive and parasitic life there with his possessive mistress. This existence drains his idealistic plans away, and when he decides he must make a break, the only path he can see open before him is that of cynical opportunism. 'It was true: the world was composed of executioners and victims, so you had to be an executioner.'[36] Madero is beginning to provide serious opposition to the government by now, and Juan reasons that 'he possessed youth, strength and intelligence, and he could get into the opposition, make ground with fire-eating articles in the opposition press, and conquer a place, possibly a prominent one, in the ranks of incipient Maderismo'.[37] But again he finds it easier to make the decision than to put it into practice, and his life continues in the same rut, as he becomes increasingly bored and indeed disgusted by Rosario.

---

[35] I, p. 67. [36] I, p. 82.

[37] I, p. 83. The Díaz government, in spite of its dictatorial methods, tolerated the precarious existence of an opposition press [p. 134n.].

The first real turning-point is when he is offered and accepts the position of editor of an opposition newspaper. At once his idealism, self-respect, and joy in life return, and he wholeheartedly throws himself into the revolutionary effort. He also significantly decides to leave Rosario for good, and to sleep in the office in order to be able to devote himself fully to the cause. But this new-found inspiration does not last. The girl who claims his attentions this time is Leonor, the young half-sister of Rosario. As soon as Juan starts living with her, all his revolutionary fervour is forgotten once again, and he returns to the carefree oblivion of romantic love. During this period Malvina, whom Juan has never forgotten, comes to Mexico City and he also meets her, in secret.

By now, however, the Maderista rebellion has broken out and Ampudia is arrested and jailed for his earlier revolutionary activity. When released during an amnesty, he comes home to find Leonor dying in giving birth to a dead child, and Malvina, now her friend, nursing her. Leonor dies, Malvina leaves him, and Rosario, he learns, has become a prostitute. On the fall of Porfirio Díaz, then, Ampudia feels his life has changed irrevocably. The first part of the novel ends here:

> I believe that my old romanticism, profoundly erotic and sentimental, has disappeared, together with the Porfirian way of life, buried in the fearful blackness of my past history. Until only a short time ago I could not believe existence to be possible without this story-book life which moves a man impulsively and irreflexively . . . I have cultivated my romanticism with still more romanticism, and my eroticism with more eroticism, just as neurasthenics cultivate their neurasthenia with more and more worries. But, luckily, I am now aware of myself and never again will I be a puppet manipulated by circumstance. This is how I seem to have reacted, just like the whole country.[38]

The self-analysis is acute, but only partially right. His judgement of his previous life as an obsessive and uncontrolled round of dalliances, an imitation of the activities of the heroes of sentimental novels, is accurate, and it is interesting to see that this sort of life is insistently described as being particularly Porfirian. But Ampudia flatters himself too much in thinking that he has renounced his romantic-sentimental-erotic obsessions. It is quite the other way about. He has not left romanticism behind: rather romanticism has left him behind, for the three women in his life are now in one way

[38] I, p. 215.

or another, all lost to him. The fact that the author of the story himself does not show any sign of realizing that this is so—indeed, Juan's final monologue looks very much as if it is meant to be a general authoritative summary of the novel and statement of its theme—is most significant and revealing [pp. 113–14]. All Ampudia's bouts of fervent radical activity spring from this kind of source: the Revolution offers him a sort of momentarily useful escape valve for emotional steam when personal romantic problems seem to have no solution. When another attractive woman appears on the scene, his life returns to its normal claustrophobic round.

By the start of the weaker second part, Ampudia has entered the world of politics, and is back in Mérida. In spite of his words at the end of part one, he has not changed, and the new resolution, like his previous one, has turned out to be no more than a whim of the moment. His thoughts have returned to his first girl, Malvina, now unhappily married, and he has decided to use the Revolution to get her back. He hopes that more disorder will soon break out so he will be able to kill her husband in the confusion; and he wants to secure an important position in revolutionary politics in order to use the power he would thus acquire to snatch Malvina away. 'To the devil with Madero, Pino Suárez, and the Revolution! He wanted to get to the top for Malvina's sake, and for her he was going to reach the heights.'[39] This new crisis sees Ampudia's old romantic urges (he himself, recalling the final words of part one, refers to his plans as his personal 'novela de folletín')[40] newly allied with political cynicism and opportunism, whereas before they had always led to retreat from any social or political involvement at all. They still prove incompatible with revolutionary idealism or any sort of effective work in favour of the radical cause, for they control his behaviour absolutely and exclusively.

Ampudia gains a seat in the Chamber of Deputies and goes to Mexico City once again in order to occupy it, which he is due to do in August 1912. After many glasses of brandy one night he visits Malvina, who refuses to go away with him; this sends him back to his old drinking habits. Soon after, he meets a pretty prostitute, María Luisa, and when she becomes his mistress he indulges with

---

[39] II, p. 23. José Mariá Pino Suárez (1869–1913) was Madero's vice-president, much criticized for his alleged ineffectuality.
[40] II, p. 31.

her in tremendous excesses of delirious erotic activity, imagining her in turn as each one of his three other women and talking to her and treating her as such. 'Between them, alcohol and debauchery are killing me.'[41] He takes his seat as a deputy in September, but all his revolutionary ideas are now forgotten, and his erotic problems occupy all his time and thought; he also fears that he is going mad.

From now on it is a relentless decline for Ampudia, interrupted only by sporadic attempts to put his life in order, which are always associated with the resolution to fight for social justice. Shortly before the *decena trágica* [pp. 30-1] he makes such an attempt, deciding yet again that 'his romantic novel was coming to an end'.[42] Yet when the hostilities break out in the city he starts drinking, abandoning himself to savagery and brutality. Always vacillating, intending to turn over a new leaf, Juan never quite manages to break through the routine of perversion. Finally he breaks into Malvina's house and when her husband returns home, triumphant from the success of the coup, in which he had played an important part, Ampudia murders him.

Another brief period of regeneration ensues, for Malvina still refuses to have anything to do with Juan: his return to revolutionary activity is, as before, no more than a momentary reaction to romantic failure. And so the miserable story of repeated vacillation between drunken delirium and fresh determination continues, with the former always much more powerful in shaping events than the latter. Between now and his death, his longest period of lucidity and political idealism is when he goes to the north of Mexico to join Carranza's revolution against Huerta—a decision which, once made, he characteristically takes about four months actually to put into practice, dallying three months in Havana on the way.[43] But when Juan finally reaches the north, and for the first time comes into personal contact with the Revolution, his idealism is shown to be very innocent and fragile indeed. He reacts to the realities of Revolution in a way altogether typical of the middle-class intellectual of these novels, for his idealism itself is so romantic and bourgeois that his first glimpse of the ugly, dirty facts of revolutionary life shatters it. 'The mob of soldiers, dressed in yellow, dirty, brutal, with the faces of murderers. They don't look

---

[41] II, p. 54.   [42] II, p. 72.
[43] Because of government control of the railway system, the normal route from Mexico City to the north in Huerta's time was via Veracruz and Havana.

like apostles to me.'[44] He immediately assumes that the Revolution
has changed nothing and is a failure, and returns to Mexico City
where he dies soon after achieving at last a reconciliation with
Malvina and marrying her.

Such is the life of Juan Ampudia, a miserable failure. As such he
is, of course, a special case, as indeed is each one of the characters
we are studying. Ancona, though, considers him typical and
representative enough to propose him as 'a specimen of our
intellectual classes';[45] so in his creator's opinion, at least, Ampudia's inadequacies are by no means peculiar to him. He is intended
to stand for the whole intellectual group we are concerned with in
this chapter.

Ampudia's lack of resolution is basic and decisive; it is what
determines his whole course of action and precludes him from
being even minimally effective as a revolutionary intellectual. His
fundamental romanticism is also worth stressing: his revolutionary
idealism, which fights a losing battle with his personal 'romantic
novel', is itself completely romantic in conception and therefore
fails the test of practice—and in any case it frequently gives way to
opportunism. His concept of revolution, in his idealistic moments,
is a wholly unrealistic one of stupendous heroes, noble and upright,
clean and tidy, fighting selflessly for the Cause of Justice (itself a
vague and undefined notion in his mind). This whole house of
cards disintegrates immediately on exposure to the harsh winds of
reality.

All of this is characteristic of the whole group of revolutionary
intellectuals as represented in the novels of the Mexican Revolution. Ampudia is like nearly all of them in his total lack of all the
qualities necessary in an efficient organizer and co-ordinator of
revolutionary action. He has no understanding whatever of the
revolutionary process; nor has he any political sense. His social
prejudices, as a member of the city middle class, alienate him
absolutely from the agricultural workers who are the actual
fighters; so that no contact or identification with them is possible
for him, and any idea of orientating them or enhancing their revolutionary fervour is quite out of the question. His lack of any sort of
steadfastness means that he can contribute nothing to any common
effort. Any qualities he does possess are not those which the revolution demands of the intellectuals who seek to further its causes;

[44] II, p. 151.   [45] II, p. 135.

this central point is so obvious as to make further insistence on it superfluous. What is perhaps peculiar to Ampudia is his particularly bohemian and neurotic listlessness and lack of will, which leads to his fatal decline through drink. We can accept him, nevertheless, as a valuable addition to the gallery of revolutionary intellectuals we are attempting to assemble; in fact the most useful of all of them, because of the detail and understanding with which his inner conflicts are examined and revealed. Ancona's sympathetic portrayal, then, corroborates the unsympathetic portrayals of Azuela, above all regarding the inability of the intellectual to make any sacrifice of his personal happiness and interests in order to fulfil his role in the Revolution. Other sympathetically drawn intellectuals, which we can look at in less detail, further substantiate this impression.

The strange and bad novel *En tierra de sangre y broma*, by Quevedo y Zubieta, presents another such revolutionary intellectual. This is Jorge Albán, in his mid-twenties like most of these figures in the novels; he returns to Mexico from Europe just as Madero's triumph is accomplished. He is also a weak-willed, undetermined character who allows himself to be carried along by revolutionary events instead of taking a hand in guiding and directing them. The novel concerns his casual flirtations with various women and political parties. Albán's political notions are limited to acute admiration for two men: Pino Suárez (because of his idealism and good intentions [p. 108n.]) and General Bernardo Reyes (because of his military quixotism [pp. 25n. and 29–30]). Albán is presented as a totally commendable character, and there is a good deal of identification with him by Quevedo y Zubieta. The account of his many failings as an intellectual, which ties in closely with all the other accounts we have examined, is the more trustworthy for this, and for the fact that Quevedo y Zubieta does not appear to realize that they are indeed failings.

The long, heavy-handed novelized history of the Revolution in Mexico City, *La ruina de la casona*, gives us another intellectual presented from a sympathetic viewpoint. Its author, Maqueo Castellanos, is conservative, Porfirista and anti-revolutionary in most of the opinions he reveals in the course of the novel, but he is able to understand the point of view of, at least, the moderate Maderista revolutionaries, even though he has no patience for the more radical movements led by Carranza and Villa. On the outbreak

of the Maderista revolt Federico Andrade is a twenty-year-old
law student from Zacatecas. His family is not rich, but he has a
brother who is a priest and who pays for his education. Federico is
honest, upright, and romantically idealistic, and consequently he is
strongly in favour of Madero. He furthermore realizes that there is
not a very rosy future for him within the Porfirian system. Already he
has found at school and in the University that ability is not enough:

Even there he found discrimination, inequality, privilege. And if, when
his studies were finished, he chose to go into the law, precisely the same
thing would happen: he would start as an insignificant little clerk,
pushed about by everybody; he would have to wait a long time for
promotion unless he could count upon people to pull strings for him.
And even if he were soon promoted, he would never be more than a
drudge, and then he'd get old, and die poor . . . unless he was prepared
to sacrifice his honesty.[46]

So he becomes a member of a Maderista club in the months preceding the outbreak of the Revolution; and when this club folds up
he founds another one. He is disappointed when Madero has
recourse to violence and the Revolution begins in November 1910;
and he loses all faith in Madero, as do most of Madero's supporters,
when the expected reforms fail to materialize during 1912. Like
Ampudia's, his idealism is far removed from reality; he expects
immediate moral regeneration from the Revolution, 'a pure,
immaculate, generous, righteous and idealistic revolution',[47] and is
necessarily disappointed: 'The whole thing smelt . . . Love,
loyalty, justice, honesty, truth, patriotism, honour, rectitude,
everything lofty and pure, holy and august, were no more than
words, words, words.'[48] The last vestiges of his romantic liberalism
are dissolved by the shocking events of the decena trágica. After
this, his disillusionment is such that he dissociates himself completely from the revolutionary movement, seeing it only as a meaningless fratricidal waste. In this he is simply giving expression to
Maqueo Castellanos's own opinions. Andrade dies, significantly
enough, not in the service of the Revolution, but at the hands of
his rival in love (for he has, of course, been involved in a romantic
affair throughout the novel).
    Andrade is, then, yet another feeble, spineless intellectual.
Maqueo, however, delivers judgement on him at the end through

46 *La ruina de la casona* (Mexico, 1921), p. 28.
47 p. 92.   48 p. 194.

the mouth of another character in the following terms: 'Poor Andrade! He was a dreamer, an idealist, tragically ahead of his times! I myself find those ideas of his attractive, too! But I moderate them, rather than going to extremes; I intend to discipline, not dissipate, them.'[49] So Andrade, like most of his colleagues in the novels a very timid, dithering intellectual by most standards, is considered by his creator—admittedly a man of conservative ideas —to be the archetypal idealist and radical, far ahead of his time. This is the third case we have encountered in these novels of the Revolution of an intellectual whose gross inadequacies are not recognized as such—and are even, indeed, considered as positive qualities—by the very man who created him (we have already observed the cases of Ancona Albertos and his creation Juan Ampudia [pp. 107–8], and of Quevedo y Zubieta and Jorge Albán [p. 111]). The phenomenon is highly significant because it is a good indication of the disorientation of the society created by Porfirio Díaz with regard to intellectual values [pp. 81–4]. Intelligent men belonging to this society consistently interpret as marks of intellectual ability certain patterns of thought and behaviour which to any outside observer are, quite clearly, proof of crippling disability. The phenomenon is also of interest as an illustration of the theory [pp. 17–18] that much of the most significant social information to be extracted from a novel is that which is far from being a reflection of the novelist's own conscious aims and beliefs.

Federico Andrade, a university student, brings us into contact with a body of young men who can be considered to form a separate category within the whole intellectual grouping. With few responsibilities or attachments to established society, the university student can afford to be violently radical, and can consequently play an important role in revolutions. The Maderista uprising was, in fact, immediately preceded by student demonstrations in Mexico City, Guadalajara, Oaxaca, Morelia, San Luis Potosí, and Chihuahua—not, however, protesting about social, economic or political conditions in Mexico but about the lynching in Texas of a Mexican citizen. The demonstrations were anti-American and there appears to have been little anti-government feeling in them. Indeed the United States Ambassador, Henry Lane Wilson (not, admittedly, the most reliable of witnesses), believed they had been provoked by Díaz himself to divert attention from Madero.[50] Azuela,

---

[49] p. 659.   [50] Ross, p. 137. Ross believes that Wilson's suspicions were justified.

however, including a description of the Mexico City demonstrations in the first pages of *Andrés Pérez, maderista*, considers them a
welcome though unexpected sign of radical independence of
thought among the young.[51] Even if this were so, the next news we
have of corporate student activity both suggests that their social
concern did not last long, and also furnishes interesting substantia-
tion of some of the evidence provided by novels. At the height of
the Maderista war, *El Imparcial* reported: 'At midday yesterday,
in the poetic "Villa of Roses", near the suburb of San Angel, the
student association gave a banquet for the eminent tragedienne
Mimí Aguglia as an act of homage expressing admiration for her
talent and her fine personal qualities,'[52] and in June 1911, the
month of huge popular acclaim for Madero and vigorous new
interest in his democratic ideals: 'To celebrate the return to
Mexico City of Mimí Aguglia, the students are preparing a demonstration of affection towards the celebrated tragedienne.'[53]

Alfonso Teja Zabre's *La Esperanza y Hatí-Ke* is a novel which
takes the reader into the atmosphere of the Mexico City student
community during the early stages of the Revolution, and paints
a remarkably similar picture to that which the above newspaper
reports evoke; indeed the novel's heroine could almost be the
beloved Miss Mimí Aguglia. The protagonist is the student, Marco
Astenia. The first part of the novel describes several scenes of
student life in late 1910 and early 1911. Marco's group of friends—
which there is no reason not to consider representative of the
student community as a whole—devote great attention to the music
hall artiste called 'La Esperanza' and engage in long and passionate
arguments about her merits. Their political interests are negligible:
a Spanish student comments 'I have been living in Mexico for two
years, and I have heard not one shout, not a single row or quarrel,
when politics has been the subject of conversation.'[54] They also
immerse themselves deeply in the ideas of the aesthetic movement,
and tend to sniff at any consideration of the social and economic
realities of life. By January 1911, however, Madero's uprising has
stimulated political thought throughout Mexico, and the students

---

[51] pp. 764–5. Each of the first two novels of the Revolution, published in 1911,
begins with violent student demonstrations; Juan A. Mateos has students
demonstrating against the vice-presidential candidature of Ramón Corral (*La
majestad caída*, 2nd ed., 1911, pp. 19–23 and 77–80).
[52] *El Imparcial*, 12 Mar. 1911.   [53] *El Imparcial*, 7 June 1911.
[54] Op. cit., p. 20.

do discuss politics among themselves; but their ideas are, as one might expect, a wild jumble of unreasoned and uninformed whims. As soon as they are reminded that Rodolfo Gaona is about to appear in the bull-ring, all is forgotten as they rush to get their tickets to see the famous Mexican bullfighter perform.

The career of Marco Astenia, a typical member of the group, is followed more closely. He is particularly fascinated by 'La Esperanza' and soon becomes the victim of what is significantly described as an 'amorous obsession which possessed him body and soul'.[55] While his friend Alex, the exception among the gang, is in favour of reform and helps Maderismo in every way he can,[56] Marco devotes all his energy to amorous pursuit. Teja Zabre describes this obsessive eroticism in a penetrating way:

> Whether because of his own natural disposition or because the books he had read had created artificial sentiments within him, Marco could not conceive love as simply another incident in everyday life; he saw it rather as an invasion of fever, of paroxysms, of blind madness, of exquisite suffering, and of happiness which possessed one's whole being.[57]

Alex rebukes Marco for the selfishness of this attitude, which all the evidence of the novels goes to suggest was widespread in students and young intellectuals generally during the Mexican Revolution: 'We are working out a tragedy, and you shut yourself inside the fortress of your egoism: you are even so rude as to be an inattentive spectator.'[58] It is only much later that Astenia performs any public action, and then it is typically blind and unreasoned. When the United States forces occupy Veracruz, Marco is sufficiently naïve to be deceived by the political propaganda Huerta creates out of the international confrontation [pp. 173–4]; and, by delivering inflammatory speeches against the invaders in meetings organized by the government to encourage enlistment into the Federal Army, he unwittingly serves the interests of the counter-revolutionary dictator.

---

[55] p. 42.

[56] He cannot be incorporated into our gallery of intellectual types, because he is not characterized in any detail—the reader is simply told he is working strenuously for the Revolution and has all the right Maderista ideas—and is anyway only created as a contrast to the central figure, Marco. Alex is not a representative of any social type, but a shadowy, background character introduced for purely literary reasons.

[57] p. 48.   [58] p. 55.

Students seem, then, to have done as little as other intellectuals to help carry the Revolution to a final triumph. The great majority of them were the sons of the wealthy—there were, of course, very few scholarships—whose concern for social problems was slight. Widespread student political involvement did not start in Latin America until after the end of the Mexican Revolution.

La ruina de la casona adds two more figures to our collection of 'bad' intellectuals, and they may briefly be mentioned. One is Federico Andrade's fellow student Agustín Chaneque. He is a dull but industrious Indio from Oaxaca, with every reason, according to Maqueo Castellanos, to be grateful to the government of Porfirio Díaz, for the money for his studies comes from a state scholarship. Chaneque becomes a Maderista, however, for purely selfish reasons, and reaches a prominent position as a propagandist for Madero; and he repeats the performance in the Carrancista camp on the fall of Madero. Maqueo Castellanos condemns Chaneque as an opportunistic bandwaggon climber.

He reserves his most hostile treatment, however, for his revolutionary politician, Austreberto Pingarrón. A middle-aged man of doubtful background, Pingarrón takes his chance on the establishment of the Maderista regime to worm his way into official favour by the frequent but judicious employment of his gift for flattery and rhetoric. He duly becomes a Maderista deputy, of the sort that Maqueo Castellanos, a deputy himself since Porfirista times, must have had ample opportunities to observe—and listen to—at first hand. He is consequently able to give a more penetrating study of Pingarrón than of his other characters. Pingarrón's attitude to politics is quite straightforward:

'How much time is wasted,' he used to say to himself, 'because people will believe in all this nonsense about the problems of peasants and proletarians, labour laws, concern for the public good and administrative honesty!' For him, politics was merely a lever, one of whose extremities must rest in the Treasury. You had to put scruples and all such irrelevancies behind you if you wanted to reach the target he was after . . . And if the people came out worst in all this . . . to hell with them! The important thing was to feather your own nest . . . What did this require? Above all, plenty of audacity. The acquisition, in the course of a campaign of spirited piracy, of a reputation as a clever and able man; and enough cynicism to deceive the masses and impose respect upon the humble, getting yourself accepted as a superior intelligence and a well of learning . . . And, on occasions, whenever necessary, the ability to 'make concessions' . . .; the equestrian agility of the good politician; the proper use of flattery; and the capacity for making a virtue out of abjection . . . You just had to be tough, and have an agile tongue.[59]

His plans for using Maderismo to the greatest possible personal advantage are well-laid and carefully thought out. He takes much care over important details like his appearance, dressing with the greatest elegance and hiring a luxurious car for all his trips to the Chamber. He devotes special attention to ensuring that his name appears daily in the newspapers, by making a great show of taking an active part in all debates. All this does not, naturally enough, prevent Pingarrón from being one of the first in the queue to congratulate Huerta after his coup; and he is quick to join Carranza once the inevitability of the latter's ultimate triumph becomes apparent. In all of this he has the greatest success, and becomes rich and influential.

Maqueo Castellanos gives us, then, a useful view of another sort of intellectual, the opportunist politician (of whom Azuela also gives a brief glimpse in his depiction of the government candidate). Even allowing for possible exaggerations because of the author's obvious distaste for this kind of person, the portrait is a convincing one, and the exaggerations are no more than the justifiable means of making the characterization stronger and bolder. It is obvious that this sort of intellectual, so exclusively concerned with personal advancement, was of no use to the Revolution.

To complete our survey of the group of intellectuals that appear in the novels, we can refer briefly to the three autobiographies and to the self-portraits found in them. We might expect these to be the most flattering pictures of all.

Dr. Miguel Galindo is another example of the phenomenon amply charted by Azuela, the totally anti-revolutionary intellectual caught up helplessly in the Revolution. He was forced into the revolutionary whirlwind in its later stages by persecution and imprisonment at the hand of Carrancistas: on escaping from jail his only possible course of action was to join the Zapatistas. He is a pedantic, academic intellectual, wholly out of place among the hordes of Zapata. His ideas about the Revolution are particularly unsound. At some points in his relation he expresses normal

[59] pp. 242–3.

IM

Porfirian hostility to the whole affair, and blames it all on to the United States: 'the war unscrupulously provoked by a few unpatriotic Mexicans, incited by the imperialistic ambitions of the United States'.[60] At others he contradicts himself completely with a grim deterministic interpretation: 'Fate is urging us to destroy each other, and if Fate is invincible we must fight; many good people will die in the fight, but so will many evil people; this is Nature's painful process for selecting the inhabitants of this part of the world, and we should help her in her work since we cannot successfully oppose her.'[61] It seems to be as an extension of this idea that Galindo puts forward the suggestion that the large number of different races in Mexico is the cause of her frequent revolutions: the only possible solution, he says (quite seriously), is widespread polygamy.[62] Galindo tells us that there were many like him, involved in spite of themselves on the revolutionary side, and mentions particularly one Fernando Celada, a poet. Galindo's highly sympathetic portrayal of the latter suggests that Azuela is not, perhaps, exaggerating very much in the picture he gives of a similar figure, his Neftalí of *Las moscas* [pp. 96-7]: the two poets, one seen in a favourable light and the other in a highly hostile one, one purporting to be a 'fictional' creature and the other a real person, are remarkably alike. Galindo epitomizes the reluctant Zapatista Fernando Celada thus: 'his heart, made to spill tears for the memory of a dead lover and to carry autumn flowers to her grave, was less well-suited for the business of lashing the enemy with his pen'.[63]

Martín Luis Guzmán is another type we have already seen in this chapter: the highly idealistic young liberal intellectual whose naïve ideals are rudely shattered by reality. Shocked by the immorality of the Huerta regime, he helped the Carrancista cause first by writing anti-government propaganda in Mexico City and then by going to join the revolutionaries themselves in the north. *El águila y la serpiente* is the collection of his personal impressions of the revolutionaries. He confirms the picture the other novels give of the naïvety of the intellectuals and their social alienation from the other revolutionaries. An example is his description of his first conversation with Pancho Villa:

At each question or answer from one or the other it was clear that two

---

[60] *A través de la sierra* (Colima, 1924), p. 176.
[61] p. 78.   [62] p. 137.   [63] p. 50.

separate worlds were here coming together; two worlds which were quite irreconcilable except for the coincidence that they were joining their forces for the fight. We, poor deluded visionaries—that's all we were at the time—had come armed only with the fragile experience of our books and our first impulsive actions.[64]

In the course of time, naturally enough, Guzmán is more and more shocked and disillusioned by rude reality. He finds the life of a revolutionary uncomfortable and indecorous, and is rather disgusted by the seething dirty masses of humanity that were the revolutionary armies;[65] and he discovers that his Maderista ideals of justice and nobility find small echo among Carrancistas. So he refuses to become actively involved in the revolution in any direct, binding way:

I could not bring myself to exchange the tough discipline of a soldier for my beloved freedom of word and deed: in part, because I could see nothing around me to justify such a sacrifice. As for me, I had not the slightest political or military ambitions; and, as for the other revolutionaries, the main leaders were far from being, in my eyes, sufficiently disinterested or idealistic for me to want to tie myself indirectly to them, with chains that would always be perilous and that it would not always be possible to sever.[66]

Guzmán's lack of social flexibility and political realism made him, like many others, unable to work effectively for the Revolution as an intellectual.

Vasconcelos's account of his life during the Revolution, contained in the first two volumes of his autobiography,[67] was written some years afterwards, and it is inconsistent and violently biased. Vasconcelos was one of the leading intellectuals of the time, the assessment of whose revolutionary activities is a subject much too large to embark on here. But it is worth throwing a quick glance in that direction, in order to take account of the Revolution's lack of convincing intellectual leaders. That as mediocre an intellectual as Madero—the personification of the counterproductive utopian idealism examined below [pp. 123–4]—could reach such prominence

---

[64] Mexico, 1962, p. 54.
[65] See, for example, his description of a train journey among revolutionaries, pp. 151–5.
[66] p. 134.
[67] *Ulises criollo* (1935) and *La tormenta* (1936), *Obras completas* (Mexico, Vol. I, 1957), pp. 287–721 and 723–1214 respectively.

as he did is itself indicative. The Mexican Revolution lacked what Brinton considers vital and calls 'the heaven storming idealist'—it had no extremist leader remotely comparable with Cromwell, Robespierre, or Lenin.[68] Both the Convención de Aguascalientes and the Congreso Constituyente were widely mocked for the poverty of their intellectual content. Of the revolutionary thinkers, indeed, only one is convincing as such, and he, consequently, appears everywhere—Luis Cabrera (1876–1954). He alone gives the impression of understanding events well enough to impose his will on them, rather than being manipulated by events like the characters of Azuela's novels. It was he, particularly, who with the expression *La Revolución es revolución*—which was first used in a newspaper article of June 1911[69] and which became a household expression during the Revolution, as the novels attest—constantly pressed first Madero and then Carranza to carry out the reforms without which real peace, *paz orgánica*, would never be achieved. Revolution is an ugly affair, he said, but there is no point in trying to deny its existence or the existence of the social and economic problems which have caused it; only continued fighting can be expected until these problems are on the way to being solved. It was he who was mainly responsible for Carranza's Agrarian Reform Law of 6 January 1915, the beginning of agrarian reform in modern Mexico [p. 35]: he had already, at the end of 1912, strongly advocated the ejido as the solution to many problems. But of course one man was not enough; Mexico needed many more Luis Cabreras at all levels of her revolutionary movement.[70]

A brief look at Vasconcelos's autobiography is useful to show how some of the common defects of the revolutionary intellectual in Mexico, as described in the novels, extend into the very tip of the iceberg. In his description of himself in Maderista times, the theme of the romantically conceived sexual obsession appears yet again: 'A nebulous period in my life, possibly because I had not yet overcome the spiritual stupor of youth in the grips of an anarchy of feeling and a delirium of eroticism.'[71] And throughout the part of the autobiography that deals with the years of the Revolution the continuous struggle in his personal life between, on

[68] Op cit., pp. 165–76.

[69] *El País* and *El Diario del Hogar*, 20 June 1911.

[70] See *El pensamiento de Luis Cabrera*, selección y prólogo de Eduardo Luquín (Mexico, 1960).

[71] *Ulises criollo*, p. 528.

the one hand, eroticism and, on the other, the desire to do great things for humanity is prominent. The theme of aestheticism appears, too: he tells how, in Maderista times, the group of young intellectuals he belonged to—the *Ateneo de la juventud* [p. 82]— spent their time 'formulating absurd theories about art, life, the after-life, or gossiping about events'.[72] They were naïvely optimistic in politics: 'We believed progress to have finally triumphed over war. An uninterrupted series of inventions was going steadily and constantly to improve human life, making it evolve in a Spencerian fashion.'[73] Indeed Vasconcelos is very proud to declare that he had no interest at all in politics—a remarkable attitude for one of the principal politicians of the Revolution, who was later to run as presidential candidate: 'I was not a politician and I didn't give a damn for that science . . . If I was mixed up in revolutionary adventures it was because extraordinary circumstances demanded extraordinary steps.'[74] His motivation for being a revolutionary was based not on social, political or economic considerations but on purely moral ones, and he confirms that this was normal among his acquaintances: 'that was why we went to the Revolution: to use the weight of the people to impose the spirit upon reality: pure men who believed in righteousness were to triumph over the perverse, the unbelievers and the merely foolish'.[75] And of course the inevitable disillusion followed: in common with so many others, Vasconcelos had expected from revolution what it can never give. *La tormenta* describes the gradual destruction of his ingenuous 'Maderista faith', and throughout it Vasconcelos frequently lapses into hysterical condemnation of the Revolution after Madero as a vast plot engineered by United States protestantism to destroy the superior Spanish and Roman Catholic civilization of Mexico [pp. 207 and 287–8].

The three autobiographical sources that throw light on the nature of the intellectuals of the Mexican Revolution corroborate the impression given by the other novels that the Revolution lacked adequate intellectual guidance. There is one further line of enquiry we can take before formulating definite conclusions. Many of the novelists themselves were members of the intellectual group. This means not only that their insight into intellectual characters in their novels is likely to be accurate, but also that their own explicit

---

[72] p. 538. [73] p. 538.
[74] *La tormenta*, pp. 741–2.   [75] *Ulises criollo*, p. 626.

or implicit ideas as manifested in their fictional works are, in themselves, useful evidence of the group's nature. The early novelists of the Revolution were not, on the whole, professional writers but unknown ones, writing principally for their own satisfaction; so their opinions can be taken as being their own, not tailored to fit any particular patron or audience. What, then, can such indirect self-portraits of intellectuals of the Revolution tell us?

Some of Azuela's personal opinions about the Revolution have already been seen earlier in this chapter. Since he wrote more novels than any of the other early novelists of the Revolution, and since he made his own position so clear, he is a good subject for analysis. We have already seen above that there is an acute contradiction within him which is reflected in all his novels of the Revolution: he sympathizes with the oppressed and the humble and would like to see a radical change in their fortunes—and at the same time he has a deterministic and anti-revolutionary belief, derived from the positivism that was the official philosophy during his formative years, in the unchangeability of mankind's destiny [pp. 87–90]. It is the latter belief that seems eventually to win the inner tug-of-war. The motivation process of his novels gives a deterministic picture of things: the Revolution is presented not as an upheaval engineered by certain groups of human beings for their betterment, but as the result of the machinations of blind, supernatural forces, which control men and make them dance to their wishes like helpless, soulless puppets. Azuela presses home this implicit lesson with judgements expressed by the characters he uses as his mouthpieces. The opinions we have already seen expressed through Andrés Pérez [pp. 88ff.], are repeated in different words by the doctor of Las moscas, talking about the parasitic bureaucrats: 'Ideas, feelings, opinions—they all take shape in their stomachs; and so they can't be blamed for anything. What is sad and deplorable is to have spilt so much blood and then to go and throw ourselves all over again into the arms of that . . . scum';[76] by Solís—repeatedly—in Los de abajo: for example: 'A revolution is a hurricane, and the man who takes part stops being a man and becomes a mere dry leaf tossed hither and thither by the wind';[77] and by Valderrama later in the same novel: 'I love the Revolution as I love an erupting volcano! I love the volcano just because it is a volcano, and the Revolution because it is the Revolution! . . . But who cares

[76] p. 876.   [77] p. 362.

which stones are left on top, and which underneath, after the cataclysm?'[78]—an image Azuela finds so apt to describe the feelings of the intellectual who finds himself helplessly caught up in the Revolution (as maybe Azuela did himself) that he repeats it word for word in his revolutionary short story *El caso López Romero*.[79] This pessimistic, fatalistic view of the Revolution[80] precludes Azuela from formulating his general sympathies for humble people into any consistent ideology or giving any suggestions about what should have happened in the Revolution, given that what did happen was not acceptable to him. Such a position is, in fact, the end of the line for thought of any sort about the problems of the Revolution.

Although not all the novelists share Azuela's particular deterministic view, they do all have in common a general pessimism about the Revolution and its effects, and a lack of any real understanding of what it was all about. These shortcomings in the novelists are, like the identical shortcomings of the intellectual heroes of their novels, partially the result of judging the Revolution with solely moral criteria. The novelist and intellectual's first experience of revolution has been Maderismo, which was repeatedly referred to as—and clearly was, to a large extent [pp. 193–4] —a pure, idealistic movement with much of the feeling of a moral crusade behind it. Such radical ideas as the novelist and intellectual grasps have been formed, then, in this somewhat chimerical and highly utopian school. What he expects of revolutions is what Madero declared that he intended to achieve by one: justice and morality. Revolutions never, in the short run at least, produce

---

[78] p. 410. Valderrama reflects in his choice of words a popular dictum of the revolutionary years, which recurs frequently in the novels: 'La Revolución es revolución'. It was an expression coined by Luis Cabrera [p. 120]. Used by Cabrera to refer to the need in revolutionary situations for real radical reform, it was diluted in popular usage into an expression of the fatality and cynicism of the moment.

[79] *Obras completas*, II, p. 1073.

[80] In two of Azuela's novels there is, at the end, some slight suggestion of hope. At the conclusion of *Los caciques* some sort of justice is done when, in the confusion caused by the entry of the revolutionaries into the town, don Juan Viñas's orphaned children avenge their father's ruin and death by setting fire to the magnificent warehouse in which the caciques had invested a large part of their ill-gotten fortune. At the end of *Las tribulaciones de una familia decente* Azuela presents us with the regeneration of the aristocratic Procopio through hard work; but he dies immediately afterwards. The general picture of the Revolution painted by Azuela is gloomy indeed.

such results, however: the immediate consequence of a revolution is, indeed, quite the opposite.[81] And while the revolution is still being fought, of course, it is absurd to expect justice and morality—in the conventional bourgeois sense of the terms—to have much say in events; yet it is precisely the attitude of the novelists that they should do so and that, since in the Mexican case they do not, the Revolution has been a disastrous failure. When the Mexican Revolution enters its more genuinely revolutionary Carrancista stage [p. 197] disillusionment is, necessarily, complete; and it is this disillusionment—that of the middle-class Maderista suddenly brought face to face with the brutalities and iniquities of a real revolutionary situation—that we find reflected in many of the early novels of the Mexican Revolution. There is, to put against the repulsion that any sensitive person must feel in the face of the inhumanity of war, no hint, even, of any compensatory political or social appreciation of the revolutionary process, no realization that, behind the façade of horror and suffering, there are important things going on which are changing society irrevocably and, maybe, for the better. The novelists have no wide view of the general panorama of the Revolution to set off their pictures of the sad experiences of various individuals; their vision of the Revolution is short-sighted and parochial, for they can see and imagine nothing but what their own limited personal contact with it has allowed them to glimpse.

This has repercussions on the novels' literary form. The style and structure of Azuela's novels of the Revolution (and of many of the others) are essentially fragmentary, and reflect a fragmentary, non-integrated view of the Revolution. Each one is a series of loosely-linked 'tableaux and scenes' (as Azuela liked to subtitle his novels of the Revolution) written in an elliptical, 'staccato' prose which prefers extreme brevity in all things—in word, clause, sen-

---

[81] A great proportion of the work of the Russian émigré sociologist P. A. Sorokin has been devoted to the detailed, if not pedantic, examination—or indictment—of the chaos that revolutions cause both to society as a whole and to individual human psychology. Sorokin can confidently claim—as, indeed, he does—exhaustively to have proved his point that man's behaviour rarely improves in time of civil war. Sociologists of revolutions who have allowed themselves wider terms of reference have agreed that a common feature of them all is a period of dictatorial rule, a 'reign of terror', when the ultimately triumphant part consolidates its victory, using methods which are often necessarily neither moral nor just (Brinton, pp. 178–200; Pettee, pp. 127–36; Edwards, pp. 156–84; Mendieta y Núñez, pp. 61–4).

tence, paragraph, and chapter.[82] There is no consciousness of any grand plan behind all these isolated phenomena that are impressionistically sketched for us: no understanding that the scenes and tableaux that are thrown out at the reader are but small parts of a great social process. The Revolution is presented as a collection of rather meaningless, even sordid, little occurrences, with only the inexorable guiding hand of Destiny behind them. The circular development of *Los de abajo* is another example of the influence of Azuela's social experience upon not only the content but also the very form of his literary expression of that social experience. The peasant guerrilla leader Demetrio Macías starts fighting at the head of a small band comprising a handful of friends in Juchipila (Zacatecas), and rapidly gains power and support as he wanders over central Mexico until he is the general of a respectably-sized army; he then falls into rapid decline, and his revolutionary career ends exactly as it started, when he and the faithful few who still follow him are ambushed and massacred—in Juchipila. The structure of *Los de abajo* embodies Azuela's fatalistic vision of the futility of the Revolution.

A further hindrance to active intellectual participation in the Revolution that is revealed in the over-all nature of the novels, and that has been seen in certain of their intellectual protagonists, is social alienation. Trotsky has shown that novelists, like all intellectuals, are bound to suffer from such a handicap, simply because they have a social background that is completely different from that of the actual soldiers of the revolution; and he has also shown that part of the measure of their success as novelists of the revolution is the extent to which they manage to overcome this handicap and project themselves into the lives of the fighting workers.[83] In the case of the Mexican Revolution, one can only note that such alienation is almost absolute. Not only do the early novelists not succeed in showing any understanding of the fighting masses: they scarcely manage even to notice their existence. Of the novels of the Revolution published before 1926 only in *Los de abajo* are the rank-and-file soldiers of the Revolution the protagonists—a

[82] *La tribulaciones de una familia decente* is something of an exception to this general rule. In his last novel of the Revolution Azuela seems to reject the style he developed in the other novels—maybe because of their failure to capture the attention of the public—and to return to a more traditional, discursive style, with fuller descriptions and a more orthodox plot structure.

[83] Op. cit., pp. 11–14.

fact perhaps not altogether unconnected with *Los de abajo*'s subsequent success at the height of the period when the socialist myth of the Mexican Revolution was being officially propagated. And even *Los de abajo*, this wholly uncharacteristic novel of the Revolution,[84] shows, for all the critical acclaim it has received, very little really sympathetic penetration into the world of the peasant. Demetrio Macías and his men are only lightly and superficially sketched characters, in spite of their prominence in the novel. There is little to distinguish between them all, as Azuela presents them: they share basic traits that Azuela evidently thinks are normal and definitive peasant characteristics—stupidity, slowness, feeble-mindedness, and gullibility, compensated for only by a certain animal courage and cunning. Azuela's attempt to create individual characters is limited to tagging on to this fundamental material a different superficial quality in each case. So Demetrio is stupid, slow, feeble-minded, gullible—and soft-hearted; Venancio's character is formed by the addition of social ambition to the four basic ingredients; Margarito's particularity is sadism; and so on. The reader concludes the novel without having formed any impression in his mind of characters with a living presence. Azuela, the only early novelist even to attempt to bridge this class-gap, failed to do so with any conviction—whatever other merits *Los de abajo* might have. In a revealing simile he perhaps unwittingly makes explicit his real attitude towards the Mexican peasant: 'those words kept battering on their clumsy brains like a hammer on an anvil'.[85] The comparison between the presentation of Demetrio Macías here, for example, and that of the lower-middle-class Juan Viñas in *Los caciques* [pp. 301–2] leaves no doubt about where Azuela's real sympathies lie.

The general conclusion to be drawn from all possible sources is unavoidably that the intellectuals in the Mexican Revolution were incapable, as a body, of performing the services of information and organization that only they could have performed.[86] One might

---

[84] It is only some of the later Mexican novelists of the 1930s who, following the example of *Los de abajo*, focus their novels of the Revolution on peasant heroes.

[85] p. 407.

[86] Tannenbaum (*Peace by Revolution*, Columbia University Press, 1933, pp. 115–19) reaches a similar general conclusion, although he explains the intellectuals' ineffectiveness solely in terms of their class alienation from the

suggest this as a reason for some of the Revolution's special characteristics.

The lack of morality and idealism by which the intellectuals were so disheartened must itself have been aggravated by their own readiness to give up the attempt to improve things and their consequent failure to do anything to remedy the situation; here is a vicious circle that probably operated throughout the Revolution. Furthermore, the Revolution's failure to create an adequate social mythology [pp. 130–82], and the general lack of organization and awareness among revolutionaries [pp. 183–239] are both attributable to the severe shortcomings of the intellectuals. Like the pin-headed monsters of prehistory, the Mexican Revolution had inadequate mental control and direction to match the mighty physical forces at play in it.

The intellectuals who have been the subject of study in this chapter had been brought up and educated in Porfirian times, and the history of their behaviour in the Revolution is a constant reminder of this fact. Since they were quite unable to make any breach in the massive class barrier which separated them from the peasant revolutionaries—and, indeed, were totally uninterested in trying to do so and incapable of making the sacrifices and concessions that such an effort would require—they could never come into any close relationship or establish any real communication with them. There is in the novels, for example, not one intellectual who actually fights on the field of battle; and many, like Azuela's Pérez, Cervantes, and even his autobiographical Solís, admit that they are cowards and take positive action to avoid danger. The precept of the division of labour applies rigidly in the Mexican Revolution, which is, then, a far cry from the modern Latin-American revolutionary tradition of intellectuals who make every effort to achieve complete solidarity with the fighting masses. It is impossible to find in the gallery of types we have considered in this chapter—different sorts, both prominent and obscure, romantic

fighting masses of the Revolution—which is surely only a part of the truth. There are indications that the intellectuals in the Zapatista movement were somewhat more satisfactory than the others (see Womack, pp. 193ff.). The southern agrarian revolution attracted idealists from all over Mexico: hardly a single one of the leading Zapatista intellectuals was from the south. This had both desirable and undesirable results: Zapatismo acquired some of the country's most able intellectuals, who then had the southerner's deep distrust of the outsider (in addition to normal class antagonism) to contend with.

and materialistic, selfless and greedy, presented from different points of view, both favourable and unfavourable—even one intellectual who can be seen clearly to have lived up to the standards of awareness and decisiveness required of him.

The intellectuals who formed part of the revolutionary forces seem, on the evidence discussed here, to fall into three main groups. One of them is composed of those who were unwillingly caught up in the Revolution simply because they had no other way to turn, who were fundamentally unsympathetic to the whole affair and who hence could offer nothing in the way of intellectual guidance. There are reasons for suspecting that these formed a larger group than might be expected: in the novels they are represented by Andrés Pérez, Neftalí Sancho, Miguel Galindo, and Fernando Celada.

The second group is that of intellectuals who did enter the Revolution by free decision, but who did so only with the thought of personal advancement in mind. The novelists, with their exclusively moral norms of judgement, apportion their most hostile treatment to these intellectuals. Consequently they do not consider the possibility that an individual might ruthlessly serve his own interests and incidentally serve those of the Revolution as well, but conceive of the two as mutually exclusive. All the indications are, however, that in the case of the Mexican revolutionary intellectual the cause of self-advancement, so single-mindedly pursued, was in fact an effective bar to the cause of communal advancement. In the novels this second group is represented by Luis Cervantes, Agustín Chaneque, Austreberto Pingarrón, and Azuela's government candidate. These two sorts of revolutionary intellectual, of at best doubtful usefulness as such, would be expected to appear in any revolution, thrown up by the social turmoil it causes.

It is the third group to which one looks for the real guidance and leadership in the Revolution—the group formed by intellectuals in whose motivation an important part is played by radical idealism. These are well represented in the novels, and are given understanding and sympathetic treatment, in the portrayal of Juan Ampudia, Federico Andrade, Jorge Albán and Marco Astenia, in the self-portraits of Martín Luis Guzmán and José Vasconcelos, and in what Mariano Azuela (and, to a lesser extent, other novelists) tell us indirectly about themselves in their writings. These intellectuals were inadequate because their idealism was not adjustable to the realities of the situation, and broke quickly under the strain of revolutionary experience. Their radicalism took no account of political, social and economic matters, and it had to compete in the individual with too powerful a body of personal feelings and pleasures. The latter were reinforced by the pervasive influence of the escapist literature that had become popular in Porfirian times. Naïve uninformed Maderista idealism—which itself seems to have owed much more to vague literary models than to actual experience —was not a strong opponent for personal happiness; and in each separate contest between the two, the latter won with ease. Not only do we not come across any Robert Jordans in the early novels of the Mexican Revolution; there is not even a Yury Zhivago to be found.

The failure of such a central and vital revolutionary group as that of the intellectuals had far-reaching and serious consequences, and sharply restricted the effectiveness of the Revolution as a whole. No section of revolutionary society could, as a result, function properly. We can see how this happened in an examination of firstly, another revolutionary group with directive functions, though of a different type—the leaders, or figureheads.

5

REVOLUTIONARIES II: THE LEADERS

THE leaders (*caudillos*) of a revolution are either civilians whose intellectual or personal qualities carry them to the top, or, more usually, men who reach their high position as a result of their abilities as soldiers and as military chiefs. In the Mexican Revolution, the most prominent representatives of the second type were Pancho Villa and Emiliano Zapata (and on the anti-revolutionary side, Porfirio Díaz and Victoriano Huerta), and of the first type, Francisco Madero and Venustiano Carranza. The fields of this chapter and the last overlap to some extent, since it is possible for a revolutionary to be both an intellectual and a leader. In the preceding chapter, however, we were concerned with the intellectuals in their function as organizers and controllers, working essentially behind the scenes in comparative obscurity, like Luis Cabrera, 'the brain behind Carrancismo' [p. 120].[1] In this chapter, in so far as some intellectuals are the subject of examination, we shall be considering them not *qua* intellectuals, but in their very different role as prominent public figures.

One of the caudillo's tasks is, of course, to command the forces under him. The study and assessment of his command is an important part of the work of the political historian, and does not primarily concern us here. The caudillo's social significance is not, however, completely separate from his political one; it is rather an extension of it. By being a successful leader he attracts the attention of both the enemy and his own side, and becomes famous; thus he turns into a figurehead for the revolutionary movement, symbolizing its ideals, aspirations, and faith in the inevitability of ultimate victory. He comes, in short, to be the centre of a whole body of revolutionary mythology. Such legendary heroes are indispensable to the success of a revolution. They provide a convenient simplification of reality: they turn its insoluble maze of cause and effect into

[1] Mariano Azuela, *Las tribulaciones de una familia decente* in *Obras completas*, I, p. 100.

a straightforward confrontation between virtuous, manly, progressive 'us', and wicked, cowardly, reactionary 'them'. Thus they make possible positive commitment and action on a large scale. Revolutionary soldiers cannot be puzzling out the rights and wrongs of a complicated situation when what is needed is for them to fight; the legend and the myth do the thinking for them and present them with clear-cut alternatives, which leave no possible choice of course of action for the man who considers himself honourable.

Indeed, it could be said that a revolution has not started seriously until it has created its heroes and its myths, and conversely that no important revolution has failed to leave for posterity (and for further myth-accumulation) its collection of heroes: for it is one of the first tasks of a successful revolution to impose its own myths on the whole of society, fuse them with the traditional body of national patriotism, and so broadcast the idea that this particular revolution has been the last one ever necessary in the country. Even revolutions which have attempted, as part of their reaction against the past, to reject traditional patriotism—like the Russian and French revolutions—have found it impossible to do so, and have had normal recourse to myths and legends. The distance between objective reality and the picture presented by the myth or legend is sometimes—but not always or necessarily—great, and is completely irrelevant, so long as people can be persuaded to believe in the myth; what counts is the comforting, stirring, encouraging fiction to which men attach their allegiances and by which they guide their conduct.

It is convenient at this point to make a clear distinction between two kinds of social symbolism: on the one hand, the myth and, on the other, the legend. Georges Sorel, and after him several American sociologists, have dealt at length with the idea of the social myth.[2] It is an imaginative creation which stands in men's minds for all their dearest aspirations and hopes for the future; examples of such social myths are the syndicalist general strike of the world's workers (Sorel's particular interest), the Marxist proletarian revolution, and the Christian apocalypse. The practical possibility of the eventual realization of the visions presented by

[2] Georges Sorel, *Reflections on Violence* (New York and London, 1967), especially pp. 41–53, 124–50 and 209–10; Edwards, pp. 90–6; Pettee, pp. 17–23, 68–71, 75–7 and 90–2; Brinton, pp. 90 and 201–18. See also Mendieta y Núñez, pp. 84–6.

such myths is entirely irrelevant: a myth cannot be 'disproved' any more than a novel or poem can be disproved. The purpose of a myth, as Sorel points out, is not that of an astronomical almanac:

The myth must be judged as a means of acting on the present; any attempt to discuss how far it can be taken literally as future history is devoid of sense. *It is the myth in its entirety which is alone important*: its parts are only of interest in so far as they bring out the main idea. No useful purpose is served, therefore, in arguing about the incidents which may occur in the course of a social war, and about the decisive conflicts which may give victory to the proletariat; even supposing the revolutionaries to have been wholly and entirely deluded in setting up this imaginary picture of the general strike, this picture may yet have been, in the course of the preparation for the Revolution, a great element of strength, if it has embraced all the aspirations of Socialism, and if it has given to the whole body of Revolutionary thought a precision and a rigidity which no other method of thought could have given.[3]

The concept of the legend may usefully be added to that of the social myth, and contrasted with it. What I have chosen to call the legend is the series of stories about the exploits and abilities of a particular revolutionary leader, which elevate him to the status of a hero in the eyes of his followers. The function of the legend is similar to that of the myth, and the two form part of the same process, strengthening revolutionary morale and unity. Yet the differences between the two are crucial. Whereas the myth is social, the legend is personal: the myth, then, is capable of achieving a much deeper and more durable unity than the legend, which is fragile in its dependence on a man rather than an idea—the legend can rapidly collapse with the death or the discredit of the hero. Legends can, indeed, create disunity among revolutionaries: if several different ones spring up they can give rise to destructive personalist struggles within the revolutionary ranks [p. 164]. The legend is a simple and immediate structure; the myth a complex and visionary one, a kind of revolutionary religion. Altogether the myth is superior to the legend. The legend can often develop into a myth, and it is, for the sake of the revolution, most desirable that it should.

The Mexican leaders of 1910–17 followed a firmly-established but not altogether honourable tradition. The nineteenth century,

---

[3] Georges Sorel, *Reflections on Violence*, p. 126.

with its continuous anarchical unrest, had been the age of the caudillo; during most of it, it was all too easy for any soldier who could command a strong force to aspire to great political power. Such conditions threw up a series of purely personalist caudillos, bereft of any civic spirit, of whom Santa Anna was the most persistent: his legend, far from being heroic, is a comic or farcical one. The real heroes of the Mexican nineteenth century were civilians and intellectuals: Morelos, Hidalgo and Juárez. Only Vicente Guerrero and Porfirio Díaz among the military leaders had respectable legends at the outbreak of the Revolution. Neither could measure up to those of the three civilian heroes, while that of Porfirio Díaz was based more on his qualities as a conservative statesman than on his early revolutionary activity: his normal epithet was 'El héroe de la paz'. In any case his legend was, clearly, not acceptable to the revolutionaries. So there was ample precedent by 1910 for the creation of radical civilian heroes, paragons of all the civic virtues; but the Mexican tradition (strangely for a Latin-American country) lacked respectable military heroes.[4] Pancho Villa and Emiliano Zapata, together with several small local leaders, were to provide abundant compensation for the previous gaps in popular Mexican social symbolism.

The novels of the Mexican Revolution provide valuable documentation of the gradual development of the legends of these and other figures. With the help of the early novels, written when the legends were taking shape, one can chart their appearance step by step. The later novels of the 1930s were an important instrument in the post-revolutionary consolidation and adaptation of these legends, to suit the needs of the new society—or at least those of its rulers—and they are worthy of study as such. We are at present concerned with the first stage of the process only. It is intended to trace, through the novels and with the support of evidence from other sources (particularly newspapers and popular songs of the Revolution), the process of the creation of the Revolution's principal legends, those which surrounded the caudillos Madero, Villa, Zapata, and Carranza. All the early novels of the Revolution are

---

[4] The only precedents for the legends of Villa and Zapata were the minor legends formed around certain brigands and outlaws of the Porfirian period, like Macario Romero and Heraclio Bernal. See Armando de María y Campos, *La Revolución mexicana a través de los corridos populares* (Mexico, 1962), Vol. I, pp. 33–4, 85–7 and 92–7.

useful in this part of the study. The elements of distortion and bias do not have to be compensated for in any way, for it is precisely such distortions of 'objective' reality that give the legends their existence. The early novels, though they never acquired a sufficiently large public to have any part in forming the legends themselves (as mural paintings, novels and films did in post-revolutionary society), accurately reflect the process. In them we can discover both the growth of certain legends and, what is just as important, the failure of other legends, though vigorously publicized, to take root in the public imagination. The novels are quite as useful for our purposes in not referring to certain legends that we know about from other sources (particularly those of Carranza and Carrancismo) as they are in fully documenting the development of others.

The first important social symbol of the Mexican Revolution was its first leader, Francisco I. Madero. He had already attracted some attention, both hostile and favourable, before the outbreak of the Revolution, in his political campaigns; the government press had dismissed him as a madman, and the opposition press had presented him as a hero and missionary.[5] From the start of the process of creation of any revolutionary social legend, the two opposing forces represented here are in play—the revolutionary force, developing the legend, and the anti-revolutionary force, creating what could be styled the counter-legend (for it attempts to do exactly the opposite of what the legend does, and to establish an image of incompetence and evil for the revolutionary leader). During the revolution there is constant rivalry and interaction between the two; it is only after the conclusive triumph of the rebels that the counter-legend is discarded and the legend itself can start to acquire firm, unchallenged national status. During the early growth of the legend in the revolution, the counter-legend plays a vital part.

[5] The Díaz government tolerated some opposition newspapers, although by regularly fining, imprisoning, and generally harrasing their editors and collaborators it ensured that they could never become dangerously influential. The whole opposition press was suppressed as soon as the Revolution broke out. The most notable of these newspapers was *El Diario del Hogar*, founded (in 1881) and heroically edited throughout the Porfirian period by Filomeno Mata (1845–1911), who paid for his independence with regular stays in jail. He was imprisoned yet again on the outbreak of the Revolution, and died shortly after Madero's victory, his release, and the reappearance of *El Diario del Hogar*. His newspaper only survived him, however, by a few months.

In Madero's case, then, the embryos of both the legend and the counter-legend were in existence before the Revolution. After its outbreak they grew from there. Since the national press was government-controlled and censorship was tightened up after 20 November, it was the Porfirista counter-legend that reached a wide audience in the early days. Porfirismo's first tactic was to accord as little importance as possible to the Maderista rebellion and its leader; to deny him a public image of any sort. However as the rebellion in the north continued and was not suppressed so quickly as the country had been led to believe it would, it became impossible to avoid references to Madero and descriptions of him. Gradually the pre-revolutionary beginnings of a counter-legend were worked on and expanded. His alleged madness was stressed again, so that he became for his opponents 'el loco Madero' or 'el loco millionario'; even the American newspaper in Mexico, *The Mexican Herald*, published (on 26 January 1911) an article declaring him a lunatic. The attack on Madero was made along these particular lines for two reasons. Firstly, it was the opinion of many that to mount an assault against the apparently invincible Porfirian order was an idea that could only be conceived by a madman. Azuela puts such an opinion into the mouth of the Porfirista don Cuco: 'No right-thinking man could judge Madero as anything but a fool or a madman. Whoever heard of such a thing as standing up to our great President?'[6] And, secondly, such a notion had the support of Madero's personal quirks: vegetarianism and spiritism.[7] On the basis of these two facts was built the whole legendary superstructure of Madero's insanity.

This basic element of the counter-legend was duly embroidered and elaborated during early 1911. One of the earliest decorations, and one which was much insisted on by the press, was Madero's failure to appear personally. His absence from the battlefield at the beginning of the Revolution was soon noticed[8] and gave rise in the press to the thoroughly unwarranted charge that he was a coward.

[6] *Andrés Pérez, maderista*, p. 780. The conversation takes place in Jan. 1911.

[7] The American Ambassador, Henry Lane Wilson, came to be convinced that Madero was mad, and included this allegation in his reports to his superiors. See, for example, his communication to the Secretary of State, Bryan, dated 12 Mar. 1913 (*Foreign Relations 1913*, pp. 775–6). Madero's own family does not seem to have been very sure of his sanity: see letters from his grandfather and his father reproduced respectively in Limantour, pp. 208–9 and *Documentos históricos de la Revolución mexicana*, V (Mexico, 1964), p. 16.

[8] *El Diario*, 26 Nov. 1910; *El Tiempo*, 28 Nov. 1910.

The accusation of cowardice is one which a Mexican counter-legend can hardly afford to dispense with, however few grounds there are for it, for it represents the ultimate humiliation of a man and the complete negation of his *machismo* [pp. 153ff.]. A second anti-heroic epithet was coined for Madero and used regularly in all the newspapers during the campaign—'el caudillo invisible'. Further material for the making of the counter-legend was provided by Madero's family background. It was most unfortunate that this high-minded advocate of purity and virtue should belong to a family whose considerable fortune was largely derived from the manufacture and sale of cheap spirits; and it is this sort of ironic coincidence that a hostile legend is bound to seize on. Surely enough Madero became, in his primitive counter-legend, not only a madman and a coward but a wicked exploiter of the vices of the weak as well: don Cuco expresses the Porfirista opinion in the conversation already referred to: 'Madero is a man possessed by vulgar ambition; a perverse charlatan who made his pile out of drink. The famous wine-merchant from Parras, who poisons the poor Mexican people with his infamous fire-water.'[9] The Porfirian press's attack on Madero extended also into an attack on his supporters, who were accused of being unpatriotic and of setting their own personal greed for power and riches above the good of the country. Most of them, it said, were no more than bandits who used political slogans as an excuse for their dastardly acts; the 'hard-working and peace-loving people', whom the revolutionaries claimed to represent, were steadfastly opposed to this violence and destruction. This was, in fact, quite true [pp. 194–7].[10] One of the more original and picturesque attacks on the Maderistas, brought out at the beginning of the campaign and insisted on throughout it, was directed at their 'underhand' and 'unchivalrous' use of dynamite. The sensational press gave great prominence to the rebels' use of this substance and what it called 'infernal machines' for exploding it, protesting bitterly at the revolutionaries' foul play.[11] The campaign seems to have made some impression: several of the novels, like *La majested caída* and *Sangre y humo*, insist, though not necessarily disapprovingly, on the Maderistas' use of dynamite.

In the later stages of the rebellion, great prominence was also accorded in the press to the presence in the revolutionary ranks of

[9] *Andrés Pérez, maderista*, p. 781.   [10] *El Imparcial*, 4 Mar. 1911.
[11] *El Diario*, 20 and 25 Nov. 1911.

American *filibusteros*, who were depicted as taking great delight in killing Mexicans with dumdum bullets and then stealing their property. Mexican suspicion of American adventurers, the result of a long tradition of border incidents, was thus exploited. The line of attack which condemned the revolutionaries for their lack of 'patriotism' was intensified, with editorials censuring them for destroying the results of years of peaceful labour and civilized life by blowing up bridges and cutting lines of communication. And of course, to the bitter end, the newspapers insisted that the revolutionaries were totally incompetent and disorganized, and that the whole business was no more than a chain of disastrous defeats for the rebels and glorious triumphs for the Federal Army—a story which after six months began to wear thin. The Porfirian press, like the right-wing press later under Huerta, did not help its own attempts to create convincing counter-legends by its constant failure to credit its readers with any intelligence.

This was the Madero counter-legend developed in a few weeks after the outbreak of his rebellion. It was, perhaps, too obviously the work of a propaganda drive; in the later, desperate stages of March and April, any rumour, however wild and unsubstantiated, was used to try to discredit Madero. This sort of careless and uncontrolled legend-making produces results contrary to those desired, for it undermines the verisimilitude and credibility of the whole legend, and hence threatens to destroy the legend itself. The Porfirian press had a reputation for being untruthful and servile, and it never had enough subtlety to make any real pretence of being otherwise. Its attempts to create a counter-legend only, in the end, served to increase interest in finding out what Madero and his men were really like, and so to prepare the ground for the positive legend. Andrés Pérez finds himself the centre of highly sympathetic attention when it is rumoured that he is a Maderista. Vasconcelos[12] says that the counter-legend had very little effect at any time outside Mexico City, the stronghold of Porfirismo. The revolutionary legend did not, at any rate, take long to gain impetus.

From the very beginning Madero was known to his supporters as 'el apóstol de la Democracia'; the midday daily *Gil Blas* made derisive reference to this epithet as early as 29 November. As the rebellion he was leading dragged on, interest grew in him—a process recorded by Mariano Azuela in *Andrés Pérez, maderista*. But

---

[12] *Ulises criollo*, pp. 657–8.

the revolutionary legend, unlike the counter-legend, had as yet no organs of widespread dissemination. Until Maderismo acquired control of them it could not develop the pre-revolutionary embryo legend in Mexican society as a whole. So Madero's legend remained at this very simple level until mid-1911 when, with general expectancy and interest at a very high level, the thirst for information about Madero began to be satisfied; Maderista newspapers like *El Diario del Hogar* began to appear again in May, and at about the same time the rest of the national press started realizing, under the pressure of events, that Madero was, after all, an acceptable political leader. *El Imparcial*, the most crudely obsequious and abject of the national newspapers, managed an almost overnight volte-face in the first week of June. Ballads or *corridos*[13] (the newspapers of the illiterate) were plentifully produced and disseminated on the subject of the rebellion of Madero and the bright future that was awaiting Mexico under his guiding hand. In April, May, and June all the conditions were exactly right for the confirmation of the Madero legend and for its elevation to the form of a myth.

Madero's social symbolism of 1911 can be seen to have three main components. Each one of them connects Madero himself with wider and greater fields of reference than the mere personal attributes of individual man alone. By being associated with these generally accepted—in 1911 at least—abstract ideal visions, bound up intimately with humanity's greatest hopes and aspirations, the man is made by the magic of mythology somehow supernatural, and the individual legend is transfigured into a whole system, a complete social myth. Madero's social mythification is a classic and complete example of the process.

One of the ideal visions incorporated into Madero's public image was that of patriotism. As an idealistic civilian leader he bore a considerable theoretical resemblance to the nineteenth-century

---

[13] The corrido is the modern Mexican continuation of the Spanish *romance* tradition, and it flourished strongly during the Revolution and in the few years before and after it. It usually relates the story of an important event, such as a battle or the life of a prominent person, often on the occasion of his death. Corridos were published, often with clear propagandist purposes, on cheap loose sheets, and sung in the streets by travelling performers who sold the word-sheets to the public after their performance. See María y Campos, op. cit.; Vicente D. Mendoza, *Romance y corrido* (Mexico, 1939), *El corrido de la Revolución mexicana* (Mexico, 1956), and *Lírica narrativa de México: el corrido* (Mexico, 1964); and Merle E. Simmons, *The Mexican Corrido as a Source for Interpretive Study of Modern Mexico (1870–1950)* (Indiana University Press, 1957).

leaders in whose tradition, as seen already in this chapter, he followed; and this resemblance was exploited sensibly. Hidalgo and Juárez, and to a lesser degree Morelos, were by 1911 firmly-established figures of patriotic hagiography: indeed, Mexican nationalism, still in an early stage of formation [pp. 278-9], was represented almost exclusively by these symbols. By making Madero appear as a member of this illustrious group of heroes, some of their brilliance was reflected on to him. His status was elevated to a place not very far inferior to theirs, as the mantle of patriotism, with its emotional attraction most men find curiously irresistible, was made to pass from their shoulders to his. Thus, in the conversation in *Andrés Pérez, maderista* to which we have already referred twice in this chapter—it is extremely valuable as a barometer of opinions of the time, written as it was so soon after the event—Toño, who defends Madero against don Cuco's allegation of his insanity, does so by comparing him with the nineteenth-century heroes:

If our country has the good fortune to see Madero obtain the triumph he deserves, all these 'right-thinking men', and you the first among them, will proclaim at the top of their voices that Madero is one of the greatest figures in our history. Madero a clown, Madero a madman! Hidalgo too was a madman and a fool, until the day he cudgelled 'right-thinking men' into accepting Mexican Independence. Juárez was an idiot until the day he cudgelled 'right-thinking men' into accepting freedom of thought. But, don Cuco, those of us who are lucky enough not to be members of the club of 'right-thinking men' have already established Madero as a figure worthy to be raised up by the side of Hidalgo and Juárez.[14]

And in *Los caciques*, the Maderista don Timoteo expresses himself in a similar way about Madero and his position in history: 'Christ, the Redeemer of mankind; Hidalgo, the redeemer of our race; Juárez, the redeemer of consciences; Madero, the redeemer of the poor and humble'[15]—ideas which we learn later are not Timoteo's own at all, but which, significantly, he has lifted verbatim from the editorial of the day's copy of *El Diario del Hogar*. The corridos put

---

[14] p. 780.
[15] p. 807. Maderistas wore, side by side on their hats, badges showing the portraits of Juárez, Hidalgo, and Madero (Frederick C. Turner, *The Dynamic of Mexican Nationalism* (University of North Carolina Press, 1968), p. 106). One of Madero's followers, Rogelio Fernández Güell, published in 1911 a study of him entitled *El moderno Juárez*.

forward a similar idea more simply and directly, by insisting repeatedly (in an expression that became a formula in Maderista corridos) that Madero had risen in arms to 'defender la Nación'. He had, then, not fought for merely personal or even political reasons, but as a patriotic duty, and had the magical authority of National Tradition for doing so.

The comparison made by don Timoteo introduces us to another abstract eternal ideal which was incorporated in 1911 into the Madero legend: the religious one. It has been pointed out that the creation of a social myth is, in itself, a process which has religious overtones [p. 132]; and it is not unnatural that this implicit religious content should be reinforced with explicit religious references. Hence don Timoteo's blasphemous association; hence also the vocabulary of the Madero myth: 'apóstol', 'redentor', and, after his death, 'mártir'. It is stressed in the Maderista corridos that God, the Virgin Mary, and the Virgin of Guadalupe (Mexico's patron saint and an indispensable ally of Mexican heroes, for she combines *Dios* and *Patria*) have all been firmly on Madero's side from the beginning of his struggle:

> Levantaremos el grito
> viva Dios, es lo primero,
> la Virgen de Guadalupe
> y don Francisco I. Madero.[16]

The third absolute vision that was used in Madero's myth was the utopian ideal that is at the centre of all fully-fledged social myths. Revolutionary myth-formation plays strongly on man's need for consolatory dreams of future bliss in a world from which all grief, injustice and pain will have been abolished. According to the revolutionary social myth of 1911, democracy was going to be the infallible magic agent by which Utopia would be rapidly settled in Mexico; and Madero was, of course, the personification of democracy (a much-repeated joke of 1911 indicated that the cheer '¡Viva Madero! ¡Viva la Democracia!' was thought by many to refer to Madero and his wife). By liberating Mexico from the

---

[16] 'We shall raise our voices and cry,
      "Long live God" comes first of all,
      "Our Lady of Guadalupe,
      And Francisco I. Madero"'.
María y Campos, op. cit., I, p. 146. For the corridos about Madero, see María y Campos, I, pp. 121–65, and Simmons, pp. 87–104.

evils of presidential re-election, the corridos suggested to their audience, Madero would also free the country from poverty and suffering and all evil generally.

The myth of Madero, at its brief and heady height in June 1911, the month of Madero's triumphal drive from the north and his hero's entry into Mexico City, presented—with its incorporation of all the best ingredients of social myths: patriotism, religion, and utopianism—the brilliant vision of a saintly hero who was going to bring heaven down to earth and put it, what was more, in the Valley of Tenochtitlán. All of this was achieved in the absence, as it were, of Madero himself, for not until his splendid arrival in Mexico City on 7 June did he start to appear personally in the public limelight. It was this very fact which made the creation of his extravagant myth possible in the first place: it meant that there was no flesh-and-blood figure to compare with the mythical superstructure, and hence no check on its growth or risk of its being refuted. The months of April and May 1911 had seen optimum conditions for the creation of a social myth—maximum public interest concentrated on a prominent person and free use of mass communications by that person's supporters, together with minimum public cognizance of the person himself. The months after June 1911 saw the ideal conditions for the demolition of such an insecurely-founded myth and for the restoration in its place of the refortified and restored counter-legend. For the result of the easy and rapid creation of Madero's myth was that the public's expectations of him were so high that no one, however able, could have lived up to them. The great danger of myth-creation in the lifetime of the mythified person is that the object of the myth is still able to give it the lie, with disastrous consequences. Madero, through a process by no means altogether within his control, had come to mean all things to all men: in an interesting pamphlet written and published in 1912 by an able and disillusioned former Maderista, the point is made clearly: 'The popularity of the revolution, in the person of Señor Madero, reached such a level that it developed into a kind of idolatry. The cry of "Viva Madero" was still, in June 1911, a sort of military anthem, a type of epic canto, in which the people crystallized all their desires and all their hopes of happiness and well-being.'[17] Such a public image would need the finest modern public relations team to maintain, as well as an extremely astute politician;

---

[17] Diego Arenas Guzmán, *Prensa y tribuna revolucionaria*, p. 3.

but the world of 1911 was not blessed with P.R.O.s and Madero was the most fallible of men.

It was not Madero's fault that his entry into Mexico City was heralded the night before by an earthquake, which many superstitiously interpreted as a bad omen or a warning message from an irate deity.[18] On the other hand, it was in his control to make a suitable first entry into Mexico City, and the aristocratic style in which the apostle of democracy chose to make his appearance in the capital was the first of a series of errors which delighted his enemies and dismayed his friends [pp. 28–30]. Not only the errors of policy but also the smaller errors of personal comportment aided the counter-legend greatly; Madero's lack of a dignified public presence is attested by claims from various sources that he bungled the swearing-in ceremony, answering with what the swearer-in was supposed to say; that he gave the bull-fighter Rodolfo Gaona a warm embrace in front of 20,000 fans;[19] that he argued with a mob of students on one occasion from a balcony of the National Palace (to achieve this his voice would have had to be more powerful than it is reputed to have been); and that he greeted Zapata when they met with a bear-hug and a speech calling him 'integérrimo' ('most righteous') which was not thought to be a very apt adjective (it was certainly not a very sincere one [p. 149]). This last was the most well-known of his gaffes, and the caricaturists made much of it. As they made clear, Madero's liberal disposal of embraces drew attention embarrassingly to his shortness (he was nicknamed 'el chaparro'—'tiny'—, 'el presidente chiquitín' and 'el presidente pingüica').[20] His slight build, together with his inoffensive gentleness of demeanour, should not be underestimated as

[18] See Maqueo Castellanos, I, chap. 8, and Lepino, chap. 6. Following the precept, presumably, that attack is the best form of defence, a Maderista song was written and popularized, interpreting the earthquake as a sign of God's favour. It was entitled: ¡Hasta la tierra tembló! (María y Campos gives the full text, op. cit., I, pp. 162–3).

[19] It should be remembered that bullfighting on foot was solely a lower-class occupation in Spain and Latin America at this time. Not even the most popular and successful torero (like Gaona) could ever hope to improve his social position; so Madero's well-meaning and charming gesture was generally considered laughably undignified.

[20] Pingüica (a word derived from the Indian language Tarasco, spoken in the state of Michoacán): the small ericaceous shrubs Arctostaphylos polifolia and A. pungens. They have many leafy branches (Madero had a black beard and bushy moustache and eyebrows) and bear a tiny fruit which has strong diuretic properties.

elements contributing towards his extraordinarily rapid loss of popularity after June 1911. They meant that he was at the great disadvantage of not being able to claim any degree of machismo [p. 153] for himself. An illustration which demonstrates how strongly this weighed against him is the cartoon that appeared in the satirical periodical *Multicolor* on 15 June 1911, commenting on Madero's triumphal entry into Mexico City a week before. It consists of two contrasting drawings of the revolutionary leader: one, under the caption 'How we were expecting to see him', shows him as a traditional military caudillo, a proud figure with shoulders thrown arrogantly back, who clasps the barrel of his rifle in a resolute grip; and the other, 'How we saw him', portrays him meekly doffing his bowler hat with an ingenuous smile, the incongruous and 'unmanly' humility of his figure accentuated by the posy in his hand.

All of this, in addition to the elements of the earlier counter-legend, particularly his frugal eating habits and unorthodox religious beliefs, led quickly to his being made the butt of violently hostile jokes and caricatures; an operation greatly aided by his insistence on establishing full freedom of the press, and so allowing the most cruel, scandalous, and rabid libel constantly to be directed at him from the columns of newspapers like *El Mañana*, founded for this sole purpose. Public admiration and veneration turned with deplorable speed and ease into public mockery, and the heroic myth was replaced by a comic counter-legend. As 1912 progressed, and Madero lost all support, charge upon charge was added to the counter-legend, which had by now completely eclipsed Madero's former heroic image; the most prominent and insistent were those of nepotism and, shamelessly, of despotic suppression of the freedom of the press.

Just as the first counter-legend of 1910 incorporated discredit of Madero's followers as well as of Madero himself, so the second version of 1912 directed attacks at Maderistas; this was achieved, and this time more effectively, with the creation of one of the most tangled legends of the Revolution, that of *La Porra*. This legend enjoyed energetic life throughout 1912 when the *Porra*'s alleged misdoings made daily news in the opposition press, but it was soon forgotten with the reinstatement of the Madero legend after his death. *La Porra* was claimed to be a gang of rioters, controlled by Gustavo Madero (the President's brother) and sent out to attack and assault opponents of the regime. It was associated with the *Partido Constitucional Progresista*, and with the Maderista daily *Nueva Era*, although another version of the legend connected it with Cabrera and his *Partido Renovador*. It was a highly successful legend in that—unlike the similar Porfirian attempts—it was accepted and widely believed, and did much damage to the reputation of the man who made such a point of the virtues of a free democratic society (although Gustavo was the target for more hatred than his brother, since the legend implicated him more directly). What roots it had in reality it is hard to assess: the anonymous author of the pamphlet *El maderismo en cueros* says that it was a horde of the city outcasts whose chiefs bluffed their way into Gustavo's confidence and could never after that be shaken off, and Maqueo Castellanos's opinion is very similar. Some historians, like Simpson and Parkes,[21] are inclined to accept the legend at face value as historical truth, though others, like Cumberland,[22] doubt whether the *Porra* ever existed at all.

The legend was originated in 1911 when the owner and editor of the newspaper *El País*, Trinidad Sánchez Santos, took the name from the Spanish *Partido de la Porra* which functioned in the time of Amadeo of Savoy.[23] Sánchez seems originally to have intended only to discredit Maderismo's left wing, but the legend's great success made it in the end into a blanket term of reprobation for all Maderistas and revolutionaries in general, and a bogey with which the undecided could be scared into opposition to Madero, just in case the campaign of mockery were insufficient by itself. It is, of course, the simplest thing to blame any act of vandalism which might occur on to such an imaginary or real group of ill-doers (it often happens that the simpler the mechanism of legend-creation, the more effective is the legend). The *Porra* legend, at any rate, succeeded in alienating Madero still further from the society he was governing, and much of the public apathy with which the treacherous events of the decena trágica and after were viewed can be attributed to it. Certainly both the terrible death by torture

---

[21] Simpson, *Many Mexicos* (University of California Press, 1962), p. 268; Parkes, *A History of Mexico* (London, 1962), p. 280.

[22] C. C. Cumberland, *Mexican Revolution: Genesis under Madero* (Austin, Texas, 1952), p. 230.

[23] See C. A. M. Hennessy, *The Federal Republic in Spain* (Oxford, 1962), p. 140, for the Spanish *Porra*. For Sanchez's coinage, see *El País*, supplement to edition of 9 Feb. 1913, and Vasconcelos, *Ulises criollo*, p. 657.

of Gustavo Madero—nicknamed 'Ojo Parado' by *El Mañana* because of his glass eye—and the burning by a mob of the *Nueva Era* buildings on 18 February must have been direct consequences of this part of the counter-legend.

The crowning moment of the counter-legend's life came in February 1913, when the ambitions that gave it life were fulfilled, and Madero was removed from power by a right-wing counter-revolution [pp. 30–1]. The fluctuations in the early growth of a legend are, as is becoming apparent, rapid and violent. The counter-legend lost its raison d'être and died on 20 February; and the revolutionary legend gained sudden and enormous impetus on 22 February, when Huerta committed the gross mistake of having Madero killed. The Madero legend—the final and more or less definitive version—emerged phoenix-like into full splendour and luxurious magnificence.

The news of Madero's death had the almost immediate effect of restoring Madero's 1911 image with the addition—of paramount importance—that the 'apóstol de la Democracia' now became the 'mártir de la Democracia'. As had already happened earlier, the ineptitude of the right-wing government and press was a great help to a legend which could hardly have failed to prosper in the circumstances: the newspapers' self-contradictory explanations of the manner of Madero's dying left no one with any doubts about the truth. In Azuela's *Los caciques* the immediate reaction of Maderistas is to weep for their dead hero, who for several months before his death had been considerably less than a hero in their eyes. Only after the death of its subject can a legend take firm and final form; and if the death is in the nature of a martyrdom, it gives great impetus itself to the legend, and virtually ensures its perpetuation.

Such perpetuation is not, however, complete until the legend is institutionalized and officially consecrated as part of the patriotic heritage of heroes. This final process cannot be properly considered to start until after the conclusion of the revolution when, during the period of normalization, the new ruling classes establish themselves and their myths and legends. Yet the beginnings of the process are, in Madero's case, present at an early stage, for his successor as the revolutionary leader, Carranza, took good care to use Madero's legend as the banner for his incipient movement: as a rallying cry Madero's name offered greater possibilities than that of the still obscure Carranza. As Madero had taken on the mantle of Juárez, so Carranza—acting very much more consciously and, perhaps, cynically[24]—took on the mantle of Madero, which, unlike that of Juárez, still needed trimming and embroidering. Within months the legend of don Francisco I. Madero was completed by Carranza's propagandists. Pamphlets appeared such as T. F. Serrano's *¡El crimen del 22 de febrero! -o-Anatema a los traidores*. Songs were composed like *El himno a Madero* by the minor poet José Varela, the marching song of the *División del sur* (the revolutionary force of Michoacán and Guerrero) in the campaign against Huerta. It is an indication of the elated feelings of 1913–14, as well as of the dearth of able ceremonial poets in the Constitucionalista ranks:

> . . . Tus ideales triunfarán
> ilustre libertador,
> y con lágrimas de amor
> tu sepulcro regado será
> En el alma popular
> tu nombre grabado está
> y ya nunca los tiranos
> lo podrán arrancar! . . .[25]

When Ugarte makes one of the characters of his novel inquire 'Is it true, is it true, that Señor Madero, the Apostle, wore a tunic that gave out light?' and says that this character 'believed in God and worshipped Madero, believing him at the very least the second emissary of the Lord',[26] one feels he is scarcely exaggerating the

---

[24] It is generally agreed that Carranza felt no admiration at all for Madero, and it was even rumoured that his revolt broke out so soon after Huerta's assumption of power because it was already minutely planned—against Madero. See Maqueo Castellanos, III, chap. 5; Romero, *Desbandada*, in *Obras completas* (Mexico, 1957), p. 164.

There was certainly a strange hesitancy in Carranza's actions after Huerta's coup. First he rejected the new regime, then he accepted it, and he finally rejected it again, alleging as his reason the fact that Huerta had refused to accept his support. See *Foreign Relations*, 1913, pp. 721, 726, 727–8 and 763–8.

> [25] Thy ideals shall triumph,
> Illustrious deliverer,
> And with tears of love
> Shall thy grave be watered.
> In the soul of the people
> Is thy name engraved,
> And never shall tyrants
> Be able to tear it out!

[26] pp. 73–4.

reactions of the common people to the final shaping of the Madero legend in 1913.

When Huerta was finally driven out of Mexico, the Carrancista leader Obregón duly performed a much-publicized journey of homage to Madero's grave and delivered himself of a highly rhetorical speech; and Carranza himself later went there, as one disenchanted novelist said, 'to weep "tears of bronze" upon the tomb . . . as a paid panegyrist vulgarly put it'.[27] Madero was now firmly on his pedestal, lifted on to it by the combined efforts of Huerta and Carranza. It is not important that after this, and especially with the split between Villa and Carranza, Madero, who was the legendary incarnation of that idealism which was so little evident during the rest of the Revolution, was half-forgotten for a time. Post-revolutionary governments were to take up the strings again and designate him as the first hero and martyr of modern Mexico.

Madero's legend is one which had a particularly full and varied revolutionary life, and is valuable in showing the full sequence of development through successive stages: firstly, the appearance of both an embryo legend and a counter-legend; then, the unstable fluctuation between the negative and the positive legends and the inflation of the latter into a full-scale social myth; and, finally, the climax in martyrdom and emergence of a definitive, officially patronized revolutionary legend, fully incorporated into the whole system of national patriotic symbolism. Madero's is the only legend which fully attained that religious status of utopian idealism that is the most effective spur for encouraging men into concerted action. This state of affairs did not last, however, for the events of 1911–12 were discrediting to Madero's ideal, democracy, which ceased to be acceptable as a key to the door to Utopia. In so far as it still continued, inevitably, to appear in Carranza's exaltation of Madero, it was as a pretty, high-sounding, but emptily rhetorical word more than as any genuine, concrete attempt to continue the social myth of June 1911. No other leader was capable of creating any alternative social myth for himself, and the Mexican Revolution was left without the revolutionary religion it needed so much.

No other legend of the Mexican Revolution is so well documented or so complete. The one which, after that of Madero, has come nearest to achieving a religious significance, is that of Zapata.

[27] Maqueo Castellanos, p. 445. See also *El País*, 18 Aug. 1914.

Because of his and his supporters' alienation by class and race antagonism from the sectors of society which provided the writers of novels and newspaper reports and articles, he is the leader that written sources tell us least about. In his lifetime he was quite unable to make a favourable impression on the country as a whole. Almost the only records we have of that period are of the growth of a counter-legend; the positive legend of Zapata as the embodiment of peasant aspirations of agrarian reform (a legend which grew extraordinarily after the end of the Revolution) sprang into life and flourished during the Revolution only among his followers, in the state of Morelos. In large part as a direct result of federal repression, which threw them into the arms of the man who at the time was best equipped to protect them, the peasants of this state rapidly came to feel a strong personal devotion to Zapata, reflected in the few early Zapatista corridos which are known.[28] It is clear, however, that Zapata's revolutionary legend was confined in his lifetime to his peasant followers, and only found its way into print and common acceptance when he became respectable and harmless by dying.

Zapata's revolutionary career started in March 1911.[29] For three months he remained, outside Morelos at least, an unknown figure. Although he was, in fact, in command by mid-April, the revolt in the south was reported in the press as having no generally recognized leader, and not even Zapata's name was known. This was the situation until June, when Zapata jumped into prominence, as Madero made it his first job to try to pacify the southern rebels, and was taken to their leader. On 17 June Zapata's name first appeared in the newspapers when it was reported that Madero had made him the Military Commander of Morelos, and that the commercial interests of that state had made a great protest against the appointment of such a man to the job. (On 20 June this report was rectified, and it was stated that Zapata had only been given the task of seeing to the demobilization of his men.) The counter-legend grew in a matter of days, the creation of the Morelos landowners, most anxious to discredit this dangerous popular leader who seemed uncomfortably close to being given a position of real power by

[28] Womack, op. cit., and Simmons, pp. 285–319. See also Oscar Lewis, *Pedro Martínez* (London, 1964), especially pp. xxx–xxxiii and 73–116.
[29] This was when he declared formal allegiance to the Plan de San Luis Potosí, although in fact he had been agitating locally for almost a year by then. (Womack, pp. 63ff.)

Madero.[30] By 20 June El Imparcial had huge front-page headlines shouting that 'Zapata is the modern Attila', and his anti-heroic epithet was immediately created: it was modified in 1912 to 'The Attila of the South'. Madero himself gave initial force to the counter-legend by publicly declaring his sympathy for the Morelos rich in the damage their property had suffered at the hands of this vandal, and by saying, also publicly, that they had nevertheless made a mistake in protesting so loudly about it because this might goad him into even worse violence—'with this action they have made an impression on Zapata's incipient [sic] brain'.[31] In the same day's reports also appeared the statement attributed to Zapata 'that he recognized no other government than his pistols', which became a catchphrase of the counter-legend. By the next day, only four days after the first mention of Zapata, the counter-legend was so complete that El Tiempo commented:

So much has been said and written about the revolutionary general Emiliano Zapata's alleged attitudes towards the government and the inhabitants of Morelos and their property, that the revolutionary chieftain has begun to appear as a terrorist.

Zapata sets fire to people's property; Zapata carries young ladies off from their homes; Zapata has distributed privately-owned land among his followers; Zapata orders his followers to attack haciendas and trains. . . .

The newspaper felt constrained to attempt a mild defensive apology for the peasant leader, assuring its readers that Zapata was really quite respectable and that he dressed decently and actually shaved and washed quite regularly. Zapata himself was reported as saying, no doubt taken aback by his dazzling rise to notoriety, 'We aren't ogres, we don't make a habit of eating live children.'

Four days were enough, then, to see the full creation of a violent black legend. Since Zapata and his men were the most persistent as well as the most socially isolated of the revolutionaries, their counter-legend flourished throughout the Revolution, and the evil doings of Zapata and Zapatistas were daily news. Even such mild defences as the early one in El Tiempo were forgotten, and the word 'Zapatista' came to be synonymous with 'bandit, murderer, and rapist'. Zapata was, in short, turned into the general, all-purpose bogy and devil for Mexican society—a most valuable weapon for all counter-revolutionary propaganda. Under Huerta the

---

[30] Womack, pp. 97–101.   [31] El Tiempo, 20 June 1911.

attacks on Zapata reached their most violent pitch, and books
appeared whose object was to increase still further the widespread
fear of Zapatistas, by describing their alleged atrocities in lurid
detail. One such work was Antonio D. Melgarejo's *Crímenes del
zapatismo* (Mexico, 1913); another was the rough and ready novel
El Atila del Sur by the right-wing extremist Alfonso López Ituarte,
who wrote it under the pseudonym of Héctor Ribot.

His prologue describes a positive legend, limited to Zapata's
supporters, and much of the sort to be expected:

ZAPATA, with his long, unkempt moustache, the rider on the dash-
ing steed which the federal soldiers can't catch, is for the proletarians,
for the eternal slaves of rural labour, the symbol of redemption, the
vendetta of centuries of anguish and sacrifice . . .

For the common people he has come to be a myth and a martyr
sacrificed on the altar of the nation's redemption. . . . There were to be
no more fatigues for them in the sugar-cane harvest, or in the processing
of sugar and alcohol. They were going to own land; they would possess
horses and arms; the overseers would no longer scold them for working
slowly or for their laziness, nor would they cut their allowances and
rations.

No more would they have to approach their masters, hat in hand and
with a humble and lowly look, to receive orders. . . .

No more would they have to buy goods on tick at the hacienda stores
at ridiculously high prices.

They dreamt a life of tranquillity, of abundance and prosperity.

Most of these ambitions, as described here, would appear to be
quite reasonable ones for a man to have; but López Ituarte makes
it plain that the Zapatistas' ideals and hopes of regeneration are
sinful. For it is the word of God that man was born to work and
suffer, and man—poor man at least, the reader is presumably
meant to suppose—should not dare to contradict what our Lord
has laid down for him.

The novel itself is a confused, badly-written mixture of accounts
of supposed Zapatista atrocities, moralizing from an extreme conservative viewpoint, and sketchy historiography, in which Zapata
himself appears as a character involved directly in the main action.
All of this is hung on a labyrinthine plot, which the author
remembers intermittently, of traditional cloak-and-dagger intrigue
mixed with the indispensable romantic love-concern; it is studded
with scenes of hacienda-burnings, the abduction and rape—in the

beautiful caverns of Cacahuamilpa—by Zapata of the heroine, of orgies, banditry, mass-killings, and torture of innocents, vicious attacks on passenger trains, and so on. The much-feared female band which operated around Tetecala under 'La China' is introduced. The novel contains, in short, all the normal ingredients of the Zapata counter-legend, as an anthology of which, even if for no other reason, it is useful and interesting.

The Zapata black legend was an unusually full and flamboyant one. But like Madero's myth of June 1911, it was created before the general public had any personal contact with the figure involved; it is as easy to paint as a black ogre as it is to paint as a shining apostle someone that none of one's audience has ever set eyes upon. *In absentia* legends tend to be extravagant and to suffer when they come up against reality. On the first entry of the Zapatistas into Mexico City, the terrified and apprehensive populace was most surprised to discover that they were just like ordinary peasants, indeed even more respectful to their betters than most. There is a well-known tale which illustrates the Zapatistas' surprising humility. In the words of one observer:

It is true that the Zapatistas did not have very good manners—the brigades were all made up of rustics—but they were not rude to anyone, either. They were armed to the teeth; yet many soldiers from those brigades in which no wages were paid, and who therefore had to depend on whatever they could obtain by their own efforts, would come up to passers-by and, hat in hand and with great humility, would request a contribution towards their sustenance with words like these: 'Please sir, would you make me a gift of ten centavos for my lunch?'[32]

But the Zapatistas' behaviour degenerated rapidly, and they soon fell back into disrepute. Their innocently immodest habit of relieving themselves in full view of the public seems to have been primarily responsible for the rapid decline in their transient popularity.

So the black legend did manage to survive in a modified version. It prevented any positive legend from finding widespread public acceptance until after Zapata's assassination in 1919 by a treacherous and cowardly trick. This had the normal consequences of the martyrdom of a public figure: consignment to the halls of legend.

[32] Galindo, pp. 65–6. See also Francisco Ramírez Plancarte, *La cuidad de México durante la Revolución Constitucionalista* (2nd ed., Mexico, 1941), pp. 247–55 and 271–85.

Large numbers of corridos appeared in 1919 and 1920. Although the press reported Zapata's death with scarcely-disguised joy, and though its first anniversary was greeted with official silence, the second anniversary, with Obregón, who wished to appear as a good radical reformer, now in power, was celebrated with all the paraphernalia normally associated with posthumous tributes to national heroes.[33] The man who, while alive, had caused people to hold their hands up in horror at the mere mention of his name, became in a short time after death a fashionable hero, a legendary son of Mexico praised by the rich and powerful as much as by the poor.

Zapata's revolutionary legend did not, then, come into its full force until after the Revolution had finished, and it is not, therefore, within the terms of reference of this study. The case of Emiliano Zapata is interesting as a particularly complete example of a sustained counter-legend, whose long life was made possible by its subject's class, race, and regional isolation from the greater part of Mexican society, and especially from educated Mexicans. It is also of interest as another illustration of the ease with which the most firmly rooted such negative legend can be quickly transformed into a positive one.

The legend of the Mexican Revolution which achieved widest circulation inside and outside Mexico and which still remains, so long after the death of its subject, as rich and ambiguous as it was in his lifetime, is undoubtedly that of Pancho Villa. The man himself had an exceptionally contradictory and elusive character, and the legend attached to him was, from the very beginning, a reflection of this inconsistency. It is at all stages confused and multifarious. Villa provides an example of another—and particularly interesting—sort of legend-creation process, in which there is not that alternation between legend and counter-legend found in the cases of Madero and Zapata, but a continuous coexistence of the two, and to a certain extent an overlapping of them. The revolutionary legend of Villa was never really concerned to deny the two principal elements of the black legend—Villa's rude ways with women and his wanton and arbitrary destruction of life—but rather to glamorize them and incorporate them into the picture it

[33] For the post-revolutionary growth, under official sponsorship, of Zapata's legend, see Carlos J. Sierra's article which forms the *Suplemento* to no. 361 of the *Boletín Biobibliográfico de la Secretaría de Hacienda y Crédito Público* (15 Feb. 1967).

presents of a he-man hero in the Mexican tradition of machismo, overpowering, dominant and larger than life.

It is impossible to understand Villa's myth or his extraordinary career without constant reference to the peculiarly Mexican idea of machismo.[34] It is a concept of a very special sort of 'manliness', at the very heart of Mexican consciousness, and it springs from the need that the Mexican feels to defend and protect his intimate being against what he feels to be a dangerous and ever-hostile outside world. To be a macho is both to keep one's defences always firmly in place, never to open oneself (*abrirse* or *rajarse*) to the world; and also conversely, to attack, to 'open' other people, to destroy their machismo as a triumphant assertion of one's own. This aggressive aspect of machismo is formulated in the verb which, in Mexico, is full of secret, magic, and forbidden meanings: *chingar*, a word constantly in the heart of Mexicans, but only on their lips when they lose the control which keeps it repressed, together with the rest of their intimate being (that is, when they let their defences fall, *se abren*). Chingar—like all taboos the key to a hidden and intimate world of sensibility—expresses violent, aggressive, destructive activity which offends and humiliates the person at which it is directed. The word is loaded with sexual meaning: when used with a strictly sexual sense, it means 'to possess by force or deceit'. So the world, for the Mexican (although he will never admit as much, for to do so means to *abrirse*) is a dichotomy of that which is invulnerable and which opens and offends—the male, the *chingón* —and that which is defenceless and which is opened and offended —the female, the *chingada*. The macho must make sure that he is, and is seen to be, resolutely in the former category.

Villa's legend had early beginnings. In December 1910 we already find him mentioned in Mexico's national press as a bandit in the revolutionary forces, and by the end of that month he was well-known enough to be referred to as 'the celebrated bandit',[35] for his idiosyncratic linguistic habits to be commented on, and for his visits each night to various women in Chihuahua City to be mentioned with some amazement. During the Maderista rebellion he was characterized in the Porfirian press as 'the brigand Francisco Villa, unhappily famous for his criminal activities' and his

[34] Octavio Paz, in his famous essay *El laberinto de la soledad* (particularly chaps 2, 3 and 4), gives a penetrating analysis of machismo, on which the following paragraph leans heavily.
[35] *El País*, 25 and 29 Dec. 1910.

illdoings made daily news towards the end of the fight against Díaz.[36] But the 'white' legend can be traced back to this stage too: in a report by the war correspondent of *El Tiempo*, Ignacio Herrerías,[37] published on 12 April, it becomes apparent that Villa had already created for himself a very passable legend among fighting Maderistas, as a steely leader who stood no nonsense from his men.

The black and white legends grew smoothly from here, and spread from Mexico abroad as they did so. Most of the United States press patronized the romantic legend, comparing Villa variously with Napoleon and with Robin Hood; and the Spanish press broadcast the black legend—Villa's sporadic turns of xenophobia were directed particularly against Spaniards and Chinese—accusing him of every dastardly act imaginable. In Mexico, where the man himself was nearer at hand, and constantly in the public eye, the legends developed along lines between these two extremes, and indeed coincided for much of the way. The black legend showed him as a ruthless criminal and womanizer, and invented or exaggerated around these two themes. The positive legend, however, was richer and subtler, accepting and trying to make acceptable that Villa was a man above the law and common morality in its depiction of him as a peculiarly Mexican sort of superman, the macho or *gran chingón*. The distinction between Villa's legend and his counter-legend disappears frequently, as Azuela's description of it in 1914 shows:

What a tale there was to be told about his extraordinary prowess, with acts of surprising magnanimity immediately followed by the most bestial deeds! Villa is the untameable master of the sierra, the eternal victim of all governments, who pursue him like a wild beast; Villa is the reincarnation of the old legend about the providential bandit, who passes through the world bearing the burning torch of an ideal: to rob the rich in order to give to the poor! And the poor create a legend for him which Time will take care to embellish, and it will live from generation to generation.[38]

---

[36] *El Imparcial*, 11 Mar. 1911. Clenenden, in *The United States and Pancho Villa* (New York, 1961), pp. 16–18, underestimates Villa's early fame in saying that he did not become prominent until the campaign against the Orozco rebellion in 1912.

[37] Herrerías was the first reporter in the national press to give sympathetic coverage to the revolutionaries. He was killed in 1912, when on a mission to interview Zapata, in a Zapatista attack on the train in which he was travelling.

[38] *Los de abajo*, p. 365.

Villa's impulsive character, his reckless valour, his personal mag-
netism, which had an uncanny effect on his followers,[39] and his
instability, provided constant factual material for the elaboration of
the legend. Behind all the accumulation of details, however, the
legend has—as must all good legends—an essential and basic
theme which its component parts elaborate, and which is socially
functional in that it contributes towards strength and purposeful-
ness on the revolutionary side.

The theme is military invincibility. Any idealism in Villa's
legend was, at the best of times, of a very primitive and rudiment-
ary sort, and did not take long to degenerate into a mere rationaliza-
tion of looting ('to rob the rich in order to give to the poor'). So
Villa's amoral behaviour was not harmful to his legend, but quite
the contrary: revolutionary soldiers would be encouraged rather
than disillusioned by reports that their leader arbitrarily threw
rich Spanish families out of all the cities he conquered, and cut off
captured American soldiers' ears, and abducted beautiful young
city ladies, and shot well-heeled gentlemen he happened to come
across for the fun of it all—without having to answer to anybody
for such actions or pay the consequences for them, as any mere
ordinary human being would have to. In all of this Villa's legend
was that of the aggressively masculine male in the Mexican tradition of machismo; and the chief characteristic of the real macho is
that he is never humiliated by anyone, but on the contrary humiliates and imposes himself on everyone who crosses his path. A
verse of the revolutionary song *La cucaracha* which was sung by
Villistas after the break with Carranza captures the whole essence
of machismo:

> Con las barbas de Carranza
> voy a hacer una toquilla
> pa ponerla en el sombrero
> de su padre Pancho Villa.[40]

The expression 'su padre' is a particularly insulting way of referring

---

[39] It was strong enough, also, to attract educated men like Martín Luis
Guzmán—whose background and attitudes should by rights have made him
violently hostile to Villa—José Santos Chocano, the Peruvian Modernista, and
the North Americans Paul Fuller, John Reed and General Hugh L. Scott.

[40] I'll take old Carranza's whiskers
And make a cockade out of them:
And then I'll stick it in the hat
Of his master Pancho Villa.

to one man's utter superiority over another. The four words 'Yo soy tu padre' are pregnant with implied offence: their basic Mexican meaning is 'I enjoy absolute dominance over you: I am the macho to one of whose chingaderas [pp. 153 and 163] you owe your very existence; and, what is more, the sufferer of that chingadera was your mother.' The modern version of the song has been bowdlerized so that the last line of this verse now reads 'del valiente Pancho Villa'.

The image of the invincible epic here is finely portrayed in a revolutionary corrido which was composed in 1914.[41] It describes the battle of Zacatecas. One must remember that Villa's military tactics of storming mass attacks, regardless of loss of life, were in themselves not only the sole way of conducting a battle that was really worthy of Mexican machos, but also highly conducive to epic heroism and so most suitable for the creation of a military legend on the old, grand scale. This corrido—representative of many others which were probably composed around the same time, but chosen here because it became very popular and is the only one firmly dated—builds on the factual base of the Zacatecas action and elaborates it artistically.

The corrido is one in which detailed description of events and naming of protagonists is an important part of the artistic procedure, as is fitting for a poem that has to convey news of an important battle to those who cannot read about it in the press. So it starts by determining the heroes of the piece, Villa of course first:

> La toma de Zacatecas
> por Villa, Urbina y Natera,
> Ceniceros y Contreras,
> Raúl Madero y Herrera.[42]

It continues with a taunt at the enemy, a theme which reappears in the middle of the piece and again at the end of it; the triumphant macho crows over his humiliated victim:

> Ahora sí, borracho Huerta,
> ya te late el corazón

---

[41] María y Campos gives the full text, op. cit., II, pp. 50–2. The corrido was written by Juan Ortega Romero.

[42] The taking of Zacatecas
By Villa, Urbina, Natera,
Ceniceros and Contreras,
Raúl Madero and Herrera.

al saber que en Zacatecas
derrotaron a Barrón.[43]

And the third verse concludes the introduction with the fixing of
the exact date of the principal action that the corrido deals with,
and the formal definition of the subject-matter (both necessary
parts of the traditional corrido technique):

> El día veintitrés de junio,
> hablo con los más presentes,
> fue tomada Zacatecas
> por las tropas insurgentes.[44]

After the short, pointed introduction the epic hero is brought
immediately into the centre of affairs, where he is to remain for the
whole of the poem in full unquestioned command of all the
revolutionaries; he is the pivot and mainspring of all action and
organizes the entire event with infallible judgement:

> Al llegar Francisco Villa,
> sus medidas fue tomando
> y a cada uno en sus puestos,
> bien los fue posesionando.[45]

The battle has already been in progress for a few days, we are told,
but as soon as Pancho Villa drops in on the scene, 'to see what was
going on', things are going to change, and the fight, it is implied,
will be won without much more fuss (stanza 5). Without actually
mentioning that the Federal defenders had already inflicted a defeat
on the revolutionary forces under Natera, it is made clear that the
fight has been a hard one until the moment of Villa's arrival. But
from now on, without the magic commander even having to take
things too seriously or strenuously, it is all going to be too easy.

---

[43] Now then, you drunkard Huerta,
Your heart is beating harder
With news from Zacatecas
That Barrón has been defeated.
[44] On the twenty third of June
—Listen, all who are gathered round—
Zacatecas town was taken
By the army of insurgents.
[45] When Francisco Villa came
He took all the proper steps,
He told each man exactly where
He must take up his position.

The theme of machismo is suggested again when Villa uses cock-fighting imagery to refer to his braves—a convincing imitation of his earthy proverbial language:

> Les dijo el general Villa:
> —¿Conque está dura esta plaza?
> ya les traigo aquí unos gallos,
> creo que son de buena raza.[46]

The scene is set, then, for the actual details of the decisive battle, and in a run of nine stanzas (7–15) we are told the particulars about how each individual leader was consigned to his position and informed about his exact duties during the battle itself. With all the revolutionaries firmly in place—their enemies have only been accorded one brief mocking reference so far, for it is not the corridista's job to present the other side's view of things (a macho cannot allow his enemies any dignity)—the sign for the commencement of the revolutionaries' massed charges is given, just as Villa had ordered:

> Al disparo de un cañón,
> como lo tenían de acuerdo,
> empezó el duro combate
> por lado derecho e izquierdo.[47]

Within three stanzas it is apparent that Villa's tactics are having the expected success, as the theme of the mockery of the enemy is renewed in four consecutive stanzas. In the machismo system the most degrading thing for a man is to show weakness of any sort, which is a feminine quality; hence, in contrast with Villa's fine '*gallos*':

> Andaban los federales
> que ya no hallaban que hacer,
> pidiendo enaguas prestadas
> para vestir de mujer.[48] (stanza 19)

---

[46] General Villa said to them,
'So this is a tough one, is it?
I've brought with me some fighting cocks,
Well-bred ones, so they tell me.'

[47] When a cannon fired a shot
(As they'd agreed among themselves)
The bitter battle was begun
On the left and right hand flanks.

[48] The men of the Federal Army
Just didn't know what to do;
They went round begging petticoats
To disguise themselves as girls.

And Villa himself presses the point home with a jeering personal challenge to a famous renegade Maderista who was fighting for Huerta:

> Gritaba el general Villa:
> —¿Dónde te hallas, Argumedo?
> Ven y párate aquí enfrente,
> tú, que nunca tienes miedo.[49] (stanza 21)

The inevitable Villista success continues, as the revolutionaries take position after position from the enemy, and the battle is over very quickly:

> Ese mismo día en la tarde,
> tan macizo le tupieron
> que, a las siete de la noche,
> casi todos se rindieron.[50] (stanza 24)

According to the classical norms of heroic poetry, the battle has been won much too quickly and easily, and the hero has not been confronted with an opponent of sufficient stature to test his strength properly; yet the point of the Villa legend is to postulate him, in contrast with his chicken-hearted enemies, as an absolutely invincible general, and as the archetypal macho—one of whose essential features is, as seen above, the exclusive and one-sided nature of his masculinity. Villa's legend, a peculiarly Mexican one, was meant to show the absolute inevitability of success of all the actions Villa was involved in; and to demonstrate the consequent advisability of becoming a Villista. There was no place in it for magnanimous praise for the other side: indeed the more ludicrous the Federales could be made to appear, the better. So after the short, sharp action and the rout of Huerta's forces, the poem enters its concluding section. It states that all the inhabitants of Zacatecas were delighted with the result of the battle, and this in pites of the sorry state of the town. But the corrido is quick to

---

[49] General Villa was shouting
'Where've you got to, Argumedo?
Come on, and show yourself out here,
You who claim to feel no fear.'
[50] That same day in the afternoon
They all fought with such a will
That at seven o'clock at night
Most of the foe lay down their arms.

assure us that revolutionaries were not to blame for the damage to property:

> ¡Ay! hermosa Zacatecas,
> mira como te han dejado;
> la causa fue el viejo Huerta
> y tanto rico malvado . . .
>
> Zacatecas fue saqueado
> por los mismos federales,
> no crean que los maderistas
> les hayan hecho estos males[51] (stanzas 27 and 29)

The poem ends with Villa's warning that any Spaniard found in Zacatecas will be shot unless he leaves immediately (stanzas 32 and 33) and with a fine concluding taunt at the remote ultimate enemy:

> ¿Cómo estarás, viejo Huerta?
> Harás las patas más chuecas,
> al saber que Pancho Villa
> ha tomado Zacatecas.[52] (stanza 36)

With corridos such as this, Villa's legend was spread by word of mouth among the people who were most likely to feel sympathy for his campaigns. It was well adjusted to its social function, for the machismo ideal has strongest hold on the lower classes of Mexican society. The effect of a corrido as well put together as *La toma de Zacatecas* must have been great both in gaining support and in strengthening the determination and the pride of the support already acquired. In 1914 the morale of Villistas was very high indeed, thanks to an efficient piece of legend-making.

---

[51] Oh, handsome Zacatecas!
   What a state they've left you in!
   Old Huerta's the cause of it all,
   Him, and all the wicked rich . . .

   The sack of Zacatecas
   Was the work of Federales;
   Don't think that Maderistas
   Could do such evil things to you.

In the fight against Huerta, the revolutionaries not only used the martyred Madero as a banner [pp. 145-7], but also occasionally called themselves Maderistas.

[52] How're you feeling now, old Huerta?
   Your legs will get more bandy still
   Once you know that Pancho Villa
   Has taken Zacatecas town.

A reference to the unsteady gait of the drunkard [pp. 175-6].

An important part of the Villa legend, in which it differs from most, is its inclusion of the followers of Villa within the general corpus. The man's magic was made in the legend to rub off on to his supporters, and give them a little dose of superhumanity as well. In the corrido Villa's men are shown to be machos like their leader; and elsewhere there is evidence that in Villa's golden year of 1914, the Villistas as a whole were regarded with great awe by other Mexicans. The special group of hand-picked Villista soldiers, the *dorados*, attracted a special legend of their own for fanatical loyalty and bravery, which found its way into songs still popular in Mexico now:

> Yo soy soldado de Pancho Villa,
> de sus dorados soy el más fiel;
> nada me importa perder la vida,
> si es cosa de hombres morir por él.[53]

In *Los de abajo* Villistas are shown to be reputedly amazingly well equipped [pp. 295–6], in painful contrast to other revolutionaries. They even possess aeroplanes, the ultimate marvel of modern science, which few Mexicans would yet have even seen:

Ah, Villa! . . . The magic word. The great man, of whom one only catches glimpses; the undefeated warrior, who, from a great distance, exercises his fascination, like a great snake . . .
Ah, Villa's troops! All men from the north, very well equipped, with their campaign hats, their new khaki uniforms and their four-dollar American boots . . .
They suffer no hunger! . . . They have cartloads of oxen, sheep, cows. Waggons full of clothes; whole trains loaded with ammunition and arms, and so much food that anyone who wants to can go and stuff himself till he bursts.
Then the conversation moved on to the subject of Villa's aeroplanes.
'Ah, those aeroplanes! On the ground, from near by, you don't know what they can be; they look like canoes, or rowboats; but then they start to take off, my friend, and there's such a din that you almost lose your senses. Then something like a motor-car, going very fast. And imagine a great, enormous bird, that suddenly seems as if it is not moving at all. And this is the best part: inside that bird there's a Yank with

---

[53] I am a soldier of Pancho Villa,
    Of his Dorados the most faithful one;
    I shan't mind at all if I lose my life—
    To die for him is a job for a man.
To judge by its nostalgic and lyrical nature, this song was probably composed shortly after Villa's death.

thousands of grenades. Just fancy that! When the time comes for fighting, it's like throwing corn to chickens, handful after handful of lead for the enemy . . . And the whole place turns into a graveyard; dead bodies here, there, and everywhere.[54]

The strong positive effect that Villa's acquisition of a few aeroplanes from the United States[55] had on his legend seems not to have been lessened significantly, as might, perhaps, have been expected, by any patriotic indignation that they should be flown, and bombs dropped from them, by North-American pilots. Indeed, Villa's whole obvious dependence for supplies on the United States might have been expected to offend nationalistic feeling, but seems not to have done so in any important way outside Mexico City [pp. 205–7].

The aeronautical theme is particularly strong in the famous Villista corrido about the Pershing expedition, *De la persecución de Villa*,[56] which gives good examples of the exaggerations and distortions which create legends and myths and epic poems. The Pershing expedition took with it, according to the corrido, two hundred aeroplanes, which seem to be largely the poet's invention (seven planes did join the expedition at the beginning of its operations, though there is no record of them after this).[57] The infantry and cavalry are soon taken care of by the difficult terrain:

> Los de a caballo ya no se podían sentar,
> mas los de a pie no podían caminar;
> entonces Villa les pasa en su aeroplano
> y desde arriba les dijo—¡*Gud bay!*[58]

Villa himself takes care of the planes with an extraordinary trick:

> Comenzaron a lanzar sus aeroplanos,
> entonces Villa un buen plan les estudió:

---

[54] pp. 365–6. The broad-brimmed felt campaign hat (or field hat) of the American army officer (after 1912), with its characteristic four dimples in the crown forming the 'Montana peak', came to be the characteristic headdress of all the northern revolutionaries [pp. 206–7 and 224]. In Mexico it was called the 'Texan hat' (*sombrero tejano*).

[55] See Clenenden, pp. 71–2.

[56] Text and music given by Mendoza, *Lírica narrativa de México*, pp. 94–5.

[57] *Foreign Relations*, 1916 (Washington, 1925), p. 498 [pp. 36–7].

[58] No longer could the cavalrymen sit down,
No further could the infantrymen march;
Then Villa, in his aeroplane, flew past,
And called out to them, from above, 'Goodbye!'

se vistió de soldado americano
y a sus tropas también las transformó.
Mas cuando vieron los gringos las banderas
con muchas barras que Villa les pintó,
se bajaron con todo y aeroplanos
y Pancho Villa prisioneros los tomó.[59]

This singular and evidently apocryphal illustration of Villa's
unusual resourcefulness seems to derive, by a process of prodigal
elaboration, from a minor incident in 1919, when a band of outlaws,
thought to be Villistas, 'captured and held to ransom two American
aviators who had made a forced landing in Mexican territory'.[60]
Such a legend was created about Pancho Villa that when he was
defeated at Celaya many found the news impossible to believe.
Azuela makes Demetrio Macías and his men react in this way
when they are told about it: 'General Villa defeated? . . . Ha, ha,
ha! . . . The son of a bitch is not yet born who could defeat General
Villa!'[61] His subsequent decline necessarily saw a depreciation of
his legend, which was no longer useful to the Revolution; it was
soon revived, however, by the raid on Columbus and the Pershing
Expedition. Both of these events, as the Mexican public saw them,
were reassertions of Mexican machismo against an iniquitous foe,
and therefore of deep patriotic significance. Villa's legend acquired
a valuable new perspective. Paz says: 'The macho performs *chingaderas*, that is to say unexpected acts which produce confusion,
horror and destruction. He 'opens' the world; on 'opening' it he
tears it apart. This tearing apart makes him give a loud, sinister
laugh . . . The humour of the macho is an act of revenge.'[62]
The raid on Columbus was a typical chingadera (and can only be
fully understood by such reference to the code of machismo); and
Villa—whom Paz does not, in fact, mention as a macho—is consequently the complete *gran chingón*. Even though Carranza's government could not, obviously, encourage Villa's reborn legend, he

---

[59] All their aeroplanes were taking to the sky
So then Villa engineered a cunning plot:
He disguised himself in Yankee soldier's clothes
And likewise he transformed his troops as well.

So no sooner had the Yankees seen the flags
Full of stripes that Pancho Villa painted in,
With aeroplanes and all, they came straight down
And Pancho Villa made them all his prisoners.

[60] Clenenden, p. 312.   [61] *Los de abajo*, p. 409.
[62] Op. cit. (Mexico, 1964), p. 68.

became once more a national hero, and was able to rebuild an army and maintain it as a decisive force in Chihuahua State until 1919. The final, decisive impetus to Villa's legend came, of course, with his murder in 1923 (the possibilities for legend-making of this event were much enhanced by the mysterious disappearance of Villa's head from his grave, shortly after burial). The wheels of the legend-machine were immediately set in motion in the normal way, with the appearance of a spate of corridos and books. [63] The difference in Villa's case was that his legend could not, under any pretext, be taken under the official wing and nurtured there; for he was in the end on the wrong side, the losing side, whatever he might have done for the Revolution before the split with Carranza, and for Mexican national pride thereafter. Official mythology could only consider Villa a puppet of the reactionaries, but it could not insist very much on this line, either, because of the huge public sympathy he had aroused. So his legend has remained after his death a non-establishment, equivocal one, perpetuated mainly in creative literature: [64] the only prominent revolutionary legend not to

[63] Puente, *Vida de Francisco Villa* (written 1919, reprinted 26 July to 8 Aug. 1923 in *El Universal Gráfico*), and the continuation of this biography after 1916, when Puente's narration ends, by Rafael Muñoz, published 9–25 Aug. 1923, all under the title *Memorias de Pancho Villa, narradas por él mismo*; Teodoro Torres, *Pancho Villa*; Guillermo Martínez, *Pancho Villa* (Mexico, undated, but evidently brought out shortly after Villa's death); Antonio Castellanos, *Francisco Villa, su vida y su muerte* (San Antonio, Texas, 1923); María y Campos, op cit., I, pp. 354–71.

[64] Novels: Benedicto, *Los guerrilleros* (Mexico, 1931); Campobello, *Cartucho* (1931) and *Las manos de mamá* (1937); Guzmán, *El águila y la serpiente* (1928) and *Memorias de Pancho Villa* (5 vol., 1938, 1939, 1939, 1940, 1964); Muñoz, *¡Vámonos con Pancho Villa!* (1931); and Puente, *Hombres de la Revolución: Villa* (Los Angeles, 1931, republished Mexico, 1937, under the title *Villa en pie*). Short stories: Baltasar Dromundo, *Villa y la Adelita* (1936); Rafael Muñoz, *El feroz cabecilla* (1928), *El hombre malo* (1930), *Si me han de matar mañana* (1934), and *Fuego en el norte* (1950)—many stories are repeated several times in these four collections; Justino N. Palomares, *Anecdotario de la Revolución* (Mexico, 1954); Hernán Robleto, *La mascota de Pancho Villa* (Mexico, 1934 and 1960); Elías L. Torres, *Veinte vibrantes episodios de la vida de Villa* (Mexico, 1934), *La cabeza de Villa y veinte episodios más* (Mexico, 1938, 1947, and 1963—the two latter editions are entitled simply *La cabeza de Villa* and reprint only a selection of the first edition's stories), and *Vida y hazañas de Pancho Villa* (Mexico, n.d.); and Juan F. Vereo Guzmán, *¡A sangre y fuego!* (Mexico, n.d.). Studies, etc: Haldeen Braddy, *Cock of the Walk: the Legend of Pancho Villa* (Albuquerque, 1955); Federico Cervantes, *Francisco Villa y la Revolución* (Mexico, 1960); Pére Foix, *Pancho Villa* (Mexico, 1950); Arturo Langle Ramírez, *El ejército villista* (Mexico, 1961); E. Brondo Whitt, *La División del Norte* (1940); Nellie Campobello, *Apuntes sobre la vida militar de Francisco Villa* (Mexico, 1940); Edgcumb Pinchon, *Viva Villa!* (New York, 1933); and Cumberland, op. cit.

be institutionalized after the Revolution. It may well, as a result, turn out to be more durable than any of the others, for its very complexity and ambiguity mean that it is unlikely to date; the more straightforward official legends of Madero, Zapata and Carranza might well, on the other hand, become stale in the course of time. Villa's legend is of the grand-scale sort that grows rather than withers with time; it follows in the tradition of the great outlaws of history, like Robin Hood and William Tell. It may well prove to have been the last of its type. On the other hand, viewed purely in terms of its revolutionary function as a booster of morale and unity, it was probably, in the end, more destructive than it was useful; for it was the enormous popular success of Villa's personal legend in 1914, together with the complete failure of Carrancista legendry and mythology, which made Villa's insubordination possible.

Villa's is, then, the super-legend, and Zapata's—before 1921— the counter-legend; Carranza is worth mentioning here only as the non-legend. The leader of the victorious faction, the First Chief of the Constitutionalist Army and first President of post-revolutionary Mexico made no favourable impact at all on the popular imagination, and an artificial legend had to be constructed posthumously for him by the post-revolutionary establishment virtually out of nothing. As a leader he failed completely in his function of providing a social symbol for men to follow and be inspired by, and he was totally eclipsed by Pancho Villa (as also was Carranza's principal general, Álvaro Obregón, even after his decisive victory over Villa at Celaya [p. 170]). This is one further aspect of the degeneration of the Mexican Revolution after 1914: the loss of idealistic mystique.

Venustiano Carranza is hardly mentioned in corridos, except some few only too obviously written for propagandist purposes.[65] The novelists that refer to him do so with unanimous bitterness and hostility;[66] it makes no difference whether they are radical or conservative in their opinions. Even such a heroic epithet as he

[65] María y Campos, op. cit., I, pp. 373–89, and Simmons, pp. 127–53.

[66] For example, Maqueo Castellanos, op. cit.; Guzmán, *El águila y la serpiente*; Vasconcelos, *La tormenta*; Galindo, op. cit.; Ugarte, op. cit.; Sanz, *La Revolución en el reino animal*; Torres, *Como perros y gatos*; Ancona Albertos, op. cit.; Lepino, op. cit.; Azuela, *Domitilo quiere ser diputado, Las moscas* and *Las tribulaciones de una familia decente*. Against all these there is but a single novel written before 1925 that gives sympathetic treatment to Carranza and Carrancistas: Bojórquez's *Yórem Tamegua* [pp. 228–30].

MM

managed to acquire among his followers was insipid: 'el hombre [afterwards marginally improved to 'varón'] de Cuatro Ciénagas' (or 'Coahuila'), which was where he came from. His anti-heroic nicknames—of much wider circulation and acceptance even among revolutionaries—were cruel indictments of his ineffectiveness as a charismatic leader: 'don Venus' and 'el primer viejo'. The only small stirrings of a legend about him that can be perceived during the Revolution spring not from his personality or actions but from the chance fact that he sported a long white beard. The act of conception of this baby legend is traced by Quevedo y Zubieta to the Huertista press's attempts to create a counter-legend: 'During Huerta's dictatorship, the editor of *El Imparcial*, Salvador Díaz Mirón, had broadcast a satirical legend about Venustiano Carranza's "goat's beard". After the fall of Huerta the legend germinated and grew [and] the vision of a bearded colossus sprang into being.' So that when Carranza arrives in Mexico City the people are quite agreeably surprised to see that his beard is of fairly normal proportions. [67] Carranza's legend was no more than his beard's legend, and his additional nickname 'barbas de chivo' (or 'barbas de ixtle') and the popular stanza of *La cucaracha* quoted above [p. 155] were among its most insistent manifestations. [68] It was from this comic counter-legend, in the absence of any better starting-point, that his modern heroic legend had later to be forged. The beard motif was ennobled, and its comic element removed; and Carranza was depicted as the modern Mexican Moses, the venerable law-giver and father of the Revolution's Ten Commandments, the 1917 Constitution. The factual basis for this highly successful myth is, of course, tenuous [p. 37].

[67] *México manicomio*, pp. 98–100.
[68] Another, less well-known stanza of the principal marching song of the Revolution was:

> Todos las mujeres tienen
> en el pecho una esperanza,
> y mas abajito llevan
> el retrato de Carranza.

> Every woman carries with her
> Hopes and fears within her breast
> And, a little further down,
> A true likeness of Carranza.

The Carrancista intellectual Isidro Fabela referred to Carranza in one of his speeches in 1913 as 'el emperador de la barba florida'. According to Vasconcelos, Carranza was so pleased that he immediately made Fabela his Foreign Secretary! (*La tormenta*, pp. 791–2).

Carrancistas were no more successful than Carranza in acquiring a sympathetic public image. Black legends about them multiplied, and they were generally feared and hated as cruel and ruthless criminals. A whole vocabulary of derogatory words sprang up around them and are used repeatedly in the novels: 'carranclán';[69] 'avanzar' ('to advance'—an ironic euphemism attributed to Carrancistas for 'to pillage'); 'avances' ('advances'—pillaged goods); 'conlasuñaslistas' ('with their talons at the ready'—for 'constitucionalistas'); 'carrancear' ('to do as Carranza does' = 'to steal'). The notorious gang of criminals of the 'grey motor-car' was popularly supposed to be under the direct orders of a Carrancista general. Rarely can a triumphant revolutionary army have been looked upon with quite such intense hostility by the populace at large.

Carrancista leaders attributed this lack of popularity to right-wing, especially Church, machinations. But this is only a small part of the story, although it is true that the Church attacked Carranza and his movement consistently and violently through sermon and pastoral letter from the very beginning of the fight against Huerta [pp. 286–9]. That its attacks and allegations could convince so many people seems to be due to the general popular feeling of disenchantment with the Revolution that set in after 1914—a feeling which ultimately hardened, naturally enough, into antagonism towards the victors. The latter then had to take the blame for all the upheaval and suffering the whole Revolution had caused, and particularly for the senseless calamities of its final years. This would be enough by itself to get the atrocities committed by Carrancistas, as by any army in war, inflated in the popular imagination into ones of particular reprehensibility. And envious resentment of the Carrancistas' assumption of positions of wealth and power from 1915 onwards added greatly to the hostility of the rest of the populace, particularly those with any social ambitions, who could only watch helplessly as the new ruling élite formed up [pp. 210–18].

The Carrancistas' attempts to counteract this black legend by

[69] Vasconcelos claims, in *La tormenta* [p. 875], to have coined the term. He says that he thought of it and spread it around at the Aguascalientes Convention; and that it gained nationwide acceptance when the generals—especially, of course, the Villista generals—returned to their forces all over Mexico taking it with them. It is an imaginative onomatopaeic formation: 'The word sounded like what they were: in action, mere clatter and noise; but voracious when it came to booty-hunting.'

creating a positive myth had small effect during the Revolution itself, though they provided the seed for post-revolutionary mythological developments. From early 1915 onwards, Carrancismo made strenuous efforts to project a social myth of extremist and uncompromising reformism (to replace the earlier, now dead, Maderista social myth of Democracy), and to establish itself as the legitimate continuation of the Mexican radical liberal tradition. It was to reform Mexico extensively, and defend the poor against their oppressors; it was to be firmly anticlerical. The earliest tangible manifestation of this myth was Carranza's Veracruz reforming legislation [p. 35], which seems to have had some immediate effect, to judge by Obregón's acquisition of six workers' battalions during his occupation of Mexico City in January–March 1915. Obregón's impositions on the Church and on rich businessmen of the city during the same period can only have had the purpose of propagating this myth. The money he demanded from them, even if it had been forthcoming, could have had no practical effect in easing the plight of the civil population, who needed food, not cash—as he must well have known. Outrages against the Church, which in the earlier part of the Revolution had been quite moderate (as such things go) increased sharply in number in the early months of 1915, and were nearly all attributed to Carrancistas. Carrancista leaders were said to have encouraged sacrilege in order to undermine the religious fanaticism of the peasant [pp. 288–91]. All this indicates a concerted campaign, dating from Carranza's early days in Veracruz, to make Carrancismo appear to be the movement of the poor and oppressed; and hence to make Villa appear a reactionary, allied secretly with the exploiters of the people. Carrancista propaganda referred to him incessantly in these terms.

All the evidence points to the conclusion that this attempt to create a social myth met with no important success before 1917, and the black legend appears to have overshadowed it completely.[70] It was a myth without roots, forced on society by a premeditated campaign; it was too transparently the product of a propaganda

---

[70] In the United States, however, the Carranza myth seems to have been propagated successfully. Much more care appears to have been put into its propagation there than in Mexico itself, according to Clenenden: '. . . the pro-Carranza propaganda in the United States was voluminous and was conducted with a skill and attention to the current prejudices of the American people that indicated that the managers knew exactly what they were doing . . .' [p. 195].

machine. A myth or legend, to be wholly convincing, seems to need to grow in the popular imagination in as organic and unforced a way as possible; and official guiding encouragement must be unobtrusive and inconspicuous. Carrancismo's myth of social reformism was soon seen to consist of little more than mere displays of rhetoric which deceived nobody, except certain of the anti-revolutionaries, who were scared by it into the Villista and Zapatista camps [pp. 208–10 and 219]. Rather, it generally increased the cynicism of the moment; only the anti-clericalism was seen to be put into practice, and this simply added more weight to the counter-legend of Carrancista crime.

The years 1915–17 saw, too, the appearance and compilation of a new revolutionary jargon which the immediate post-revolutionary governments were to find extremely convenient for their use, in their successful campaign to create the myth of a socialist Mexico. Azuela shows the early stages of this process in his short novel *Domitilo quiere ser diputado*.[71] The action takes place at the end of 1915. In his caricature of a Carrancista general in this novel, Azuela lays particular stress upon his hypocritical use of the rhetoric of radicalism. From the general's very first words in the novel its gratuitous nature is stressed: 'Please forgive me, Antoñita, for a certain lack of moderation in my language; but since I'm so radical . . . Oh, yes, a great radical! . . . You can believe me.'[72] The general's name used to be Dolores Cebollino, but he has recently changed it to Xicoténcatl Robespierre Cebollino,[73] and his two children are provisionally named Uno and Dos. He talks in a way no Maderista, Villista or even Zapatista ever did:

We who bear the glorious ensign of Constitucionalismo are on the point of undertaking the Holy Crusade. . . . We are going to carry out the great work of cleansing Mexico of the leprosy of clericalism.
We are astounding our brothers in South America with our portentous work of social renovation; we are asserting ourselves against the insolent Yankee. We shall, yet again, be a guiding light for senile Europe; yet again shall we strike terror into crowned heads.
Reactionaries should either be left naked, or strung up from the nearest telegraph pole, or both. . . . For verily, verily, I say unto you: you need

---

[71] *Obras completas*, II, pp. 926–50. Only the page number will be given in subsequent references to this novel.
[72] p. 928.
[73] Xicoténcatl was the name of several figures of Aztec history, notably two of the most important members of the resistance movement against Cortés.

no gun to hang a friar . . . you need no gun to strangle a científico.[74]

He emulates Obregón's actions in Mexico City, issuing a decree attacking big business and ordering the free distribution of pulque. And from the very beginning it is made constantly clear that Cebollino really means and believes not one word of all this, that it is no more than a façade for the frauds and bribery by which he is making a fortune; so that when, at the end of the tale, he reveals that he had been an ardent Huertista and, as a policeman in Porfirian times, had hanged Maderistas by the score, it comes as no great surprise.

Azuela's caricature is an incisive analysis of Carrancismo's unconvincing attempts to clothe itself in radical fancy-dress. An ineffectual social myth—one which is rejected by the public—is much worse than no social myth at all, for it only discredits the revolution in the people's eyes, and ruins, at least for the time being, any further chances of creating a revolutionary mystique or religion. And so the Mexican Revolution was left, after the fall of Huerta and the decline of Madero's myth, empty of idealism. It had no equivalent to the liberalism of the French Revolution, the puritanism of the English Revolution, or the Marxism of the Russian Revolution; its mythology had to be created later by post-revolutionary governments, as we have already seen above in Chapter 3.

There remain, finally, some minor legends of the Revolution to consider briefly. Alvaro Obregón, perhaps a little surprisingly, had no legend to speak of; he was seen as a rather colourless military tactician, and was completely overshadowed by the spectacular actions of Villa. Some attempt was made, with no immediate success, to exploit for mythological purposes his loss of an arm in winning the battle of Celaya. His only real chance of acquiring a legend was in his role as the chief instigator of Constitutionalist anti-clericalism, but this campaign, as seen above, misfired completely, and, far from gaining support, only succeeded in alienating it still further. Pascual Orozco, who was the principal military leader in the Maderista revolution and attracted much more attention than Villa at that time, forfeited his legend by his counter-revolutionary attempt in 1912 and his later support of Huerta.

The Revolution also had its miniature heroes who, without occupying positions of importance in it, acquired small legends as

[74] pp. 928 and 936. 'Crowned heads' refers to the Emperor Maximilian [p. 20n.].

a result of significant or symbolical actions. The most important of these were Aquiles Serdán, María Arias and José Azueta. Serdán, the first martyr of the Revolution, is its most important minor hero. The siege of his house in Puebla by the army, the gallant resistance put up by the handful of men and women inside, and the death of Serdán himself [p. 26] all provided that initial symbolic spark which, according to Edwards,[75] is necessary to get a revolution under way. The siege of Santa Clara Street is, then, the Mexican equivalent of the Boston Tea Party, the storming of the Bastille, the attempt on the five members, and the St. Petersburg strike. The government press helped the process by attempting to make the Army appear in a heroic light when it was perfectly clear that the incident pointed, on the contrary, to gross inefficiency in the Army;[76] and the shooting of Serdán—though there was little heroism really involved, for he was found hiding in a cellar, given away by a sneezing fit—handed the Maderista revolution a martyr on a plate. Serdán was never, however, a prominent enough person in his own right to attract a complete legend; he was completely overshadowed when Madero himself became a martyr. María Arias Bernal was one of the middle-class women who maintained a cult around Madero's grave in Mexico City during Huerta's dictatorship. During Obregón's speech by the martyr's grave [pp. 147 and 266–7], he praised her action in the highest terms and, to put the male population to shame for their apathy in the face of the usurpation, presented her with his pistol. She became popularly known as María Pistola, but her legend shone but briefly; and she died when Carranza was president, in complete obscurity.[77]

Such, then, were the heroes and would-be heroes of the Revolution, and the unsteady growth of their myths and legends, which the governments of the 1920s and 1930s took over, tidied up, and institutionalized by fusing them into the whole apparatus of national patriotic mythology. But no epic is complete without its villain; he is almost as necessary to it as the heroes themselves. There has to be a symbol of wicked reaction, in contrast with which the symbols of the revolution may shine the brighter. Saints cannot exist without devils; the Sheriff of Nottingham was indispensable

---

[75] pp. 96-9 and 107-9.
[76] See Azuela, *Andrés Pérez, maderista*, pp. 771–3.
[77] See Quevedo y Zubieta, *México manicomio*, pp. 54–5 and 132–3; Ramirez Plancarte, pp. 65–7; and Ugarte, p. 93. For Azueta's Legend, see below, p. 275.

to Robin Hood, Herod and Pilate to Christ. Our study of Mexican revolutionary mythology would be incomplete without a mention of its black villain, Victoriano Huerta, the growth of whose legend is, in its way, as colourful a story as that of Pancho Villa.

On coming to power in February 1913, Huerta, realizing the need to set himself up as a symbol, made immediate and flamboyant attempts to create a vivid public personality and to make himself appear, in the confusion of the moment, as a leader acceptable to both revolutionaries and anti-revolutionaries. The image he sought to establish was that of the honest, straightforward, and dependable old soldier, behind his rough exterior a human and sincere man. From the beginning he made a point of dispensing with the formalities of parliamentary procedure (before dispensing with parliament itself), speaking very much out of turn because, he said, his overwhelming candidness forced him to.[78] He laid great stress upon the virtues of patriotism, calling the deputies and senators 'my brothers' when he opened Congress on 1 April—not in fact celebrated in Mexico as All Fools' Day—for 'it is necessary, even if only for a moment, for those present here to be not senators and deputies, but sons of Mexico'. He even tried to make himself a martyr in his own lifetime by anticipating for himself a heroic death, in words which were to become notorious: 'From this place and in the presence of the Nation's representatives I guarantee to the Republic that the Executive will find a way to restore peace, so dearly longed for, whatever it costs to do so, in spite of life itself, and even if he who is addressing you has to sacrifice his own!' And he attempted to attract radical support by devoting many words to the need to regenerate the indigenous races—he was the only leader in the Revolution, apart from Zapata, to lay any claims to serious concern for this question[79]—and also stating that his

[78] *El Imparcial*, 2 Apr. 1913.

[79] Huerta was a *huichol* Indian (the *huicholes* are an independent tribe who inhabit the mountains of north-east Jalisco). Molina Enríquez considers that he lost much support because of race prejudice (*Esbozo de la historia de los primeros diez años de la Revolución agraria de México*, Mexico, 1932–6, Book V, pp. 120–50); and this conjecture is substantiated by Maqueo Castellanos's novel, in which Huerta is repeatedly referred to by certain of the characters with disparaging expressions of race antagonism. His lower-class extraction, tastes, and habits—among them the tendency regularly to inebriate himself in public—which he made no attempt to dissemble, also served to alienate the support of the wealthy and aristocratic interests he came to represent (see Azuela, *Las tribulaciones de una familia decente*, p. 509, and Torres, *Como perros y gatos*, II, chap. 1).

government would incorporate the ideals of the Revolution into its policies.[80] In all this—much of it probably perfectly sincere—he made it clear that God was on his side; 'We are in the presence of the Republic, in the presence of humanity, in the presence of God. And I invoke His name because I know that it will lend strength and greatness and sincerity to my words'—a claim to which the Mexican Roman Catholic Church gave the full weight of its endorsement [pp. 286–8]. No well-intentioned Mexican could possibly fail to rush to Huerta's side and help the grand old man in his selflessly undertaken task of restoring peace to the country.

Huerta's attempt to create a positive legend for himself met with scant success from the beginning, but it continued along the same lines throughout his period of rule. When the United States invaded Veracruz his attempts to establish himself as the hero of Mexican patriotism and independence were intensified. On 22 April 1914 El Imparcial, in announcing the news of the occupation, headed its front-page report with a large engraving in a heavily sentimental style of Huerta, holding aloft the Virgin of Guadalupe banner, in a staunch pose, at the same time saintly and heroic, with a woman imploring at his feet; all against a background of the Mexican eagle and prickly-pear tree. The report, under the headline 'A Great Wave of Patriotic Enthusiasm Excites the Republic', said that war had been declared and that Mexicans had already invaded the United States and captured Eagle Pass and Laredo.[81]

[80] Three prominent land reformers, at least, were convinced that Huerta's administration was, or could be turned into, a radical one. Andrés Molina Enríquez accepted a post in the government and maintained to the end of his life that Huerta, if given a chance, would have implemented radical agrarian reform and policies generally favouring the indio and mestizo (op. cit., Book V, pp. 120–50). Otilio Montaño, the brain behind Zapata's Plan de Ayala, accepted Huerta's government for a period. And Toribio Esquivel Obregón, who had been for many years a leading advocate of radical land reform, was a member of Huerta's cabinet as Financial Secretary from 20 Feb. to 26 July 1913. Luis Cabrera evidently had similar ideas for a few weeks at least: on 6 Mar. 1913, El Imparcial published a letter from him advising renovadores to accept the new situation for the time being.

[81] The Huertista press campaign was now directed in El Imparcial by the powerful if bizarre modernista imagination of its new editor, the famous poet Salvador Díaz Mirón (1853–1928) [p. 166]. The most notorious of his many highly-coloured contributions to Huerta's legend was his description in El Imparcial of a visit to the newspaper's offices by the drunken old Indian soldier: 'Yesterday General Huerta visited our offices, leaving the perfume of glory in his wake' (see Azuela, Las tribulaciones de una familia decente, p. 509; Vasconcelos, La tormenta, p. 766; and Ramírez Plancarte, p. 49).

It was the sacred duty of all Mexicans now, the press and particularly *El Imparcial* went on to say in the next few days, to forget merely political arguments and unite behind Huerta to defend the motherland against the vile and infamous invader. Those who, like Villa and Carranza, failed to do this and continued to fight their fellow-countrymen when there were gringos to be driven out, were, declared *El Imparcial* (on 9 May 1914) 'bastardized sons, whose eternally infamous names will be borne in shame and abomination by their descendants, like foul stains which all the water in the five oceans could never wash clean!'

It is clear that this press campaign had, at best, only transient effects. Woodrow Wilson certainly played into Huerta's hands by the occupation, and he seems to have been extraordinarily badly informed about Mexican society not to have realized that such an invasion of Mexican territory by United States forces was bound to arouse violent patriotic wrath to a hysterical pitch—and therefore to boost the strength of whoever occupied the Presidential Chair at the time, even without the help of a propaganda campaign. If Huerta had been a less unacceptable president, and if he had handled his legend-creation generally, and particularly the press campaign after 21 April, with a little subtlety and commonsense, the occupation of Veracruz could have been made into a fountain of strength for him. As it was, the style of the anti-American propaganda, like that of Huerta's whole attempt to create charisma, was so ridiculously histrionic that its effect, far from increasing the spontaneous xenophobia of the moment, was to discredit and deaden it; so that within a week or two it appears already to have died down. People were, at the beginning, undoubtedly stirred into acts of patriotism such as enlisting in the Federal forces and encouraging others to do so with fiery street-corner speeches, like Marco Astenia [p. 115]—and thus, perhaps without realizing it, strengthening Huerta; but the fact that the press was lying tirelessly, and that anyway those who did enlist were sent to fight not Yankees but Mexican revolutionaries, was known almost immediately and can only have dampened fervour in a way that no soothing overtures by the Colossus of the North could have succeeded in doing. Huerta's entire attempt to create a personality cult was widely regarded as the inane buffoonery that it was. None of the novels portray anyone, not even Huerta's supporters, as accepting the legend he sought so strenuously to propagate; there is scarcely,

in fact, so much as a single derisory reference to it by any of the
novelists, even those who sought to justify his actions or make
excuses for them. The legend about Huerta that, according to the
novels, was accepted by his supporters of the anti-revolutionary
ruling classes (and presumably spontaneously created by them too,
since Huerta had not tried to put it about) was very different from
the one he broadcast: it represented him as the strong, ruthless
right-wing dictator—the 'iron hand'—that a country in the grip
of anarchy needs to put it firmly under control, by whatever means
are necessary; and also, of course, to restore to it the situation
obtaining before the Revolution.[82]

Huerta's heavy-handed attempt at legend-fabrication was, then,
an absolute failure; so he became an open and large target for a
black legend which was created by the Revolution, with, of course,
the greatest help from Huerta himself. Both his domestic policies
and his notorious personal behaviour were such that even the
staunchest counter-revolutionaries could not support him for long
without qualms. A likely supporter, Maqueo Castellanos, calls him,
with obvious regret, 'the man who seemed determined to lose
prestige and become divorced from public opinion'.[83] There cannot have been many legendary villains who have personally contributed so much—more perhaps, in this case, because of imbecility
than wickedness—to form their own legends. The act of treachery
by which Huerta came to power would have been a bad enough
initial disadvantage in any event. By killing Madero and botching
his excuses for the deed, allowing one explanation to be published
one day and a contradictory one the next, he ensured that the whole
thing was made unforgettable. It became the foundation stone for
his black legend: his normal epithets were 'El usurpador' and 'El
chacal', alongside 'El tirano' and 'El pelón'. As Madero's white
legend grew under the auspices of Carrancismo, so did the black
one of the man who had betrayed and foully murdered him:
treachery and disloyalty are unforgivable when inadequately dis-
sembled. Huerta's alcoholism added a second important ingredient
to the black legend: it was soon ensured that Huerta's name could
not be mentioned without his dipsomania's immediately being

[82] Azuela, *Los caciques*, p. 849; *Domitilo quiere ser diputado*, p. 948; and *Las
tribulaciones de una familia decente*, p. 425. Also Maqueo Castellanos, p. 385. It was
likewise the standpoint of most of the United States community in Mexico, as reflected in *The Mexican Herald*, and of many Americans at home (Clenenden, p. 48).

[83] Op. cit., p. 395.

brought to mind. From this factual base grew the legendary elaboration that Huerta was addicted to marijuana also, and the old
song *La cucaracha* was given new revolutionary life and meaning
as new words were accordingly fitted to its chorus:

> La cucaracha, la cucaracha
> ya no puede caminar,
> porque no tiene, porque le falta
> mariguana que fumar.[84]

The theme of Huerta's treachery and addiction to drugs were
reinforced in the making of his black legend by his physical aptness
for the role of knave and scoundrel. His face and his whole presence
seemed to radiate evil: in the documentary of the Revolution
Epopeya de la Revolución[85] he flashes at one stage across the screen,
dressed in top hat and long black cloak, looking every inch the
sinister villain of an early film melodrama.

When Huerta was defeated and fled the country his black legend
was strengthened still further by the inclusion in it of the charge of
cowardice. Such a charge is even more damaging in Mexico than
elsewhere, and it was made still more telling in Huerta's case by
the palpable contrast between his final flight and his blustering
attempts while in power to make himself appear to the very last
moment as a man who, in the best military tradition, would
sacrifice his very life before renouncing his mission. As the newspapers, now that he was gone, publicized facts about his political
crimes, the legend was completed. The spate of corridos that were
written and published by revolutionary propagandists on Huerta's
flight into exile rounded off and gave definitive form to the black
legend, in their compilation of all its elements: Huerta was the
villainous drug-addict who usurped the presidency by vile treachery

---

[84] The cockroach, the cockroach
      Can walk not one step more:
      He's run out of supplies
      Of marijuana to smoke.

The last line of the pre-revolutionary version of the song was 'cuartilla para
almorzar'. For two different accounts of the rebirth of *La cucaracha*, see Lepino,
chap. 12, and Rafael Sánchez Escobar, *Narraciones revolucionarias mexicanas,
histórico-anecdóticas* (Mexico, 1934), pp. 188–94, where the author claims the
credit for introducing the song to the Revolution, in April 1914 in Monterrey.
See also Vasconcelos, *La tormenta*, p. 828.

[85] Put together in 1961 on the basis of film taken in the Revolution by Jesús H.
Abitia, the official photographer of the Constitutionalists (see Guzmán, *El
águila y la serpiente*, pp. 337–40).

and murder, who retained possession of it by a further series of murders and other crimes, and who was not even man enough to stay and face the consequences when he was defeated. Like the heroes of the Revolution, the villain of the Revolution continued to have a functional mythological purpose after his departure from the scene. While he still occupied the National Palace, the point of the legend was to make him as morally repulsive as possible to as many people as possible, and so to remove popular support from him. When the legend achieved its purpose and Huerta went, it was not abandoned but intensified, as the production of the corridos shows. Its somewhat less self-evident but no less important purpose now was to convert Huerta into an all-purpose whipping-boy, the embodiment of the evils of the Revolution; so that he could be charged with the responsibility for all the suffering it caused to the Mexican populace, and take the entire blame that people were inclined to distribute among many of its leaders, in particular Carranza. This continuation of the Huerta legend had, then—as it still has—the function of distracting attention from other black pages of the Revolution and making its heroes appear, in contrast with Huerta's evil nigritude, even more spotlessly white than their respective legends could, alone, have made them. By appointing him the Drunkard, the Usurper, the Traitor, the Murderer, the Coward of the Revolution, it is strongly suggested that none of its other prominent personalities possessed any such undesirable qualities. That this legend-technique was not altogether successful during the Revolution itself can be inferred from the fact that during the Revolution's later stages—though Huerta's crimes were known to all—Carranza seems to have had a general repute scarcely any less black. That the reputations of these two are very different nowadays is witness to the post-revolutionary effectiveness of Huerta's black legend.

The Mexican Revolution gives good examples of a wide variety of different sorts of legend-creation, as each of its principal individual legends has its own distinct style of growth. We have the rapidly-fluctuating but quickly-consecrated legend of Madero; the counter-legend of Zapata, which only became a positive legend later; the non-legend of Carranza; the variously unsuccessful or only partially-successful attempts of these three to create social myths; the ambiguous legend of Villa; and the black legend of

Huerta. But in spite of the differences, there are certain interesting common features. General conclusions can be reached, on the basis of this study, about the formation of myths and legends in revolutions.

A society in revolution provides good conditions for the creation of myths and legends. The actions of war throw up heroes and the breakdown in communications makes for the easy spread of rumours and for the distortion of facts. A revolutionary society, furthermore, has a particular need for a mythology, a need which is bound to be satisfied since the means of satisfaction come from within that society itself. The emergence of myths and legends is, then, inevitable in revolution, and they have a very real, often decisive influence on events, which, because it works under the surface, is not always immediately obvious. No social study of a revolution can be complete without a methodical examination of its mythology and its legendry; and no theory of revolution is adequate if it fails to pay careful attention to the processes of myth- and legend-formation.

A legend must be given some factual basis by the personality and actions of the man at its centre. An attempt to create an artificial one out of nothing fails, often with disastrous consequences, for such a failure fertilizes the counter-legend. The leader must, in himself, have some attractive quality, in order to excite the public's imagination in the first place—and the more he can, by his own efforts, catch the public's eye, the better. The first growth of the legend must be spontaneous, or at least have a large element of spontaneity. In certain circumstances a legend can develop very quickly in an extremely short period of time: the commonly-held idea that the amount of exaggeration contained in a legend is proportionate to its age is fallacious. All legends are extremely unstable in these first moments of their existence, and their course can change suddenly; but legends created before the general public has come into any contact with the legend-figure are the most precarious of all, and can die sudden deaths upon the appearance of the man himself.

The legend-seed must not only be fertile, however, but must also fall on rich and receptive ground. It has already been pointed out that, in general, revolutions provide such a predisposition for the growth of legends; for legends answer the psychological need to idealistically inflate one's own situation, a need which is felt strongly in times of strife. In particular, however, a legend or myth must correspond to the special requirements of the moment if it is to prosper. In 1911, after Mexico had been ruled for over thirty years by the same dictator, a young hero who promised Valhalla by the means of effective suffrage and no re-election was acceptable, both because of the attractive novelty of the idea and because no one had actually undergone the disenchanting experience of parliamentary democracy in practice. By 1914, the democratic myth had lost its relevance and no Madero could have flourished then: instead it is the exclusively military legend of the invincible warrior, with few, if any, idealistic overtones, that carries all before it. In 1916 and 1917, it could be argued that general disillusionment and bitterness was so rife that no positive legend at all, however attractive, could have taken root in such stony soil. And throughout the Revolution the legend of a man who promised redistribution of land in southern states might thrive among the peasants of that region, but was hardly likely to find many adherents elsewhere or in other social classes.

Once the legend has sprouted, official hands must guide its development in the required direction. If performed skilfully and unobtrusively, such an operation can give the legend the strength it might not be able to acquire with continued spontaneous and unaided growth. The official training of the young legend is an important part of the task of the intellectuals, and the principal means of bringing it about are by newspaper and pamphlet campaigns for the literate and by songs and corridos for the illiterate. The aim at this stage is to elevate the legend or social symbol to the status of a social myth, fusing the person with an idea and so adding to the legend that mystique which is essential for the maintenance of idealism and optimism among the revolutionaries. If the intellectual guidance is deficient the mythological or religious mystique will probably not come into being or survive. Such was the case of the Mexican Revolution.[86]

[86] *After* 1917, of course, the legends which grew up during the Mexican Revolution and which have been the subject of this chapter have been most successfully converted into social myths. Indeed it is upon these myths—the myth of agrarian reform, the myth of the socialist Revolution, the myth of indigenismo, and, above all, the myth of the never-ending Mexican Revolution —that the social and political stability of post-revolutionary Mexico principally rests (see F. C. Turner, op. cit.) But the subject of this book is the military phase of the Revolution, the years 1910–17; and the failure of the Revolution to develop a mythology during this period is an important part of any explanation of its degeneration after 1914.

During this secondary stage of growth the legend can still fluctuate drastically, though it is now more stable than in the first, seeding period. It has at all times to contend with the counter-legend, which can take over at any point. The growth tends, indeed, to be a continuous dialectical interaction between legend and counter-legend; and each one, in its attempts to contradict the other, can in fact contribute to it.

The third, flowering stage of the legend's growth comes with its confirmation and, if necessary, its elaboration or modification by the triumphant revolutionaries after the revolution (the process can, as in Madero's case, have its beginnings during the revolution itself). A martyrdom much enhances the legend's final form, as is well known, because it makes a natural appeal to the public's sympathies. An important part of the legend-making process which usually works strongly at this stage is the system of the reflection of glory, which prominent men know all about: take a previous outstanding man and his legend or myth, enhance the legend as much as possible, and then declare oneself the immediate successor of the praised person. This system creates a chain-effect throughout a nation's history, keeping its social symbolism in constant evolution, and ensuring that one century's heroes are unfailingly passed on to the next. In twentieth-century Mexico the links of the chain have been solidly forged: Hidalgo and Juárez-Madero-Carranza-P.R.I., and Morelos-Zapata-Obregón-P.R.I.

The final stage is that which follows confirmation or consecration and is that of preservation. The revolutionary legends, with the men themselves safely in the other world, take their positions in the dusty hall of patriotic fame. Full membership of the State Mythological Club takes time to achieve, for a prerequisite of it is that the counter-legend should be completely forgotten, that there be nothing to challenge the purity of the legend. Not, perhaps, until the last of the old men who lived through and shortly after the Revolution are dead—perhaps two or three generations later—can this happen. The only legend which still manages to retain any vitality over a long period after the end of the Revolution is the one which, for one reason or another, has escaped preservation and institutionalization, and has been vigorous enough to continue growing unaided. The unofficial hero seems to be the only one, in the end, who, by not being made respectable and tidy, can avoid being fossilized.

The revolutionary legend or myth is an artistic creation—constructed, in turn, out of many individual works of art from various genres—with a direct social purpose. It is an example of the direct influence of art on society—concrete proof that literature, particularly, is no mere escapist luxury for the cultured individual, but that it is centrally and materially involved in the most fundamental processes of social life. The study of social symbolism is an area of sociological and historical research where the scholar trained in the techniques of literary criticism can make a very real contribution. This is presumably why historians and sociologists, who are not normally so trained, tend to neglect this important subject.

Artistic, particularly literary precepts apply, then, to myths and legends. As with all literary creations, what is important in them is not the extent to which they actually 'reflect reality' (as Sorel pointed out), but rather the extent to which they convey the illusion of reflecting reality, by presenting a satisfactorily coherent and complete structure of relevant meanings (the myth is superior to the legend precisely because its structure is much more complex and complete). To be effective, a modern legend or myth must be both convincing and aesthetically pleasing. It must have verisimilitude: in other words, it must not be excessively fantastic, or self-contradictory, or in obvious variance with reality. It must achieve exactly the right balance between the extremes of objective truthfulness—which could prevent it from being a legend or myth at all—and extravagance—which would make it lose its relevance to life—and in all of this it must be consistent to itself. It has, then, to be developed with subtlety, style, and artistic flair. It must also have artistic unity, and embody a central theme of widespread social appeal. Simplicity is more essential to it than to other, more sophisticated types of literary creation, for its whole purpose is to reduce reality to black-and-white terms, to create absolutes out of a relative situation. It is not concerned to portray life in all its depths and facets, and there is no room in it for displays of human weakness in the hero, or of expiatory traits of goodness or valour in the enemy. There is room in some legends, however, for considerable ambiguity, as the fascinating case of Pancho Villa shows (there are also reasons for believing that the ambiguous legend is more durable than the straightforward one). The legend or myth must be elaborated with dramatic and epic elements to stir the imagination; lyricism

NM

is largely, but not wholly, superfluous to revolutionary symbolism, and comic elements are, at best, very dangerous, and probably destructive—the barbed arrow of humour is best kept for firing at the enemy. In all of this it must appeal principally to the emotions and seek to convince through them. Myths and legends are not rational; rather they are meant to befuddle the brain.

The revolutionary legend or myth, in short, is a sort of modern magic, and performs precisely the same social function, in a way more consonant with modern civilized life, as the war-dance of the primitive tribe. That such magic is not by any means restricted, as the twentieth-century mind likes to think, to savages or even to societies in abnormal states, is shown by the creation in recent years of highly-regarded and well-remunerated professions devoted exclusively to this kind of magic-making. We prefer to call them public relations officers and advertising agents, rather than witch doctors or mythologizers.

In the Mexican Revolution, the leaders failed to give birth to durable myths. Some, like Carranza and Obregón, failed even to create legends. This failure can, in part, be attributed to shortcomings in the leaders themselves; but even more, perhaps, it can be blamed on the inadequacies of the Revolution's intellectuals, an important part of whose job it was to propagate and cultivate legends and myths. The intellectuals' weakness did not, however, affect only this revolutionary group, preventing it from efficiently performing its social function. The other revolutionary groups, which can conveniently be collected together and called 'the fighting masses', were affected just as drastically, as the next chapter will attempt to show.

6

REVOLUTIONARIES III: THE FIGHTING MASSES AND THE MIDDLE LEADERSHIP

THE prime requisite for a revolution is widespread deprivation and discontent in society. A revolution, as opposed to a *coup d'état*, can have no possibility of success if it does not possess the necessary numerical, physical strength to defeat the enemy in the field of battle. This material force is provided by the third and last component of a revolutionary army, the fighting masses.

The term 'masses', although it is the most convenient and normally used one, is here possibly a little misleading. Though the major part of a revolutionary army will normally be recruited from the poorest and most deprived sectors of society, it is an error to assume that, apart from intellectuals and leaders, all revolutionaries are always bound to be proletarians or peasants, as the expression 'fighting masses' suggests. What is really meant by the term 'the fighting masses' is all those, regardless of class extraction, who are on the revolutionary side and whose main function there is to fight, not to think or to lead. The most useful definition is, then, a negative one: 'fighting masses' are all revolutionaries who are neither intellectuals nor caudillos. They include not only the rank and file, but also the minor, secondary leaders who are not of sufficient importance to become revolutionary symbols.

With this provision in mind, it is safe to say that in all probability the fighting masses will, in fact, be principally derived from the lower classes of society. There are three distinct groups: the agricultural workers or peasants, the industrial workers or proletariat, and the rejects and outcasts of society, or the mob. Other fighters for the revolution will come from a variety of different sources: deserters, both officers and men, from the Regular Army; foreigners—mercenaries, adventurers, or heroic idealists; and men in a reasonably comfortable social and economic position who, out of personal convictions or grudges, decide to fight, or whom circumstances force into the fray. Many of these, but not necessarily all, will become revolutionary intellectuals rather than fighters (the distinction between 'revolutionary intellectual' and 'fighter' is not, of course, an absolute one; there is no reason why an intellectual should not fight as well as think, although, in fact, the intellectuals of the Mexican Revolution appear, on the whole, to have carefully avoided the battlefield [p. 127]). Crane Brinton has come to the conclusion that revolutionists are, in general, a representative cross-section of common humanity.[1]

It is the job of the fighting masses not only to fight but also, for their own good, to try to protect their common interests and ensure that the sacrifices they make are properly recompensed by the ultimate achievement of their goals. This latter object is never more than partially attained in any revolution; for the fighting masses tend to be inarticulate, anonymous, and intellectually passive, while the revolutionary soldiers' representatives, the intellectuals and caudillos, have considerable independent power to modify or alter the revolution's ideological direction to suit their own or others' interests.[2]

The story of the plight of the Mexican poor at this time is well enough chronicled not to need repetition here at length [p. 120].[3] In spite of the industrial progress before the Revolution, and the steady migration from the country to the cities at the end of the Porfirian period, agricultural workers still formed by far the largest part of Mexico's working population, and consequently the largest part also of the fighting masses of the Revolution. After 1820 the peasant's lot had steadily worsened as the land allowed him by the Spanish government for subsistence was taken from him, a process only hastened by the strict enforcement after 1880 of the Reform laws, with their insistence on legal ownership of property [p. 19n.]. He consequently was more defenceless than ever against the large

[1] p. 133.
[2] For this reason Sorel [p. 241] rejects the concept of the revolutionary intellectual in favour of the idea of a revolution in which each fighter is inspired by his own innate zeal for the cause. This unrealistic notion is similar to Marx's vision of an industrial proletariat automatically organized into a revolutionary force by the capitalist means of production.
[3] See for critical contemporary accounts, Andrés Molina Enríquez, *Los grandes problemas nacionales*, especially Part 2, pp. 101–347; and—an exaggerated and somewhat hysterical account—John Kenneth Turner, *México bárbaro* (originally published in English; reprinted by I.N.J.M., Mexico, 1964).

The fullest historical account is by M. González Navarro in *Historia moderna de México; el Porfiriato*, ed. Cosío Villegas, vol. 4 (Mexico, Buenos Aires, 1957), pp. 187–380.

landowners, and debt-peonage became a normal part of the country life. An inefficient farming system furthermore meant that he had insufficient to eat. One of the six ills to which Luis Cabrera attributed the Revolution, in an analysis he made in April 1911, was predictably 'Peonismo: that is to say the effective slavery or feudal servitude which is the lot of the rural day-labourer, particularly those who have been "recruited" or transported from South-East Mexico, and which subsists due to the economic, political and judicial privileges enjoyed by the hacendado.'[4] Poverty was made an even worse burden by the injustices which could be committed with impunity against rural workers by their masters and by district authorities: another evil to which Cabrera draws attention is 'Caciquismo: that is to say the despotic pressure exerted by those local authorities who are in contact with the proletarian classes, and which is exerted by means of the military contingent, of arbitrary imprisonment, of the Law of Flight [p. 31n.], and of many other types of harassment and obstruction of freedom of labour.' And any sort of an education was out of the question for them, unless the local hacendado happened out of the kindness of his heart to provide a school. Altogether it was a brutish existence for the Mexican peasant, for whom one of the few joys of life was the pulque[5] that he was kept plentifully supplied with at the hacienda store. Yet a working class that is so completely and systematically degraded is unlikely to have enough spirit to start a revolution by itself. Men who are as broken as the Mexican peasants appear, by all accounts, to have been in the early years of this century, offer small peril to their oppressors. The writer of the following description did not envisage the peasants as budding revolutionaries:

They live on land which does not belong to them and which they cannot work as they want and according to their needs; rather, they work for their master, from whom they receive house, clothes, food, and protection, but only in sufficient proportion to keep them alive, which concerns their master as much as keeping one of his cows or horses alive; they are losing all initiative and ambition, and they lack any sense of duty or notion of responsibility; their passivity grows daily and they

[4] El Tiempo, 17 Apr. 1911. Reprinted in Blas Urrea, Obras políticas (Mexico, 1921), pp. 176–80, and in El pensamiento de Luis Cabrera, pp. 121–46.
[5] The unmatured fermented sap of the agave; the main alcoholic drink of the Mexican working classes, particularly in the central region of Mexico, where conditions are best for the cultivation of the plant.

are progressively relinquishing their will. With each day that passes they are more servile and more incapable of becoming citizens.[6]

A revolution is only to be expected from unsuccessfully tyrannized men. That the Mexican peon had not only been broken by his servitude, but had also indeed come to be psychologically dependent on it, is a thesis put forward by E. A. Ross,[7] who tells of the American who bought an hacienda and freed his peons from all their debts; the result was that the peons soon left him. The whole master-servant relationship was defined and symbolized in their minds by the existence of the debt which tied the two together; so that without it they felt that they had been deprived of security and protection.

A section of the rural working classes that had equally good reason to be rebellious and more scope for doing so was composed of the small landowners who worked their own property, held either individually or communally, the *rancheros*. They also had suffered greatly from the intolerable powers that the hacendado was allowed, especially under the Díaz regime, and a third of Cabrera's points was '*Hacendismo*: that is to say the economic pressure and the unfair competition which the large property exerts over the small, aided by inequality of taxation and a host of privileges which the former enjoys in economic and political matters, and which result in the constant absorption of the small property by the large.' By virtue of their possession of property, rancheros had more independence, personal pride and dignity, and were more inclined than peons to be rebellious. It was a combination of peon and ranchero discontent that Andrés Molina Enríquez, one of the few not surprised by the outbreak of the Revolution, said in 1909 would cause civil war unless land redistribution were effected by peaceful means.

The other two groups of the lower class played much smaller roles in the Revolution. The mob of Mexico City had been a traditional source of unrest since colonial times; but at the time the

---

[6] *El Imparcial*, editorial of 31 Mar. 1913. That such a critical analysis should appear in a Mexican paper at this time, particularly in the one whose editorial policy was always to reflect the sentiments of whatever government was in power, supports the suggestion [pp. 172–3] that Huerta's government had, in the first few weeks of its life, some serious reforming intent. It also strengthens the assertion that neither Madero's rebellion nor his regime affected the lower classes in any discernible way [pp. 189–97].

[7] *The Social Revolution in Mexico* (New York and London, 1923), p. 73.

Revolution started it had no power to cause more than street riots. The Revolution itself was fought decisively in rural areas, where the mob could have no influence, though it had its say now and again in the capital. It is, then, to the third of the groups mentioned above that some historians have looked for the main source of revolutionary discontent, for an industrial working class is commonly more restless, better organized, and less resigned to its fate than an agricultural working class.

The industrial poor—a class in formation in Mexico from about 1870 on—were almost as badly off as the rural poor: Cabrera calls this evil 'Fabriquismo: that is to say the personal and economic servitude to which the factory worker is effectively submitted, because of the privileged position in economic and political matters enjoyed by the boss as a consequence of the systematic protection which it has been thought necessary to bestow upon industry.' But over their rural counterparts the factory workers had two advantages. They were in contact with the outside world, and particularly with the United States of America, because of the great use made in Mexican industry of skilled foreign labour; and they earned much higher wages—about five times higher, in fact, though their living costs were vastly greater.[8] Hence they were able, in the last decade of the Díaz regime, to form unions and organize a few strikes, which were brutally repressed [p. 24]. But in spite of the steady migration into the cities—which made the lot of the industrial poor all the worse—the proletariat did not have the numerical strength to make, by themselves, anything greater than the isolated strikes of the first years of the century. It seems to be a mistake to attribute the popular discontent which made the Revolution possible to any single section of the poor; it was, rather, the result of the coming together of a whole complex of different grievances, of which the principal ones have here been mentioned.

[8] In 1912–13 it was calculated that the peon earned an average of between 18 and 25 centavos daily, paid in kind at the hacienda store (*tienda de raya*), and the unskilled factory worker about 1 peso 50 centavos, though a skilled worker could earn much more (*Nueva Era*, 25 Jan. 1913; Arenas Guzmán, chap. 1; Luis Cabera, speech of 3 Dec. 1912, fragments of which are reprinted in Silva Herzog, I, pp. 267–84). The peon's miserable living accommodation was provided free, but his wage was still insufficient to support a family; it was supplemented with periodical loans which amounted, on average, to 30 pesos each a year, which no peon could hope ever to be able to repay. A man's total debts, divided on his death among his children, could amount to 500 pesos or more (Cabrera, op. cit.).

None of these social ills alone, nor even all of them together, seem to have been able to generate enough impetus to set the heavy wheels of revolution in motion. They needed a starter to release the full force of their destructive energy.

One might reasonably expect all of this, and more, about the nature of the fighting masses of the Mexican Revolution to be most revealingly illustrated in the novels in which it is depicted. It is precisely this aspect of social history, that which is concerned with the humblest sectors of society, that is least well documented in orthodox sources and therefore most difficult to approach. The socially-concerned realistic novelist can often do something to fill this gap, as, for example, in the European tradition, do Zola, Galdós, and Dickens. This is not, alas, true in the case of the Mexican Revolution, as has already been indicated [pp. 125-6]. The fighting masses do not, in the early novels of the Revolution as a whole (or even in the novels of Azuela as a whole), play a prominent role, in spite of the fact that the success of *Los de abajo* has led to the general acceptance—even by literary critics who ought to know better—of the contrary idea. What the novels can tell us about this part of revolutionary society is mainly contained in scraps of information that have to be gleaned here and there, compared and fitted together. Negative evidence is important too: the comparitively minor role played by the fighters in the novels is itself an indication not only of the intellectuals' class and race alienation but also, conversely, of the failure of the masses to make their voice heard in the upper levels of the hierarchy of the Revolution, and to secure adequate representation of their interests among the revolutionary leaders. The similarly negative evidence to be found in the novels about *indigenismo* [pp. 222-35] and the *mestizo* question [pp. 202-5] point likewise to conclusions about the Revolution's social content very different from those which many students of the subject have reached under the influence of post-revolutionary myths. The novels are not altogether as disappointing from our sociological point of view as a search in them for merely positive facts about the participation of the fighting masses might indicate.

The Revolution went through different stages of development and had different characteristics in various parts of the country. It seems vital, then, to take notice of its chronological and regional diversity as carefully as possible in the study of the fighting masses. There is little that can be said very usefully about them *en bloc*, and one has more probability of getting close to the truth by dividing the mass participation into the Revolution's four principal movements: Maderismo, Carrancismo and Villismo (in connection with which it is convenient to study the mestizo question) and Zapatismo (under which general heading the subject of indigenismo may be considered). In doing so, an attempt will be made to distinguish between the legends surrounding these movements—studied in the last chapter—and the 'objective' truth about them. Such a distinction can never, however, be absolute, for the dividing line between myth and reality cannot ever be traced with precision. A myth or legend itself becomes a part of reality as soon as it is widely accepted and many people believe in it.

The novels do not have a great deal of information to furnish about the overall social nature of the Maderista revolutionary movement. At no stage was it a full-scale revolution; its numbers were very small and it was confined, until the very moment of success, to the northern frontier of Mexico. No one who did not actually go north and join the revolutionaries of Madero could have anything but second-hand information about them, and none of our novelists did this; so for them, as for the rest of the Mexican populace, the first revolutionaries were a remote and mysterious enigma.

The small size of the Maderista revolt itself indicates that it was not a working-class movement. Photographs of groups of Maderista fighters show that a large proportion of them were men of some small social status at least.[9] The eye-witness reporter Ignacio Herrerías indicates the same fact indirectly when he says that most of the revolutionaries are of mature age, for they are heads of families who have come to the Revolution leaving their lands in the charge of their sons.[10] Vasconcelos, of the novelists the one who came nearest to the original Maderista revolutionaries, stresses over and again that they were, most of them, men

---

[9] *Historia gráfica de la Revolución mexicana* (ed. Gustavo Casasola, Mexico, 1964), Vol. I, pp. 224–51. The clothes, features and complexion of very many of them are not those of the peon.

[10] *En el campo revolucionario* (Chihuahua, 1911), p. 12.

who had sacrificed a great deal to fight for their ideals in the Revolution (Vasconcelos's prejudices must, however, be expected to lead him to exaggerate the high-mindedness of Maderismo to make Carrancismo—his pet hate—appear the more despicable by contrast): 'In one way or another each one of us was sacrificing something for the cause. It was reserved for Carrancismo to turn the revolution into a lucrative business.'[11] Not much weight can be attached to the evidence found in Juan A. Mateos's novel, but it, also, shows the Maderista fighters as men of property and social respectability.

The exclusively political—and liberal—motivations and aims of the Maderistas were a natural consequence of the revolt's social content; there is none of the drive for basic economic reform associated with a revolt of the lower classes. From the declarations of Madero down, it is clear that the reason for the revolt was the desire to establish liberal democratic freedoms, which culminated and found concrete symbolic expression in a wave of middle-class indignation at the vice-presidential candidature of Ramón Corral.[12] The protest against the undemocratic habits of the Porfirian regime was materialized in two important myths of Maderismo: that of the científicos and that of the caciques, the supposed tyrants respectively of economic power and local political power. To call them myths is not, in fact, to suggest that both terms did not represent a portion of truth, for there can be no doubt that the Porfirian government did actively encourage both the unfair monopolistic concentration of economic power in a few hands and the acquisition of political power by unscrupulous and corrupt men, unworthy to exercise it. They are here called myths because the use of such all-inclusive labels postulates the existence of sinister tightly-knit politically-motivated groups of men plotting silently and invisibly behind the scenes, whereas the reality is simply that both caciques and científicos were merely individuals, with few formal connections with each other, each one working

---

[11] *Ulises criollo*, p. 632. See also pp. 594–7, 626 and 643–4.

[12] Ramón Corral (1854–1912), a member of a northern family of rich hacendados and a faithful and long-standing collaborator of Porfirio Díaz, was Vice-President of Mexico from 1904 to 1910, when he was re-elected together with Díaz. His re-election was considered even more of an imposition than that of the President, because of the special private interests he was believed to serve [p. 191] (see Limantour, pp. 293–5). For reflections of the situation in the novels, see particularly Lepino, chap. 6, and Mateos (where the re-election of Corral appears as the sole reason for the Revolution), pp. 17–23 and 146.

more or less in competition with the others to accumulate a fortune.

Much wrath was stirred up against the científicos.[13] They constituted another of Cabrera's fundamental Mexican social evils, '*Cientificismo*: that is to say commercial and financial monopolization and the unfair competition which large businesses exert over small ones as a consequence of official protection and of the political influence wielded by the directors of the former.' But few people defined the term in such a wide way, as a general social and commercial phenomenon, as Cabrera did on this occasion. The científicos were rather believed to constitute some sort of secret and unofficial political party, created to protect and further the business interests of its individual members. Much of the opposition to Corral was derived from the belief that he was one of the heads of the group, which was rumoured to have the old and bumbling Díaz caught up in its steely tentacles. The notorious *El Imparcial* was, according to the myth, the científicos' organ, backed up by Finance Minister Limantour with the nation's money. The científicos were the more unpopular because many alleged members of the group were not of old Mexican stock, and were thought to be the representatives of European interests in Mexico. In a remarkable correspondence between the American capitalist Henry Clay Pierce and his agent in Mexico, Captain Sherburne G. Hopkins [p. 271], it appears that Hopkins was active in propagating this aspect of the científicos' myth in order to discredit Pierce's rival for control of Mexican Railways, Lord Cowdray. The científicos became, then, the chief public enemy in 1910 and 1911, and the cry of '¡Mueran los científicos!' was common; several attempts were made by the mob to set fire to *El Imparcial*'s buildings. The desire to rid Mexico of this mythical party was an important part of the motivation for the Madero revolt: as well as being a continuation and re-vindication of traditional liberal principles, it seems to have been a kind of crystallization of the various grievances of those Mexican commercial and landowning groups that did not consider themselves as belonging to the científicos' party—that is, those that felt that they were not

---

[13] The name arose around the turn of the century, as a jocularly colloquial term, from observation of the frequent recourse of Mexican financiers and their spokesmen to positivist sociology [pp. 81–2] and its famous 'criterios científicos' to justify their stony-hearted pecuniary attitude to life.

making money as successfully as they should. What is evident is that the myth had no working-class roots. There are few references to científicos in the novels of the Revolution. General hostility to them is reflected in *La ruina de la casona*, by Maqueo Castellanos (who had been named by Cabrera as a científico himself[14]) and in Quevedo y Zubieta's *En tierra de sangre y broma*, where two wealthy Mexicans anathematize them in a conversation.[15] No científicos appear as characters in the novels, which is not surprising in view of their essentially mythical and 'invisible' nature.

One of the few men who appear to have seen the científicos as a myth is Maqueo Castellanos (who had some personal interest in the question): he had an article published in *El Tiempo* on 12 April 1911, refuting attacks Cabrera had made on them, by declaring (as did Limantour[16]) that no such organization existed. But the myth continued to flourish after Madero came to power, even though it became strangely confused and self-contradictory: for one of the most widespread criticisms of Madero in 1912 was that he had allied himself with the científicos and allowed himself to be controlled by them as much as Díaz had; yet the Orozco revolt—against Madero—was popularly supposed to be financed by these omnipresent gentlemen!

The caciques are less justifiably called a myth, perhaps, because their activities were more directly experienced, less shadowy and remote. There was, however, a strong tendency to use the word in a somewhat similar way as an all-embracing and undefined blanket-term to refer in general to the oppressors of the people, without specifying enough to make detailed individual identification possible. The word was most commonly taken to refer to the jefes políticos (district prefects), or at least the unprincipled ones among them—of which there appear to have been a great many. They were local political chiefs appointed by the government, men put into positions that offered them the opportunity to become petty tyrants and despots and to enrich themselves in various dishonest ways [pp. 241–2]. Such is the cacique, for example, that appears in *Los de abajo*, don Mónico, who is responsible for Demetrio Macías's becoming a revolutionary. Yet another of Azuela's novels of the Revolution, *Los caciques*, is not about political bosses at all, but about a family business organization—del Llano hermanos,

---

[14] *El pensamiento de Luis Cabrera*, p. 81.
[15] pp. 99–100.   [16] p. 235.

S. en C.—which has, in various unscrupulous ways, monopolized the commerce of the region around a provincial city; and when many of the novel's characters express the hope that Madero will rid Mexico of caciques, it is to sharp, double-dealing businessmen that they are referring, not to political bosses at all. In fact the caciques here are rather closer to being científicos, according to the normal definition of the term—except that científicos can never actually be seen doing their dirty work, as the del Llano family are, and function on an altogether much grander scale. In Oscar Lewis's case-study of a peasant who fought under Zapata, the caciques are defined as a landed local aristocracy, created by the distribution of Church lands after the Reforms of 1857 [pp. 19n. and 243–7].[17] The word clearly had a wide range of possible meaning. As the científicos became the mythical symbol of the evils of monopoly, so the caciques became the mythical symbol of the evils of injustice, and were widely attacked, even in the press, as such. This was a safe target, for it was undefined, and shooting at it did not involve any attack on the higher levels of the Porfirian establishment, in the way that printed attacks on científicos did; the latter are consequently not to be found until the triumph of Madero.

Just as the Maderista rebellion had middle-class motivations, and seems to have had a much greater proportion than most revolutions of middle-class participants, it appears also to have been conducted in a thoroughly middle-class way; by all accounts it was a very clean, gentlemanly affair. Some students of the mechanics of revolutions—without alluding to the Mexican one—have discerned that there is usually, at the beginning, a successful moderate movement led by wealthy men, and they call this initial stage the 'honeymoon period'.[18] Maderismo has all the characteristics of just such a movement, and indeed Juan A. Mateos talks of 'the honeymoon of the triumphant revolution'.[19] Vasconcelos repeatedly stresses the decent, respectable nature of Maderismo: 'We all felt generous, we were all abdicating with triumph within our grasp. Public office—the refuge of the mediocre—was not considered an appropriate reward. Glory, singing its melodious strophes to our names, was enough for us.'[20] Madero's behaviour throughout was that of a man concerned at all costs to preserve

---

[17] Op. cit., pp. liii, 7 and 75.
[18] Brinton, pp. 99–100 and 134–62; Pettee, pp. 115–18; Edwards, pp. 128–9.
[19] p. 217.   [20] Ulises criollo, p. 644.

chivalry and avoid suffering, and his eagerness to sign what seemed to many to be a premature peace treaty was just one aspect of the generous and urbane nature of his bourgeois movement. There was no question, for example, of any shooting of prisoners, which was to become the normal procedure in the Revolution from 1913 on. There is hardly a hint of anti-clericalism in these early times, either, in spite of its prominent place in the Mexican liberal and revolutionary tradition; neither the novels which refer to the Maderista revolt nor the critical writings of revolutionaries before 1913, like those of Cabrera and Arenas Guzmán, lay any stress on the iniquities of the Church, which were to be such an important target of attack later. Cabrera's analysis in 1911, for instance, does not mention the Church, while his pamphlet published in New York in 1915, *La cuestión religiosa en México*, is a comprehensive attack on the Church's activities in Mexico since the middle of the nineteenth century. Azuela's *Los caciques* is anti-clerical and is concerned with this period—but it was written later, when anti-clerical feeling was already strong and widespread. Neither of the two novels actually written in Maderista times—*Andrés Pérez, maderista* and *La majestad caída*—though they both show sympathy for the Revolution, draw any attention to the Church as one of its enemies.

So the fighting masses of the Maderista part of the Revolution were not really 'masses' at all in either of the two main meanings of the word: neither were they principally working-class, nor were there many of them. The important social effect of the Maderista revolution was very slowly to stir Mexico's populace out of its long sleep so that by the next stage of the Revolution there would be real fighting masses to wage full-scale war with. In 1910 Madero had little popular support. Serdán's stand, for example, was followed up by no auxiliary movement of the Puebla workers, as had been hoped and expected, nor did Madero's call to the country as a whole to rise up on 20 November meet with any significant response. Simply by not being caught, however, Madero made Mexicans realize that there were possible alternatives to the *Pax Porfiriana*. Latent radicalism was stirred, and by April 1911 many parts of the country were up in arms. *El Tiempo* of 25 April 1911 reported that there were rebellions in every state in Mexico, except Colima and Querétaro, and that the whole of the states of Guerrero, Morelos, West Oaxaca, south Puebla, Michoacán, and the Federal

District, except the cities, were in rebel hands. Maderismo, for the first time, became a popular movement, just as its triumph was assured.

The whole of this process is examined, as it happened in one part of central Mexico, in *Andrés Pérez, maderista*, the novel of Azuela which provides such a remarkably complete analysis of the whole development of Maderismo. The social composition of this second stage of Maderismo, the gradual acquisition of sympathizers, is, as Azuela describes it, rather different from that of the first. In the cities Maderista political clubs grew in numbers: in *Los caciques* such a club is largely composed of semi-literate small tradesmen, with a baker for its president, a municipal musician for its vice-president, and a small shopkeeper and a newspaper-seller among its leading lights; and another such club, presented in *Andrés Pérez, maderista* as being absolutely typical, is made up 'of cobblers, barbers, bakers, etc.'[21] But such clubs provided only moral support of doubtful validity for Madero, and it was not from here, according to the novels, but from rural areas that the armed uprisings of March to May 1911 hailed. In *Andrés Pérez, maderista* it is the idealistic hacendado himself who raises the local Maderista band, and who thus follows the pattern of the main movement of the north. His active and committed followers are all men of some standing in rural society, but of a rather lower status: his major-domo, who is a revolutionary because he had, many years earlier, been turned off his small-holding by a local large landowner with the aid of Porfirian laws; his clerks and secretaries; a travelling cattle-dealer; and a ranchero who is unfairly overtaxed for his small parcel of land. Maderismo, on this evidence, appears at this stage to start to find support lower down the social scale, and some economic motivations—and, of course expectations [p. 27]—begin to encroach on its original political motivation. Azuela makes it plain that Maderismo has still acquired no peasant support; the peons are so scared of the Revolution, and of the possibility of being forced to fight in it, that they have dug holes in the ground in which to hide when it comes. When the actual uprising occurs, however, the hacendado Toño Reyes arms all the men in his power. One can assume that this also would have happened in the north, and that any peasant participation in Madero's early main movement would principally have been acquired in this way. Thus

[21] pp. 828–30 and 797.

the peasants, too, are given the revolutionary habit, very much against their will and inclinations, and forced into it by their master. According to Azuela, then, the first workers to take part in the Mexican Revolution were tyrannically compelled to do so by their oppressors![22]

All this happens in the state of Zacatecas: in Michoacán a very similar process is recorded by Jose Rubén Romero in his memories of early life, *Apuntes de un lugareño*. The revolutionary movement of which Romero and his father were among the leaders, starting there in early May (by which time, although Romero does not say so, the whole state was already in revolutionary hands), is led by the poorer middle-classes, and its troops are peasants; the 'campaign', however, at this late date, is no more than a succession of triumphant welcomes and celebratory receptions and dinners laid on for the movement's leaders by the hacendados of the state, anxious to be in the Revolution's good books. The Maderistas do not have to fight so much as one battle.

It would appear on the evidence of *Andrés Pérez, maderista*, and *Apuntes de un lugareño*, that the awakening by Maderismo of the Mexican people was a process that started at the top of the social ladder and moved, step by step, down it. Such a hypothesis has the support of the likelihood that, in general, the more oppressed a section of society is, the longer it will take to react to opportunities for revolution and to indulge in the unfamiliar activity of protesting and rebelling.

This second stage of Maderismo as a revolutionary movement merges easily into its third and final one, the 'bandwaggon' stage. A triumphant revolutionary movement is bound in any circumstances to attract turncoats, but Maderismo—and the evidence for this is abundant and unanimous—did so in an exceptional way. Nearly all novels that describe any aspect of Maderismo draw attention to the general cynical rush to become a Maderista as soon as Madero's success was assured.[23] Newspapers pointed it out imme-

[22] The situation was quite different in the state of Morelos, where there was clearly a state of acute revolutionary unrest in the last years of the Porfirian period. This is, perhaps, the only part of Mexico where there was a full-scale revolution from 1910 onwards. See Womack, especially pp. 28ff. In this and many other ways Zapatismo shows itself to be not so much a part of the Mexican Revolution as a separate and independent revolution in its own right [pp. 21n. and 23n.]

[23] See particularly Azuela, *Andrés Pérez, maderista* (above all the conclusion, pp. 797–801); Romero, *Apuntes de un lugareño* (Mexico, 1955), pp. 100–16;

diately: *El País* drew attention on 2 June to the appearance of large numbers of 'last-minute heroes', and on 8 June, commenting upon Madero's triumphant entry into Mexico City the day before, it mentioned 'faces which, with no great surprise, we saw in the parade yesterday surrounding and acclaiming Madero, just as only hours ago they were acclaiming and surrounding the *científicos*'. This third stage of Maderismo, its institutionalization, was interrupted by Huerta's counter-revolution in 1913.

The Maderista movement was, then, a moderate one and quite unlike the majority of revolutions in its lack, until the last moment, of widespread active popular support. Its fundamental significance was, more than anything else, that of a social catalyst, the starter without which the real Revolution could never have got under way. Without, in itself, changing much, it set off reactions within Mexican society which on reaching their climax some time later would change a great deal.

The movement against Huerta was from the beginning a very different affair, a full-scale Revolution with no punches pulled. There was a feeling of hatred about it that Maderismo had never known:

> It was impossible to forget Laredo, almost destroyed by the fury of the Huertistas, and other towns that had been burnt or blown up by the hatred of the defeated troops, destroying their own cities and killing their inhabitants, even those who had taken no part in the fighting, with implacable rage; and it was impossible, too, to forget the martyrdom of revolutionaries, initiated in Mexico City by the murders of Madero and Pino Suárez. The Revolution . . . was the Nation's Vengeance, which was to grow in intensity, as long as Huertista crime continued. Land redistribution, free elections, and all those trivialities? All that would come later, after the triumph.[24]

Ancona Albertos's analysis of the atmosphere of 1913 shows just how effective the Maderista catalyst had been.

Ancona Albertos, Part II, pp. 1–22; Maqueo Castellanos, Part I, chap. 7; Lepino, chap. 6. Also Azuela, *El novelista y su ambiente* (*Obras completas*, III), pp. 1069–72.

[24] Ancona Albertos, II, pp. 155–6. For similar reflections of the widespread thirst for vengeance felt at this moment, see Vasconcelos, *Ulises criollo*, pp. 720–1, and *La tormenta*, p. 730, where he records that the expression 'Everyone from lieutenants upwards is to be shot' was much heard in revolutionary circles for the first time in 1913; Teja Zabre, *La Esperanza y Hatí-Ke*, pp. 77–8; and Bojórquez, chap. 11. It also finds violent expression in Carrancista propaganda pamphlets.

To split up the Revolution after 1913 (leaving the special phenomenon of Zapatismo aside for the moment) into the two distinct
movements of Villismo and Carrancismo gives an altogether too
schematic and straightforward view of things. As well as the three
main Northern Divisions of the Revolutionary Army under the
generals Pablo González, Pancho Villa, and Alvaro Obregón, there
were all over Mexico smaller local movements which had no direct
connection with any one or other of them, and whose allegiance
after the rupture between Villa and Carranza tended to be purely
fortuitous. Indeed all the armies of the Revolution, including the
large ones, were personal armies, owing their first allegiance to a
man rather than to a cause. Just a few of them, those of Zapata,
Villa, Obregón, and González, grew into the great fighting forces
that won and lost the major battles of the Revolution; but most
remained relatively small and obscure, each one fighting its own
minor battles and skirmishes within the limited area it could cover,
independently of the main forces. Azuela's famous short novel
Los de abajo, for all its limitations, is particularly valuable as an
eye-witness account, which attempts to be sympathetic, of one
such obscure and forgotten, but nevertheless sociologically relevant, movement. It provides the only inside information about
this neglected backwater of the Mexican Revolution. It must be
handled with care: for because of Azuela's often uncomprehending attitude towards peasants, as well as his prejudices as a whole,
there are some subjects on which its testimony cannot be accepted
—for example, the personality, characteristics, abilities, and intelligence of the revolutionary soldier [pp. 125–6]. But it is a unique
document, and can tell us much.

The guerrilla band of Demetrio Macías is formed in late 1913
and operates in Central Mexico, in the states of Zacatecas, Guanajuato, Jalisco and Aguascalientes. With the exception of the
intellectual who joins it a little later, it is composed entirely of
illiterate members of the working class, mostly indigenous agricultural workers from the highlands of Zacatecas. They have become
revolutionaries for a variety of motives. Demetrio himself is a
ranchero who, after arguing with the local political boss and insulting him, was branded, in revenge, as a revolutionary; his house was
burnt down, and he was forced to become an outlaw and a rebel.
Most of his officers are also rancheros, and are in arms for similar
reasons; one stole some jewels, another knifed a captain of the

Federal Army. Demetrio's band only numbers twenty-five at the beginning, but with its success it soon grows: most of the new-comers who swell the ranks appear to be peons, attracted by the freedom of the revolutionary life:

They all filled out their lungs as if to breathe in the wide horizons, the immensity of the skies, the blue of the mountains and the fresh air, perfumed with the aromas of the sierras. And they made their horses race, as if in that unbridled gallop they were trying to take possession of the whole earth. Who now remembered the stern police commandant, the grumpy policeman, the presumptuous cacique? Who remembered the wretched hut, where you live like a slave, always under the vigilance of the master or of the sullen, bad-tempered foreman, with the inescap-able obligation to be up before sunrise, shovel and basket or plough handle and share in hand, to earn the daily bowl of corn-mush and plate of beans.[25]

That the anti-Huerta revolution was a genuinely lower-class one is reflected in the taunting shouts that the federal soldiers would direct before and during battles at the revolutionaries, and which Azuela, like several other novelists, records: *comevacas* or *robavacas* ('cow-eaters' and 'cow-robbers', referring to their need, in the absence of any regular provisions or pay, to support and feed them-selves off the land) and *nixtamaleros* (eaters of *nixtamal*, tortilla-dough—the staple diet of the Mexican poor).

If we can believe Azuela, the motivation of these guerrillas never had anything directly to do with revolutionary ideals of social reform. The Revolution is never, for these revolutionaries, a way of changing society, but rather an enticing release from society into anarchy. And even after the arrival of the intellectual, who tries—albeit half-heartedly and cynically—to preach to them the message of permanent and social redemption, rather than merely temporary and individual liberation, their attitude does not change. They all continue to fight long after there has been any purpose in doing so, and only death stops them; for the Revolution becomes for them a way of life, an end in itself, from which a return to the restrictions of a peaceful society is unthinkable. When one of Demetrio's men observes, towards the end of the novel, that it seems silly to con-tinue to fight now that Huerta has gone, most of the revolutionaries 'laughed at his ingenuity. For if you've got a rifle in your hands and a belt full of cartridges, they must be for fighting with. Who

[25] pp. 352–3.

against? Who for? No-one worries about that!'[26] There is as little
room for social idealism in their aims in fighting as there is in their
motivation. At the beginning they are spurred by hatred of the
Federal Army and the caciques, and all through the story they are
fiercely possessed by strong class-hate of *curros* and *catrines*
(elegantly dressed city dwellers: this word reveals the close connection between class conflict and the conflict between city and
country [pp. 264–8]). But the main goal soon becomes the acquisition of booty, and the principal incentive the orgiastic opportunities
that are constantly held out to successful armies. After their
participation in the taking of Zacatecas until the final ambush in
which they are all killed, they are involved only once in a military
operation (a minor mopping-up expedition), and all they do for all
the rest of the time is to sate themselves daily with food, drink and
women—all stolen from the poor as well as the rich—and indulge
in wanton destruction and sadistic cruelty: all of which naturally
turns the initial friendliness of the non-fighting populace into
embittered hostility. Demetrio Macías himself, far from attempting to impose any discipline or order on his followers, indulges
more than most of them in licentiousness. Even allowing for some
exaggeration by the pessimistic Azuela, the impression conveyed is
one of a revolution in which large numbers of the participants had
not the smallest idea that the fighting was for any common goal
at all.

The parochiality of the peasant guerrilla group is also reflected
in its isolation. News of what is going on in the country at large
takes months to reach them, if it ever does reach them at all. The
other revolutionary forces seem to be unaware that they exist—
never does Demetrio receive orders from any main body of the
revolutionary army, and he only joins in the attack on Zacatecas
because he happens, by chance, to find out about it in time and
decides, on his own initiative, to go there. The United States'
occupation of Veracruz, for example, which caused such fierce and
universal excitement in Mexico, and occurred in the middle of the
period of time covered by *Los de abajo*, is not even mentioned in
the novel. Demetrio and his men find out about the battles of
Celaya, by chance, two months after they were fought. They only
inform themselves about the impending attack on Zacatecas in
time by coming across two muleteers who happen to have heard

[26] p. 407.

about it. When Macías learns about the rupture between Villa and Carranza on going to Aguascalientes for the Convention in October 1914, he has not the vaguest notion about why it has happened, what it means, or how to choose between the two. His men become Villistas only because the local revolutionary leader Pánfilo Natera —at whose side they had fought at Zacatecas—is one.

Such, then, were the smaller guerrilla bands and armies in the Mexican Revolution, according to Azuela. On the evidence of *Los de abajo* they show to an extreme degree all the shortcomings and failings of a peasant movement—disorganization, indiscipline, lack of fixed objectives, parochiality; and, because of the poor use they are put to, they are given small chance to display or employ the virtues of one—bravery and decisiveness in battle, toughness and resilience, evasiveness. The band portrayed in *Los de abajo* reflects many of those features of the Revolution which have previously been noted in this book: principally its lack of co-ordination and directing purpose, and its consequent degeneration into anarchical and blind destruction. The general inadequacies of the whole Revolution reproduce themselves successively at each of its levels: Macías and his men can only follow their inclinations and roam and maraud unchecked because there are never any superior orders to tell them what their precise duties are; and the lack of these superior orders is due, in turn, to the lack of co-ordination in each of the higher reaches of the Revolution's hierarchy. This particular and central failing of the Mexican Revolution seems to have been automatically self-perpetuating all the way along the line.

It is apparent that the fighting masses cannot, in such conditions, fulfil their two functions properly: their energy as a fighting force is squandered, as the Revolution fails to deploy them efficiently, and it is quite impossible for them even to start trying to defend their class interests, for they have no idea what such interests are, and there is no one to enlighten them on the subject. Of course all revolutions tend to be wasteful, destructive, and irrationally fought, and one cannot expect them to conform to certain logical laws and reasonable theories which an academic student of the subject might evolve in the comfort of his armchair; yet it is surely to be preferred that the waste, destruction, irrationality, and disorganization be minimized, and that the Revolution be as efficient as possible in achieving its aims. This did not happen in the case of the Mexican Revolution.

Los de abajo is, of course, just one short novel dealing with one sector of the revolutionary soldiery. There are no other early novels concerned primarily with the fighting masses with which to substantiate the evidence given in it by Azuela. His microcosm of peons in revolution is acceptable, however, because it matches the general patterns of the Mexican Revolution observable from other sources and, indeed, can only be understood and explained in terms of these patterns. The inductive-deductive method which we are using in this study seems to work fruitfully here.

Much of what Azuela observes about the guerrilla band—social composition, motivation, and so on—is likely to apply to the *constitucionalista* and *convencionista* fighting masses as a whole. One might expect, of course, somewhat more effective organization within the three principal divisions of the north; but it seems safe to suppose that their social content would be in many ways similar to that of the small army of Demetrio Macías. Unfortunately there is no early novel written about any of the northern movements with which to judge this hypothesis, so it will have to remain a hypothesis which general observable facts about the conduct of the Revolution tend to confirm. Martín Luis Guzmán's *El águila y la serpiente* is the novel which is closest to the northern movements, but it does not, however, attempt to give any sympathetic portrayal of the fighting masses. All sources give the same general picture of a complete lack of any higher purpose and a very fragile discipline among the soldiers of Villa and Carranza, and hence corroborate the detailed analysis of Azuela.

It is possible, in addition to this, to glean in the novels and elsewhere various other relevant pieces of information about the special characteristics of each of the three principal revolutionary movements fighting after 1914: Villismo, Carrancismo, and Zapatismo. The two northern movements had much in common, and it is only after the definitive rupture that their ways divide significantly in a social sense. They can best be considered together until that point, particularly with regard to the regional and racial significance that the Mexican Revolution has been widely given.

It has been accepted by many students of Mexican history that the nineteenth century saw the rise of the half-caste, the mestizo— the new Mexican of the future, ambitious, restless, progressive, and independent because of his non-aligned racial position.[27] The

[27] For this kind of interpretation, see particularly Parkes and Tannenbaum.

Reforma is often seen as a mestizo movement, and mestizos are considered to have been liberals in politics. This racial interpretation of Mexican history appeals very strongly because it supports the pleasing picture of a modern Mexico in which both the indigenous and the Spanish elements have been fused into one homogeneous and truly Mexican whole.[28] The new monolithic Mexican race is seen emerging hand in hand with the new monolithic Mexican culture.

According to this view of Mexican history, the Revolution is the final, definitive triumph of the mestizo. The Revolution was a movement from the north; the north is a region full of mestizos, specially half-caste rancheros; the Mexican Revolution therefore represents the ultimate conquest by the mestizo of the country as a whole. So goes the chain of reasoning.

That this racial theory of modern Mexican history has found any acceptance is due in part to the fact that it is central to the brilliant analysis of Mexican society made shortly before the outbreak of the Revolution, Andrés Molina Enríquez's *Los grandes problemas nacionales*. Under the strong influence of positivism, Molina Enríquez tries to explain the characteristics and attitudes of all sectors of society in terms of race heredity and ethnic development, and consequently he feels obliged to make each social group correspond to a separate ethnic sub-division; society's middle reaches—rancheros, skilled industrial workers and so on—are identified as mestizos. In doing this, Molina Enríquez started a durable tradition in modern Mexican historiography.

It is surprising that such a fallacious argument should be accepted so readily and unquestioningly by some historians. Although, as part of the colonial legacy, people of European stock have certainly tended to occupy the highest positions in Mexican society, and the Indios the lowest, there has never been a precise enough correspondence all the way up the social ladder to justify this confusion between social and racial status. The difference between indio and mestizo is, anyway, impossible to establish in absolute terms.[29] What writers after Molina Enríquez really mean

---

[28] Daniel de Guzmán argues this thesis extensively in *México épico*.

[29] Eighteenth-century Spanish colonial governments commissioned a series of paintings—called 'Cuadros de mestizaje'—of the results of various racial mixtures, in order to classify all possible grades of half-breeding. The sets were made up of pictures of several dozen different types, of which the most complicated were given names which seem to bear witness to the impossibility and

when talking about mestizos has little to do with race: they are referring simply to certain social categories below those of hacendado and industrialist yet above those of peon and unskilled proletarian. That there is a large proportion of people of mixed racial derivation in these sections of Mexican society is not surprising in view of the fact that mestizos form the largest part of Mexican society as a whole: 'blood' was already well mingled in all Mexico in 1910.[30] Andrés Molina Enríquez's bequest to later scholars of race obsession merely seems to confuse things.

The novels reflect this. Although the novelists who wrote before 1925 about the Mexican Revolution have relatively little to say about the levels of society commonly associated with mestizos, it is noticeable that when they do mention the middle and lower rungs of the social ladder, the question of ethnic definition is one which concerns them very little. To discover the racial derivation of the peons, rancheros and modestly-positioned people in general who appear in the early novels is sometimes impossible, and even when it can be done, it usually requires deductive effort from the reader: very few of the Mexicans who lived through the Revolution and wrote about it appear to have seen in it the racial significance subsequently attributed to it by some historians. Even where the racial nature of these so-called mestizo groups can be determined in the novels, individual members of them very often fail to conform. The ranchero Demetrio Macías appears not to be a mestizo but a 'full-blooded' Indio, for his skin is dark, he has no facial hair, and his eating and dressing habits are those of one [p. 226]; and many of his men are Indios too. To Azuela—who is particularly vague about racial distinctions in practice—the División del Norte of Pancho Villa seems also to be full of 'pure-

futility of the whole exercise—and the headaches it must have given those who had to carry it out—like *Ahí te estás*, *Tente en el aire*, and, most revealingly, *No te entiendo*.

[30] Molina Enríquez (op. cit., p. 203) calculated that a half of Mexico's population was mestizo, without ever defining exactly what he meant by the term. The problem of definition is well illustrated by Tannenbaum's confused attempt to solve it (pp. 16–17, 19–20 and 21), by saying that it is not really racial at all: 'Indios' are all those who live in predominantly indigenous communities, he says, whether they are 'pure-blooded' or not, and 'mestizos' are all those with some Indio ancestors at least who do not live in such indigenous communities, regardless of whether they have any white forebears or not. In this case, one might question the wisdom and logic of using racial terminology in the first place, and going on to build a whole interpretation of historical events on the alleged mechanics of race-heredity.

blooded natives'.[31] The Huastecan rancheros don Cipriano and don Florencio Izaguirre of Lepino's *Sangre y humo* are not mestizos but Spanish and of pure Spanish pedigree respectively. In *En el sendero de las mandrágoras* the character who has all the mestizo characteristics as defined by Molina Enríquez and others— he is poor, ambitious, unscrupulous, sharp, socially unattached, and emerges at the end of the Revolution on top of society, as a general [pp. 213–16]—is in fact an outlawed member of an extremely respectable and wealthy family which seems to be of exclusively Spanish extraction. And so on.

If one discards the confusing and unhelpful racial theory, it becomes apparent that the Revolution of the north had primarily regional—as well as class—significance. As has been indicated more than once, there are many Mexicos: regional differences count for even more, perhaps, in Mexico than in other countries. The central part of Mexico is the richest agriculturally, the most densely populated, and the most dominant politically, and it is looked on with envy and misgiving by other regions. The north has poor soil, and it is a region of large landholdings: even rancheros can possess a sizeable tract. It is better suited to cattle-raising than any other agricultural activity. At the beginning of the century it was much more closely than other parts of Mexico in contact with the outside world, especially the United States of America, not only by reason of being on the frontier but also because railways and mining centres there had brought many workers across the border. The north had, furthermore, little colonial tradition, as it was left largely uninhabited until the eighteenth and nineteenth centuries. All this produced there a hard, relatively free and independent breed of men, who felt contempt for the inhabitants of the south, and resentment of their privileged status in the country. It was in this north of Mexico that the Revolution —Maderista, Villista, and Carrancista—had its nucleus, and from here that it moved into the centre of Mexico and took it over. Mexico was ruled after the Revolution until 1934 by what has been called[32] 'the Northern Dynasty' of Carranza, Obregón, and Calles.

Just as the 'mestizo' interpretation of the Mexican Revolution finds no support in the novels, so their evidence shows that its

[31] *Las moscas*, p. 906.
[32] Howard F. Cline, *The United States and Mexico* (Harvard, 1953), pp. 192–203.

regional significance was widely appreciated during the Revolution itself, as well as by some later historians. The early novelists were almost without exception men born and bred in the centre or 'core' of Mexico, and they reflect the somewhat apprehensive reaction of this region to the invasion from the north of these hordes of strange men, packed menacingly like swarming bees into the compartments of the trains which conducted the vast migration. Eduardo Pallares gives a less self-defensive opinion than most in a pamphlet bravely published in Mexico City in 1913: 'The government believes it is defending legal institutions; but it is wrong: what it is really defending is a certain social idiosyncrasy, a certain collective temperament, the interests of a certain group—the refined, delicate, hypocritical culture of the bourgeoisie of the centre of the Republic.'[33] Quevedo y Zubieta, a more able social analyst than novelist, provides the fullest discussion of what he calls *el nordismo* as seen from the standpoint of the inhabitant of the centre:

In our northern states there predominates a race of adventurers, the worthy descendants of those avid Spaniards who went up into the plains under which lay copper, silver and gold. Up there is a pool of men who are always restless; either they direct their restless feelings upwards, and we have smuggling, or predatory expeditions to the United States frontier, an inexhaustible source of indemnification for our neighbours, or they direct them downwards, and we have revolutions, invading the centre of Mexico. The inclement weather, the ugly townships, a drunken existence studded with hangovers, are all recommendations for the life of smiling valleys. . . .

Around the figure of Venustiano Carranza, Nordismo is becoming more complicated. It is no longer a circumscribed phenomenon, but one extended to all the frontier states—Sonora, Chihuahua, Nuevo León, Coahuila and Tamaulipas. Then Nordistas of the second rank—from Sinaloa, Durango and Zacatecas—participated. It was a vast political and military pilgrimage, of greater proportions than the one the mini-christ Madero initiated in 1910. The pilgrims knew from experience that at the end of the journey their toils would be richly compensated with honour and wealth.[34]

Quevedo y Zubieta had already described the Maderista revolution in similar terms: 'An avalanche of khaki clothing, wide-brimmed felt hats, riding boots, revolvers and cartridge-belts; types halfway

---

[33] *La inmoralidad de la prensa*, pp. 7–8.
[34] *México manicomio*, pp. 113–14.

between the Yankee and the Mexican, the soldier and the civilian; the whole herd of frontier rancheros, avid for booty from central Mexico.'[35] Attention is drawn frequently by these apprehensive core-dwellers to the palpable influence of the United States on the revolutionaries. One of the most condemnatory references is made by Maqueo Castellanos: 'rough soft-collared coffee-coloured shirts, made fashionable by Carrancismo . . . , khaki trousers, each with its pair of leggings, military blouses carried over the arm, for the heat made it impossible to wear them, and campaign hats on the back of the head. . . . A caricature of a U.S. army officer— which the revolutionaries took so much pleasure in copying.'[36] Vasconcelos—writing some time after the Revolution—brings together the idea of nordismo with that of the Revolution as a creation of United States protestant imperialism. The men of the north, he says, are corrupted by living near the border with the United States, and are, indeed, not real Mexicans at all but *pochos* —those who deny their Mexican blood and ape American manners and habits (a word normally applied only to the inhabitants of the southern United States who are of Mexican descent). They are, then, he goes on to say, the agents of the protestant and Anglo-Saxon imperialists of the north, whose sinister plan—'Latin dissolution as a preparation for Saxon occupation'—they are unwittingly carrying out [pp. 121 and 287–8.][37] And in general the novels display the hostile and timorous response of the inhabitants of the centre, particularly those of the cities of the region, and above all those of Mexico City itself [pp. 254–68], to the new presence among them of large numbers of proud, strong, untamed men from the north. This regional hostility is mixed with class hate, as Pallares points out, for the centre had become identified with Porfirian interests. Whatever the significance of the regional invasion might have been in post-revolutionary developments, there is no doubt that during the Revolution itself it was seen as a vital—and from the standpoint of the inhabitants of the central plateau, highly disturbing—factor.

After the rupture between Villa and Carranza their two movements diverged and acquired distinct social characters. Villa, anxious to attract support and increase his numerical strength at all costs, enlisted large numbers from the disbanded Federal Army—

[35] *En tierra de sangre y broma*, p. 104. [36] p. 519.
[37] *La tormenta*, especially pp. 779–82, 797–8, 805–10, 818, 821–2, 884.

Quevedo y Zubieta gives us an interesting scene of the competition between Villista and Zapatista recruiting officers (*enganchadores*) to re-enlist the Federal soldiers as soon as they are demobilized.[38] Villismo consequently moved noticeably to the right, and this tendency was accentuated by Obregón's open declaration of war on the Church and the rich, which threw many conservatives into the Villista camp. Azuela's *La moscas* is a novel devoted to the examination of this momentary rightward trend of Villismo. Its action is concentrated into a few days in mid-1915 and shows the infiltration of reactionary interests into the movement, their brief courtship with Villismo, and their rapid defection after Celaya. The 'flies' are the parasitic crowd of bureaucrats and other conservatives who attached themselves to Villista forces in the hopes of the prize of a respectable and well-paid position in society at the end of the Revolution. Carrancistas have thrown them out of their jobs, and they have been frightened away from Carrancismo still more by its propaganda and acts against Capital, on whose side they naturally consider themselves:

Rubén . . . comments, 'The Carrancistas' flag carries the motto "Extermination and Death to Reaction". . . . And since, for them gold and reaction are synonymous . . .'

'That,' says Matilde trenchantly, 'is why, since they can't shoot gold, they satisfy themselves with carrying it off. They certainly punish it effectively enough; for in the simple process of passing into their pockets it stops being reactionary!'[39]

As the less horrible of two evils they have, then, been forced into Villa's arms, and indeed Villa has accepted their support. As a result the Villista forces are surfeited with anti-revolutionaries, both civilians and ex-federales, described by Azuela as 'young gentlemen dressed up as soldiers'.[40] Azuela shows a similar situation obtaining at this time in the now Villista band of Demetrio Macías: 'The few officers that are left, old comrades of Macías, are indignant because casualties in the general staff are replaced with nobs from the city, scented and foppish.'[41] The alliance of these conservative newcomers and the original Villistas of the north is naturally enough an extremely uneasy one, as the former secretly despise the rough soldiers and only flatter them because it is necessary to remain on good terms with them; and the soldiers

[38] *México manicomio*, chap. 6.   [39] p. 873.
[40] p. 885.   [41] *Los de abajo*, p. 413.

have the normal northerners' contempt for the flabby city dwellers of Central Mexico.[42] Villismo, then, in 1914 and 1915, was sheltering a dangerously large proportion of the sort of people that the Revolution was supposed to be being fought against.[43] What Azuela, who had no reason not to record reality faithfully on this point, clearly depicts as the most perilous aspect of this infiltration is the profusion of ex-federal officers, petulantly cultivating their resentment at the ignominy of defeat and disbandment, and unable for a moment to forget the blow to their military pride that has been administered by this wretched army of peasants. All this comes to the surface in a snatch of conversation between two such former Federal Army officers of *Las moscas* who are now Villistas: '"Can it be, sir, that this rabble defeated our glorious Federal Army?" "The Federal Army was never defeated, my friend. We were betrayed, that is all. With fifteen men I turned hundreds of these wretches to flight on many occasions."'[44] A second counter-revolution could have been in the making here; but Villa was already irretrievably lost, and nothing developed out of this potentially hazardous situation. That such a hope of resurgence was not far from the minds of Villa's new supporters is seen in the joy with which they greet the rumour that a counter-revolution has indeed broken out under the leadership of Huerta, Orozco, and Félix Díaz, and in the readiness with which they ascribe to this rumour the status of uncontroverted factual truth.[45]

Villa's conservative support only remained with him, however, so long as there was still hope of his triumphing in the Revolution. As soon, in *Las moscas*, as the news of the disaster of Celaya becomes known, the ex-federals and others realize that this is not, after all, the place for them, and decide that Obregón and the Carrancistas are not as bad as all that. The bureaucrats and job-seekers leave the Villista train immediately, hoping to be able anonymously to filter into the Carrancista force which is about to arrive; and the ex-federals literally change their jackets. Villa's courtship with the right is finished and the potentially dangerous concentration of

---

[42] *Las moscas*, pp. 887–90.
[43] See also Ramírez Plancarte, pp. 224 and 273–5. Villa himself was fond of the federal general's uniform and wore one often, as, for example, on the occasion of the División del Norte's triumphal entry into Mexico City on 6 Dec. 1914.
[44] *Las moscas*, p. 889.
[45] Ibid., p. 913 [p. 299].

counter-revolutionary groups under his wing is finally dispersed. From now on Villismo loses national significance, except as a legend [pp. 162–4].

One of the most socially significant things about Villismo after the fall of Huerta is, then, the final attempt of the right to take control of the Revolution through it—the last fling of the lower levels of the old ruling-class. The particular feature of Carrancismo that is most important from a sociological point of view during the same period is, conversely, the gradual emergence of a new ruling élite from its ranks. The Carrancista forces, as the finally victorious ones, had to provide post-revolutionary Mexico with its leaders, and the early novels of the Mexican Revolution show several interesting facets of the primitive stages of the development of a new ruling-class. This is the process that Azuela described later as no more than daylight robbery on a vast scale:

It was in the times when the victorious Carrancistas had brought the country to the extreme limit of poverty. Rapacious politicians and corrupt soldiers invented a diabolical trick, which right up to our own days is a source of enrichment for shop-keepers and parasites: seizing possession of the most basic goods and of the means of transport, in order to fix the highest prices for them in the market. We all saw how pickpockets were converted overnight into owners of motor-cars and sumptuous residences and shareholders in the wealthiest concerns— and all the fruit of the poverty and hunger of the working classes. How strange it seemed to me then that, when I pointed out these vices in my books, I should be branded with a white-hot iron as a 'reactionary'. Pickpockets and murderers could find no better defence than that hollow word.[46]

Azuela himself, together with Ancona Albertos and Maqueo Castellanos, give us more detailed histories of the development of the new ruling class in individual cases, in the novels *Las tribulaciones de una familia decente*, *En el sendero de las mandrágoras* and *La ruina de la casona*.[47]

---

[46] In his series of lectures *El novelista y su ambiente*, *Obras Completas*, III, p. 1090.

[47] Another individual case is the old scoundrel don Domingo of José Asunción Reyes's *El automóvil gris*. Since this novel is so badly written and so violently hostile to Carrancismo as to be quite unreliable, it seems advisable to dispense with such evidence as it can provide about the Revolution, as far as possible; don Domingo does, as a matter of fact, share the characteristics of the Carrancistas to be examined in the following pages, though he is given very much more aptitude for devilry of every kind than any of them.

Azuela makes it quite clear where he stands; so one knows what to expect from him. His Pascual is the most contemptible of those who came to the top in the Revolution, and our consideration of him can be a brief one. He is a caricature; but caricatures depend on a reality which, to portray the more vividly and pointedly, they exaggerate. The reality itself can, with care, be pieced together from the overstatements.

Pascual is of humble family background, but well-educated and nimble-witted. He had arrived in Zacatecas with no more assets than his astuteness, his education, and the clothes he wore, but had soon ingratiated himself with the city's high society and wriggled into the favour of the richest and most influential members of the community. By always playing his cards in the most advantageous way he had finally, in 1912, crowned his successes by marrying into the rich landowning family, the Vázquez Prados, whose misfortunes in the Revolution the novel describes. When the family's decline starts in 1914 with the fall of Huerta, Pascual makes himself indispensable to them. They migrate to the safety of Mexico City where, removed from the source of all their income, and incapable, because of their aristocratic habits, of working to support themselves, they come to rely absolutely on Pascual's guile to carry them through. He procures loans for them, and they are so overcome with gratitude that they scarcely notice that he makes them sign for the receipt of metallic currency when what they are being given is paper money.

When Huerta flees and the revolutionaries take the city over, Pascual is only momentarily disconcerted and, using to the full his knowledge of how to turn any situation to personal advantage, he makes himself within a week the bosom friend of a group of young Carrancista officers, and is able to offer the Vázquez Prados their protection. When Carranza moves to Veracruz, Pascual goes with him, ready nevertheless to return immediately if Villa turns out, after all, to be the victor in the national conflict. When Carranza finally returns to Mexico City to stay, Pascual comes back too; he is by now the friend of generals and ministers and on good terms with Carranza himself. He holds a prominent government position and acquires a palatial residence in the Avenida Chapultepec, which he furnishes with fine objects taken from the homes of former Porfirista ministers like Iñigo Noriega and José Limantour (the occupation by the Carrancista generals and intellectuals of the mansions that the Porfirian rich had left empty on their flight from Mexico City into exile was a normal occurrence in these years, a symbol of the process of élite substitution that was taking place). Pascual moves into the business world and further increases his fortune by acquiring his wife's family's lands: he manages to do this without much difficulty, by threatening them both with the many I.O.U.s signed by them that he possesses, and with the divulgence to the authorities of a secret loan they had made to Huerta. He reaches one of the highest positions in the new society, becoming in 1917 a minister in Carranza's government, and moving to a still more luxurious house on the Paseo de la Reforma. It is only the moral convention that evil characters in literature must be punished that makes Azuela contrive a death in a drunken brawl for Pascual on the last page of the novel.

Although Azuela has obviously exaggerated the ruthlessness and unscrupulousness of the new ruling classes in the caricature he makes of them in the figure of Pascual—particularly as regards his callous treatment of his wife and his heartless and unnecessary abandonment to poverty of the people on whose backs he had climbed to the top—he puts him forward, by implication, as a case wholly representative of a widespread social movement of the years 1915–17. Pascual typifies, in Azuela's contemporary view, which will have to be compared with others, the process of the formation of Mexican society's new élite.

Azuela gives a brief view of another member of the new ruling class, the Carrancista officer, Pepe Covarrubias. He belongs to a rich family from the far north of Mexico, and he has joined the Revolution to protect his family's interests. He has a vicious, murderous inclination, and so he thrives on the chances for killing that the Revolution offers him. He is only a captain when Pascual becomes his friend in late 1914, but by the time of the return from Veracruz he has also caught Carranza's attention and become a prominent general, involved with Pascual in his shady business ventures. The Carrancista generals are caricatured even more boldly by Azuela in the figure of Xicoténcatl Robespierre Cebollino of *Domitilo quiere ser diputado* [pp. 169–70]. But the fullest portrayal from a hostile standpoint of this Carrancista military élite is given by Maqueo Castellanos. He was even more violently opposed to Carrancismo than was Azuela; so similar allowances have to be made when considering his account of the rise of the new ruling class through its ranks.

Melchor Tenorio is, at the beginning of the Maderista rebellion, a student in Mexico City, sharing lodgings with Federico Andrade, who is later to become a revolutionary intellectual [pp. 111–13]. He is twenty years old, and the son of the administrator of an hacienda in Pachuca; he is a bad student, and a hot-headed gambler and ladykiller. His hatred of the old order, and particularly of the Federal Army, leads him to accompany Andrade in his democratic and Maderista ventures in 1910 and 1911. Yet a much stronger force in him is the lust for power and riches, and he grasps his chance for personal advancement during the confused 'band-waggon' period of Maderismo of April, May and June 1911 [pp. 196–7]; he leaves the city for the battlefield, where he steals all he can lay his hands on, calls himself 'colonel', and invents a history of heroism for himself. On not being recognized by Madero, however, he joins the revolt of Pascual Orozco, who does recognize his rank; and the decena trágica finds him among the rebels led by Félix Díaz. But when the *coup d'état* succeeds, official rewards for his help again fail to materialize; so he joins the revolution against Huerta, and by the end of 1914 he has reached the rank of general in the Carrancista forces. When in 1915 he is well on the way to taking his place in the upper levels of the new society in formation, the novel ends and Tenorio has to be killed, for the same reasons that obliged Azuela to dispose of Pascual.

All of these depictions of successful Carrancistas are the work of authors who condemn Carrancismo and all who took part profitably in it, and they present only the negative and unworthy aspects of certain men's rise to the top of Mexican society. The only novelist with tolerance enough to depict without bitter hostility an individual instance of the rise of the hated new élite, and so to give a sympathetic and understanding analysis of the phenomenon, is Antonio Ancona Albertos. He is by no means sympathetic to Carrancismo as such, and he does not attempt to idealize it or to gloss over its many morally reprehensible facets; but one of the important merits of Ancona Albertos as a novelist and observer of society is his ability—found in none of the other early novelists of the Revolution—to recognize, beneath their surface appearances of gratuitous wickedness, genuine and understandable human motivation in the most seemingly despicable of people. Ancona's portrayal of the Carrancista Romualdo García, then, is as unique and helpful as the one he gives of the intellectual, Juan Ampudia [pp. 103–11].

Ampudia meets and becomes friendly with Romualdo García when he is imprisoned in early 1911. García is a man who has come down very sharply in the world—he is a drunkard and a pick-pocket, although he had been born into a respectable family (which has disowned him because of his criminal activities), and had received a good education. Like Azuela's Pascual, he has a very sharp and astute brain, and he serves Ampudia well as his accomplice in his various intrigues, without ever ceasing to pick whatever well-filled pockets come his way. As Ampudia's faithful companion he naturally goes with him to the Revolution in the north after Huerta's usurpation of the Presidency. When Ampudia dallies in Havana on the way, Romualdo goes on ahead. He starts his revolutionary career as a sergeant in the troops of the Villista leader, Lucio Blanco, in Tamaulipas, and advances rapidly from here. As a petty thief in peaceful times he has become accustomed to an uncertain and miserable life, and to grasping each chance of enrichment immediately and uncompromisingly; it is quite under-standable, indeed inevitable, that he should take a wholly oppor-tunistic view of existence. The Revolution is important to him, then, only in so far as he can extract wealth from it, and any other consideration is superfluous. He fights bravely, because it is one way to success; and he has never prized his life very highly anyway. Without any scruples or idealism—and yet never a repulsive character like the others of his kind we have seen—he moves from success to success, since he happens not to be killed. Ampudia himself summarizes Romualdo's attitude to the Revolution and his behaviour in it: 'Guided by his rashness and his insouciance, the lad triumphs. He runs between the bullets after honours and rank, at the risk of his life, "lousy life", in his own words, "which is not worth living except in the midst of comfort and pleasure." He's doing well. With a clear conscience and a lively imagination he spends his time playing hide-and-seek and grasping whatever comes within his reach.'[48] Romualdo García continually changes from one revolutionary force to another during battles, a fairly common and accepted practice in the Mexican Revolution; and in this way he is able to gain rapid promotion by the judicious use of lies about his rank in whichever battalion he has recently left and about his feats as a warrior. By mid-1914, Jesús Carranza (the brother of Venustiano) has found out about Romualdo's trick of

[48] *En el sendero de la mandrágoras*, II, p. 139.

gaining personal advancement through a succession of desertions, but, far from being angered by such underhand behaviour, he admires García for his bravery and cool-headed astuteness and extends his personal patronage to him. By October 1914 Romualdo has already reached the rank of brigadier and is a man of some influence, surrounded by his own coterie of flatterers seeking their niches in Carrancismo, and by wealthy property-owners attempting to remain in his favour and to distract his covetous gaze from their possessions. He is, inevitably, corrupt in his position of power, and Ancona makes his reader realize that it would be totally unreasonable to expect him to be otherwise.

The novel ends in 1915, as Romualdo orders a fine military funeral in Mexico City for his friend Ampudia, to whom he had always retained his dogged loyalty. The opportunist has triumphed and the idealist—or, more exactly, the occasional idealist—is dead. Since García has finally thrown in his lot with Villa and become a brigadier of the División del Norte, one might suppose that his subsequent emergence into the post-revolutionary élite is doubtful, though not impossible by any means; but the novelist draws no attention to this, and we are left solely with Romualdo García's success in the achievement of his goals, which is all that is relevant since it is all that the novel itself shows us.

The move towards the top of Carrancismo is reflected by three novelists in the detailed individual cases of Pascual, Covarrubias, Cebollino, Tenorio, and García.[49] As our sources present the emergence of the new élite, what is important is not that aspirants to it have determined social origins. There seems to be no question of the underdogs of the Porfirian world's taking over the reigns of power; indeed, there seems to be a tendency for this middle leadership of the Revolution (which became the post-revolutionary élite) to be made up of individual members of the middle classes who were social misfits in one way or another. Romualdo García is a particularly interesting example of this phenomenon. The really vital factors in each individual case are the driving ambition to get to the top and the smartness

---

[49] A fine study of a man's rise to the top of Carrancismo and his consolidation of his position in post-revolutionary Mexico is made in Carlos Fuentes's novel *La muerte de Artemio Cruz* (Mexico, 1962). It is not included here as a novel of the Revolution because it is mainly concerned with post-Revolutionary Mexican society: only incidental short scenes deal with the military phase of the Revolution.

and ruthlessness necessary to do so—qualities which one might, perhaps, expect to find in a middle-class outlaw. These characters —each one in the eyes of his creator representative of the whole caste—all have the will and the ability to thread their lone way through the Revolution, grasping with both hands all the chances for personal advancement that its confusion offers.

In particular, there were two main paths to success: the civilian way, taking a position in Carranza's train of personal advisers, and not having to risk one's life at all (like Pascual, as well, for what he is worth, as don Domingo of *El automóvil gris*), and the military way, reaching high rank in return—maybe—for the constant risk of death (like Covarrubias, Cebollino, Tenorio, and García). As a consequence the everlasting distrust between soldiers and civilians was felt especially keenly in the Carrancista movement, as the former despised the smooth-talking and easy-living members of *el corte de don Venustiano*, and the civilians considered themselves superior to the rough and uncultured generals. The military path to success seems to have offered more scope than the civilian one, and more of the leaders of modern Mexico appear to have travelled this route: certainly it was the Carrancista generals rather than the Carrancista courtiers who, after 1914, attracted the indignant attention of Mexico City. This might also be explained, however, by the prudent behaviour and good manners of the civilians, compared with the conspicuously rowdy demeanour of the generals, who made no bones about the fact that they considered Mexico City and all it contained to be fair prey, booty well won in the war.

Carrancismo's principal social significance is, then, the emergence through its fighting masses of those few who, in the jungle-like conditions of revolution (particularly one as confused and anarchical as the Mexican Revolution), possessed the largely animal qualities of quickness, astuteness, voracity, and (in some cases) bravery or recklessness which enabled them to fight their way up to the top of the new society—as well, of course, as the luck to survive. A modified social Darwinism would seem to have some application in revolutions. One of the most important tasks of post-revolutionary governments was to be the taming of these young, successful, disorganized, and highly dangerous Carrancista generals, avid for power, loot and a good time.

Every coin has its reverse. As the process examined in the last few pages went on—and was seen by all to be going on—with constantly increasing impetus after 1914 (in individual cases it had, of course, been in progress ever since the Revolution's start in 1910, but as a definable social phenomenon it is best dated from the first firm appearance of the party that was to win), so that vast majority of the Carrancista fighting masses who knew that there was no chance of making any great personal profit out of their sufferings could only sink ever more deeply into despondency, and acquire an intensified vision of the futility of it all. Large parts of the Carrancista soldiery were as disillusioned after 1914 as were most of the rest of the Mexicans—particularly at the very end of the Revolution when there was no more booty to be had, even on a small scale. This disenchantment is given anguished and moving expression in the only camp-fire tale of the Revolution that seems to have survived. It was collected by the painter and folklorist Gerardo Murillo (whose pseudonym, 'Dr. Atl', is more well-known) and it was told him, he says, by an illiterate indigenous fighter during the Revolution. He does not give any indications of date or place, but, to judge from its content and tone, it can only refer to Carrancismo in 1915 or after (Murillo was a prominent Carrancista intellectual). It is one of the most expressive pieces of creative literature about the Revolution, and in spite of its technical soundness and structural strength, Murillo's attribution of it to a popular source seems to be genuine. It tells its story so eloquently that no comment is necessary in addition to that which has already been offered:

The flight (*Indalecio's tale*)

We got caught up in a dog-fight. There were seven of us and we hadn't noticed them. They caught us by surprise, but we returned their fire, very hard. We resisted for a bit, and then we ran. And there we go over that endless plain . . . and such a sun that the earth was burning.

And there we go, on and on and on, on and on, and the others right behind us, and us at a wolf-trot, covered with earth, and bullets buzzing all around . . . and on and on and on we go . . .

All day along we trotted on, until, when the sun was setting, we caught sight of a wall, and we ran to hide behind it. But the others turned us out, and we moved on to get a drink of water from a well. And here comes another shower of bullets, even harder and thicker than before, like hail. And here fell one bullet and there another, and the ground began to boil just like when the first drops of rain fall after a time of drought.

The others felt like finishing us off, and they really went for us, and after a while all you could hear was crackle, crackle, crackle, crackle, like when my old woman used to fry corn for me.

The companion who was by me kept jumping from one side to another and I said to him, 'Don't try to dodge them, chum, that's the worst thing you can do.' Until he got one in the head that left him staring at the sky. And some other companions were also left staring at the sky. And those of us that were left got behind a fence, and off we go again, sir, on and on, and the others right behind, until night fell.

And by dawn we were at the foot of some mountains, where there was no water and nothing to eat.

(The Indian took the pot from the fire and, as he stirred the coffee, he said in a tone of the deepest bitterness:)

And what was it all for? All that running, all those frights, all that hunger—what for? For the colonel to have rides in his motor-car with a girl he calls his wife![50]

The enigma of the Revolution, about whose social content little can be discovered in detail, is Zapatismo [pp. 147–52]. There are only isolated and incidental references to the movement in the novels. This fact itself suggests that the popular notion of Zapatismo as a wholly peasant movement—and therefore one unable to find expression in the written word—is accurate, at least as regards the years before its decline. The early novels of the Revolution, in their neglect of Zapatismo, reflect its alienation from the rest of Mexican society.

There are three exceptions. López Ituarte's *El Atila del sur*, although it is about Zapatismo, is not an attempt to depict the movement of the south at all, but a crude piece of Huertista propaganda [pp. 150–1]. López-Portillo y Rojas's *Fuertes y débiles* is nominally concerned (in part at least) with the Zapatista movement in the southern part of Mexico State. The account it gives rings so false, however, that it only convinces the reader of the author's total ignorance of his subject matter [pp. 76, 101–2, and 251–2]. Miguel Galindo's *A través de la sierra* is the one contemporary account of Zapatismo from within, but it only deals with a few months in late 1915, when the movement was firmly set in decline. It is the story of the author's participation in a Zapatista expedition to the Isthmus of Tehuantepec to fight Carrancistas. The author is as incapable as anyone else of penetrating the surface of the Zapatista movement and discovering in meaningful

[50] 'Dr. Atl', *Las artes populares en México*, 2nd ed. (Mexico, 1922), II, pp. 129–31; reprinted in *Cuentos de todos los colores*, Vol. I (Mexico, 1946).

detail its driving force, but at least he was the only novelist in personal contact with Zapatismo.

The principal fact of social relevance that his book brings to light is that, like Villismo, Zapatismo suffered, in the later years, a large right-wing infiltration, especially into the officer classes. Galindo himself was a gentleman of the old school, frankly Porfirian in politics and poles apart in everything from the peasant soldiers [pp. 117–18]: this is why he can say so little about them, except give the description that appears in a hundred other places: 'with wide-brimmed hats, shirts, loose trousers, sandals, their chests almost covered with well-filled cartridge-belts, and rifles in their hands'.[51] And Galindo is no isolated accidental case: he mentions many other Zapatistas from the most respectable families, who have joined up as the only way to fight against impious and wicked Carrancismo and restore Mexico to the golden age of Porfirismo. Zapatismo, like Villismo, also attracted many ex-federal soldiers.[52]

About the original peasant Zapatistas Galindo's observations are limited to the appalling lack of organization and discipline among them: 'numerous soldiers wander in streets and squares with no leader to obey and no fighting orders. So they would sometimes be seen to hurl themselves at the enemy with great courage, and at others to flee headlong.'[53] Each Zapatista general considered himself his own master, responsible to nobody else, and felt very jealous of his own power and suspicious of those who might be in a position to take it from him: Galindo tells the tale of the capture of some of his fellow officers by another Zapatista general, a move instigated by such mistrust. There were great divisions between those who were supposed to be fighting under the same flag, and the expedition to Tehuantepec itself collapsed in confusion and mutual recrimination after only one minor skirmish with a few Carrancistas.

Galindo's account can be allowed but a limited importance, for it is only about the period of Zapatismo's decline, and Galindo himself, because of his rigid class position, is not a very reliable or perceptive observer. What he does tell about Zapatismo's lack of

[51] p. 20.
[52] Ramírez Plancarte, p. 284. There were many defections from the federal ranks to Zapata even before Huerta's fall (see Womack, pp. 159–90).
[53] p. 64.

organization is consonant with the entire revolutionary history of the southerners—their inconsistency and general unreliability as a fighting force, their capricious acts of terrorism; and his witness to the rightwards turn of Zapatismo in 1915 is well supported by other evidence. In the novels, for example, we have the anti-revolutionary figures of Archibaldo in *Las tribulaciones de una familia decente*, Florencio Izaguirre in *Sangre y humo* and Manolo Mandujano in *La ruina de la casona* who become Zapatista officers: the first, because he can find no job in Mexico City and has to make a living somehow, Izaguirre because he is one of Benjamín Argumedo's men [p. 159], all of whom turned Zapatista after the demobilization of the Federal Army, and Mandujano because his family in Morelos had been badly treated by the federal forces fighting Zapata in 1912 (when repression was particularly brutal) —though this case is rather special for being such an early one.

Zapatismo's social relevance within the whole context of the Mexican Revolution is limited and secondary, for it was never at any stage any more than an isolated trouble-spot, albeit a large and extremely persistent one. For the rest of the Revolution it was more of a running sore than a complementary revolutionary movement, and even when it did finally form an alliance with one of the main revolutionary forces the association was an uneasy and brittle one. There was a world of difference between the brash, extroverted northerners of Villa and the chary, circumspect Zapatistas, which caused mistrust to hold them apart from the very beginning of their alliance. The contrast was personified in the figures of the two leaders, whose clashing personalities are caught beautifully in a sequence of Abitia's documentary film *Epopeya de la Revolución*, that which records the banquet held in the Palacio Nacional on the occasion of the entry into Mexico City of the División del Norte and attended by the entire diplomatic corps. Villa and Zapata sit on either side of the president, Eulalio Gutiérrez. Villa launches immediately into his meal, with un-disguised hearty appetite; he talks continuously as he eats, and he enjoys himself thoroughly, with not the smallest concern for etiquette to hinder his enjoyment. Zapata, on the other hand, his head bowed and his hand rising nervously again and again to his mouth, throws out embarrassed and furtive glances at the other guests, acutely aware, it seems, of his ignorance of the art of hand-ling the multiplicity of cutlery laid out before him—and also, apparently, afraid of an assassination attempt. Vasconcelos, in his description of the banquet,[54] says that he had the job of requesting both caudillos to leave their many bodyguards at the door of the hall in which the banquet took place. Villa readily acceded, taking only two gunmen in with him to stand behind his chair throughout the meal. Zapata, however, took no notice of Vasconcelos and, ordering every member of his large escort to follow him in, lined them up with their backs against the long wall immediately behind the table. 'The diplomats and their wives', says Vasconcelos, 'behaved in a valiant and helpful manner, pretending not to have noticed the military array . . .'

The southerners were never able, during the Revolution itself, to overcome the regional, racial, and class barriers that separated them from other Mexicans; and the lack of information about them in the novels, itself a consequence of this isolation, does not leave a vitally important gap in the panorama the novels provide of revolutionary society. The fleeting pictures they occasionally give of a remote, frightening, anonymous, and inscrutable mass of men in sandals, loose white cotton clothes, and large hats, carrying the banner of the Virgin of Guadalupe—unfortunate though it is that they go no deeper than this—do, at least, accurately reflect the vision that all the rest of Mexican society had of them. Since the Zapatistas were unable to communicate with the rest of the Revolution and make it aware of the truth about their movement, the black legend formed about them [pp. 147–52] became, for all practical purposes, the truth, in the sense that it was what was generally believed. So the only section of the Revolution which seems to have had a well-defined, commonly shared, and genuinely revolutionary aspiration—land reform—remained, until the Revolution was well over, very much in the background of events. On the evidence of what people were actually doing and thinking during the Revolution, interpretations of it as a straightforward fight for land, like, notably, that of Tannenbaum,[55] seem to hold

---

[54] *La tormenta*, pp. 900–5.

[55] *Peace by Revolution*, especially chap. II. '[The Revolution] is essentially an agrarian movement. The other aspects of the Revolution have been incidental by-products and trimmings.' (p. 127). This sweeping statement is contradicted by Tannenbaum himself in the same book twenty pages later, with the altogether more sensible and perceptive judgement that

It is best to think of the Mexican Revolution as a movement made up of a series of waves having more or less independent beginnings and independent

little water. As far as the conscious ideas and motivations of its participants are concerned—with the sole exception of the Zapatistas, who were far from being representative of the Revolution as a whole—it appears, indeed, to have been almost everything but a fight for land redistribution.

Tannenbaum advances another point of view that has fairly wide circulation: that the Revolution was fought by, or at least for, the indigenous races of Mexico—of whom Zapata has come to be the symbolic leader—to redeem them from the Spanish legacy of oppression. This is an interpretation of the Revolution that has been circulated by the post-revolutionary artistic representations that have been made of it in novels, films and, in particular, the mural paintings of artists such as Diego Rivera. It is an integral part of the socialist myth of modern Mexico. What, then, is the history of the rise of this indigenismo during the Mexican Revolution?

A survey of the Mexican national press just before the outbreak of hostilities in 1910 reveals, in direct contradiction of the pattern of development that indigenistas and many other interpreters have laid down, the existence of a widespread concern for the fortunes of the indigenous races of Mexico. Indios were considered by all to be beneath contempt, an inferior race, incapable of any sort of advance, who should either be enslaved or eliminated, and their place in society taken by immigrants, according to conventional analyses of Porfirian society—all of which seem to follow Molina Enríquez in much of what he said.[56] And yet in the first half of November 1910, alone, we find that the first *Congreso Indianista*, composed of 'people from the most select classes of our society',[57] devotes days to discussions and studies of the Indian problem, and calls urgently for concerted attempts to regenerate the Indio by educating him and controlling the activities of his worst oppressor, the cacique; long reports of the Congress's activities, written in sympathetic and approving terms, appear in prominent

objectives. At times these movements fused together for a while, and then separated again. Some of the rebellions were initiated for one purpose and then, for political reasons, assumed a direction not inherent in them in the beginning. So rapid and varied have been the cross currents that have come to the surface in the Revolution that it is difficult to discover any given direction in the movement as a whole [p. 147].

[56] Cumberland, p. 6; S. R. Ross, pp. 29–31; Tannenbaum, pp. 31–3.
[57] *El Tiempo*, 3 Nov. 1910.

places on the pages of all the national newspapers; even *El Imparcial*, the semi-official voice of the government, prints several editorials devoted to strong and enlightened attacks on the belief that Indios are racially inferior;[58] on 12 November the same newspaper calls in an editorial for real Mexican art, inspired not in European styles but in pre-conquest themes, and on the 14th it publishes a poem, *Espera a Quetzalcoatl* by one Prisciliano Maldonado, lamenting that the Indios should be a downtrodden race and calling vigorously for their resurgence; and *El País* ('Catholic daily') criticizes the Congress for not being precise or radical enough in its recommendations, in an outspoken editorial on 11 November. Although this impressive indigenista sentiment had its limits, and, in particular, not many advocated economic or legislative reforms to revindicate the Indios as *El País*'s leader-writer did—*El Imparcial* printed a curt dismissal of any suggestion of 'fantastical agrarian laws for protecting the Indian's property and labour'[59]—it is still what one is led to expect only from the men who fought the Porfirian ruling classes, not from the Porfirian ruling classes themselves before the Revolution even started. And yet it was the government of Porfirio Díaz, not any revolutionary regime, that erected (in 1887) Mexico City's bulky monument to the hero of Aztec resistance to the Spanish conquerors, Cuauhtémoc—and it never put up any monument to Hernán Cortés.

The indigenista interpretation of the Revolution seems to be on shaky ground from the start, for there is proof that indigenismo was not initiated by the Revolution at all, but that it existed in a fairly lively form before it began. Maybe, however, it was strengthened and intensified by the social upheaval that started in 1910? But it has already been seen above that Zapatismo—said to be the indigenous movement *par excellence*—was never more than

---

[58] According to Martín Luis Guzmán, the Mexican ruling classes had recently become aware of the frightening ignorance and brutishness of the Indios, and decided that this was the only disconcerting anomaly that marred the perfection of Porfirian Mexico; so they were coming to the conclusion that the Indio would have to be educated in order that absolute perfection could be achieved (*La querella de México*, Madrid, 1915, p. 46). Martin T. Stabb, however, has shown that considerable indigenista feeling can be found in creative writers, essayists, educators and social philosophers throughout the second half of the nineteenth century ('Indigenism and Racism in Mexican Thought: 1857–1911', *Journal of Inter-American Studies*, I, 4 (1959), pp. 405–23).

[59] 20 Nov. 1910.

a parochial uprising which attracted no sympathy from other Mexicans until after 1920. All this hardly suggests a mass crusade of redemption for the sons of Moctezuma.

There were even more exclusive indigenous forces in other sectors of the Revolution, and most notably the Yaqui tribe, from Sonora in the north of Mexico. The Yaquis had always been keen and warlike defenders of their fertile lands, and had been particularly harshly oppressed under Porfirio Díaz; and when Madero's revolt broke out, they soon rose up, fighting at first with bows and arrows. It was later, however, that they came to national prominence as they were incorporated into the command of the Carrancista general, Obregón, and moved through the republic to Mexico City with his Army Corps of the North-west; and it is as Carrancistas that they appear in the novels. And again, it is as a strange, utterly foreign species of beings, just like the Zapatistas, that they are described. In the revolutionary camps they kept, and were left, very much to themselves:

> The courtyard was filled with different sounds of people chatting and people enjoying themselves. In a group of Yaquis a tabor beat out the cadences of their indigenous dances. They were corpulent, sallow-complexioned men, with enormously long legs; they spoke their own language and they came together to enjoy themselves alone. The tabor exalts them to either fury or joy, and it cannot be missing from either battles or fiestas: so the tabor sounded. [60]

And on their entry into Mexico City with the Constitutionalist forces on 15 August 1914, the inhabitants reacted with even more timorous apprehension than they did when faced with the Zapatistas—with some justification, according to the description of the scene made by Francisco Ramírez Plancarte: [61]

> After the cavalry, which was in the vanguard of the column, came the Yaqui Indians, who made up the infantry; they were tall and corpulent, with bronzed skins and emphatic features; they wore campaign hats held on with chin-straps, fairly tight-fitting ankle-length trousers, and sandals with only one thong which, passing between the big toe and the next, went over to the heel and finished up wound round the ankle; tied round their waists were three or four belts full of Winchester ammunition. They moved forward in long strides emitting inarticulate bestial shrieks whenever they heard the harsh rolling of their small tribal war drums.

[60] Ugarte, p. 118.   [61] pp. 63–4.

'The Yaquis! The Yaquis!' exclaimed the crowds, drawing back nervously in instinctive fear. Their reputation of bravery and terrible bloodthirstiness in battle, which had preceded them, had been known for a long time before they arrived in the city. Many anecdotes were told about them and their daring, some of them truly incredible; like one about how once when they were in a fever of fury, having put paid to the enemy and mercilessly finished off all the wounded, in their war-like zeal to continue fighting and not having anyone to fight against, they discharged their wrath against each other, until they were all either destroyed or exhausted. Only in the midst of the whistling of showers of bullets, it was said, when the rattle of the dying, the moans of the wounded and the awe-inspiring and fearful shrieks of the combatants are heard, and when danger menaces them and death is all around, do they feel a sweet sense of enjoyment and a happy urge to laugh.

But what everybody affirmed unequivocally was that the Yaquis were the backbone of the Constitutionalist Army: that is why, it was added, General Alvaro Obregón is invincible.

The Yaquis were viewed as demons let loose from hell rather than fellow-countrymen, and indeed the Villista bureaucrats of *Las moscas* call them 'estos yaquis del infierno'.[62] When, in *Las tribulaciones de una familia decente*, César, the effeminate youngest member of the aristocratic family whose downfall Azuela's novel traces, is caught one night in Mexico City by some Yaquis who mistake him for a Villista, his description of the incident has the atmosphere of an encounter with Martian monsters in a science-fiction tale:

Suddenly a heavy hand came down on my shoulder.
'Is that you, Archibaldo?' I groaned.
The reply came in a language I could not understand; then I was grasped in a strong grip and dragged, almost, to some unknown place....
An intense cold penetrated my bones. I shuddered, moaned weakly and opened my eyes. How horrible! Enormous men, with faces like Aztec idols, had me up to my neck in a trough of icy water.
'God! Where am I?' ...
I could not understand the babbling of these monsters from hell. They were talking all around me and showing me their perfectly white teeth in horrible grins.[63]

The occasional reference in the novels to the Yaquis tends to confirm, then, the conclusion that might be reached after examining the treatment given in novels to the Indios of the south: that

[62] p. 871.   [63] p. 454.

the indigenous movements in the Mexican Revolution were banished to social isolation, and that whatever the overall aims and aspirations of the Revolution, indigenismo was far from being one of them.

What the novels and other sources thus suggest in their description and treatment of the indigenous movements, of the Indios *en masse*, is confirmed by an examination of the novelists' descriptive technique in the presentation of individual Indio characters. It is reasonable to assume that a society which is seriously concerned about the aboriginal groups within it will produce novelists who take care to delineate in detail at least their customs and appearance. In the early novels of the Mexican Revolution, however, there are only a comparatively small number of characters identified as Indios; it has already been observed that the novelists do not concern themselves primarily with the lower classes, to which most Indios belonged. Azuela, who does so more than most, confines himself mainly to a few favourite formulae in his description of Indios. He does little more, in fact, than use certain bald clichés simply to indicate that a given character is an Indio. His favourite expressions are 'pure-blooded native', 'Aztec idol', and 'of Cuauhtémoc's race'.[64] His language here is purely literary, remote, and abstract, and he conveys no sense of any actual contact with living people of the twentieth century: the indigenous races are envisaged as fossilized remains of pre-colonial times, not as human beings made of bones, flesh, and blood.

Los de abajo attempts some closer approximation to Indios as men with a present-day life of their own. In it Azuela describes an indigenous settlement, and makes some brief reference to the dress and customs of the inhabitants, and of the Indio revolutionaries who billet themselves there. Demetrio Macías himself is seen as the novel opens eating in the Indian style: 'he was eating in a corner, squatting on his haunches, with an earthenware dish in his right hand and three rolled-up tortillas in the other',[65] and is dressed in 'rough cotton shirt and trousers, a wide-brimmed palm-leaf hat and sandals'.[66] The village where he and his band stay is composed of 'a few hovels of straw, scattered along the bank of the

---

[64] See *Los de abajo*, pp. 352, 359, 368, 381 and 408; *Las moscas*, pp. 875, 888 and 906; *Los caciques*, p. 814; and *Las tribulaciones de una familia decente*, p. 454 [p. 225].

[65] p. 320.   [66] p. 320.

river, among small seed-beds sprouting corn and beans',[67] and appears to be inhabited only by women (the men having been forcibly recruited into Huerta's army [pp. 294–6]), whose only special trait of character that Azuela draws any attention to is their superstition: they believe, among other things, in the healing qualities of a split pigeon applied to a wound to the accompaniment of prayers. There is little more than this: a few minor touches of superficial depiction of customs are all that Azuela's attempt to characterize his Indios amounts to. There is no genuine penetration into the Indio's world, no intuition of his particular problems and psychology *qua* Indio, that could compare with the interest in indigenous matters reflected in many novels of the 1930s such as López y Fuentes's *Tierra* or *El indio*, for example.

The only slightly sustained description of Indio physiognomy that is to be found in Azuela's novels appears in the passage from *Las tribulaciones de una familia decente* referred to above, which is very far from being indigenista in tone: 'I noticed how much they all looked alike: the same dark olive colour, the same high cheekbones, with skin stretched taut over them, the same inexpressiveness in their small, browless eyes and in their thin, beardless lips, the same long, straight, shining hair. But, since they moved, they were not idols: what were they, then? Which were men and which were women?'[68]

Most of the other novelists who wrote before 1925 about the Revolution are even less interested in Indios and less specific in the portrayal of them. López Ituarte draws no attention at all to the fact that the Zapatistas, with whom his *El atila del sur* is concerned, are Indios: they are just bandits and murderers, and their racial derivation is irrelevant. The same author's *Satanás* has an Indio as the hero, but he is just labelled as such and there is nothing specially indigenous about him or his actions. The same is true about Eduardo Luquín's shoddy, sentimental novel, *El indio*. The revolutionary movement which has an important part to play in López-Portillo y Rojas's *Fuertes y débiles* is, one supposes from its geographical location, a branch of Zapatismo. No mention at all is made in this novel, however, of any particularly Indian features or, indeed, of Zapata. When the hero of Lepino's *Sangre y humo* joins the Zapatistas and the novel follows his exploits closely, the ethnic characteristics of his comrades in arms are similarly denied any

[67] p. 329.   [68] p. 455.

importance. And, in general, the most the novelists can do is to show a vague awareness that there are such things as Indios. Only Quevedo y Zubieta, López-Portillo y Rojas and Ugarte venture on isolated short pieces of gentle description of customs which, like Azuela's, go no deeper than the surface.

Among all the novels of the Mexican Revolution written before 1925, real sustained interest in the native population of Mexico is found only in two exceptional cases. One is the novel which has already been seen to have other outstanding features, *En el sendero de las mandrágoras*. It appears to reflect a wave of much more advanced Indianist feeling in Yucatán during the Revolution than in the rest of Mexico.[69] The novel's hero, Juan Ampudia, as a Maderista candidate for a deputyship, addresses a political meeting in Mérida, the capital of Yucatán, and the description of the audience's reaction to his speech is the only example in these novels of a genuine attempt to penetrate the world of the Indio and imagine things from his point of view:

Religious attentiveness and sincere enthusiasm in the audience. The Indians, particularly, screwed up their faces in their visible desire to understand, to benefit from what they were being taught and to discover the advantages of the Revolution. They had never believed white men's promises, but now they seemed inclined to pay attention to them. And Ampudia glimpsed the awakening of the race, and put vigorous colouring into his speeches when he referred to it.[70]

And although Ampudia makes this particular speech in a mood of cynicism, without meaning a word of it, he later becomes seriously preoccupied with the problem of the regeneration of the Indios.

The other exception is perhaps less noteworthy and of less relevance to this study, as it was published in 1923 when the govern-

---

[69] There are several factors which could have contributed to this. The Yucatán peninsula is separated from the rest of Mexico by forests, and it is culturally quite separate too. Yucatán was, before the conquest, the centre of the advanced Maya civilization, and the Indian element has always, since, been basic in its cultural complex. Two important socialists figure prominently in its revolutionary history: Felipe Carrillo Puerto (1872–1924), who founded the Socialist Party of the South-East of Mexico during the Revolution, and Salvador Alvarado (1879–1924), a Carrancista general from Sinaloa, and governor of the state from 1915 to 1917, when he promulgated many far-reaching socialist decrees (among them the liberation of hacienda workers from their peonage), which, if they changed very little in practice, gave radical ideas an effective airing in Yucatán.

[70] II, pp. 18–19.

ment-inspired Indigenista campaign had already started;[71] so it is a document not of the Revolution proper (which it partially deals with), but of the early years of post-revolutionary Mexico. It is just as the first Mexican attempt to write an indigenista novel, and consequently as a precursor of the later indigenista movement in Mexican literature, that Juan de Dios Bojórquez's *Yórem Tamegua* (Guatemala, 1923) can be briefly mentioned. It is the story of an imaginary Yaqui settlement in Navojoa, Sonora, and its development from pre-revolutionary days—as typified by a few scenes set in 1895—through the Revolution itself—1915—and into an imaginary future—1935. The Indios are seen in an excessively idealized and romanticized way, and the attempt that is made to depict their world is a failure. There is little in feeling or tone—as opposed to external trappings and local colour—of Yaqui life as portrayed here to distinguish it from the rural round in any other part of Mexico, or, in fact, of the world. The nineteenth-century Mexican literary tradition of dependence on European models is a strong influence on this novel, so that—although the author probably had close experience of what he was describing, as he was himself from Sonora—the *costumbrista* depiction of healthy, noble, hard-working country lads going brightly about their business often seems closer to the South of England, as it has sometimes been seen through romantic eyes, than to Sonora. The Yaquis, as they are shown here, certainly have none of the fierce and warlike qualities that gave so much fright to the inhabitants of Mexico City. One of Bojórquez's principal reasons for writing the novel appears, in fact, to have been to give the lie to the Yaquis' bad reputation, and to show them to be normal, peaceful people: he explicitly states at one point in his narrative that Yaquis are widely considered to be bloodthirsty savages not as a consequence of their observed deeds but because of the intensive propaganda campaign that was waged against them in the press by the enemies of Carrancismo. Bojórquez has deprived his account, however, of all conviction, by taking it too far towards the other extreme in his efforts to dispel the Yaquis' black legend. The novel, written by a faithful Carrancista, idealizes the Revolution and its achievements

---

[71] This indigenismo is also reflected in 'Dr. Atl's' long and detailed work in praise of *Las artes populares en México*, which was commissioned by the Mexican government (Mexico, 1921); and in the exhibition of indigenous art held in 1921 (opened on 19 Sept. by President Obregón) to celebrate the centenary of the consummation of independence.

QM

enormously; it makes it appear that most of Mexico's problems had already been solved by 1915, and it ends in a radiant utopian vision of a communist future in which the Indian settlement has been converted into a co-operative, where evils like Roman Catholicism and alcohol have long been banned, and where nothing is amiss. In its optimism, as well as its Indianism, it is unique among the early novels of the Revolution.

As regards indigenista content, then, there is little in all the early novels which goes even so far to express interest in and concern for the special problems of the Indio as the newspaper articles of November 1910. There is certainly nothing that can compare, for detailed and sustained literary attempts to come to grips with the realities of Indio life and psychology, either with the novels of the Mexican indigenista movement of the 1930s or with the English works that anticipated them, D. H. Lawrence's *Mornings in Mexico* (1927) and *The Plumed Serpent* (1926). Illustrative passages from them will serve to throw into relief the inadequacy of the early Mexican novels' treatment of Indios.

Mornings in Mexico, a series of short notes and sketches of Indian life in Oaxaca and New Mexico, shows at times a penetration into the Indio consciousness that few indigenistas have been able to emulate. Lawrence's theme is the gulf, which can never, in his opinion, be bridged, between the white man and the Indio; and he approaches it from the latter's standpoint. 'To them a white man or woman is a sort of phenomenon, just as a monkey is a sort of phenomenon; something to watch, and wonder at, and laugh at, but not to be taken on one's own plane.'[72] He shows how, for the Indio, the white man's habits and whole way of life are foreign and incomprehensible—his insistence on the exact measurement of time and distance, his notions of personal property and his attitude to death, his working habits and disciplines—so that the Indio must always remain on the outside of industrial society, only collaborating (without ever understanding) because it is the white man who runs society. Lawrence's conclusion, dogmatically pessimistic, is invalid because it depends on the false postulate that there are racial characteristics in man that can never change or be changed; but on the way to reaching it he has revealed much more about the Mexican Indian's psychology than any previous author. He also reveals that in Oaxaca, at least—the notes

[72] Harmondsworth, 1967, p. 33.

were written in 1924—the Revolution had not changed the Indio's position in society in any appreciable way.

In *The Plumed Serpent* Lawrence puts most of these ideas and observations into novel form, by imagining a mysterious revolutionary movement to regenerate the Mexican Indians by ousting the Christian religion imposed on them by their Spanish conquerors and bringing back in its place the old Aztec deities, Itzpapalotl (the god of motherhood), Huitzilopochtli (the god of war) and Quetzalcoatl (the god of creation). The movement's hymns, composed by its leader—a projection into the novel of Lawrence himself—give poetic expression to Lawrence's visualization of the Indio's attitude to the white man's civilization. The fourth one, entitled *What Quetzalcoatl Saw in Mexico*, starts:

> *Who are these strange faces in Mexico?*
> *Palefaces, yellowfaces, blackfaces? These are no Mexicans!*
> *Where do they come from, and why?*
>
> Lord of the Two Ways, these are the foreigners.
> They come out of nowhere.
> Sometimes they come to tell us things,
> Mostly they are the greedy ones.
>
> *What then do they want?*
>
> They want gold, they want silver from the mountains,
> And oil, much oil, from the coast.
> They take sugar from the tall tubes of the cane,
> Wheat from the high lands, and maize;
> Coffee from the bushes in the hot lands, even the juicy rubber.
> They put up tall chimneys that smoke,
> And in the biggest houses they keep their machines, that talk
> And work iron elbows up and down,
> And hold myriad threads from their claws! . . .[73]

Lawrence's willingness to try to envisage the Indio's world from within—the consequence of his belief in the corruptness of life in an industrial community, and in the rightness of the elemental, natural life—sets perhaps excessively exacting standards for judging the Mexican novelists' treatment of Indian characters in those works that appeared before 1930, when the indigenista movement first started to make a decisive impact on Mexican literature. But the early novelists of the Revolution are incapable even of writing any passages of sustained and sympathetic description of Indios

[73] *The Plumed Serpent* (Harmondsworth, 1961), p. 269.

from a simple external viewpoint that can withstand comparison with the following, which is a typical, if early, specimen of the newly committed approach to the Indian that became normal in Mexican prose fiction after 1930. It is taken from a novel of the Revolution which is not chiefly concerned with Indios, and describes the quiet and resigned death of a guide, driven by a revolutionary soldier to complete exhaustion:

A man sitting on the ground. Completely alone. Neither seeking nor getting brotherly sympathy from anyone. His head hangs over his chest. His hat covers his eyes, as if the bright light of the bonfire bothered him. His rough cotton clothing makes him look like a rag thrown on the floor. Occasionally he coughs. He is an Indio.

In paternal tones, the leader speaks to the Indio. He tells him to come up to the bonfire to have some coffee and to warm his tortillas. They have to speak to him a second time before he realizes that it is him they are talking to. He had so few hopes that they would do so. The Indio thanks the leader in his own language. He picks up his sandals, placed by his side. He gets up slowly. As he comes to the bonfire he shows signs of not being able to walk or of walking with great difficulty. He limps. Nevertheless, his face bears an impassive look. . . .

The Indio, now seated by the bonfire, makes no attempt to help himself to coffee or to warm his tortillas. He must have come up to the bonfire simply out of obedience. His jet-black eyes glint as they reflect the nearest flames. His protruding cheekbones make him look very thin. When he coughs, his teeth can be admired, as perfect as those of a wild animal.[74]

This degree of real sympathy and will to understand the Indian races is quite beyond any of the Mexican novelists who wrote during the Revolution or shortly after it, and also, we must assume, beyond Mexican revolutionary society as a whole.

The Indians of Mexico, far from being regenerated during the Revolution, continued to occupy their lowly and despised place throughout it. There appears not even to have been anyone sufficiently troubled about the fact to draw attention to it in novels or any other sort of literature, in the way that López y Fuentes, for example, did later in the passage just quoted. The Indio was still, for most people, not really fully a human being. This applied particularly to those Indians who remained submissive, fatalistic, and unrebellious during the Revolution. It is, perhaps, for this

[74] Gregorio López y Fuentes, *Campamento* (Madrid, 1931), pp. 79–81.

very reason that attention is so rarely drawn by the novelists to the racial peculiarities of Indian revolutionaries, with the exception of the Yaquis; it might well have been felt that those Indios who showed enough spirit to rebel had, by doing so, somehow stopped being Indios. Many Mexicans held the opinion expressed in Martín Luis Guzmán's contemporary essay on the Revolution, *La querella de México*: 'the Indio can only have one function, that of the faithful dog who blindly follows his master's wishes',[75] an exact description of the role in which Indios appear in Alberto A. Rodríguez's novel of the invasion of Veracruz, *Don Pascual*—faithful mindless servants who know their place, who obey every whim of their masters without question, and whom all address with the pronoun of familiarity, *tú*, thus ascribing to them the same status as children and domestic animals.[76] Rodríguez chronicles this, of course, as the eternal way of things, which he does not think for a moment to question. Rather than the racial optimism implied in indigenismo it is racial pessimism, the legacy of nineteenth-century Latin-American thought, that regularly appears in the novels: Azuela talks about the Mexicans as a race fated always to be inferior, through the mouth of Solís in *Los de abajo*;[77] and several other novelists, like Lepino and Galindo, insist on the 'genetic' inclination of the Mexican race to war and barbarity [p. 118] or, like Maqueo Castellanos, on the general ethnic backwardness of the Indio.[78] The general antipathy with which Victoriano Huerta was faced probably had much to do with such racial prejudice against Indios, as well as with his personal and political ineptitude [p. 172n.].

In the Mexican Revolution itself, the indigenismo which already

---

[75] p. 25.
[76] Perfectly normal practice. In *Los de abajo* Demetrio and men, although they themselves are Indios, arrogate to themselves the white man's privilege of addressing submissive Indios with the *tú* form (pp. 353–4). An hacendado always addressed his peons as *tú*; they had to reply with the archaic pronoun of extreme respect, *su mercé* (see, for example, López-Portillo y Rojas, *Fuertes y débiles*).
[77] p. 362.
[78] The positivist essayist Francisco Bulnes (1847–1924) was probably the man most responsible for spreading this idea in Mexico during the Porfirian period. In particular he developed, in his book *Las grandes mentiras de nuestra historia*, the theory, which became extremely fashionable, of the three racial categories: the superior (white) races whose diet is based on wheat, the secondary (brown) races whose diet is based on maize, and the inferior (yellow) races whose diet is based on rice.

existed before it seems rather to have diminished and receded than to have grown. People who, in 1910, had made high-sounding speeches in general terms about the need to regenerate the Indio were probably frightened away from such views when it became a possibility that the Indio himself might take his regeneration into his own hands and achieve it in a more direct and effective way than that envisaged by the members of the Congreso Indianista: that this was not, in fact, going to happen would not have been apparent to the Mexicans in 1912, for example, as they read in their newspapers about the Zapatistas' marauding activities, or in 1914, as they quaked at the tones of the triumphant Yaquis' drums and war-cries.

Indigenismo was restricted in the Revolution itself to the Zapatista intellectuals who, at the Convention of Aguascalientes, stated unequivocally that they considered the movement's prime aim to be the regeneration of the Indio. Their wishful indigenista thinking had, at best, a cool reception from the Convention, and at times, a violently hostile one. At no time did it echo their sentiments (until the Zapatistas themselves became the dominant faction in the Convention in 1915), and they were patently preaching in a wilderness.[79] It is only from these intellectual spokesmen that we find any sort of indigenismo during the Revolution, and there are strong indications that even the southern revolutionaries did not attach much weight or importance to their words: it is fairly certain that the Zapatista fighting masses themselves did not think of their movement as an indigenista one.[80]

Indigenismo appears as a widely accepted social creed in Mexico only after the Revolution, as part of the redemption and consecration of Zapata and Zapatismo [pp. 151–2]. Its development may have been made possible by the Revolution, but to construe this Revolution as one fought consciously or even unconsciously on behalf of Mexico's aboriginal population is to misinterpret it. Even the indigenismo of the last forty-five years has been, in the tradition of the Congreso Indianista held in Mexico City in 1910 by the most

[79] For eye-witness accounts of these lively scenes—during which a leading Zapatista intellectual, Antonio Díaz-Soto y Gama, came very near to being shot as a result of a particularly fiery indigenista speech—see Ramírez Plancarte, pp. 144–61; Silva Herzog, II, pp. 131–2; Vasconcelos, *La tormenta*, pp. 872–3; and Guzmán, *El águila y la serpiente*, pp. 310–25.

[80] See Womack, pp. 70–1 and 302. Zapata himself knew no Náhuatl (the Indian language of the region) at all. Only one of the twenty-six Zapatista representatives at the Convention was a native of Morelos state (Womack, p. 216).

select members of Porfirian society, very much more formal and theoretical than real and effective, more a question of fine words than of genuine remedies. The Mexican Indios of today, though certainly better off than many of their brothers in other Latin-American countries, are still far from bearing the proud look of a redeemed race.

Of the various theses which seek to explain the Mexican Revolution as a co-ordinated mass movement, fired by a single ideal or aspiration, none seems to emerge intact from a study of the various movements and of their social content. The idea that it was a socialist revolution, of the enslaved workers rising and crushing their oppressors, as put forward afterwards by Mexican governments, mural paintings, and films, is evidently false. Socialist ideas —of any sort—did not achieve wide popular circulation before 1917 in Mexico, in spite of the labours of the *Casa del Obrero Mundial*.[81] There had not been sufficient preparation of the way before the Revolution; and the rural workers were too disunited, and the industrial workers too few in number, for any sort of socialist doctrine to be able to make much headway during the Revolution among the fighting masses. There is scarcely a mention of socialism in the novels under examination, and members of the industrial proletariat do not make more than one or two brief and incidental appearances in the whole body of novels written before 1925 about the Mexican Revolution.[82] Socialism, however

[81] Founded in July 1912 as a general Trade Union and a loudspeaker for radical and revolutionary thought. Well-known Mexican orators spoke there to the workers of the capital. The *Casa* had no fixed ideology, and the ideas of Kropotkin, Bakunin, Marx, and Engels were propagated there—highly simplified for popular consumption—together with more moderate doctrines. It gave its support to Carrancismo and was, in turn, briefly favoured by the Constitutionalist authorities in 1914 and 1915, when its influence on the population of the capital became considerable; but it could never reach further than Mexico City, and the six Red Battalions that were sent to fight for Obregón and other Carrancista generals in February 1915 were but so many drops in the ocean of the fighting masses as a whole. (Silva Herzog has more to say about the *Casa* than most historians of the Revolution—I, pp. 225–6; II, pp. 11, 40–6, 80, 127–8, 142–4, 174–80, 198. See also Ramírez Plancarte, pp. 53, 68, 328–30, 349, 355–62, 369, 371–2, 562–3.)

[82] Juan A. Mateos, somewhat surprisingly, introduces a worker from Río Blanco into his novel [pp. 142–5], and Ugarte mentions some foundry workers from Cananea [p. 118]. The prize-winning novel of Gustavo Ortiz Hernán, *Chimeneas* (1937), is concerned with the industrial working classes in the Revolution.

important its influence may have been on the thought of, for example, the creators of the Constitution of 1917, was not widely divulged among the fighting masses, and was not, therefore, socially relevant until after 1917.

Other common interpretations of the Revolution are scarcely more acceptable. Both racial ones seem to be as mistaken as racial interpretations of history usually are: there is no evidence that there was anything more markedly 'mestizo' about the fighting masses than about the Mexican populace as a whole, and no one conceived of the Revolution as a movement to regenerate Indios except some of the spokesmen for the Zapatistas—and whether they really represented the opinions of the southern revolutionaries is open to grave doubt. The agrarian interpretation can obviously claim much more serious attention—there certainly was a grave land-distribution problem in Mexico on the outbreak of revolution, and many men joined the fighting masses for individual reasons springing from it—but it is, nevertheless, by no means the whole story. The regional interpretation also contains some truth, but it is not fundamental—the Revolution was not, primarily, a civil war between the northern and central states of Mexico. It was simply that for various incidental reasons, in particular the frontier with the United States of America, the northern states were the best starting place for a full-scale revolutionary movement, and, as a logical consequence of this, many of the revolutionaries were northerners.

As far as the conscious motivations, aims and hopes of the Mexican fighting masses are concerned, it appears that the Revolution totally lacked any sort of common concerted goal at all. It was more the negative force of a general undefined ill-ease than the positive one of a corporate wish that made the wheels of revolution turn. And they turned very slowly at first. There was no spontaneous mass uprising of the Mexican people to protest against an intolerable iniquity or to reconquer some human right which had been withheld from them. The Revolution started as a flickering and puny candle-flame, which any moderately efficient counter-action could have snuffed out without much difficulty, and it only achieved the significant proportions of a social conflagration a full three years after it had started. And it could be argued that the events and conditions of those three years would inevitably have set a revolution in motion almost anywhere, however unpromising the social situation. For the seeds of revolt are present in the most skilfully organized societies: even in those whose stability is based on a degree of justice and equality most people still have some serious grievances which could perhaps, in certain conditions, be magnified in their minds and become adequate reasons for rebellion; and in those, like that of Porfirian Mexico, whose stability is based on thoroughgoing and efficient repression, the effects on society—both unsettling and stimulating—of a period such as that which started with Madero's revolt and ended with his murder are enough, in the end, to encourage the most securely shackled peasant to do what he had never previously dreamt of doing and throw off his chains. Men rose up, when the pressures upon them to do so became impossible to resist, for a multiplicity of more or less petty individual reasons, mostly personal grievances springing directly or indirectly from one or more of the basic injustices and social ills of the Porfirian world; and they continued to fight more because fighting had become a habit—as well as, for some, an opportunity to make a fortune—than for any other motive.[83] Each revolutionary seems to have been fighting his own private war to avenge the wrongs committed against him, and if possible, to get rich; the individuals never appear to have been brought together under the banner of an effective idealism professed in common by many.[84]

The fighting masses, because of their lack of awareness and

[83] In all of this Zapatismo is an important exception. Womack makes it clear both that the southern revolution was a full-scale mass movement from the beginning, in 1911, and that it was fired throughout by a common goal, land redistribution. The comparison between Womack's description of the ferment in Morelos in 1911 and what we know of the state of the rest of Mexico at that time shows, by contrast, just how unrevolutionary the situation in the country as a whole was when Madero rebelled.

[84] The anarchical individualism of the fighting masses in the Mexican Revolution is reflected in the marching songs which were adopted by them: songs which expressed not revolutionary fervour or hopes for a glorious future, but instead man's purely personal and subjective aspirations of romantic sexual bliss. The revolutionaries marched along singing sad love songs, which do not even mention the Revolution, like *La Adelita, La Juanita, La Julia, La Valentina, La norteña, El abandonado*, and *El desterrado* (most of which date from the Porfirian period and are still popular in Mexico); the only exception of importance was the burlesque *La cucaracha* [pp. 33–4, 155–6, 166, 176, and 307–9] which is as far as the others from expressing progressive sentiments. Against their competition, more appropriately revolutionary songs like the *Himno a Madero* [p. 146] or the Spanish translation of the *Internationale*, and other socialist songs of the Red Battalions (recorded by Ramírez Plancarte, pp. 356–62), could make no impact at all.

cohesion, were unable to secure adequate protection for their group interests. They did not even really know what these interests were. Consequently, although peasants formed by far the greatest part of the fighting masses, the leadership of the Revolution was never for a moment in peasant hands and did not, in the end, primarily serve peasant interests. Whatever the ultimate achievement of the Revolution, it was not the ennoblement of the peasant, the relief of working-class misery, the establishment of democracy or justice, or the suppression of corruption. It could be argued that the Revolution gave birth to nothing but xenophobia; or that it pushed Mexico rapidly into the modern world [pp. 38–9].[85] Whichever is true, it can be safely assumed that not a single member of the fighting masses had the smallest suspicion that anything like this was the real underlying meaning of the Revolution. The cliché 'cannon fodder' is an exact and correct descriptive term for the soldiery of the Mexican Revolution: the fighting masses in the Revolution, if they are viewed not in the light of the careers of individuals but as a class of revolutionary society, were no more than pawns on a chess board, with no will of their own, to be sacrificed freely for the realization of a goal of which not even the chess-masters themselves seem to have been cognizant.

The Mexican Revolution was, then, an unconscious revolution, in which hardly any one of the participants was aware of what was really happening, of what had caused the war in the first place or of what sort of changes it was likely to bring about in Mexican society. The shortcomings of the fighting masses are all attributable to the intellectuals' failure to organize them. The revolutionary soldiery seems to have shown no lack of innate qualities like bravery, toughness, and general fighting ability. The discipline and general coherence that were missing from the movement could not have come from the peasants themselves, and could only have been imposed from without—by the intellectuals, who were not equipped for this task. The Mexican Revolution was consequently an inefficient revolution: it consumed too much energy in proportion to the work it did.

If the Revolution was so inefficient, though, how was it that it

---

[85] It must again be stressed that these comments apply to the Revolution as a whole, within which Zapatismo was an exceptional and separate movement. In Morelos the conscious aims of the peasant revolutionaries were achieved to a large extent, once Obregón, who was highly sympathetic to them, became President in 1920 (see Womack, pp. 331ff.).

succeeded in overthrowing the old order at all? If its ultimate triumph cannot be explained positively, in terms of the excellence of the revolutionary movement as such, then the only explanation possible is a negative one, in terms of the incompetence of the anti-revolutionaries. Let us now examine the latter.

7

ANTI-REVOLUTIONARIES

IT is proposed in this chapter to examine those social groups which were generally hostile to the Revolution, whether they made any direct contribution to the anti-revolutionary effort or not. They represent the old order of things, the Porfirian hierarchy which the revolutionaries sought to destroy. The importance of the forces working against a revolution in determining its course and its ultimate success or failure has not always been stressed as strongly as it should be.[1] The positive factors which make a revolution possible (widespread discontent, inspiring leaders, able politically-minded subversive intellectuals) cannot function if they are not complemented by some serious degree of élite inefficiency or incompetence. In the Mexican Revolution, as has been argued above, the positive factors were altogether much weaker than is to be expected in such a movement; so the negative factors consequently acquire even greater importance.

Each one of the groups which constituted the anti-revolutionary sector in Mexican society suffered as a group during the Revolution, and some were dissolved altogether, although many individual members of them were able to find a satisfactory place for themselves in post-revolutionary society. It is not, however, with special individual cases that we are concerned, but with such typical features of each group seen as a whole that we can discern in the novels and other sources. The anti-revolutionaries, those who considered themselves well-off in the Porfirian system and who felt that they had more to lose than to gain by its destruction, can conveniently be divided into six groups: the rural ruling classes, the urban ruling classes, foreigners, the Church, the Army, and the lower-middle classes. Let us examine these groups one by one to discover what the novelists of the Revolution can tell us about their characteristics and their decline.

[1] See Stone, p. 167; and Eckstein, especially pp. 145–58.

(a) The Rural Élite: Hacendados, Caciques, Rurales

Under Porfirio Díaz, power in the countryside was in the hands of the large landowners (*hacendados*) and their allies the rural political leaders (*jefes políticos*) and the rural police force (*rurales*). A class of large landowners had been in existence since the conquest, when the conquistadores, once having pacified Mexico, settled on large estates. The local Indios were placed under their control in *encomiendas*, allotments of natives for whose spiritual and economic welfare the Spanish *encomendero* was responsible. In return for this service the encomendero could demand tributes and personal service from the Indians in his charge. During the colonial period a social structure developed in rural areas which had some affinities with the medieval feudal system; it was based on the hacienda, the large, self-sufficient, enclosed estate, within which the hacendado enjoyed virtually absolute power over the men and women who lived and worked there. Nineteenth-century political changes did nothing to reduce the power of the hacendados, who rather flourished in the anarchical atmosphere of the times; the Reforma's insistence on legal rights to property tended to strengthen their hand all the more [p. 19]; and Porfirio Díaz, as part of his general policy of keeping all powerful interests satisfied, allowed them to do much as they pleased with a minimum of outside interference—exactly the situation that the hacendado preferred, for it enabled him to preserve and strengthen his autonomy, the basis of his power. Any attack on that autonomy was an attack on the continued existence of the hacienda system.

As the basis of Mexico's agricultural system the hacienda was weak and insufficient. The average hacendado had a medieval disregard for the virtues of productivity, expansion, and technical advance. He was concerned simply to maintain his estate as a provider for his many personal needs, but no more [pp. 120–1]. The stable and continued enjoyment of possession was what was important to him, not increasing profits. Many landowners rarely visited their estates, but, leaving an administrator in charge of them, lived in Mexico City or even in Madrid or Paris, if they were wealthy enough. Those who lived in Mexico City were absorbed into the way of life of the capital, and adopted its mores; and they can be considered as belonging more to the group of the city élite [pp. 254–68] than to the rural élite, although the basis of their wealth was in the country. Here the hacendados that concern us are those who remained closely connected with their estates, living on them some of the time at least.

If the hacendado needed any help from the outside world to maintain his power, he could count upon the good offices of the local jefe político (district prefect) and of the local force of armed rurales (mounted police). The jefe político was the political authority of the area around the town to which he was appointed by the government. Under the Díaz regime the institution flourished, and the corrupt, unscrupulous jefe político became a highly unpopular figure [pp. 192–3]. The rurales, a Porfirian creation (they were given official status in 1874), had a more ambiguous position. As the tools of the hacendados and caciques, used principally as a disciplinary force against recalcitrant peons, they were much feared; yet they also had a certain romantic appeal, for their uniform was the flamboyant and attractive *charro* dress. The Porfirista Maqueo Castellanos romanticized the rurales as follows:

The classic, typical rurales, who entered deep into the soul of the people as something completely theirs, genuinely Mexican, with their broad hats, their short leather jackets, their red neckties, their clinking spurs, their cowboy-style saddles with long straps curling down by the side of the ropes, and riding sinewy horses with fine coats, on which the riders showed off their skills in a speedy gallop which drew sparks from the paving stones and an enthusiastic cry from the hearts of the multitudes, who broke out in a loud 'Viva México!'[2]

The rurales were, furthermore, themselves recruited from the lower classes—many of them were former criminals—and in the country of machismo [p. 153] their ability to rise to a position of power by reason of their toughness and skill as horsemen and gunmen would be admired by their former peers.

The rural situation and the changes it underwent during the Revolution are most fully illustrated among our novelists by Azuela in *Las tribulaciones de una familia decente* and López-Portillo y

---

[2] Op cit., p. 298. Revolutionaries were not so enthusiastic about charro dress. Dr. Atl, for example, dismisses it as 'ugly, uncomfortable and ridiculous' (*Las artes populares en Mexico*, I, p. 291), and Martín Luis Guzmán refers to it as 'representative, outside the theatre and the hacienda, of the degradation of culture' (*El águila y la serpiente*, p. 316). Zapatista leaders, however, were fond of wearing charro dress (there was no Zapatista uniform). This originally counter-revolutionary symbol is now, ironically enough, accepted as the Mexican national costume.

Rojas in *Fuertes y débiles*, although several of the other novelists of the Revolution touch on it. Azuela is highly critical of the hacendado family he portrays, and he caricatures its members; but his largely hostile portrayal is balanced by that of López-Portillo y Rojas, who is well-disposed towards his hacendado, though by no means altogether uncritical. When accounts provided by these two novels and the passing references in several others are pieced together, there emerges a reasonably complete general picture of the nature and career of the Porfirian rural élite in the Revolution. The hacendados are, in the novels, the aristocracy, or the would-be aristocracy, of Mexico. Other groups among the anti-revolutionaries had strong aristocratic pretensions too [pp. 254–68 and 300–11]—indeed, such pretensions were the most marked feature of the Porfirian élite—but the hacendados, as the longest-established section, set the style for the rest. Many individual hacendados had no pedigree to boast of at all—large numbers of them were sons of men who only acquired wealth and power during the Reforma—but such new members of the class were even more fervently aristocratic in their attitudes than the rest. The aristocratic hegemony of pre-revolutionary Mexico was a strong influence upon all groups who had any claims to, or hopes of, prominence in society: no sooner, it seems, had a family reached a position of even the most moderate social respectability than it started creating for itself a whole complex of aristocratic norms of behaviour and systems of thought. This is something that the Revolution has modified but not altogether eliminated: a similar tendency can be observed in the history of the post-revolutionary élite of Mexico [p. 268].

Azuela's family of hacendados, the Vázquez Prados, represent these features in their most extreme form. Their descent dates only from 1857 and from a caudillo who made a rapid fortune in the same sort of way as many individual Carrancistas were to make theirs in the Revolution [pp. 210–16]. Azuela intends the Vásquez Prados to be typical members of the ruling élite in this respect, as he shows when he makes Procopio exclaim, on seeing a car full of revelling Carrancistas: 'Ever since the War of Independence, people of that stamp, murderers and bandits, have been the foundations on which the successive aristocracies of this country have been based.'[3] In their insecurity it seems that they feel all the

---

[3] *Las tribulaciones de una familia decente*, p. 421.

more obliged to demonstrate to the world that they are true aristocrats. Their concern about this vulnerable point was well-founded,
for the long-established hacendado families were slow to accept as
their equals the many parvenus who joined their ranks in the mid-
nineteenth century. The extreme right-wing journalist Alfonso
López Ituarte gives a notable example of this blood-snobbery
when he explains the wickedness of the hacendado don Rodrigo,
who plays a central role in his novel *Satanás*, by the fact that he is a
'descendant of the rabble, one of those men who are after money
and for whom, in order to make their pile, all means are valid'.[4]
The prominence that López Ituarte gives, in his condemnation of
his upstart hacendado, to his appallingly non-aristocratic interest
in financial matters is most significant. Don Rodrigo has just raped
the wife of his faithful personal servant, but for López Ituarte the
fact that he is a capitalist is far more damning than the fact that he
is a rapist.

For the Vázquez Prados, then, the most important thing in life
is to convince the whole world—and themselves as well—that they
really are genuine aristocrats. Their ethical system is based solely
and exclusively upon the needs and interests of the family. Azuela
puts the narration of the first part of the novel into the mouth of
the youngest member of the family, the weak and effeminate
César, and makes him relate events in a style which parodies this
peculiarly aristocratic vision of the importance of the family. For
César, the whole world revolves around his family, and is properly
organized to his family's convenience; that which maintains this
well-ordered scheme of things is, by definition, and regardless of
all other considerations, good, and that which tends to disrupt it,
bad.

The Vázquez Prados had succeeded in conquering for themselves a position of eminence in the society of Zacatecas (near
which city their hacienda was situated) mainly by lavish spending,
which of course was basic to the successful maintenance of aristocratic appearances. It was indispensable to show at every possible
moment that one lived in a world of comfort and opulence; as
Vasconcelos indicated, 'according to our topsy-turvy ethical
system, anyone who didn't spend money like water, even if he had
to live afterwards on tick . . . didn't know what living was, and
wasn't a real man.'[5] The family's flight to Mexico City in the face

---

[4] p. 11.   [5] *Ulises criollo*, pp. 559–60.

of the advancing revolutionary armies, on the fall of Huerta
[pp. 34 and 153] is a disturbing experience for them, for it means
the loss of the social position they had spent so much money
and energy in conquering. César's first reaction to Mexico City
upon arriving there is to question himself bitterly: 'Where is the
gloved hand raised courteously to greet us with affection as we
pass? Where is there a single head bared respectfully or humbly
bowed on seeing us? Glacial, disdainful, indifferent, insolent faces.
That's all. How odious is the metropolis! Here, we are no more
than a tiny drop of water in the immensity of the oceans.'[6]

An important part of the way of life of these aspirant aristocrats
was the ostentatious cultivation of indolence and helplessness:
shortly after the Revolution an American observer reported that 'no
Mexican gentleman will consent to be seen toting his hand-
luggage. . . . The abundance of servants has made most upper-class
Mexicans spiritual cripples, morally incapable of looking after
themselves.'[7] And so it is that the Vázquez Prados, living in Mexico
City separated from their source of income, bereft of servants, and
dependent upon their own abilities and resources, are utterly
incapable of helping themselves, and go into inexorable decline.
Their Zacatecas life has psychologically predisposed them to
prefer the most abject poverty to the indignity of doing useful or
remunerative work. They quite pathetically depend upon the
opportunist Pascual [pp. 211–13] to see them through their difficulties, and are helpless prey to his cynical machinations. Meanwhile, in the face of possible starvation, they pass their days in a
suitably aristocratic way: 'Visiting churches and shop-windows
in the mornings, and telling each other what we had seen
for the rest of the day, time passed painlessly.'[8] The elder son,
Francisco José, an aspiring poet, 'in his ivory tower, devoured the
latest books'.[9] When finally, after a long struggle with his pride,
the head of the family, Procopio, takes a job as a cashier, his wife
and son, far from being relieved and thankful that the family has a
steady income again, are shocked and outraged:

'Who can any longer doubt that Procopio is set on being the dis-
honour of our forebears? He is dragging the immaculate name of our
house through the mud!'

---

[6] *Las tribulaciones*, p. 433.   [7] E. A. Ross, p. 28.   [8] *Las tribulaciones*, p. 437.
[9] Ibid. Lyric verse was the most fashionable form of literature at this time in
Mexico [p. 83].

RM

'He has descended to the condition of a wage-earner!'
'And he obliges his family to follow him in such an ignominious fall.
I can't do that, I can't: I'd sooner die! I hear the voices of the Generals
Prado protesting in their cold tombs.'[10]

Procopio is a key figure in the novel. His position in the Vázquez
Prado family is, from the beginning, a discordant and contentious
one, for he has no claim to any aristocratic background at all: the
much-invoked Generals Prado are his wife's ancestors, not his, and
he is never allowed to forget the fact. He was the administrator
of the hacienda when it was owned by his future father-in-law,
with whom he ingratiated himself so successfully that he was able
to marry his master's daughter. Although Procopio has absorbed
many of the aristocratic customs of the family into which he has
married, he has not been entirely won over to their way of life; and
so it is he alone who is able to realize what the Revolution is going
to mean for the family, to see through Pascual's trickery, and finally
—albeit after a protracted inner conflict—to redeem himself and
regain his human dignity by throwing aside his aristocratic
prejudices and taking a job. In contrast with Procopio's perceptive-
ness and final salvation, the obstinate blindness to reality of the
other members of the family and the consequent hopelessness of
their position are the more manifest.

In *Las tribulaciones de una familia decente* Azuela attempts to
demonstrate that the hacendados were an undesirable section of
society, because of their unproductive and parasitical lives, and
that their only hope of salvation from the moral degradation of their
useless existence lay in the complete rejection of their aristocratic
pretensions: in other words, in the rejection of that very code of
beliefs and behaviour by which they guided their every action. He
shows that the Revolution gave the hacendados the choice of either
making the necessary transformation or perishing, but indicates
that it was impossible for the complete hacendado to escape from
the influence of the beliefs inculcated into him by his past training
and environment and to make such a drastic change in his way of
life (Azuela's determinism is evident here [pp. 122–3]). Only
those, Azuela seems to be saying, who are already in some way
partially dissociated from hacendado ethics and mores are capable
of making a successful effort to break free from their influence.

It is worth referring, in passing, to the class overtones of the

10 p. 556.

word 'decente', as it is used in the title of this novel. By the nine-teenth century this adjective had undergone interesting semantic change, and both in Spain and in Spanish America it had come to mean not only 'decent' but also 'aristocratic' (clearly because of the conviction that ruling classes normally have that they alone are honourable and respectable—indeed the latter word has in English acquired comparable, though less marked, class signifi-cance). Many of the novelists of the Revolution use the word with its second meaning (which became quite independent of its original moral sense), but none more than Azuela, who constantly exploited the ironic possibilities of this linguistic situation. The most notable example (among dozens) is a scene in *Los de abajo*, where a woman begs money from the revolutionary soldiery, claiming that her suitcase has been stolen: 'Gentlemen, a *señor decente* stole my suitcase at Silao station.'[11] The fact that the alleged robber was a well-dressed, wealthy-looking person makes the Villista soldiers indignant, and the beggar-woman's appeals are well answered.

José López-Portillo y Rojas's *Fuertes y débiles* is complementary to *Las tribulaciones de una familia decente* in that it portrays other aspects of the rural élite, although it illustrates the same general process of its decline. Whereas Azuela's novel is about the hacen-dados' sufferings after their flight from their estate and only refers obliquely to their normal life, *Fuertes y débiles* describes the rural situation in rather more detail.

Juan Nepomuceno Bolaños, nicknamed 'Cheno', owns an hacienda ('San Víctor') near Toluca (in the state of Mexico, to the south of Mexico City). He lives on his hacienda, but, because of its proximity to the capital, he is able to make frequent visits there in his motor-car, which López-Portillo y Rojas considers an 'aristo-cratic vehicle'.[12] He is unmarried, and in some ways not a typical hacendado: he is irreligious and iconoclastic, having received a positivistic education, and as a farmer he is a progressive. These details are not, however, important in the novel; they are just mentioned in passing, and do not subsequently play any part in the development of the theme or action. What are important are features of Cheno's character and life that are altogether more representative.

Cheno has secured absolute dominion over his property by

[11] p. 402.   [12] p. 17.

adding to his authority as hacendado that of the position of *presidente municipal* of the nearby town of Isota, 'whose jurisdiction extended several leagues all around, and included numerous farms of various sizes and about a dozen small villages'.[13] The municipal council is composed of local men of humble condition, and Cheno is able to impose his wishes upon them much as he likes. The elections which put Cheno and his colleagues into office were rigged by Cheno himself without difficulty.

Since San Víctor was the largest and richest hacienda in the area, it was the one which possessed the most electoral resources. . . . From which it followed logically that this hacienda and its owner called the tune in all political arrangements and rearrangements that were projected, developed and carried out in that small and defenceless world of Isota. Cheno, who was no fool in these matters and who would not tolerate being second to anyone in this his theatre of operations, had adopted an extremely effective tactic of elementary simplicity in order always to be the most influential voice in public affairs: it was to get elected as councillors his dependents, peons, partners, or debtors, who would not think with their own brains but with his, and to put himself at the head of them all as their president, whenever the law permitted. When this was not possible, he seated some blockhead of his close acquaintance in the stately presidential chair, and managed him as he wished.[14]

Cheno has, then, in effect solved the problem of maintaining an alliance with the local political boss by becoming the boss himself. Within the Isota district, which is all that interests him, his control is absolute, although in less important matters he leaves room for his underlings to satisfy their power-lust.

Primary education, the provision of drinking water, the construction of benches and a bandstand in the town square, and, in general, all material improvements, depended exclusively on his own personal management, and he was usually behind fines, the committal of wrong-doers to prison or to armed service, and all impositions on people and property, when it was in his interest to have a finger in such affairs; although they were more commonly governed by the petty passions of the councillors, and, in particular, by those of the secretary.[15]

By extending his political power beyond the limits of his hacienda, to the area immediately surrounding it, Cheno has created a small but sufficient buffer-state, as it were, which encloses his property, and which, protecting it from any outside interference, ensures him of that personal autonomy so precious to

[13] p. 208.   [14] pp. 208–9.   [15] pp. 209–10.

the hacendado. His position as the absolute lord of his estates is unquestioned and unchallengeable—until the Revolution destroys his carefully organized little world.

On his hacienda Cheno is an active and vigilant master. He does not, of course, himself do any physical work, but he takes a detailed interest in all the activities of his workers and controls them closely. Since he efficiently manages his lands himself, his *administrador* is reduced, in effect, to the position of foreman, not entrusted with any decision-making at all but taking all orders directly from Cheno. On other haciendas—like that of the Vázquez Prados—the administrador had very much more personal responsibility for the day-to-day running of the estate.

Cheno's practical abilities as a gentleman farmer might seem to contradict much that has been said above about the aristocratic norms and values of the hacendado class. Unlike the Vázquez Prados he does not make a cult of ineffectuality; quite on the contrary, he takes considerable pride in his ability to organize and control personally, in every detail, not only his hacienda, but also the municipality of Isota. The difference is not, in fact, fundamental: it is one of means rather than ends, for Cheno's business-like practicality is, as we shall see, directed solely at a strictly aristocratic goal; but it is nevertheless significant. It reflects an important division within the hacendado class that has already been referred to—between the long-established families and the parvenus.

The Vázquez Prados are newcomers to the rural élite and are consequently obliged to exaggerate their claims to be considered as aristocrats. They carry aristocratic behaviour to ridiculous extremes, and dare not do anything which might be reminiscent of their plebeian origins. The Bolaños family, on the other hand, have been members of the Mexican élite for much longer, and they feel quite secure in their social position. Possessed of an unspoken inner conviction of their own superiority, they have no need to prove it to anyone. And so it is that Cheno can be active and efficient without qualms; can pit his personal machismo against that of his subordinates without feeling that he is lowering himself in any way; and can make certain concessions to country ways, becoming an expert horseman and dressing, when on his hacienda, in the country style—albeit in a very luxurious version.[16] It

16 pp. 210–11.

would be difficult for a member of the '1857 aristocracy' to feel sure enough of himself to do any of these things.

His less exaggeratedly aristocratic behaviour does not, however, affect Cheno's basically aristocratic outlook; in a sense, as we have seen, it rather confirms it. He manages his hacienda himself not to increase efficiency, productivity and profits, but simply to ensure the smooth running of the estate in general, which in turn serves the traditional interests of the hacendado: a steady income for lavish personal spending and secure possession of land and men. His totally aristocratic view of the land, and of the men and women who cultivate it, is well caught in the scene in which Cheno, accompanied by his personal servant, rides through the settlement of peons on his hacienda:

He rode along in his usual proud and self-satisfied manner, holding the reins in his left hand and with the other caressing the arched neck of his steed, which beat the ground like a drum with its hoofs, and which moved as if dancing to some gay, rhythmic music. Cheno glanced to one side and the other with the look of a lord and master, to see how things were going, and if anything was missing that ought to be there, or if anything was there that ought to be removed; and he frequently stopped to speak to some passer-by, to ask for information about the hacienda's chattels and livestock, or about the name, provenance and origin of any stranger who turned up.[17]

Since Cheno has made his lordship so strong and absolute, it is not difficult for him to indulge his only serious vice: lust. Using a wide range of tricks and wiles—but principally by appointing the objects of his desires as his successive housekeepers—he has succeeded in conquering many of the most attractive young women who live on the hacienda: and many of the children there bear a marked resemblance to him. It is one of Cheno's conquests—of a relation of his administrador—which gives rise to the novel's main action: the uprising of his peons under the administrador, and the capture and execution by them of Cheno.[18]

---

[17] p. 211.

[18] This type of story has many literary precedents. It is to be found in large numbers of Spanish Golden Age plays—like Lope de Vega's *Fuenteovejuna*—and, more recently, in the nineteenth-century Mexican realistic novel. Even if the plot of *Fuertes y débiles* is, in fact, derived from literature rather than life (and this is the sort of incident that could well happen in a revolution), the consequences for our analysis are not important, for the details of the story do not affect the presentation of the rural situation in this novel.

At the heart of López-Portillo y Rojas's novel there is an interesting contradiction. The author was a convinced conservative and anti-revolutionary, and thoroughly in favour of the hacienda as an institution. He attempts to portray the peons as living wholesome and happy lives within the hacienda, lacking no essential nor even some luxuries[19], and to present the Revolution as a movement caused not by real social grievances but by a few plotting malcontents [pp. 101–2]. And yet in his novel he gives a detailed analysis of the inordinate powers enjoyed by hacendados, the grave injustices that this situation could lead to, and the impossibility of changing it by any peaceful means—in other words, he demonstrates that the hacienda system was morally indefensible and that a revolution was necessary to destroy it and the iniquities it caused. He seems at one point to notice this discrepancy between his explicit opinions and the unavoidable implications of his novel, but his attempt to gloss over it is weak in the extreme:

Don Ireneo avouched that cases of medieval abuse were not general, but exceptional and unusual on haciendas for, although it could not be denied that some landowners paid their peons miserable wages, that they fleeced them in the hacienda stores and iniquitously seized from them their small plots of land, it was also true that the vast majority of hacendados did not behave in such a bad way, and that there were some . . . who were so just and clement that, more than anything else, they seemed like their servants' diligent fathers.

Although it is clear that López-Portillo y Rojas is here using the venerable Don Ireneo de la Paz as the mouthpiece for his own opinions, he is plainly dissatisfied with this explanation (as well he might be) and feels obliged to reinforce it with direct comment, which leads him into still deeper waters:

Señor de la Paz was completely right: the ill was far from being general and widespread. . . . The slavery of the peons . . . was no more than a fable, and the arrogation of their plots was not so commonplace as to have become systematic. The excesses committed by some hacendados

[19] He describes a normal, everyday meal of hacienda peons as follows:

A deep bowl of broth, which was duly seasoned with hot peppers, lemon juice and slices of banana; boiled meat with a hot sauce; rice and chick-peas; fried beans swimming in melted butter, with more chili sauce and hot tortillas; many jars of water to cool the palate, burning from the hot peppers . . . And that was all (*Fuertes y débiles*, p. 268).

Other contemporary witnesses give strikingly different accounts of peasant life before and during the Revolution [pp. 184–6].

on people or on property could be remedied by recourse to the law, which condemned and persecuted such excesses, and no revolution was therefore necessary.[20]

The novel, then, is here a direct and detailed rebuttal of the novelist's own beliefs; the realities of a social situation shine through an individual's attempts to distort and deny them [pp. 17–18].

Here, then, is the hacendado class as it appears delineated in two novels of the Revolution. Both show, in different ways, why it was necessary and inevitable that the Revolution should do away with this class. The details of its decline are also furnished by the novels, and may be rapidly summarized. They form a consistent and recurring pattern.

The armed movement and subsequent government of Madero did nothing whatsoever to disturb the hacendados. Indeed, many hacendados were Maderistas and took an active part in the movement, some even leading their peons into battle [pp. 195–6]. Andrés Molina Enríquez interprets Maderismo as a movement which represented the interests of the hacendados against those of the científicos,[21] and reports Madero as declaring categorically: 'I have always advocated the creation of smallholdings; but that does not mean to say that any landowner is to be deprived of his property.'[22]

Reactions to Huerta's coup seems to have been divided. In *Fuertes y débiles* Cheno is quite happy with the way things are going under Madero; but a young woman, a member of the city élite [pp. 254–68], involves him in the plotting to depose Madero and by a process of sentimental blackmail obliges him to give his support to the plot and help to finance it. The coup was, however, in López-Portillo y Rojas's view, the work of the city élite; and Cheno later regrets his action, particularly when, to everyone's surprise, it is not Félix Díaz but Huerta who takes over the presidency [p. 31], and throws the country into complete anarchy by his incompetence. The Vázquez Prados of *Las tribulaciones de una familia decente* are more wholeheartedly on Huerta's side, hailing him as 'an iron hand—just what the country needs'

---

[20] pp. 345–6.

[21] *Esbozo de la historia* . . ., Vol. IV (1935). He calls Maderismo 'a counter-revolution, skilfully brought forward'.

[22] Op cit., pp. 167–8. Molina Enríquez is quoting from a letter written by Madero to the national daily newspaper *El Imparcial* on 27 June 1912.

[p. 175], and making a large loan to his government to help in the fight against Carranza.

It is during the first half of 1914, with the imminent fall of Huerta, that the decline of the hacendados commences. The constitutionalist armies had none of the Maderistas' respect for property, and their advance meant the looting and sacking of all haciendas in their path. Panic-stricken hacendados flocked to Mexico City from all over the country, seeking the shelter and the protective anonymity that it offered (a process recorded in detail by Azuela in *Las tribulaciones de una familia decente*). Cheno, more resolute than most, stays on his hacienda to protect it, underestimating the power and importance of the Revolution. The state governor appoints him security chief of Isota and dispatches a contingent of rurales to fight under his orders and to strengthen his resistance. As the rebels advance, the hacienda is virtually besieged, and the final attack, leading to Cheno's capture and death, comes before he can make his escape to the city.

For those who did manage to flee in time, life in Mexico City could be hard. The richest and most influential hacendados could move on into exile with Huerta, taking a good part of their fortune with them. Some others, no doubt, by careful and astute action, could wriggle through the net and into the post-revolutionary élite. But the tribulations of Azuela's family of hacendados are representative of the ordeal many such families must have gone through. They take rooms upon arrival in a luxury hotel, but as their funds diminish they are forced to live more and more humbly until at last they occupy one squalid unfurnished room in the slums. They are defenceless in the big world of the city, and at the mercies of anyone who wants to take advantage of them. Their pride and wealth take blow after blow: news reaches them of the sacking of the hacienda; Carranza's invalidation of the currency and imposition of a new one hastens their ruin still more; and their fall is complete when they are tricked and blackmailed into parting with all their lands. At the end of the novel, friendless, helpless, and with nothing left to pawn, a bleak and miserable future awaits them.

We can observe, then, a single pattern in the demolition by the Revolution of the old rural élite, the hacendados: a mass convergence upon Mexico City followed by a variform dispersion from there. This demolition was an important achievement, for it removed a barrier—both economic and cultural—to the formation of an authentic progressive bourgeoisie. The hacendados had not only retained so strong a hold on a large part of Mexico's material wealth as to constitute a serious obstacle to industrialization, but also—and perhaps even more importantly—permeated the industrializing bourgeoisie itself most successfully with its own outlook on life, thus converting what should have been an economic foe into a close cultural ally. The exact manner of this conversion is one of the subjects of the next section of this chapter.[23]

(b) The Urban Élite

Under Porfirio Díaz Mexico City flourished spectacularly. The peace and stability of Porfirian Mexico, and the government's policy of favouring the rich and powerful, created conditions ideal for economic expansion and the rapid enrichment of individuals with enough ability, drive, unscrupulousness, or luck to take advantage [p. 20]. This new band of capitalists made their homes in Mexico City and brought to it great and flamboyant prosperity. They created for themselves what has been aptly called an 'overworld'—a highly privileged and powerful pocket within the country, making an ostentatious display of all the trappings of modern civilization in order to prove to the world at large its full membership in the civilized section of mankind. Here was to be found the real economic power in Porfirian Mexico.

It was not altogether a coincidence, then, that the first two novels to be written about the Revolution should open with references to the sumptuous celebrations in Mexico City of the Centenary of Independence, the climax of these efforts to demonstrate Mexico's progress and prosperity to the world. The spectacle of such pride before such a fall offered too many dramatic possibilities for a novelist to miss. After a very brief introductory chapter, Mateos continues lyrically:

---

[23] Another feature of the rural situation is examined by Azuela in *Los caciques*. Here the theme is the ravaging effects of modern capitalism, ruthless and unchecked, upon a traditional rural society which has no way of defending itself against this new menace. By exploiting and abusing the system of mutual trust and responsibility upon which traditional provincial life depends, the capitalist newcomers—the caciques—are able to accumulate fortunes at will [pp. 301–2]. This is an aspect of the conflict in late Porfirian society between modern capitalism and traditional neo-colonialism which, it has been suggested, was a basic cause of unrest [pp. 21–2].

Great Tenochtitlán is on holiday, adorned with the most dazzling and magnificent jewels that prodigal nature and civilization have given her. . . . The immense square, with its beautiful gardens and fountains, illuminated by manifold Venetian lamps, echoing everywhere with the enthusiastic clamour of military music. The National Palace illuminated *a giorno* with shining stars and thousands of incandescent spotlights embroidering its manifold balconies and cornices; and, in the centre, waving majestically, the national flag.[24]

Azuela, in contrast, is characteristically sardonic and critical. *Andrés Pérez, maderista* begins with a quotation from an imaginary newspaper report of the preparations for the fiestas:

Cereals have reached an unprecedented price. The day-labourer lives on maize and beans: he earns 37 centavos a day and maize costs seven pesos a hectolitre and beans fourteen. But the government will spend more than twenty million pesos on building the National Theatre, twenty millions on embellishing Mexico City, twenty millions on regaling the foreign delegates who have been invited to the celebration of this first centenary of our national independence. At least the diplomats will be satisfied about the overflowing prosperity of the inhabitants of the Republic of Mexico.[25]

The inhabitants of the Mexico City overworld had a variety of different backgrounds and occupations. The group as a whole can be described as that of the newly prosperous bourgeoisie and its allies, within which there are many sub-groups: businessmen, industrialists, financiers, rentiers, bankers, politicians and top-ranking civil servants; other professional men, like lawyers and doctors; army officers; absentee hacendados [p. 241]; and other miscellaneous elements, like the descendants of successful caudillos, living off fortunes inherited from them, and families whose wealth and social prominence were more long-standing, but who were incorporated, albeit rather uncomfortably [pp. 258–64], into the new Porfirian city-based ruling group. The group can be most profitably considered as a whole, as the sociological differences

[24] *La majestad caída* (1911), p. 7. Tenochtitlán was the Aztec city on whose ruins Mexico City was built. The word is used here simply as a sonorous synonym for 'Mexico City'.
[25] *Andrés Pérez, maderista* (1911), p. 764. The Teatro Nacional, the most grandiose and ambitious architectural project of the Porfirian period, was begun in 1905 in the centre of Mexico City. It was designed by Italians, built by Americans, its sculptures made by Italians and Spaniards, and its elaborate stage machinery provided by Germans. The Revolution halted its construction and it was not concluded until 1935—by Mexicans. It was renamed El Palacio de Bellas Artes.

between the various individual sub-groups are not, as the novels show them, very significant.

The novels of the Mexican Revolution are particularly rich sources for a study of the life and ways of this Porfirian urban élite. Many of the novelists who published before 1925 had either been born in Mexico City or lived there for a long time—unlike the members of the later school of the 1930s[26]—and, whether they themselves belonged to the overworld or not, they were in a good position to observe and analyse it at first hand. Two novelists among them are exceptionally useful for our purposes: Carlos González Peña and José López-Portillo y Rojas. Both occupied respectable social positions and were, consequently, near enough to the élite to be able to observe its activities closely; both were, at the same time, of sufficiently independent mind to be critical of those activities, without damning them absolutely. Both *La fuga de la quimera* and *Fuertes y débiles*—and particularly the latter—give, then, detailed and perceptive descriptions of the anti-revolutionary Porfirian urban élite.

It is most significant that this overworld of Mexico City, when seeking a term to use when referring to itself, should have chosen to borrow one from English: *la high-life* (something of an international term, in fact). González Peña describes the group as follows:

Bankers, businessmen, ministers, journalists, all mixed in with families of the upper-middle class who, in Mexico, call themselves 'la high-life', in spite of the fact that they are far removed from the semi-aristocracy in their old houses of colonial pedigree. The rabble of upstarts, who had risen thanks to adventure or to money, swarmed there; the grandfather of one had been a mason enriched by his contracts, another's a general who prospered as a result of a pronunciamento, another's a lawyer whose office thrived under the protection of dictators . . . *e tanti altri!*[27]

Antonio Ancona Albertos describes them from an even more hostile viewpoint:

Here, in the elegant suburbs, our aristocracy, born of yesterday's rebels, hatched in revolutions, in riots and in barrack-uprisings: the sons of the generals and the national heroes whose austere portraits fill the pages of history books, turned into fops and rascals; spendthrifts who dissipate in orgies what, not very long ago, their grandfathers appropriated in

---

[26] See M. P. González, pp. 223–4.   [27] *La fuga de la quimera*, p. 251.

raids, forays, sieges, and so-called battles. . . . And now the fragile residents of Colonia Roma are getting alarmed, because in the north of the country property is being appropriated, and there are forays and raids.[28]

La high-life was characterized, then, by its newness as a social group. In a manner typical of *nouveaux-riches* its lack of any solid historical foundations, of any common traditions consecrated by constant usage, obliged it to fabricate a hybrid style of life by imitating the mores of other, well-established élites. Furthermore, the insecurity it felt as a group made it not only copy but also exaggerate what it copied, in a desperate effort of self-assertion. La high-life turned to two sorts of already-established élites in its search for models for social living: the Mexican aristocracy (or pseudo-aristocracy)—the hacendados—and the ruling-classes of European countries, particularly those of France and England.

The aristocratic hegemony of Porfirian Mexico has already been commented on [p. 243]. Although many members of the city overworld, as businessmen, financiers, and capitalists, had an entirely non-aristocratic attitude to the making of money, this hegemony was so strong and pervasive that many of them—or their wives and daughters [p. 260]—came to adopt a thoroughly aristocratic attitude to the use of it, once acquired. Such an attitude put severe limitations upon Porfirian Mexico's capabilities for continued development, for it resulted in a considerable curtailment not only of the accumulation of capital for re-investment but also of the middle sectors' interest in reform and modernization. The city élite's emulation of the hacendados' aristocratic love of display and luxury was, then, an important weakness in the economic structure of pre-revolutionary Mexico [p. 39].[29]

The influence of foreign élites upon the Porfirian overworld was the result of two factors: nineteenth-century Latin America's general admiration for European, particularly French, culture and civilization; and the particularly strong European influence upon the Porfirian business world. The flow into Mexico of foreign capital, carefully engineered by the policies of Díaz's government [p. 20], brought with it, as would be expected, many foreign

---

[28] *En el sendero de las mandrágoras*, II, pp. 117–18.
[29] Claudio Véliz considers this to be a feature of the middle groups in Latin America as a whole. Post-revolutionary Mexico is, however, according to Véliz, something of an exception. (See 'Introduction' to Véliz, ed., *Obstacles to Change in Latin America*, Oxford University Press, 1965.)

investors in person [pp. 268-79], and also an overwhelming influence of foreign, especially European, culture.

Such, in general terms, was this awkward mongrel creation, which was so open to ridicule, and which made itself the more ridiculous by trying to pass itself off as a thoroughbred. Examples of its hybrid ethos in practice—on which this preliminary analysis is based—are found in abundance in the novels of the Revolution, particularly in the two already specified. Although the Revolution ruined this class—or more precisely, perhaps, realigned the individual members of it [p. 268]—it seems to have continued in virtually undisturbed existence until the end of 1914 at least; so there was room for it in the novels of the Revolution. It is José López-Portillo y Rojas who gives the most complete and detailed account of la high-life, and we shall concentrate upon his description of it.

One way in which the presentation in *Fuertes y débiles* of the Porfirian city élite is made interesting and convincing is by the comparative element which is introduced into it. The descriptions of city life in the novel revolve around two axes. One is the Montalvo family, with one of whose members—the daughter Clara —the novel's protagonist Juan Nepomuceno Bolaños is romantically involved. The other is the Téllez household, with whom Cheno (as he is nicknamed) stays on his sporadic trips to Mexico City from his hacienda: it comprises Cheno's aunt and her daughter Anita, with whom he falls in love when he tires of Clara. The former family is typical in every way of la high-life, and López-Portillo y Rojas seeks to give a complete and representative picture of this Porfirian creation in his depiction of the Montalvos. The Téllez family, on the other hand, has a longer history, and observes with dismay the antics of the *nouveaux-riches*. The division in the ranks of the élite between veterans and parvenus has already been noted in the rural situation; it was clearly also a significant one among the city élite. The difference is that in the countryside the old-established hacendado families were preponderant, and could therefore impose their norms upon the newcomers to their ranks; whereas in Mexico City the situation was reversed, and the older families could only watch with some resentment and annoyance as their domain was invaded and transformed by Porfirian upstarts.

Doña Carlota Bolaños, viuda de Téllez, belongs to a family

whose huge fortune was founded upon its possession of enormous estates in the north of Mexico. Her husband, the owner of a rich silver-mine, had been from an equally wealthy and aristocratic family. She has an immaculate pedigree and is intensely proud of it: she is 'a shoot on a tall, noble and leafy family tree, as testified by a picture, drawn in pen and ink, hanging by the head of her bed'.[30] Strokes of misfortune have drastically reduced the wealth of the family, but doña Carlota has managed her affairs well, and lives a life of moderate luxury: her large house is finely furnished with beautiful antique pieces, impressive mirrors and chandeliers; she has kept possession of the family china, silver and jewellery; and she is, in spite of everything, still a comfortably affluent woman.

Don Pablo Montalvo, on the other hand, can boast no glorious family history; in place of that, however, he has a massive and constantly growing fortune derived from a chain of haciendas he owns in central and southern Mexico, devoted to the lucrative business of producing pulque and tequila. His house in Mexico City is correspondingly sumptuous: it is a veritable mansion, hugely overdecorated and overrun with servants. Each one of its many halls, rooms and salons is furnished in modern European styles, the walls are covered with tapestries and silks; everything in the mansion is from Europe, having been brought over at huge expense, and there is not a single article of furniture of Mexican make.[31]

Doña Clara regards the Montalvos with the utmost scorn, because of their lack of a family tree and the indecorous speed with which they have become so inordinately rich. These two factors added together can only mean one thing for doña Clara: that the Montalvos are unsavoury, dangerous and unscrupulous opportunists, to be avoided at all costs. She has always maintained a suitable distance between herself and the Porfirian *nouveaux-riches*, lamenting that not all those of her class have done so: '"We who belong to older families have preferred to live in seclusion,

---

[30] p. 5.
[31] 'They nearly always wear European or American hats and American shoes, and use American or European carriages; they decorate their rooms with European objets d'art and, in short, they prefer everything foreign to what is Mexican; even the painting, literature, and music with which they gratify their tastes and occupy their spare time have to bear a foreign stamp.' (Molina Enríquez, *Los grandes problemas nacionales*, p. 230.)

unbudging in our own homes, lamenting the fact that some of our number have rubbed shoulders with the parvenus, and have consented to figure in the dictator's retinue." '32

Doña Clara's scorn is directed particularly at don Pablo Montaño's wife, doña Mónica, and his daughter Clara. Don Pablo himself has remained relatively unaffected by his immense wealth; it is his womenfolk who have been led by it to adopt an extravagant and flamboyant style of life (a similar situation is presented in *La fuga de la quimera*). Doña Mónica's weakness is jewels: her excessive self-adornment is immediately seized upon as a subject for ridicule by the Téllez family: ' "They say she won't even take off her jewels to get into her bath, that she wears rings over her gloves, and that she looks like the window of a jeweller's shop, full of rings, necklaces and bracelets." '33 She does, indeed, give herself away to the experienced and knowledgeable eyes of an 'old aristocrat' by her lack of discretion and *savoir-faire*:

Necklace and earrings of fine pearls, a profusion of rings on her fingers, and, particularly, a cheap, thick one on the middle finger of her right hand. When he saw it Cheno thought that perhaps the matron's background was not all that noble or respectable, for her excessive love of jewels and the atrocious taste with which she wore them made it seem questionable and shadowy: above all because of that monstrous ring she exhibited on that finger, her middle finger, precisely the one which, according to the rules of good taste and elegance, should never be used for that purpose. The opulent lady would have been capable of decorating her toes with rings and perhaps even of piercing her nose and putting a golden ring through it.34

In contrast, doña Carlota's fine collection of antique jewellery, old possessions of the family, is only aired on very special occasions.

The contrast between Clara Montalvo and Anita Téllez is even more pointed. Anita is an ideal aristocratic beauty: 'white, very white, and always pallid, as if she were ill, even though she suffered from no malady'.35 Her temperament is also ideal for a woman of her position: serene, discreet, and immaculately respectable. Clara, on the other hand, is a typical high-life young woman, with very different attitudes and behaviour. Her greatest efforts are devoted to achieving in her person a perfect imitation of the Parisian woman, as certain novels have led her to imagine the latter to be: 'She had set her heart on being a complete Parisienne,

32 p. 335   33 pp. 335–6.   34 p. 285. See also pp. 114–15.   35 p. 7.

like those who appear in the novels of Paul Bourget and Marcel
Prevost: insouciant, luxury-loving, a trifle disenchanted, and
capable of the greatest recklessness.'[36] Her free and frivolous
behaviour—and desirable body—have conquered for her a court of
admirers. She dresses to please them:

Tight-fitting clothes and vaporous fabrics had become fashionable, to
the great displeasure of some fathers, husbands and brothers, but to the
great satisfaction of well-built and shapely girls. Among the latter was
Clara, who, in the knowledge that her body was like a beautiful statue,
strived not only to show off as much of it as she could, but also to make a
display and spectacle of it. There was no one in the whole city who wore
fewer clothes than Clara.[37]

Such behaviour shocks and outrages Carlota and Anita, and adds
more weight to their condemnation of the new Porfirian pseudo-
aristocracy:

'She lets all her admirers kiss her . . . and she calls that flirting, just
flirting. . . . What nice customs this makeshift aristocracy brings us
from over the seas!' concluded Doña Carlota emphatically.
    'It's unbelievable,' murmured Anita quietly, shaking her head as a
sign of her disapproval.[38]

    López-Portillo y Rojas vividly illustrates the differences
between the customs of the traditional élite and those of the
parvenus by juxtaposing detailed descriptions of the Christmas
celebrations in the Téllez and the Montalvo residences. Doña
Carlota 'loved tradition and clung on to it with the desperation of a
drowning woman'.[39] And so in her house the *posada* is celebrated
on Christmas Eve in the time-honoured manner, deeply religious
and traditionally Mexican. The proceedings are initiated by
prayers; there follows a candle-lit procession around the house;
then a concert and recital of poetry by the guests; and a formal,
elegant, and lavish dinner, finished by midnight in time for all to
attend mass in the private chapel before returning home. A
lovingly prepared crib, permanently set up in a special room in the
house, is the focal point of the Christmas celebrations.
    The Montalvos, as good members of la high-life, have rejected
all these elements of the traditional posada, for they are greatly
concerned to keep in line with the latest European fashions: 'The
cultured upper classes . . . are as fickle and changeable as the leaves

<hr>

[36] p. 115.   [37] p. 117.   [38] p. 337.   [39] p. 144.

of a tree or as the weathervanes on towers, which turn with the wind and fold over at the slightest breeze. La high-life is transformed under the influence of a fashion.'[40] Their posada is designed more to impress their guests with their wealth, nobility and fashionableness than to celebrate the birth of Christ. They have their mansion specially illuminated for the occasion. The guest, upon arrival, is greeted by two porters, dressed in lackeys' uniforms, and two other such lackeys take his hat and coat. He is then shown into a large, brilliantly-lit salon—*el hall*—where the guests are assembled, the women in evening gowns with daring necklines, overloaded with jewellery, and the men in evening dress. The main activity of the evening is the ball, and the most modern European dances (particularly two-steps) are played by the orchestra. Clara is superciliously amused when her father, somewhat more traditional in his tastes, orders the orchestra to play a few older pieces like polkas, *danzas* and *contradanzas*. The dancing is momentarily interrupted at midnight by a quick buffet supper, and then it continues until daybreak. The bar is well attended.

Young people are predominant at the Montalvos' posada, and it is in them that the high-life ethos is taken to its most ridiculous extremes. Many of them, like Clara, try to convert themselves into imitation Parisians; others copy the English:

Two youths, their hair well combed and oiled and groomed. One of them, educated in France, was called Raúl Duval, and he signed his name 'Raoul du Val' in order to give it an outright noble and Gallic character; and the other, whose name was Tomás Robert, signed 'Thomas Robert' so that he should be taken for an Anglo-Saxon. The former wore a small beard à la Boulanger; the latter a monocle. Neither liked Mexico. Raoul said that his country was 'un pays tout à fait sauvage', and Thomas referred to everyone as 'very common people'. Whenever he sat down, Raoul was specially careful to pull his trouser legs half way up his scrawny calves to display his long black silk socks, like a woman's stockings; and Thomas dropped his monocle continuously, in order to give himself the pleasure of fixing it once again between nose, eyebrow and right cheek-bone, making horrible grimaces like a tormented mask.[41]

---

[40] p. 5.

[41] pp. 188–9. López-Portillo y Rojas, whose own position is close to that of the old aristocracy, attacks cosmopolitan tendencies by exaggerating and caricaturing them. All caricatures, however, must have a solid basis of truth; and maybe the exaggeration is not so great in this case as it might appear.

The adoption of English christian names by young Mexican members of la high-life seems, according to López-Portillo y Rojas, to have been common. At the Montalvos' posada we come across Jack, Dick, Ellick, Hal, Netty Quintero, Lilly Rubio and Patty Miranda, 'all Mexicans, and some of them half-Indian; but, having passed through the United States or England like birds in migration, they had adopted those extravagant, absurd diminutives in order to pass themselves off as foreigners'.[42] The general linguistic influence of French and English on the Spanish spoken by la high-life is, of course, great.

The life these young people chose to lead was, as illustrated by *Fuertes y débiles* and other novels, resolutely idle and unproductive. The principal occupation was the endless and sterile cultivation of transient romantic and vicariously erotic attachments with members of the opposite sex—the two allied but different games or rituals known as *el flirt* and *el galanteo*. Flirt was more frivolous and more overtly erotic, and galanteo more indicative of a genuine personal relationship—but no less ritualistic. Flirt was more properly the activity of the high-life youth, and galanteo more traditional and Hispanic: Clara indulges in flirt; Anita in galanteo. The singularly futile play-acting involved in these pursuits—for which the principal settings appear to have been the ballroom, the salon, and the tennis court—seems to have occupied all the time, ingenuity, and energy of the sons and daughters of the Porfirian *nouveaux-riches* of Mexico City. The thought that there might possibly be something more worth while to do with their lives never threatened to disturb the peaceful lethargy of their dulled minds. Given the environment into which they were born and in which they grew up, it was difficult for such a thing to happen.

Such, then, in broad outline, is the picture of the élite of Mexico City given by *Fuertes y débiles* and also, but with less wealth of detail, in other novels like *La fuga de la quimera*, *La majestad caída* and *El terror*. Azuela's Andrés Pérez [pp. 92–5] is a product of la high-life. If López-Portillo y Rojas's convincingly realistic account needs any corroboration, it is well provided by the

[42] p. 296. 'There are fools who, although they are Mexicans, affect not to use the country's language, but rather some other language imperfectly learnt abroad. . . . Everyone receives English publications; everyone advertises in English; everyone learns English; everyone even wants to think in English.' (Molina Enríquez, op. cit., pp. 312–13.)

reappearance of the same scenes and situations and the same over-all atmosphere in the other four novels. Although López-Portillo y Rojas is hostile to la high-life—he clearly speaks for the hacen-dados and the long-established families in the Mexican élite—his hostility has not led him to distort his account in essence, but only to magnify, for the sake of more effective criticism, the real traits he observes.

The Mexican overworld, then, as we can observe it in several novels, was a new élite that already showed many signs of deca-dence and degeneration while it was still being formed, even before it had firmly established itself as a ruling class. It was principally the inescapable aristocratic hegemony of Porfirian Mexico that made it such an inadequate élite (as well, perhaps, as the general tendency for economic power without direct political power to produce irresponsibility). It seems generally accurate to say that while la high-life's details of behaviour, dress, fashions, and so on, were derived from its observance of European life, its basic attitude—that inexorable need to be ostentatiously extravagant and idle—was home-bred, the result of the absorption of the aristocratic norms and values of the ruling élite that had tradition-ally held sway in the country. Thus Mexico's economic expansion under Porfirio Díaz, was, in a sense, doomed before it could get properly under way, for it was led by a class who believed that the purpose of making money was to buy one's way into the aristocracy and retire—oneself, one's ideas, one's money, one's family, one's descendants—from active and productive life. The main aim was, as with the hacendados, to buy and maintain as high a level as possible of status and prestige. A capitalist group whose members subscribe to this belief is surely not a sufficient base for steady and sustained economic expansion. The evidence of *Fuertes y débiles* suggests, furthermore, that the sons of the new Porfirian capitalists —entering adulthood, approaching the time when they would take over their fathers' concerns, as the Revolution broke out—had developed an even more aristocratic and parasitic approach to life than their parents. Another totally unproductive ruling élite was rapidly being developed to add to the one already in existence. Such, at any rate, is the analysis of Mexico City society in about 1912 that *Fuertes y débiles* and other novels invite us to make.

The relationship between the City and the rest of Mexico was inevitably strained. There were other inhabitants of Mexico City,

of course, than the ruling élite—and most notably the bureaucrats [pp. 300–11]—but it was the élite who set the tone and the
example for the rest to follow. It is, therefore, convenient to consider the characteristics and responses of the City as a unit in this
part of the study. The inhabitants of Mexico City came, under Porfirio Díaz, to
assume an even more condescending attitude towards the inhabitants of the rest of the Republic than the inhabitants of capital
cities usually do towards their fellow-countrymen:

In General Díaz's time [Mexico City] was acquiring a striking majesty.
It was regarded as one of the world's great cities by some; those who
were born there considered themselves superior to the mere mortals
born in the provinces: and, with a certain pride and in an affectedly
high-pitched voice, women would ask, on being introduced to someone,
'are you from the capital?' Because being from the capital was something
great.[43]

The rest of Mexico was, of course, fully aware of the City's disdainful exclusiveness, and the capitalinos were widely disliked as a
consequence. The way was well prepared, then, for a bitter confrontation between the Porfirian overworld of Mexico City and the
resentful remainder of the inhabitants of the Republic.

One could summarize the clash between the revolutionaries and
the City by saying that the latter was made, in the end, to pay for
its sins, but that it defended itself tenaciously and left its mark on
its aggressors. Its defence—it is difficult not to resort to personification here—was a simple yet subtle and effective one for which
it was well endowed: seduction. All triumphant leaders and their
followers were always greeted by cheering crowds, and all the
City's many pleasures were made available to them: 'The Mexican
capital is the city of intermittently gushing enthusiasm for whoever
arrives with the credentials of a caudillo.'[44] And then the newcomers had to confront the enervating effects of the City, just as
the provincial journalist (from Yucatán) Juan Ampudia does: 'The
opulent, vice-ridden metropolis rejects new vitality as if it were
some disease.'[45] Many caudillos and their men, by all accounts,
were unable to resist the blandishments of this new-found
courtesan; until the situation was reached when, after too much

[43] Galindo, A través de la sierra, p. 41.
[44] Quevedo y Zubieta, En tierra de sangre y broma, p. 142.
[45] Ancona Albertos, En el sendero de las mandrágoras, part I, p. 101.

repetition, her wiles lost their magic, and she was punished for her infidelity.

When Madero entered triumphantly in June 1911, he was received with the same enthusiasm as had been accorded to Porfirio Díaz months earlier. One novelist, describing the scene, comments: 'It was the atavistic cry of "Viva", accorded to whoever arrives in triumph.'[46] Madero lost his popularity, however—perhaps one could suggest that his dogged uprightness, his refusal to be seduced, might have had something to do with it—and by the beginning of 1913 plans were being hatched for his removal [p. 30]: as Quevedo y Zubieta puts it, 'towards the end of January 1913, the Federal District was conspiring'.[47] The population of the City took no part in the decena trágica, and were widely criticized for their passivity: Andrade, the hero of La ruina de la casona, 'roundly condemned the people's apathy in the face of the catastrophe, for they went neither to the side of their apostle to defend him, nor to that of his enemies to discredit him'.[48] The triumph of Huerta was next hailed as rapturously as had been Madero's before.

Nothing that had happened so far posed any threat to Mexico's overworld. As the fight against Huerta got under way in the north, la high-life saw no reason in these new circumstances to alter their mode of living: 'These moments are, indeed, tragic ones, and we inhabitants of the Valley of Mexico witness the drama with the tranquillity of self-centred bourgeois. Public entertainments go on uninterrupted: kermesses, banquets, theatres, everything continues as if we were living in an eternal spring.'[49]

It was a fool's paradise, however. As Huerta became weaker and weaker, the movement of large numbers of provincials fleeing from the revolutionaries to Mexico City commenced, and with it the deterioration in living conditions in the capital. By the time Obregón made his victor's entry, food and money were scarce; and the reception this time was slightly less ecstatic. Perhaps there were also premonitions that the day of reckoning was near.

The knell was sounded by Obregón, in a remarkable speech he made, three days after his entry, at the tomb of Madero [pp. 147

---

[46] Quevedo y Zubieta, En tierra de sangre y broma, p. 108.
[47] Op cit., p. 303.   [48] Maqueo Castellanos, p. 333.
[49] Eduardo Pallares, La inmoralidad de la prensa, p. 6. This article is dated 3 Aug. 1913.

and 171]. He charged the male inhabitants of the City with degeneracy and lack of manliness for having failed to bestir themselves during the decena trágica, and, to shame them, presented his pistol to a woman who had, running considerable risks, tended Madero's grave ever since his murder. His words were: 'Since I admire valor, I cede my pistol to Señorita Arias, who is the only one worthy of bearing it.'[50] The capitalinos were shocked and petulant, and one of them comments: 'These undeserved and offensive words, discharged against the populace of the capital, who had suffered so much during the government of Huerta and who had just lavished demonstrations of such ostensible respect, affection and enthusiasm upon the revolutionaries, caused a profound effect of stupor and displeasure, and were much commented upon.'[51] Carranza's entry, shortly afterwards, was still less triumphant than Obregón's (accounts of it vary considerably—some reports state that he was enthusiastically received, but it seems probable that any enthusiasm was artificially generated).

The next few months were disastrous. As the city was successively occupied and abandoned by the rival factions its life came to a standstill. Famine and epidemics raged; carts were sent out every morning to collect dead bodies from the streets.[52] The city population could expect no sympathy from the revolutionary soldiers, among whom the contempt expressed by Obregón was normal. A Yaqui colonel in one of the novels expresses the general feeling: 'These puppies from the Valley of Mexico are such simpletons.'[53] Constitutionalists came to refer to Mexico City as 'the corrupt city', 'the accursed city', 'the city of infamy'. The general misery was increased by the rapacity of the occupying troops who, given the undeniable wickedness of the place, saw no reason for self-restraint [p. 216]. Even when most of the fighting had stopped, the

[50] Ramírez Plancarte, La cuidad de México, pp. 65–6. [51] Op. cit., pp. 66–7.

[52] Numerous and repeated reports of bad conditions in Mexico City throughout 1915 are to be found in Foreign Relations 1915 (Washington, 1924), pp. 649–763. See also Ramírez Plancarte, op. cit., pp. 223, 237–9, 253–5, 316, 366–7, 382, 396–8, 423–8, 440–9, 456–9, 500, 502, 509, 523, 525–7, 531–4 and 537–540; and Azuela, Las tribulaciones, p. 489. It was rumoured at the time that the Constitucionalistas were carrying out a deliberate policy of starving Mexico City to punish it for its crimes: Foreign Relations 1915, pp. 654, 660 and 666–8. It is worth noting that at precisely the same time Morelos State, a little to the south, was enjoying an idyllic period of peace and plenty—simply because the main Revolution was too occupied with its own problems to persecute Zapatistas (Womack, p. 241).

[53] Quevedo y Zubieta, En tierra de sangre y broma, p. 128.

commercial life of the city—and that of the Republic—had been so catastrophically disrupted that the situation did not start returning to normal until 1917–18.

Those among the anti-revolutionaries who suffered the most atrociously during this terrible period were not, of course, the city élite but rather the completely unprotected lower-middle-classes, whose life was precarious enough even in times of peace [pp. 300–11]. But even la high-life could not escape such devastation, and this period of about three years saw its disintegration as a group, and its replacement by the new Carrancista élite from the provinces of Mexico and particularly the north [pp. 205–7]: 'By now [1924] it has been seen that the men of Mexico City are quite useless, and that outsiders have come to dominate in all fields. . . . If one searches out the provenance of each one of those with important positions, one finds that they are from the provinces.'[54]

Resourceful individual members of the old élite could save themselves, some by going into exile with their fortunes—like the Montalvos in *Fuertes y débiles*—and others by staying on and astutely insinuating themselves into the new élite in the process of formation, like the businessman Ulpiano Pío in *Las tribulaciones de una familia decente*, who is able to retain his wealth by making himself useful to various fortune-hunting members of the Carrancista élite. As a class, however, la high-life was finished; not without leaving, nevertheless, a durable and influential tradition. The patterns of behaviour it had established for itself were, in turn, extensively drawn upon by the new post-revolutionary élite in its search for a suitable ethos; and modern Mexican newspapers are still graced with a profusion of reports of 'elegant weddings between members of highly distinguished families from the best society of the capital held in aristocratic temples', and of many other such exciting events. The great metropolitan courtesan continues to seduce many of those who approach her.

(c) *Foreigners: Gringos and Gachupines*[55]

Porfirio Díaz's policy of attracting foreign capital to Mexico at almost any cost [p. 20] created powerful interests, particularly American ones, which had much to lose by a disruption of the

---

[54] Galindo, p. 41.

[55] *Gringo*: a North American. *Gachupín*: a Spaniard. Both derogatory slang words of doubtful origin.

peace or a radical change to the Porfirian system. The influential
and privileged foreign communities in Mexico formed, then, a
significant part of the anti-revolutionary side, even though on the
whole they respected convention and took no active part in the
effort against the Revolution. It is worth giving some brief consideration to the position of these foreigners, particularly the
Americans, in the Mexican Revolution.[56]
Even before the Revolution broke out, the United States
citizens resident in Mexico were generally regarded with resentful
hostility. The reasons are not hard to find. Fear of the United
States' power and her imperialistic intentions were general
throughout Latin America in the early twentieth century. By this
time virtually the whole territory of the United States had been
occupied, and expansion beyond the national frontiers commenced.
This new imperialistic spirit was notably manifested in United
States interventions in British Guiana in 1895, in Cuba and
Puerto Rico in 1898, in Panama in 1903, in Nicaragua in 1912, and
in Mexico in 1914 [pp. 273–6]; and in the Roosevelt Corollary
to the Monroe Doctrine in 1904, which announced that the United
States were an international police power for the whole American
continent. Life so close to such a powerful and aggressive neigh-
bour was bound to be hazardous—Porfirio Díaz is credited with
the statement: 'Poor Mexico, so far from heaven and so near to the
United States!' (the clear light in the Valley of Mexico used,
before industrial pollution, to make the sky seem higher there than
elsewhere). This uneasy proximity created, inevitably, a succession
of episodes that served to make the Mexican people suspicious of
all Americans: the war of 1845 and the annexation of Texas; the
stream of adventurers that came from the north during the nineteenth century to exploit Mexican uprisings and make a fortune
out of them; constant border incidents, and so on.[57] But above all,
perhaps, the privileged position that Americans were granted
under Porfirio Díaz in Mexican society gave rise to strong feeling.
A popular epigram around 1910 was 'blessed are the Yankees, for
theirs is the Republic of Mexico';[58] Luis Cabrera, in his analysis in
1911 of the causes of Madero's revolution, includes in his list

[56] For the political relationship between the United States and Mexico, see
Cline, *The United States and Mexico*, and Clenenden, *The United States and
Pancho Villa*.
[57] See Clenenden, chap. 1, and F. C. Turner, pp. 35–44.
[58] *El País*, 8 Nov. 1910.

'*Extranjerismo*: that is to say, the predominance and the unfair competition exerted in every kind of activity by foreigners over Mexicans, because of the privileged position which they enjoy thanks to the excessive protection afforded them by the authorities and the support and vigilance of their diplomatic representatives.'[59] The Revolution was immediately preceded in November 1910 by anti-American riots in Mexico City and elsewhere in the republic [pp. 113–14]. The demonstrators protested against the lynching of a Mexican named Antonio Rodríguez in Rock Springs, Texas, and certain daily newspapers (notably *El País*, *El Diario del Hogar* and *El Tiempo*) added their voices to the protest, pointing out how American wrongdoers in Mexico were virtually immune from punishment. Molina Enríquez, in *Los grandes problemas nacionales*, repeatedly draws attention to the friction caused by the excessive privileges enjoyed by Americans in Mexico.

As the Revolution progressed, hostility towards the United States increased. The widespread belief arose that the Revolution itself was a vast American conspiracy, contrived in order to cause anarchy in Mexico and leave her defenceless in the face of invasion and conquest. The United States policy, initiated by Taft, of careful surveillance of revolutionary Mexico, which led to the concentration of troops near the Mexican border and the stationing of ships near the Mexican coast, added extra weight to fears of an American imperialist invasion.[60] Anti-revolutionary propaganda took up this fear, and encouraged and stimulated it. The Díaz regime attacked Madero for being a puppet of the Americans from the beginning of his revolt. The *Pacto de la Empacadora*, the manifesto of the 1912 rebellion of Pascual Orozco [p. 29], specifically charged Madero with making a secret deal with the Waters, Pierce Oil Company. The charge that Madero was in league with American oil companies became commonplace.[61] Huertista propaganda later took up this line of attack, directing it against Carranza; the campaign reached its climax in the very last days of Huerta's rule, when the Huertista newspaper *El Independiente*, in a despairing last effort to save the regime by discrediting the revolutionaries, published translations of letters exchanged between Henry Clay Pierce and his agent in Mexico, Sherburne G.

[59] *El Tiempo*, 17 Apr. 1911.   [60] F. C. Turner, pp. 218–20.
[61] See Maqueo Castellanos, *La ruina de la casona*, pp. 254–8, and Vasconcelos, *Ulises criollo*, pp. 668–9.

Hopkins [p. 191].[62] The correspondence started appearing on 12 July 1914 on the front page under the boldly printed headlines: 'The Revolution Has No Ideals. It is the Vile Slave of North-American Interests.' Successive translations of the Pierce–Hopkins letters continued to constitute the leading story of each day's edition, until on 16 July the front page brought the news of Huerta's resignation. The letters mainly consist of instructions from Pierce to Hopkins to try to persuade Carranza to organize the Mexican railway system according to the American financier's liking, reports from Hopkins to Pierce on his activities, and insistent complaints from the former to the latter about his meanness and slowness in paying him for his work. They are dated from January to May 1914, when the smooth progress of Pierce's plans was unwittingly frustrated by Villa, who refused to allow Carranza to organize the railway system in the part of north Mexico that was under his control.[63]

The allegation that the revolutionaries were agents of United States imperialism finally became something of a cliché in the conversation of anti-revolutionaries. A minor character in *Las tribulaciones de una familia decente*, the businessman Don Ulpiano Pío, expresses these typical sentiments:

It's useless for you to deny it: Carranza has promised President Wilson to hand over the nation without a single inhabitant, because the Yankees want Mexico without its costing them a single drop of blood. That's why each Carrancista soldier has the obligation of killing ten Mexican civilians: after which those of us that remain will be starved to death, and that will be that. This is the explanation of so many robberies, so many murders, such brutal taxes, the considerable rise in the price of

[62] Hopkins is a shady but important figure who appears at several junctures in the Revolution, in both the Maderista and the Carrancista stages. Of him Vasconcelos (op. cit., p. 635) says: 'By making and unmaking Central American revolutions and conspiracies from Washington, he had made himself an expert in organizing newspaper propaganda and in securing the tolerance of filibusterism.' See also *Who was Who in America*, Vol. I, 1897–1942 (Chicago, 1943), p. 587. The correspondence with Pierce was originally acquired in a mysterious way by the *New York Herald* and printed in its columns at the end of June 1914.

[63] In the Madero–Hopkins correspondence which is printed in *Documentos históricos* it is clear that Madero felt that he owed a considerable debt of gratitude to the American (VII (Mexico, 1965), p. 251, and VIII (Mexico, 1965), pp. 206–8, 210–12, 246, 248–9, 259, 263–7, 286–9, 298–9 and 310). See also Limantour, pp. 203–4. For correspondence between Hopkins and Carranza, in which the former tries to persuade the latter to favour various American interests, see *Documentos históricos*, I, pp. 49–54, 56–7, 76 and 146.

goods and the way life has become impossible for all people of any social standing.[64]

Such was the growth of anti-American feeling during the Revolution that it became, by its latter years, a professional obligation for any Mexican politician or leader to adopt, in public at least, a staunch anti-American posture.

American characters do not appear prominently in novels of the Revolution—the United States community in Mexico isolated itself in its own exclusive world, and kept contacts with natives to a minimum—but those who do appear in minor roles are not very flatteringly portrayed. No American appears in Azuela's six novels of the Revolution; he does, however, make pointed criticisms in *Los caciques* of the unscrupulous commercialism which he believes to have corrupted Mexican businessmen and to be a direct import from the United States.[65] The same theme appears in Mateos's *La majestad caída* (a novel which shows strong American influence), where the financier Mr. Williams is so coldly obsessed by money that when the ship bearing his wife and son is wrecked with the loss of all passengers he only thinks of the financial losses the disaster has caused him! In Maqueo Castellanos's *La ruina de la casona* there is another unpleasant financier, the shady conspirer symbolically named Jim Remington, always seeking to increase his wealth by exploiting the disturbed Mexican situation in every way. Other American characters are: the egoistic, hypocritical, and treacherous plantation owner Tom Warloo (= Barlow?) in Lepino's *Sangre y humo*; the naïvely enthusiastic, empty-headed Mrs. Stephenson, who after twenty years in Mexico is still incapable of putting a single sentence together in Spanish, in López-Portillo y Rojas's *Fuertes y débiles*; and the unpleasantly severe and joyless

---

[64] p. 512. In fact, of course, Carranza was always very careful to maintain a resolute patriotic stance. See also Galindo, p. 176.

[65] Azuela's mouthpiece in this novel, Rodríguez, attacks the caciques' assistants: 'Your oracle is the Yankee; you know, and need to know, no other definition of the word "business" than that which the Yankee has taught you.' [p. 809]. The latter make much use of the expression *'business es business'* in order to justify their unethical procedures [pp. 811 and 864], stating that 'a concern's probity, my friend, is secured in its safe, and not in the tongue of the first fellow who comes along' [p. 809]. Indeed the semi-official newspaper *El Imparcial* had stated plainly on 23 May 1911 that 'the nation's honour is its credit'. Andrés Molina Enríquez attacks the invasion of the Mexican business world by American methods and attitudes in very similar terms (*Los grandes problemas nacionales*, pp. 310–11).

puritan, Betty Porras, in Quevedo y Zubieta's *México manicomio*. The event during the Revolution which brought anti-American feeling to its greatest intensity and which more than anything else ensured that anti-Americanism became an official posture was the occupation of Veracruz in April 1914 [pp. 33–4 and 173–4]. It seemed to confirm Mexicans' worst fears and suspicions about the United States' intentions towards them, and it created, for a short time at least, rabid xenophobia in Mexico City and Veracruz especially. Its long-term effects were less extreme, but decisive nevertheless. After Veracruz for many years no Mexican in public life could afford to show friendly feelings towards the United States.[66]

Alberto A. Rodríguez's *Don Pascual*, although an exceedingly badly written novel, is a useful source of information about the growth of xenophobia during the American occupation of Veracruz. The author was himself from Veracruz and seems, in part at least, to have written this book as a refutation of allegations made by inhabitants of Mexico City that the *veracruzanos* had not shown sufficient ardour in the defence of their city. He had every reason, then, to exaggerate in his depiction of the nationalistic fury that the invasion produced; and, indeed, he writes in an absurdly over-emphatic style which only makes the hysterical patriotism that is his theme look even more gauche and laughable than it otherwise would. But the mere fact that he is able to take these histrionics as seriously and uncritically as he does makes them highly significant as a guide to the mood of the society be belonged to and described.

The novel describes how, when the Americans invade Veracruz, the city populace heroically defends it. Prominent among the defenders is a prosperous tradesman, don Pascual Ramírez. When the Americans finally take the town, don Pascual and other volunteers establish a camp a little to the south (at Boca del Río) to prevent the marines from advancing any further.[67] Various minor

[66] The complicity of the United States ambassador, Henry Lane Wilson, in the conspiracy against Madero, and his subsequent support of Huerta [pp. 30–1], was to add to popular hostility towards America a little later, when the full facts of his implication became widely known. This did not happen, however, until after Huerta's fall.

[67] This camp of civilian volunteers seems to be wholly fictional. The army garrison, under Maas, withdrew to a camp at Tejería, ten miles to the south, in order to blockade the city and to prevent an American advance on the capital. Rodríguez appears to have elaborated on this (see Quirk, *An Affair of Honor*, pp. 92–7 and 125–6).

adventures and traditionally sentimental love affairs are inter-
spersed, with the intention of leavening the historical narrative.
Finally everything ends happily as the Americans leave in November and all the young people are married off, don Pascual returning
to private life.

The furious patriotism that is instantly aroused by the invasion
knows no limits. The narrator and his characters repeatedly refer
to the Americans with expressions like 'our eternal enemies the
Yankees', 'miserable foreigners', 'despots and tyrants', 'envious
and selfish hypocrites', and 'the pirates of the Americas'. The
author accuses the Americans of being cowards and murderers for
firing on the defenders of Veracruz (who were not, of course,
unarmed). When a girl shoots and kills two American soldiers who
try to arrest her for disobeying an order to halt, her action is completely justified by the author and by all the other characters; for
to fall into the hands of these barbarians 'who seemed to have come
from the savage depths of Africa'[68] is an indignity and an outrage
that no decent Mexican woman can permit: 'Luisa . . . in spite of
being a young lady, was forced to commit murder twice, because if
she had not done so, she and Carolina would have been abused,
just as her respectable mama and her no less respectable sister
Graziela had been abused.'[69] The two latter ladies were not raped,
as this quotation might lead one to imagine, but were merely taken
briefly into custody by the Americans, who treated them with the
utmost respect. This strange and significant equation between the
Americans' territorial violation of Veracruz and a purely imaginary
sexual violation of individual *veracruzanas* occurs again and again
in the novel. As soon as the marines first appear, it is automatically
assumed by all that their intentions are to bomb Veracruz, rape all
the women, and then proceed to conquer all Mexico. When
Luisa's boyfriend sees her limping, his immediate assumption is
that she has been raped. As a slight variation on the theme, the
perfectly reasonable decree ordering the temporary confiscation
of arms from civilians (to bring a halt to sniping) is interpreted
as a measure designed to enable the invaders to 'give full vein
to their cannibal instincts at the expense of defenceless civilized
citizens'.[70]

In this way a social myth was created—or, more accurately,
resuscitated, for all its basic elements had been in existence for

<hr>

[68] p. 242.   [69] p. 242.   [70] p. 280.

many years. Its most notable features are its extraordinarily rapid growth and its basis in mass hysteria, although its early pitch of fervour seems to have declined fairly quickly, in part because of the counterproductive effect of Huerta's clumsy and blatant attempts to turn it to his own ends and use it as an aid in defeating the revolutionaries [pp. 173–4]. This, the only social myth—apart from Madero's short-lived democratic myth [pp. 138–41]—to achieve any significance during the Revolution, was anti-revolutionary rather than revolutionary. Its implications were that all Mexicans, of whatever political beliefs, should rally together and repel the invader; and also that those whose cause was helped by this very invader—as, arguably, was the revolutionaries'—were despicably anti-patriotic. The myth of patriotism is one which only becomes unequivocally useful to revolutionaries once they have won their fight and firmly established themselves in power.[71]

Like all myths, the one which developed in Veracruz and then in the rest of the country in 1914 had its legendary hero. Unlike the federal garrison, commanded by General Gustavo Maas, which withdrew rapidly from Veracruz when the Americans announced their intention of occupying the customs-house, the young pupils of the naval school stayed on to help repel the invader. Among the cadets, one José Azueta held the Americans at bay for a time with a machine-gun. He was finally wounded and dragged away from his post. A few days later Admiral Fletcher (who was in charge of the initial occupation) went to visit the boy, to congratulate him for his bravery, and to offer him the services of his own doctor; Azueta rejected this 'insidious idea', as Rodríguez calls it,[72] and later died. The Revolution had another minor hero and martyr [p. 171].

Such, in broad outline, were the attitudes to Americans during the Revolution. The general contempt that they attracted was, in large part, due to the naïve tactlessness and insensitivity that characterized, as it still tends to, both the behaviour of individual Americans and the policies of their government. Although the Revolution was immediately preceded by somewhat ambiguous anti-American riots in Mexico City and elsewhere, the hostility to the United States that had been smouldering quietly for many decades only burst into flames as a result of the Americans' most

[71] This does not mean that the revolutionaries made any serious attempt to attack the myth itself: the invasion of Veracruz put this out of the question.
[72] p. 322.

ill-considered occupation of Veracruz.[73] After that, things could never again be the same. And so it was possible, for example, for Villa's blatantly criminal raid upon the innocent American border town of Columbus [pp. 36 and 163], to be greeted with undisguised pleasure by large sectors of the Mexican populace.

The Spaniards resident in Mexico during the Revolution can occupy less of our attention. They are only worth mentioning because the Revolution has sometimes been interpreted as a movement to assert Mexican nationalism by eradicating Hispanic influence and traditions from the country.[74] If this interpretation were correct, one would expect to find evidence in novels and other available sources of widespread hostility to Spaniards.

The fact is that there is little such evidence to be found. Spaniards in Mexico certainly tended to be fiercely anti-revolutionary, as would be expected from the position they occupied in society: 'The Spaniards are the traders of Mexico. They keep the countless pawn-shops (empeños); they are the usurers and money-lenders of all kinds; they are the overseers on the haciendas and, incidentally, they keep all the grocery shops; in fact, they control the sale of nearly everything in Mexico.'[75] The novelists are not, however, very interested in Spaniards. One very typical one appears briefly in *La ruina de la casona*: the owner of a small general store in Mexico City, Rafael Menendezorra y Rendueles. He sells adulterated and falsified goods, lends money at very high rates of interest, and uses his premises for any other purpose, however shady, that can be of financial advantage to him. Other early novelists of the Revolution appear not to have considered the Spaniards important enough to put into their books. There are two exceptions that must be considered separately, for there is clearly a direct Spanish influence at work on both of them, and they consequently give flattering portraits of Spaniards. These two are Lepino's *Sangre y humo* and Rodríguez's *Don Pascual*.

[73] There are no reports in, for example, *Foreign Relations, 1911, 1912,* and *1913* of any significant anti-Americanism during Madero's rebellion or his regime, or during the decena trágica. For the post-Veracruz increase in anti-American feeling and acts, see Ibid., *1914,* pp. 659–90; *1915,* pp. 837–1004; and *1916,* pp. 465–626 and 650–708. See also F. C. Turner, pp. 207–31 and 236–48; and Quirk, *An Affair of Honor,* pp. 107–10.

[74] Frank Tannenbaum, especially, advances this interpretation (see, for example, his *Peace by Revolution*).

[75] Edith O'Shaughnessy, *A Diplomat's Wife in Mexico* (New York and London, 1916), p. 94.

The untraced K. Lepino (possibly a pseudonym) certainly knew Mexico well and had lived there for many years, as his accurate descriptions of Mexican life and fluent use of Mexican Spanish show: he very likely was a Mexican. A strong Spanish influence, however, is shown in the author's habit of self-consciously putting every *mexicanismo* between inverted commas and in the inclusion of a glossary explaining every one of them—although the novel was published in Mexico. It is in no way surprising, then, that the Spanish ranchero don Cipriano who plays an important role in the novel should be a thoroughly upright, sensible and noble man, with none of the less attractive qualities ascribed by Maqueo Castellanos to Spaniards in Mexico; nor that the equally admirable hero of the novel, don Florencio Izaquirre, another wealthy and industrious ranchero, should be given an exclusively Spanish pedigree by his creator. It is significant, perhaps, that *Sangre y humo* is the most fiercely right-wing novel of the Revolution—the only one which seeks positively to defend Victoriano Huerta (Spain was one of the countries which recognized Huerta).

Rodríguez, like Lepino, may or may not have been a Spaniard but he displays a strong Spanish connection (it seems probable that both were sons of Spaniards but born in Mexico). The intense patriotism of *Don Pascual* argues, of course, in favour of its author's Mexican nationality. There was a large Spanish colony in Veracruz, though, and Rodríguez is evidently close to it; for he refers to it constantly in the most glowing terms, assuring the reader that its members are as devoted to Mexico as the Mexicans themselves, and that they participated valiantly in the defence of Veracruz. The attitudes reflected in *Don Pascual* are also extremely conservative and anti-revolutionary.

The largely negative evidence provided by the novels about feelings towards Spaniards between 1910 and 1917 must be qualified by one or two positive facts from other sources. During the famine which struck Mexico City in 1914 and 1915 the traders in foodstuffs—mostly Spaniards—were accused, rightly or wrongly, of hoarding supplies. The wrath of the starving city populace was attracted towards them, and bitter anti-Spanish feeling grew; Spaniards were abused in the streets, and hostile demonstrations formed outside their closed and shuttered shops.[76] And evidence

---

[76] Ramírez Plancarte, pp. 315, 324 and 346–53.

of further anti-Spanish feeling is found in the notorious activities of Pancho Villa, whose first action on conquering new territory was always to expel all Spaniards from it.

Spaniards were not popular during the Revolution, and as individuals they suffered from it. Their reputation as unscrupulous money-grubbers made them, under certain conditions—the famine in Mexico City, the personal hostility of Villa—into open targets for attack. Yet there is a vast difference between the anti-American feeling which, after 1914, attained the proportions of a full social myth and the anti-Spanish feeling which was never more than sporadic and occasional. There is no evidence to suggest that, over the country as a whole, dislike for Spaniards became very much more acute during the period of the Revolution than before it (Mexican liberalism had always been strongly anti-Spanish). Spaniards, when they aroused the wrath of Mexicans, did so because of their reputation and activities as individuals. As individuals they were more or less integrated into the society with which they had much in common—language, customs, religion, traditions. Spaniards never posed the concerted and powerful threat to Mexicans that Americans did; and they never attracted hostility, as the Americans did, as an exclusive, privileged and wholly alien community living in their midst. The only people who, during the Revolution, thought the Spaniards significant enough to conceive of the Revolution as a crusade against them were Pancho Villa and the Spaniards themselves, who complained vociferously about their sufferings in the columns of the right-wing Spanish press.[77]

The long-term importance of the foreign presence in Mexico during the Revolution and of Mexican reactions to it at that time consists in its setting of foundations for that fierce nationalism which has characterized post-revolutionary Mexico and which has been a vital element in its political stability. National pride had not been strong in pre-revolutionary Mexico, with its official deference to foreign interests and its élite's constant preference of foreign

---

[77] The monarchist *ABC* gave much publicity to the plight of Spaniards in Mexico. Letters, reports, and articles on the subject—of a uniformly petulant tone—were published frequently. *El Liberal*, however, pointed out that maybe the Spaniards resident in Mexico had brought much of this hostility upon themselves by their own misguided actions, alleging (on 25 July 1914) that the Spanish community in Torreón had gone so far as to hold a banquet to celebrate Madero's death.

culture, foreign products and foreign ways of behaving [pp. 254–68]. A reaction against these tendencies was an important part of the revolutionary process, and Mexico emerged at the end of its Revolution as a nation with a firm belief in its own importance and value. This new nationalism sprang, in particular, from the bitter anti-American feeling that grew during the Revolution; and its origins can be even more precisely traced to the invasion of the city of Veracruz in April 1914, which turned a general unspecified grudge into a full social myth. Dislike of Spaniards undoubtedly contributed to the growth of xenophobia and, out of it, nationalism; but it does not appear to have been a basic factor. Hostility to *gachupines* seems only to have become a vital part of Mexican nationalism after the Revolution; particularly, perhaps, after 1927, when the improvement in relations between Mexico and the United States made it desirable for the government to dampen Mexicans' hostility to *gringos* and find something else to put in its place.

(d) The Church

When the Revolution broke out in 1910 the Church in Mexico was in an equivocal position. During the colonial period it had accumulated great wealth and power, which it had consolidated after independence, during the first half of the nineteenth century, until it came to be the most powerful institutionalized force in the country (at the same time as the public treasury was empty). It had consequently become one of the principal enemies of liberalism in Mexico, and took its place firmly in the conservative camp. The Reforma laws and the 1857 Constitution were strongly anti-clerical [pp. 19–20], and signified a defeat on paper for the Mexican Church and its removal from the political scene. But the clergy fought quite ruthlessly for its traditional privileges; and then Díaz, following a policy of compromise in order to keep all influential sectors satisfied, turned a blind eye to the Church's failure to comply with the law. On the outbreak of Revolution, then, the Church still had considerable interests to defend, although its position had been extensively undermined and might collapse if a government came into power that was prepared to enforce the law. Its attitude to Porfirio Díaz was consequently ambiguous: on the one hand, it welcomed—indeed depended on—his studied neglect of anti-clerical legislation: on the other, it disparaged his failure to suppress this legislation (as well as his encouragement of positivist philosophy). The Church was acutely aware of the instability of its position. A change of government could mean either a disastrous collapse in its fortunes or a glorious return to the situation obtaining in earlier and happier times. There were high stakes to play for in the Revolution.

The early novelists show a disappointing, and somewhat surprising, lack of interest in the history of the Church during the Revolution. They have little to say about the activities either of the institution as a whole or of individual members of it. Our account will, therefore, be based principally upon Mariano Azuela's *Los caciques*, the only one of these early novels in which any attempt is made to portray the Church's social role in the Revolution. Azuela's attitude is extremely hostile, and he resorts to constant and violent caricature in order to make his attacks more effective; but there is enough other evidence to suggest that his exaggerations are not arbitrary or unfounded.

Father Jeremías is the youngest of the Del Llano brothers, the ruthless speculators and caciques [p. 25n.] who are in control of a provincial town. He is in close collaboration with his family, using the weighty authority of the Church to support its many interests; Azuela seeks to symbolize in him the Church's alliance with the powerful and wealthy sectors of society and its furtherance of causes favourable to them. Above all, Father Jeremías constantly preaches the virtues of patience and resignation. He urges on everyone the unquestioning acceptance of his lot and of the belief that suffering and hardship must be passively accepted by those who experience them as a necessary qualification for their later enjoyment of an eternal life after death. So successful is Father Jeremías in his defence of the *status quo*, indeed, that even the chief victim of his brothers' machinations accepts his complete ruination by them without a murmur of protest: 'It is God's will. Let no one oppose the designs of Divine Providence! Blessed be His holy hand!'[78] Priests do, of course, enjoy unique powers of persuasion in a religious society, as the Mexican Church of the time was very well aware:

No word is so efficacious as the word of the Catholic priest. The priest when he is ordained receives a very special grace to stamp his language

---

[78] *Los caciques*, p. 258.

with a supernatural talisman [sic] which has the power of attracting all
who listen and of sealing his sermons with a divine character which has
admirable powers of suggestion over his audiences, however refractory
they may appear. For when the priest speaks, there speaks truth, there
speaks reason, there speaks philosophy, there speaks unfalsified History,
virtue, abnegation, good example; and he lends such persuasion to his
words that, like a magnet, he pulls the masses towards him.[79]

Father Jeremías's extreme conservatism means, of course, that
he opposes any suggestion of social reform, going even so far as to
accuse the mild democrat Madero of being a communist. It is
interesting that he should immediately think of communism when
theories of social equality are mentioned. Communism was not
strong in Mexico at the time of the Revolution; and only the
Church seems to have considered it a really serious menace (a
reflection of the international rivalry between the two organizations). The strong impulse given to Catholic workers' organizations from 1908 onwards [pp. 284–5] was designed expressly to
combat its possible influence on the poor. In November 1914 a
collective pastoral letter written (in exile) by seven archbishops and
five bishops forbade Mexican Catholics to attend any meetings or
read any publications of the *Casa del Obrero Mundial* [p. 235].[80]
The Mexican clergy repeatedly stressed that social peace and
harmony depended, above all, on the maintenance of rigid divisions between the classes, and especially on keeping the working
classes in their place: 'The basis of the tranquillity of society is
without any doubt the clear division of classes, conscious of their
rights and mutual obligations. His Holiness Leo XIII said in his
Encyclical *Rerum Novarum*: "To expel social differences from the
world is impossible." '[81] Thus, when Father Jeremías hears in 1911

[79] Dr. José Castillo y Piña, *Cuestiones sociales* (Mexico, 1934). This is a collection of lectures given by the author, a prominent church spokesman on social
questions, between 1910 and 1934. The lecture quoted here is dated 1921.

[80] *Carta pastoral colectiva a los católicos mexicanos sobre la actual persecución
religiosa y normas de conducta para los mismos católicos* (Nov. 1914).

[81] 'El sindicalismo cristiano' (1912), in Castillo y Piña, op. cit. In the same
volume a study of women's education, dated 1915, stated that the important
subjects for females were cooking, mending, dressmaking, ironing, sweeping,
'lighting fires, sewing buttons . . .'; that physical, moral, and religious education should be stressed more; that girls should be prepared for life by being
taught in school to suffer (Castillo y Piña does not elaborate on the particular
pedagogical system to be employed in this branch of education); and that 'classes
about Arithmetic, Grammar, Reading, Writing, Calligraphy, Lessons about
Things [sic], etc., etc.', if given at all, should be relegated to a very minor role
(op. cit., pp. 187–218).

of some discontent among the poor, caused by their lack of basic foods, he laments 'I don't know who has awakened such ambitions among the masses; no one now is satisfied with the lot that God gave him.'[82]

When Madero's rebellion breaks out, Father Jeremías is not quite sure what to think of it. As we have already seen, the Church was equivocal in its attitude to Porfirio Díaz; and it was equally equivocal in its attitude to the man who toppled him. On the one hand, any disturbance of the peace was, in principle, undesirable from the Church's point of view: ' "Social disintegration! No more respect for society, for the family, or for Religion!" exclaimed Father Jeremías, still trembling.'[83] On the other hand, this rebellion might bring about an improvement in the Church's position: 'I don't utterly disapprove of this revolution, for it could give back to me many of our lost rights.'[84] Madero's personal beliefs, however, hardly recommend him to Father Jeremías: 'The Church and Our Lord God would be more honoured if this movement were not led by this poor fellow Madero, infected with the leprosy not only of freethinking but also of masonry, spiritism . . . and who knows what else.'[85] In non-fictional sources, however, one finds records only of Church opposition to the Madero revolt (in the period prior to its success). The hierarchy published various pastoral letters condemning the revolt for its transgression of the fifth commandment; and on 3 April 1911 the faithful gathered in the Basilica of Guadalupe (the national shrine, near Mexico City) in order to pray for the suppression of the rebellion. The uncertain feeling that the Revolution might well turn out to be good for Church interests and ought, perhaps, to be welcomed rather than condemned—the other side of the coin, that Azuela bears witness to—was, naturally enough, kept well concealed.

The Church made her first definite move when, with Madero's victory, the politically ambitious of all kinds started raising their heads: in 1911 the Partido Católico Nacional was founded (its formation was announced in the press on the same day as the resignation of Díaz).[86] Although it was illegal, according to the Constitution, for priests to play any part in politics, such was Madero's concern for democracy that he not only did not oppose the P.C.N., but was even reported as expressing strong approval

---

[82] *Los caciques*, p. 825.   [83] p. 831.   [84] p. 831.
[85] p. 831.   [86] *El Imparcial*, 18 May 1911.

of it: 'Its programme reveals progressive thinking and a desire to collaborate in the country's progress in a responsible and constitutional way'[87]—wishful thinking, perhaps.

To defend its re-entry into politics, the Church employed the specious reasoning to which it was to have recourse several times during the next few years. It claimed, by reference to Article 9 of the Constitution, that Mexican Catholics were quite legitimately defending their rights by forming the P.C.N. Alleging discrimination against Roman Catholics in Porfirian Mexico, it said that the P.C.N.'s sole aim was to right this wrong. It protested that the P.C.N. would respect the Constitution—in all those parts where the Constitution was acceptable to the P.C.N.: 'Catholics accept and will defend with all their energy the Constitution in all those aspects which are organic. "Organic" means establishing God as the foundation of civil society and as the origin of all authority.'[88] And it affirmed that the P.C.N. was a fully democratic party—'with the proviso that nothing be understood or practised in a way which infringes on the order assigned by God to individuals, to the family and to society'.[89]

In *Los caciques*, Azuela attempts to take us behind this—not very convincing—façade of moderation and to show us the real truth about the formation of the Partido Católico Nacional. He presents it as the outcome of close and cynical collaboration between the clergy and the wealthy landowners and industrialists, in which the former agreed to use those exceptional powers of persuasion we have already referred to, and the latter to furnish material aid, in order to promote the common interests of the two groups. In fact, although the clergy made nominal protestations that they were not directly concerned in the P.C.N.—there were no priests among its officers—no one had any real doubts that they controlled it (the Archbishop of Mexico, Mora y del Río, was widely known to be the party's principal organizer). Azuela depicts a meeting held shortly after Madero's victory, of Father

---

[87] *La Nación*, 8 Jan. 1913.

[88] 'Concepto católico de la política mexicana' (dated Aug. 1911), in *El resurgimiento mexicano. Cuatro opúsculos sobre algunas cuestiones que ha suscitado el ingreso de los católicos a la vida pública* (Mexico, 1913), p. 5. See also 'La Iglesia Católica y la cuestión social' (dated 1912), in Castillo y Piña, op. cit. Pope Leo XIII's encyclical, *Rerum novarum* (1891), and his letter, *Graves de communi* (1901), were much quoted by Mexican church spokesmen seeking to defend their entry into politics at this time.

[89] Ibid., p. 6.

Jeremías and another priest with some twenty representatives of the local rich. Well supplied with French brandy—on which Father Jeremías becomes increasingly drunk—all twenty people present swear loyalty to the new party. They are not prepared to follow Jeremías's suggestion of personally forming the organizing committee of the local branch of the party, for they do not want to commit themselves too openly. But each assures him that all his employees will be induced to vote for the party's candidates, and the meeting ends in cheerful conviviality.

Another feature of the Church's sally into public life under Madero, of which Azuela makes no mention, was the formation of Catholic Workers' Circles. The Catholic Action movement had, in fact, started during the last years of the Porfirian period;[90] on 23 February 1910 the Mexican clergy had received a letter of congratulation from Pius X himself, in which he defined Catholic Action's principal purpose: 'And so that you may the more readily make the workers persevere in their duties and assist them in remaining unharmed by socialist snares, you will see to it that, under your authoritative guidance, uniting their resources under the leadership and auspices of Religion, they themselves can provide for their necessities.'[91] The movement was, however, considerably intensified during the regimes of Madero and Huerta. The aim of the circles, according to one of their most active organizers, Dr. José Castillo y Piña, were in fact threefold—and not, it seems, very realistically adjusted to the actual needs and potentialities of Mexican workers: to give religious instruction to workers, to stamp out their vices and inculcate into them a love of their labours, and to improve their economic condition by encouraging them to save.[92] The self-help schemes were the basis of the Circles' economic organization, and do not seem to have been a very viable proposition, given the low wages earned by workers at

---

[90] In 1907 the few dispersed Catholic workers' circles that existed in Mexico City had been united, and in October 1908 the Unión Católica Obrera was formed with the Mexico City circles and one each from Saltillo (Coahuila), Aguascalientes, Oaxaca, León (Guanajuato) and Cuidad Camargo (Tamaulipas). The first national assembly of the Union was held in December 1911. The Archbishop of Mexico, Mora y del Río, and the Bishop of Oaxaca, Gillow, presided over it. See 'El sindicalismo cristiano' (Mexico, 1912) in Castillo y Piña, op. cit.

[91] 'La Iglesia Católica y la cuestión social', in Castillo y Piña, op cit., p. 54. Pius X's encyclical, *Il fermo proposito* (1905), had laid down the principles of Catholic Action; it was much referred to by Castillo y Piña and his colleagues.

[92] 'Círculos católicos de obreros', in Castillo y Piña, op. cit.

the time [p. 187n.]. They scarcely appear to have been over-generous: 'members who over a period of 50 years have frequented the Circle and have not received any aid have the right to withdraw all the money they have deposited.'(!)[93] The movement of Catholic Action seems only to have had small success: in 1912 it could claim only forty circles and 20,000 members altogether, and at the height of its fortunes in 1913 it claimed fifty circles and 30,000 members.[94] None of the novelists mention it.

The Partido Católico Nacional had more success. On 1 June 1912 its official organ, the daily *La Nación*, first appeared. Its readers were regaled with advertisements for 'the latest novelties in ecclesiastical dress' and editorials condemning liberalism. Its attitude to Madero was, true to form, highly ambiguous. Although, as head of a liberalizing administration—and as a heretic—he should theoretically have been the target for fierce attack, the P.C.N. was well aware that another president might well not be so tolerant of anti-constitutional Church interference in political affairs. So, although the Partido Constitucional Progresista and its newspaper *Nueva Era* (as well as *El Imparcial* when it turned Maderista) were the objects almost daily of violent attacks by *La Nación*, it kept prudently quiet about Madero himself (who had been the P.C.N. candidate in the presidential elections of 1911)—a policy it retained right up to Madero's fall, in marked contrast with the rest of the non-Maderista press [p. 143]. The Church hierarchy issued edicts instructing the faithful to vote for P.C.N. candidates in the elections for deputies that were held in 1912,[95] and the Catholic party duly acquired nearly thirty per cent of the seats in the lower chamber.

[93] Castillo y Piña, op. cit., p. 225.
[94] Castillo y Piña, op. cit., pp. 54, 229 and 259.
[95] See, for example, the edict issued on 12 June 1912 (reprinted in *La Nación*, 22 June 1912) by Orozco, Bishop of Chiapas:

> All Catholics should . . . as soon as possible join the Partido Católico Nacional which, based on justice, on true liberty which ennobles man, and on the most sincere patriotism, can only guarantee the designation of men who will make for the happiness of the people . . . Parish priests should note that the obligation we have indicated to them of not becoming involved in politics does not exclude the obligation which presses them, according to what has been laid down by the Holy See, to explain and make the faithful fully understand the duties and rights which are theirs as Catholic citizens, as we have just explained.

The Archbishops of Mexico, Oaxaca, Puebla, Michoacán and Linares issued a similar edict a few weeks later (*La Nación*, 25 July 1912).

With Madero's downfall and death and the accession of Huerta, the attitude of the Church, characterized so far during the Revolution by watchful, non-committal ambivalence, became for the first time explicit and unequivocal. Emboldened, perhaps, by recent successes, the whole Catholic sector hailed Huerta as Mexico's saviour. He seemed to them to promise the kind of strong right-wing government that best served the Church's interests; and the frequent mentions in his speeches and in his conversation of the Almighty [p. 173] appeared to indicate that he was a devout Roman Catholic himself. *La Nación*'s first editorial after the decena trágica, on 25 February, welcomed Huerta effusively. The official Catholic newspaper felt that moral judgements and references to the fifth commandment were not, now, called for: 'To attempt to criticize would, at these times, be to throw more fuel on to the still-smoking undergrowth, and we do not believe such action to be either patriotic or prudent.' Azuela makes Father Jeremías, in his welcome for Huerta's triumph, take the same sort of sophistry even further:

'You are in error judging the execution of Madero as a crime', intervened Father Jeremías. 'Regicide itself is approved by the Church, as I can show. The learned men of the Company of Jesus have brilliantly sustained this thesis. But what am I saying! All of you, as good cultured Catholics, know the exquisite little work of Father Sardá y Salvani. One may wound, injure, kill, whatever one wants, if the result is beneficial to us and *ad majorem Dei gloriam*.'[96]

Huerta gave the P.C.N. due rewards for its loyalty: Francisco León de la Barra and others of its leaders took important places in his cabinet; and in October 1913, when the dictator closed the lower chamber and imprisoned the deputies, the P.C.N. members alone escaped detention.

Perhaps the most remarkable demonstration of Church support for Huerta came in January 1914 with the *Homenaje a Cristo Rey*, the precedent for the *cristero* revolt of 1926–1929. When the special prayers for Huerta's triumph that the hierarchy ordered to be said during masses failed to establish Huerta's regime, a more drastic way of enlisting God's support for the dictator's cause was

[96] Op. cit., p. 849. Sardá y Salvani was the author of a book violently attacking liberalism to which Azuela refers here, *El liberalismo es pecado*. The book's intransigence clearly had a strong effect on Azuela, for he had already referred to it at some length in his earlier novel *Los fracasados* (1906) (*Obras completas*, I, pp. 62–3).

essayed: Christ was formally, and with great pomp and ceremony, proclaimed in churches throughout Mexico as the Supreme King of Mexico's destiny. [97] The Revolution, it was declared, was God's punishment for the secularism of Mexico's Constitution; so the country's only hope of salvation was to perform the solemn act of prostrating itself at Jesus's feet. In Mexico Cathedral, cries of 'Viva Cristo Rey!' mingled during the ceremony with others of 'Viva el señor presidente!'; and the Jesuit, Eduardo de la Peza, preached a sermon pledging the Church's eternal support for Huerta, condemning the Revolution, and inviting his public to work with all their strength for 'the restoration of peace and the Kingdom of God'. [98]

A more lastingly successful piece of anti-revolutionary propaganda, however, was the spreading in 1914 of the myth that the Revolution was a foreign conspiracy, a massive protestant crusade originating in the United States. This myth is the theme of the collective pastoral letter to Mexican Catholics of November 1914 [p. 281]. It talks about 'the intimate relationship that this persecution has with protestantism' and, with reference to the outrages committed by Carrancistas against the Church, it asserts that 'contrary to what has been claimed, these acts are not natural consequences of the unruliness of troops entering a town; these deeds obey a plan which has been previously forged in connivance with Freemasonry and with certain Protestant corporations of the United States'. It concludes by forbidding Roman Catholics to enter protestant churches, read protestant books, or listen to protestant propaganda; and lamenting that 'while Catholic priests are persecuted and their churches closed, the masters of error, the Protestant ministers, enjoy complete liberty and take advantage of it to activate their propaganda, which is both heretical and unpatriotic'. [99]

[97] Castillo y Piña, 'Homenaje a Cristo Rey', op. cit.

[98] *El Imparcial*, 12 Jan. 1914.

[99] p. 29. This complaint was much repeated at the time by Church spokesmen. See also, for example, *Apuntes para la historia. La cuestión religiosa en Jalisco. Homenaje de respecto y adhesión de la colonia jalisciense de la ciudad de México al Ilustre Mártir de la persecución religiosa en Jalisco el Exmo. y Rmo. Sr. Dr. y Maestro don Francisco Orozco y Jiménez Dignísimo Metropolitano de Guadalajara* (Mexico, 1918), especially p. 2. The allegation that the Revolution was a protestant crusade seems principally to have been based on the fact that Moisés A. Saenz (1888–1941), a fairly prominent Carrancista intellectual, was a protestant lay preacher. This slight factual base was all that was needed for

The myth of the Revolution as a protestant crusade was influential enough to convince four of the novelists of the Revolution. Lepino describes the Carrancista leaders as men who were failures in life and envious of those who by their own efforts and merits had been successful; he gives special mention to small traders, schoolmasters and protestant ministers. Quevedo y Zubieta, in *En tierra de sangre y broma*, conveys the impression that he believes the Revolution to have been dominated by homosexual protestant schoolteachers.[100] Correa, in *El dolor de ser máquina* (Mexico, 1932), also presents the Revolution as a great protestant conspiracy. And Vasconcelos repeatedly denounces Carrancismo in precisely the same terms [pp. 121 and 207].

Besides spreading this particular myth, Church spokesmen took every opportunity generally to denigrate the revolutionaries, particularly the constitucionalistas. Many of their accusations were undoubtedly true, but they only increased revolutionary anti-clericalism.

The Mexican Church, in supporting Huerta so openly, had backed a loser; and it was made to pay dearly for its error, with harsh persecution which lasted for many years after the end of the Revolution. Before 1913 there had been little anti-clericalism. Cabrera, in his six-point summary of the ills which caused unrest in 1911 [pp. 185–7, 191, 194, and 269–70], made no mention at all of clericalism (in 1915 he was to write the pamphlet *La cuestión religiosa en México*, a reasoned but bitter indictment of the Church). Maderista revolutionaries never made any attacks on clergy or churches; the old hostility between liberals and Catholics remained dormant throughout the Maderista uprising—another indication of the genteel nature of the latter [pp. 189–97]. It was

the mythical elaboration. The fact that the Y.M.C.A., which was established in Mexico in 1901, had had a fairly successful career there had sharpened Roman Catholic fears.

    100 Op. cit., part I, chaps 12 and 13, and part II, chap. 2, where he describes Saenz (who was an educator) in a hostile and contemptuous manner. López-Portillo y Rojas also mounts a violent attack on schoolmasters (op. cit., pp. 216–18) and describes the perverse and subversive Zapatista intellectual Alcocer [pp. 101–2] as a typical member of the profession. López-Portillo's hostility springs, however, from rather different roots—his point of view is that of the hacendado, for whom all teachers are merely impertinent meddlers who threaten the lethargic calm of the hacienda by putting ideas into the minds of the young. Hacendados formed, of course, an important part of the traditionalist Catholic sector of Mexican society. There may also here be a reference to the leading Zapatista intellectual, Otilio Montaño, who was a schoolmaster.

when the Church re-entered public life by forming the Partido Católico Nacional that liberals returned to the attack, and the traditional rivalry was renewed. The attack was, as yet however, solely verbal, and largely confined to the more radical of the liberals.

It was not until the constitucionalista revolution that the wrath of all revolutionaries was brought to fall on the established Church in Mexico. The years 1914 and 1915, especially, were characterized by daily attacks on churches and on their contents. Obregón and other leaders made anti-clericalism a point of policy [pp. 167–70], imprisoning priests and exacting forced 'loans' from them[101] (many priests and most of the hierarchy prudently scurried into exile upon the fall of Huerta, from where they wrote pastoral letters telling their flock to be heroic in the face of persecution and martyrdom).[102] The activities of Catholic Action in Mexico were brusquely curtailed. The violent pronouncements of the Carrancista general in Azuela's *Domitilo quiere ser diputado*, Xicoténcatl Robespierre Cebollino [pp. 169–70], are, in fact, no great exaggeration of the feelings of the time. Altogether, the price the Mexican Church had to pay for its sins was a high one indeed: during the period of severe persecution which started in 1914 and was still not finished twenty-five years later, its power was much undermined.

And yet there is a strong note of ambivalence about even this fierce wave of anti-clericalism. The same soldiers—Carrancistas as well as Villistas and Zapatistas—who sacked churches and imprisoned priests wore medals depicting the Virgin of Guadalupe in their hats, and did not omit to visit her shrine, the Basilica of

---

[101] For first-hand reports of Carranza's anti-clerical policy see especially *Foreign Relations 1914*, pp. 560 and 569; *Foreign Relations 1915*, pp. 1004–30; Ramírez Plancarte, pp. 325ff.; and *Memorándum del Arzobispo de Guadalajara* (1917), where the persecution in Jalisco, a particularly staunch Roman Catholic stronghold, is described.

[102] Notably the long *Carta pastoral colectiva a los católicos mexicanos sobre la actual persecución religiosa y normas de conducta para los mismos católicos* (Nov. 1914), signed in exile by seven archbishops and five bishops. The acute irony of such expressions as 'Happy those who did not defect at the moment of trial!' [p. 18] appears to be quite unconscious. Orozco, Bishop of Chiapas (1902–12) and Archbishop of Guadalajara (1913–36), was more resolute than most in the face of persecution, and he consequently became a key figure in the fight between Church and State.

The gathering of Mexican Church dignitaries in Mexico City, in order to be able to go without delay via Veracruz into exile upon the fall of Huerta, is reported in *El Independiente*, 10 and 23 July 1914.

Guadalupe, on reaching Mexico City. According to one novelist, Carrancista shouts of 'Death to the clergy!' were often qualified by others—from the lips of the same Carrancistas—of 'Long live the village priests!'[103] The painter and revolutionist 'Dr. Atl' reports:

The revolutionary who was fighting against the clergy and against the Church, on the instigation of others or simply because he did not know who he was fighting against, remained profoundly religious and profoundly Catholic. After sacking a church he would carry small images off to his barracks or his home in order to perform a triduum, to light a candle to them, or to ask them to protect his family.[104]

In *Los de abajo*, Demetrio Macías and his guerrillas constantly have the names of saints and of God on their lips, and they instinctively recite the Lord's prayer on finding the bodies of companions. The vendor of prayers and lucky charms in Aguascalientes—'All good Catholics who devoutly recite this prayer to Christ Crucified will be freed from tempests, plagues, wars, and famines'[105]— does a roaring trade during the Convention, Demetrio's men being among her best customers:

La Codorniz . . . asked the vendor to extract a tooth for him; Margarito bought the black stone of a certain fruit, which has the property of delivering its owner from thunderbolts and any other disaster; and Anastasio Montañés bought a prayer to Christ Crucified, which he carefully folded up and, with great piety, placed next to his chest.[106]

And yet when, near a village in Jalisco, they come across the local priest at the head of a group of faithful, armed—not only with guns —to resist marauding revolutionaries, they do not hesitate for a

---

[103] Lepino, *Sangre y humo*, pp. 259–60. *El clero*—often personified as '*don Clero*'—was a conventional liberal term of abuse, referring more particularly to the upper ranks of the Church hierarchy. *Padrecito* was, in contrast, a widespread term of endearment reserved for humble village priests.

[104] *Las artes populares en México*, II, p. 91.   [105] p. 404.

[106] p. 404. Civil wars provide conditions in which superstition can flourish. The prophecies of la madre Matiana, a set of predictions allegedly made by a woman on her deathbed at the end of the seventeenth century, enjoyed a revival in popularity during the Revolution. La madre Matiana had prophesied wars, mass extermination and invasions, and, more particularly, had predicted that a time would come when four Franciscos would govern Mexico, the first three of which would soon be deposed. After the short periods in office of Francisco León de la Barra, Francisco Madero and Francisco Carvajal (the Interim President after the fall of Huerta), this prophecy was widely interpreted as meaning that Francisco Villa would be President of Mexico (see Azuela, *Las moscas*, pp. 890 and 892; Quevedo y Zubieta, *En tierra de sangre y broma*, p. 115; Maqueo Castellanos, p. 335; and O'Shaughnessy, p. 154).

moment in massacring them all, and sacking the priest's house and the church:

> A few federal soldiers and a poor devil of a priest with a hundred or so deluded fools, all united under the ancient banner, 'Our Religion and Our Privileges'. The priest was left swinging from a mesquit tree, and on the ground were scattered corpses bearing on their breasts little shields of red flannel and the words: 'Stop! The Sacred Heart of Jesus is with me!'
> 'I've made up all my back-pay, with a bit of bonus,' said La Codorniz showing off the cloaks and gold rings he had taken from the priest's house.
> 'That kind of fighting's a pleasure!' exclaimed El Manteca, with obscenities between every other word. 'At least you know what you're risking your skin for!'
> And he seized with the same hand that held the reins a glittering brilliant that he had torn from the Divine Hostage in the church.[107]

This curious duality, the combination of fierce anti-clericalism and strong, even superstitious religious faith, is best exemplified by the mock confession with which Macías tests Luis Cervantes on the latter's appearance at the revolutionary camp, early in the novel. He has Cervantes arrested and tells him he is to be shot as a spy; he then dresses one of his henchmen in stolen priest's clothing and sends him to give Cervantes his 'last confession'; and when Cervantes fails to say anything self-incriminatory, he is immediately welcomed as a genuine revolutionary. It does not even cross Macías's mind that Cervantes could possibly profane a sacrament by telling lies in the 'confession'; yet he has absolutely no qualms about committing the outrageous sacrilege of faking a sacrament himself.

Even fanatical revolutionary anti-clericalism was insufficient, then, to sweep away the religiosity implanted in men's minds by constant indoctrination. This fact did not, perhaps, help the Church very much in its plight during the many years of intense persecution, for religiosity appears to have done nothing to temper the fierceness of the persecution itself. It was, however, a major factor in the Church's resurgence after the years of persecution to its present, once again highly influential, position.

The Mexican Church followed a course during the Revolution which was neither very intelligent nor very Christian. It behaved,

[107] p. 390.

perhaps, much as one might expect a powerful established Church to behave in the circumstances; its behaviour is, nevertheless, indefensible in terms of the Church's own teaching. It came badly out of the Revolution: it scarcely deserved any better. For post-revolutionary governments, however, the unpopularity the Mexican Church attracted upon itself was most useful, for they were thus provided with a very convenient Aunt Sally on which to blame Mexico's misfortunes and with which to distract attention from their own shortcomings. Thus the years 1912–1915 saw the sowing of the seeds of the anti-clerical myth and the religious persecution of the 1920s and 1930s, which came to a climax in the cristero revolt of 1926–1929.

(e) The Army

In any revolution a vital role is played by the Regular Army, the ruling classes' principal physical means of imposing their will on the rest of the country. If the government has insufficient force, or fails to make efficient use of force to put the revolution down, especially in its early stages when the latter is at its most vulner-able, then the work of the revolutionaries is made very much easier.[108]

The part played by the Porfirian Army during the Mexican Revolution provides a good illustration of the above thesis. During the first half of the nineteenth century, with its almost constant civil war, an irresponsible and predatory military caste had come to be the dominant sector in Mexican public life. The Army became a safe, lucrative, and easy career, which offered the best—usually the only—chance of social improvement. During the long years of Porfirian peace, however, the Army had little to do besides putting down the occasional strike and staging colourful parades and pro-cessions. Furthermore, Díaz was careful not to let his army become strong enough to offer him any serious challenge. At the same time as he brought the military to heel by creating a central-ized national army, he studiously failed to make any real effort to modernize and professionalize it—in a period when rapid advances in military technology made such modernization necessary in any effective fighting force. Díaz appeared to have been successful in curing Mexico of her apparently endemic militarism; but in doing

[108] Pettee, pp. 89 and 104–6; Brinton, pp. 94–9; Stone, p. 167; Johnson, pp. 14–22; and Eckstein, pp. 153–8.

so he had made the fatal error for a dictator of depriving himself of adequate armed protection, and leaving himself very vulnerable to violent opposition.[109] In 1910 the Mexican Army's 4,000 officers (mostly from the middle and upper sectors of society) and 20,000 enlisted men (mostly illiterate Indios) were out of practice, inadequately trained and equipped, and totally unprepared for serious fighting; and thus the Madero revolt, which had such an inauspicious and feeble beginning, was allowed, simply because of the Army's inability to stamp it out, enough time gradually to gain momentum and force, and finally to topple the government [pp. 23–4 and 26]. And the remainder of the Federal Army's career, until it was finally demobilized in 1914, was no more distinguished. One receives the same impression of ineptitude and tiredness from the Porfirian Army as from the Porfirian administration itself during its final years.[110]

The early novelists of the Revolution do not provide very abundant or detailed information about the Federal Army. None of them displays any close knowledge of it, and there is no sustained attempt to portray the Revolution from the Army's viewpoint (this does not happen until later, and most notably in the short stories of Rafael Muñoz and in Urquizo's *Tropa vieja* (1943) [p. 66n.]). In the contemporary novels of the Revolution one only sees the army as outsiders—revolutionaries and non-combatants —saw it. From these various opinions it is possible, nevertheless, to extract some worthwhile evidence about, mainly, the Federal Army's reputation during the Revolution. This is of considerable relevance, since in any war each side's opinion of the other is an important factor in the formation of its morale.

A central part of the propaganda of each adversary in a war is devoted to ridiculing the other side. We have already seen, in Chapter 5, the various ways in which the Porfiristas and Huertistas attempted to discredit the revolutionaries. The Federal Army, on the other hand, seems largely to have discredited itself, without the help of revolutionary propaganda. At the very beginning of the Revolution its reputation seems already to have been low, as is

---

[109] For the pre-revolutionary history of Mexico's army, see John J. Johnson, *The Military and Society in Latin America* (Stanford, 1964), pp. 13–90; and Edwin Lieuwen, *Arms and Politics in Latin America* (3rd. edn., London, 1963), pp. 17–35 and 101–21.

[110] Limantour (pp. 187–8, 247, 252–6 and 267–9) lays much emphasis upon the ineptitude of the Army as a vital factor in the Revolution's success.

indicated by the nicknames, all of them with disparaging overtones, with which regular soldiers were referred to: *mochos,
pelones, juanes, catrines, federales*.[111] The incompetence of the
military campaign against Madero and the clumsiness of the
government propaganda lowered the army's reputation still
further: according to Azuela in *Andrés Pérez, maderista* it was
above all the mishandling by army and press of the Serdán incident
which brought great discredit upon the forces of order [p. 26].
After the victorious Madero had refused to accede to revolutionary
demands for the demobilization of the Federal Army, his betrayal
by the great part of the latter in February 1913 brought it into even
greater disrepute. One novelist, the Porfirista Maqueo Castellanos,
puts unconvincing excuses for the army's disloyalty into the mouth
of the hero of his novel: 'Is not the Army an integral part of the
social organism, with rights and duties like any other? When has it
ever agreed to support an unpopular and tyrannical government?
And are not the people it now attacks the same ones who were but
yesterday inviting it to be disloyal?'[112] The Maderista revolution,
according to Maqueo Castellanos, produced among the military a
rebirth of the political ambitions which had been stilled by Díaz.
This analysis was probably accurate. As a justification to the
Mexican public of the military's role in the *decena trágica*,
however, it was ineffective.

The tragic ten days irrevocably linked the Army's destiny with
that of Huerta; so the decline of both followed the same course.
Huerta's frantic attempts to build up the numerical strength of his
army by forced conscription—which was not unknown previously
but which appears to have reached massive proportions during
1913 and 1914—only made things even worse than they would
otherwise have been. The unhappy victims of *la leva*, transported
untrained to the battlefield, put all their efforts into deserting

---

[111] *Mocho*: standard peninsular Spanish, 'lacking in horns'; modern Mexican
colloquial, 'right-wing, Roman Catholic'. The semantic change possibly came
about as a result of jocular references to the followers of the nineteenth-century
conservative caudillo Santa Anna as *mochos*, after the much-publicized incident
in which he lost a leg. *Pelón*: a reference to the military hair-cut. *Juan*: more
specifically a rank-and-file soldier (cf. English 'tommy'); now romanticized, but
used disparagingly by revolutionaries during the Revolution. *Catrín*: (Mexican
colloquial) 'one who is dressed with meticulous elegance'; used generally for all
Federal soldiers, but no doubt originally applied to the officers (who had some
reputation at the time as effeminate dandies [p. 298]).

[112] *La ruina de la casona*, p. 308. See also p. 273.

rather than fighting; and the morale of the whole army was affected disastrously. In *Los de abajo* one of the federal soldiers confides to Cervantes:

I am a carpenter; I lived with my mother, an old lady stuck in her chair for ten years past, because of her rheumatism. Three policemen took me from my home at midnight; next morning I was in the barracks and by nightfall I was twelve leagues from my village. . . . A month ago I passed through it with the troops. . . . My mother was dead and buried! . . . She was my only consolation in this life. . . . Now no one needs me. But, by God in heaven, these bullets they are handing out won't be for the enemy. . . . And if I am granted a miracle (the Holy Mother of Guadalupe will concede it to me) and I get to join Villa . . . I swear by the sacred soul of my mother that I'll make these federals pay.[113]

Later in the novel, when Macías and his men prepare to attack a federal garrison, a local sympathizer tells them that there are many soldiers but 'that doesn't matter. Most of them will be forced conscripts, and all they can think of is turning their backs and leaving their officers alone. They took my brother and he's here with them.'[114] With the general loss of morale in the federal ranks, stories of the superiority of the revolutionary forces, particularly of the Villistas, spread fast. It was rumoured that the latter were superbly dressed, fed and equipped, and that to join them was to acquire an unprecedented opportunity to become rich easily. Other federal soldiers tell Cervantes:

'Listen, chum . . . the others . . . those on the other side . . . they ride the finest horses from the north and the interior, their harnesses weighed down with silver. . . . As for us . . . on sardines, good only for raising buckets in a draw-well. . . . See what I mean, chum? They get shining silver pesos; we get celluloid tickets from the murderer's factories.' All of them said the same sort of thing, and there was even a sergeant who ingenuously related: 'I volunteered, but that was the biggest mistake in my life. What you can't achieve in peacetime during a whole life working like a black, you can achieve in a few months on the sierra with a rifle on your back. But not with this lot, mate . . . , not with this lot.'[115]

[113] p. 333.

[114] p. 356. The *leva* and its consequences are described in other novels: Maqueo Castellanos, part III, chaps 2, 4 and 7; Matamoros, *El terror*, p. 171; Azuela, *Las moscas*, p. 908. See also O'Shaughnessy, p. 65; Ramírez Plancarte, pp. 45–6 and 50–3; and *Foreign Relations 1913*, p. 802: American Ambassador H. L. Wilson (an ardent supporter of Huerta) to Secretary of State Bryan on 15 May 1913—'Huerta . . . has enlisted by one process and another somewhere between 15,000 and 20,000 soldiers during the past month'.

[115] *Los de abajo*, pp. 333–4. See also Lepino, chap. 12.

The Villista legend was clearly very successful [pp. 161-3]; it induces Cervantes himself to desert and become a revolutionary [pp. 96-7].

The large numbers of women who could be found accompanying army contingents were another factor which worked to the detriment of military efficiency and discipline. These *soldaderas*, each resignedly serving her man as concubine, cook, baggage-porter, and personal servant, were to be found with all armies in the Revolution;[116] but a regular army, whose only answer to the enemy's superior knowledge of the terrain is better training and discipline, must be more severely hampered by a large female following than a revolutionary one would be. The large influx of irregulars which Huerta's press gangs produced meant not only a drastic lowering of standards and morale but also a disproportionate increase in the number of soldaderas; for the wife and family of a forcibly conscripted man would often choose to share his sufferings and misfortunes in the field rather than be left alone and helpless.

A description by Ramírez Plancarte of the Federal Army's last withdrawal from Mexico City, on 15 August 1914, gives a graphic picture of the pitiful state it had been reduced to by the end of Huerta's period of rule:

They were surrounded by a profound and bitter sorrow, which gave out a cloud of desolation and woe. All that could be seen on those faces was the dejection and the despair of the vanquished; so much so that those few who were up early enough to witness the withdrawal watched with a pitying smile that was loaded with contempt. . . . In the bronze of the soldiers' faces not a muscle moved, and in the impassivity of their looks not a single thought was reflected. They were the product of the leva, the victims of the *razzias* of the mounted police, recruited to support a government born of crime and treachery.

At the rear, singly or in groups, walked the soldaderas, burdened with a profusion of shoddy cooking implements and large bundles of clothes, and most of them with two or three children. They were following their

---

[116] General Juan F. Azcárate claims categorically in his memoirs that only the Federal soldiers had soldaderas, and that revolutionary soldaderas are an invention of the cinema (*Esencia de la Revolución*, Mexico, 1966, p. 80). As permanent attachments to an army, and as defined exactly here, it may be that soldaderas were more typical of the federales than of many revolutionary forces; but all revolutionary factions certainly had their share of female camp-followers, and many eye-witness descriptions of them exist. See, for example, Ramírez Plancarte, pp. 58-9 [pp. 296-7], 364-5 and 549. There is a romantic portrayal of juanes and soldaderas in Maqueo Castellanos, part III, chap. 9.

husbands, whom they had not left since they had been carried off from home. Suffering had erased all graceful softness of line from their faces and all expressions of sweetness from their eyes, leaving in their place the august marks of grief and the sublimity of resignation. They were just starting the march and they already showed a marked feeling of fatigue and tiredness. It was a sad caravan of suffering. The women were miserably dressed; some went barefoot, most wore sandals and very few had rough, worn-out shoes. The children were half-naked, barefoot, filthy, dressed in rags, many of them with nothing to cover their heads, their little faces numb with cold and emaciated by repeated fasts. Their look was inexpressive, like that of an idiot. Many of them wept in a heartrending manner.[117]

The revolutionaries of 1913 and 1914 felt only scorn and contempt for such an enemy. Although the Federal Army was out of training in 1910 and 1911, it was at least loyal. There were few desertions during the Maderista revolt; many soldiers probably felt like Captain Tajonar of *La ruina de la casona*, who has his sympathies for the rebels but whose rigorous professionalism makes him persevere in his duties. By 1914 even the virtue—or the habit—of loyalty had been undermined, both by the revolutionary experience in general and by Huerta's abuse of the press gang. By this time the particular charge of cowardice had increased the general unpopularity which the Regular Army suffered; the hasty withdrawal of the Veracruz garrison in the face of the American occupation [p. 275] gave special weight to this charge. Even a right-wing novelist like Lepino, who does all he can to speak kindly of the Federal Army, includes scenes of gross cowardice on the part of officers and men, even though he seeks to balance them with scenes of bravery.

It is no surprise, then, that in *Los de abajo* Macías and his men should feel supremely confident of their chances in fights with federales. They can depend not only upon a detailed knowledge of the land on which they fight and upon their fine marksmanship to give them an advantage over the enemy, but also upon the active and willing help of the local population of poor villagers, who are bitterly hostile to the federales because of their repeated depredations: 'God bless you all! . . . Today you are off; tomorrow we too will be running, fleeing the press-gang, persecuted by these accursed government troops, who have declared war on all poor

[117] Op. cit., pp. 58–9.

people, who steal our pigs, our hens and even the maize we eat, and who burn our houses and carry off our womenfolk.'[118] In the actual fighting, the federales are regularly found to be cowardly and easy to beat. The officers set the example of cowardliness which the men follow. In an attack upon a Federal Army garrison, the first tentative sally of Macías's twenty men is repulsed:

The federal commander was a youth with blond hair and a curled moustache, and exceedingly vain. So long as he did not know for sure how many assailants there were, he had kept extremely quiet and prudent; but now that the enemy had been so successfully repelled that they had been given no time to reply to a single shot, he made a great show of unprecedented bravery and temerity. While the soldiers hardly ventured to peep out from behind the veranda railings, he, in the pale dawn light, displayed his elegant silhouette and his dragoon cape, which the breeze occasionally billowed out.

'Oh, what memories of the Ciudadela!'

Since his experience as a soldier was restricted to the adventure in which he was involved as a pupil at the Mexico City military school, when the betrayal of Madero was carried out, he brought up the subject of the Ciudadela whenever an opportunity presented itself.[119]

He mentally composes his dispatch, stating that the assailants numbered five hundred, that the battle lasted two hours, and that the enemy was routed, leaving twenty dead behind in their flight. He feels sure that promotion will automatically ensue.[120] When the revolutionaries' real attack comes, however, the unprepared federales are massacred to a man. The last one to be caught and killed 'is the young blond captain with a Burgundian moustache, white as wax, who, leaning in a corner by the entrance to the spiral staircase, has stopped because he lacks the strength to descend it'.[121] In the end, Macías and his men become so bored with easy

---

[118] *Los de abajo*, p. 328. In this novel it is the abusiveness of the federales which starts the hero Demetrio Macías on his career as a revolutionary leader [p. 198]. Just one year later, the revolutionaries themselves have acquired exactly the same bad reputation, and similar hostility is now directed against them [p. 200].

[119] pp. 356–7.

[120] Muñoz's short story *El feroz cabecilla* is an amusing satire of the exaggerations in military dispatches, which in this case convert the capture and execution of a sole prisoner (left behind by retreating revolutionaries because he has lost both legs in action) into a bloody battle with a fearsome rebel leader, widely reported in the press and incorporated into official mythology.

[121] pp. 359–60. There is another cowardly *federal* on pp. 390–1, and a very similar scene of cowardice in Ancona Albertos, II, pp. 153ff.

victories over federales that an order to go and fight some *oroz-quistas* is greeted with jubilation: 'Demetrio was speechless with pleasure. "Ah, a fight with Orozquistas!... A chance to get to grips with some real men ... No more killing federales like you kill hares or turkeys!" '[122]

The revolutionaries' scorn for their enemy is also a keynote of many of the corridos of the period. The federal soldiers' cowardice is the subject, for example, of laughing taunts in *La toma de Zacatecas* [pp. 156–60], where they are even portrayed as dressing up in women's clothing in order to escape from their enemy. The corridos and some of the novels obviously exaggerate the defects of Huerta's army—there must have been some good officers and some brave soldiers—but there is equally obviously enough truth in their allegations for one to be able to conclude both that the Regular Army was a poor and inefficient fighting force (and became increasingly so as the Revolution progressed) and that the extremely low reputation of the Army was an important factor in the raising of revolutionary morale, especially during 1913 and early 1914, and hence in the victory over Huerta.

The Federal Army was finally demobilized on 18 August 1914. Many individual members of it joined revolutionary bands, especially those of Villa and Zapata, where they attempted to keep the cause of the right alive and hopefully awaited the counter-revolution which would restore their fortunes [pp. 207–8 and 219–20]. As late as March 1919 the former general and Minister of War under Huerta, Aureliano Blanquet, issued from Veracruz a *Proclama a los miembros del antiguo ejército federal mexicano*, calling on them to rise up in arms and overthrow Carranza. Félix Díaz [pp. 30–1] had issued a similar manifesto the year before (he had been rebelling in Veracruz since 1916). No such resurgence was to come, however. The Army was one sector of Porfirian society which was totally destroyed by the Revolution, unlike other sectors studied in this chapter, which were able to recuperate some of their strength, after the Revolution. The post-revolutionary Regular Army was to be a completely fresh body, formed anew from the ranks of the triumphant Carrancistas.

[122] p. 389. *Orozquistas*: the followers of Pascual Orozco, a Maderista leader who turned against Madero and became a Huertista [pp. 29–30 and 31]. The Orozquistas acquired a reputation as tenacious fighters.

(f) *The Lower-Middle Classes*

In section (*b*) we have discussed the part played in the Revolution by the small but influential urban ruling class composed largely of the prosperous bourgeoisie. In this final section of the chapter it is proposed to deal with the remainder of the bourgeois sector, which can loosely be labelled 'the lower-middle classes', or 'the poor bourgeoisie': those whose possession of material comforts and social respectability was, at best, precarious and partial. Individuals from a large number of different occupations make up this sector, but the most important single group within it is that of the rank-and-file bureaucrats, or functionaries in general.

The Mexican lower-middle classes of the revolutionary period are different from the other anti-revolutionary groups we have considered in that the Revolution was not fought directly against them and in that, as a group, they showed no open hostility to the revolutionaries (indeed, many of the Revolution's leaders came from this group [pp. 215–16]). It would be possible to categorize them as 'neutrals' rather than as 'anti-revolutionaries'. Yet 'neutrality' can scarcely exist in a revolution, for indifference to the revolutionaries' cause amounts to tacit acceptance of the *status quo* and is a weighty factor in favour of those who seek to preserve the old order. The principal concern in the Revolution of the Mexican bureaucracy and the rest of the lower-middle classes was for a return to normality, for as individuals they stood to lose everything in social upheaval—their jobs, their savings, above all the general security which they prized most dearly.

The rapid growth of this group in Porfirian Mexico is reflected both in pre-revolutionary novels and in novels of the Revolution, where members of it appear frequently. The whole atmosphere of *La ruina de la casona* is markedly lower-middle-class: the characters in the novel are all residents in a decaying boarding-house in Mexico City, and most of them fall within the category we are dealing with here—the boarding-house owner and her husband, an unsuccessful lawyer, four sisters who make and sell dresses, a wig-maker, a retired army officer and his family, a book-keeper and his family, a piano teacher. There is, however, a strong influence of Balzac's lower-middle-class characters upon many of these, and although they are interesting and are depicted in some detail, there is more reliable evidence to be found in other novels. It is often difficult to distinguish between features of Maqueo Castellano's lower-middle-class characters that derive from direct observation and features that are taken from Balzac; so it is preferable to turn to other novels in which literary sources are not so important. The hero of Rodríguez's *Don Pascual* could also be considered to belong to the lower-middle classes. He is a retired colonel who set himself up as a port agent in Veracruz, and he and his family show many of the traits typical of the group under consideration here; especially an obsession with respectability and strong aristo-cratic pretensions. Yet his business has prospered and he is now quite wealthy, though not sufficiently so to move into the Mexico City overworld. He is, then, on the borderline between the upper and the lower bourgeoisie: a special, non-typical case, whom it is not therefore very profitable to study. The novel in which he appears is, furthermore, an exceedingly bad one, and Don Pascual himself is idealized to a sometimes ridiculous extent.

Azuela's *Los caciques* deals with a provincial community of small traders (the town is not named, but it has many of the charac-teristics of Lagos de Moreno, in the state of Jalisco, Azuela's home town). Prominent among them is Don Juan Viñas, who is portrayed in great detail and with much sympathy. He is a self-made man who, from humble beginnings, has moved up into the lower-middle classes by dint of twenty years' unstinting hard work and thrift. His personal motto is 'patience, tenacity, and probity'. He owns a grocer's shop and has enough money saved—40,000 pesos —to invest in the construction of a housing estate. He is respected and admired by his fellows, but scorned by the powerful and wealthy family of caciques who control the commercial life of the region. He, in turn, holds them in the most deferential respect. He has a pathetic faith in their honesty, based on an unquestioning acceptance of the social hierarchy and on the belief that financial success must be a reflection of moral rectitude. The caciques find it easy to ruin him and to appropriate his possessions, including the nearly-finished housing estate.

To demonstrate the vulnerability of the honest small traders in the face of the new, unscrupulous capitalism represented by the caciques, Azuela makes Viñas so naïve, credulous, and upright that he becomes a thoroughly unreal and ultimately tiresome character. Azuela is more successful in depicting the details of Don Juan's domestic life. In spite of his small fortune, which makes him the

richest man—apart from the caciques—in town, his obsession
with the accumulation of capital makes him continue to live as
frugally as he always has. His clothes and those of his wife, Elena,
and his two children are shabby and dirty. They eat the same
humble food as they did before their success. Family celebrations
are strictly rationed: 'He allows himself one beanfeast per year.
It's his turn, then Elena's, then Esperanza's, then Juanito's, in
strict order of rotation. But the expense is not quite so great as
might be imagined. Elena makes it her job to borrow what is
needed: she even borrows the pot that the turkey is cooked in. And
Viñas, for three months beforehand, is looking out for a chance to
buy the bird at almost half-price.'[123] His family has to conform to
his standards of industry and thrift: 'He makes his wife work more
than a mule; but he loves her dearly. He loves Esperanza too, so
much so that he has bought her a fourth- or fifth-hand Rosenkranz
piano; and he gives Juanito ten centavos every Sunday to go to the
pictures. But, still, Esperanza makes up for the piano darning and
ironing, and Juanito pays back the price of the cinema collecting
bad debts.'[124]

There is interesting information in *Los caciques* about the lives
of the provincial small bourgeoisie at the time of the Revolution.
Azuela indicates that this traditionally sober, honest and hard-
working sector of Mexican society was, at this time, in danger of
being squeezed out of existence by the new, ruthless capitalist
spirit represented at the highest levels of Porfirian society by the
científicos [pp. 190–2 and 254 n.]. He also indicates, however,
that they had nothing directly to do with the Revolution, neither
influencing it nor being affected by it in any specific way (the
Revolution neither halts nor hastens Don Juan's ruination). In a
study of the social history of the Revolution this provincial bourgeoisie—one group, it is well worth noting, which appears to have
remained unaffected by the all-pervading aristocratic ethos of
Porfirian Mexico—is of relatively small importance. Let us pass
on to novels which deal with members of the lower-middle class
who were more involved with the Revolution.

The other novels of the Revolution in which members of the
'poor bourgeoisie' play central roles are González Peña's *La fuga de
la quimera* and Azuela's *Las moscas*, both of which give pictures of
the Mexico City bureaucracy. Azuela's attitude to his bureaucrats

[123] Op. cit., p. 846.   [124] p. 847.

is one of bitter hostility; but, as is usually the case with Azuela, the caricatures that he draws are both accurate and justified enough for the real features they exaggerate to be easily recognizable. González Peña's portrait of the family of a bureaucrat is, furthermore, much more sympathetic, and consequently it not only adds details to Azuela's depiction but can also be used to check it. *La fuga de la quimera* is, however, a novel with marked literary affiliations, and it has to be used with care, especially since the sort of lower-middle-class family situations it describes appear frequently in nineteenth-century European fiction. Azuela's novel, with no perceptible direct source influences, can be used, in turn, to check *La fuga de la quimera*. The two novels complement each other most usefully.

The state bureaucracy, as might be expected, formed a large proportion of the urban population of Mexico, and especially of the population of the capital city. The Porfirian policy of 'poca política, mucha administración' increased the bureaucracy's importance, and the boom that Mexico City enjoyed in Porfirian times further added to its contingent of functionaries. They and their families, as close observers of the urban élite and completely dependent upon them, imitated their manners as well as they could. Their most notable trait in the novels is their wholehearted acceptance of the aristocratic ethos that has been described earlier in this chapter. But the bureaucrats did not, of course, possess the wealth that the pursuit of the aristocratic way of life demanded, and the central conflict of their existence arose from this situation. Thus the incompatibility between the wish to maintain an image of prosperous respectability by the acquisition of status-symbols, and the lack of sufficient means to do so, which characterizes lower-middle classes in many societies, was aggravated in the Mexican case by the luxury and extravagance of the way of life that was emulated.

The family of Jacobo Lavín, in *La fuga de la quimera*, provides a typical example of the precariousness of the bureaucrats' hold upon the material comforts they value so much. Lavín worked in minor positions in the Home Office, and after thirty-eight years he had achieved promotion to the rank of Head of Department. He had managed to acquire a good house in a respectable suburb of Mexico City, and to furnish it well, ensuring that it was equipped with all those symbols that would demonstrate his position in the upper sectors of society—carpets, curtains, servants, metal beds (as opposed to the lower-grade wooden ones), and a piano. He bought elegant clothes for his family and—the ultimate status-symbol—he had a box in the theatre. All of this was achieved, however, only by incurring an enormous debt; and when Lavín died suddenly his wife, Eduvigis, and his two children were left in a desperate position. They had to move immediately from their residence to rooms in an old, dilapidated colonial house in the centre of Mexico City, where they are living as the novel begins in 1910. Their neighbours are tailors, cobblers, seamstresses who work as prostitutes by night, an unemployed opera singer, and dozens of children who overrun the gloomy corridors of the house. Eduvigis and her two daughters consider themselves superior to their neighbours and will have nothing to do with them.

A similar picture is given in less detail by Azuela. His novel concerns bureaucrats caught up in the whirlwind of the Revolution in 1915, and we only know of their normal life through isolated reminiscences. Thus the legal bureaucrat, Señor Ríos, sitting on the floor of a compartment of a Villista train, contrasts his present predicament with the comforts of his previous life: 'Señor Ríos savours the delights of a soft, luxurious bed, the freshness of pure white linen sheets, and dreams that his departure from Mexico City in a train full of animals was a dream, a horrible nightmare.'[125] The principal protagonists of *Las moscas* are, however, Marta (the widow of the janitor of the National Palace) and her three children Matilde (a library worker), Rosita (a stenographer), and Rubén (who is still at college). They, too, have known hard times since the death of the head of the family, who served all occupants of the National Palace from Emperor Maximilian to Madero. In spite of their present predicament, however, their social pretensions and aristocratic hankerings have not been modified. Their inappropriate clinging to past glories is neatly symbolized by Azuela in the canary in a gilded cage which, as the novel opens, Matilde is cherishing in the midst of the bustle and the turmoil of a railway station crowded with revolutionary soldiers. They constantly use the word 'decente' [pp. 246–7] to describe themselves, proudly refer to their family pedigree, and dream of the times when Matilde used to give piano recitals at their home, which were attended by the State Governor himself.

[125] *Las moscas*, p. 878.

The detailed similarities in the composition of the families in these two novels are curious. In both cases we have an elderly widow with adult children whose interests she relentlessly advances. In both cases, too, there is an elder daughter who is particularly frivolous, pretentious, and ambitious. The impression thus given is one of a sector of society in which women are particularly dominant; and such an impression is confirmed by various details in the novels. The men are shown, especially in *Las moscas*, as pusillanimous and faint-hearted, a breed to which the code of machismo [p. 153] can have no application at all. Señor Ríos, whom Azuela presents as a typical bureaucrat, gives an unexpectedly honest description of himself:

Donaciano Ríos, age forty, married, a government employee since losing his last milk-teeth. Record of service: impeccable since starting as a message-boy in a minor law-court right up to present position as State Attorney.

Work: an Underwood. Moreover: the typewriter requires cleaning, overhaul and repairs; he only needs a little alimentary oiling in order always to function impeccably. Preponderant faculties: abdication of will, intelligence gagged and muzzled, unlimited moral elasticity, absolute castration of individuality: the ideal government servant.[126]

Years of blind obedience and conformity to the Porfirian system— a system which emasculated its bureaucracy even more than others[127]—have taken their toll of the likes of Señor Ríos. All he and the other male bureaucrats on the revolutionary train can do is helplessly to sit about bemoaning their fate and sighing for the good old times of Díaz and Huerta.

In sharp contrast, Marta, Matilde, and Rosita show such resilience and resourcefulness that one feels that even Azuela, with his declared hostility to these hangers-on, has considerable admiration for their ability to survive. These women, and especially Marta, the mother, face doggedly up to suffering, hardship, and degradation, and are resilient enough always to find some way of coming through each new trial. They are ruthless and unscrupulous in using any method available—usually, in fact, either hypocritical flattery or shameless flirtation—to enlist the aid of

[126] p. 879.
[127] A central feature of the system was the Minister's private lackey, popularly called the *achichinque* (from Nahuatl *atlchichihuintzi*, 'a wet nurse'). He was the centre of all the petty intrigues employed by those in search of jobs depending on public ministries, and dealt especially with the Minister's audiences.

those who can be of use to them (they even manage to wheedle money out of Villa himself). Although Azuela clearly intends us to condemn them for this immoral behaviour (the title of the novel is itself an expression of his extreme distaste for their parasitical activities), he does, in spite of himself, show that there is something positive to be admired in these women. He also shows that the hypocrisy that marks their behaviour is virtually forced upon them by circumstances—even if it does, admittedly, seem to come quite easily to them.

A very similar picture emerges from *La fuga de la quimera*. In contrast with Jacobo Lavín, who is referred to as having been little more than an office slave—'that meek, silent, stooping, badly dressed man'[128]—his wife shows the greatest strength of character after his death in paying off the debt and establishing the family in a moderately respectable position again, even managing to give her daughters an education. They are thus, she feels, prepared for the favourable marriages which, as she hopes, await them in the future. Her ambitious and attractive elder daughter Sofía is consequently able to become a shorthand typist and finally to marry her wealthy employer, Miguel Bringas, whom she subsequently ruins by her lavish spending.

Eduvigis achieves all this by taking up one of the peripheral money-making activities which emerged as by-products of the turmoil of the times—that of the *corredora de alhajas*. In the uncertain times of 1915 onwards in Mexico City, hitherto wealthy families who were finding it hard to make ends meet employed women to make discreet enquiries among the new Carrancista élite to whom they hoped to sell their jewellery. These jewel-peddlers were another facet of the transference of power and wealth from the old élite to the new. One of the minor characters in Azuela's *Las tribulaciones de una familia decente*—la Tabardillo—is also a corredora de alhajas. It is worth noting that she, just like Eduvigis de Lavín, is the wife of a bureaucrat. Although her husband—Payito—is still alive, he is totally insignificant and does not even appear in the novel (the diminutive in his name reflects his feebleness). La Tabardillo, on the other hand, is a resourceful and dominating woman; there is indeed much of the Celestina about her, in the almost sinister and magical power she seems to exert over the women into whose homes her trade takes her. Here the

[128] Op. cit., p. 26.

Mexican Revolution curiously gives new life to a tradition dating from the Middle Ages: in the *Libro de buen amor*, doña Urraca is a 'corredera de las que venden joyas' and is thus able to act freely as a go-between.

Like all the inhabitants of Mexico City, the bureaucratic sector suffered badly during the Revolution and particularly in 1914 and 1915. The brief survey above, in section (*b*) of this chapter, of the decline of Mexico City refers equally relevantly to the lower-middle-class inhabitants of the capital as to the urban élite. According to Ramírez Plancarte, their sufferings were particularly atrocious. He describes how, by March 1915, many bureaucrats were reduced to selling firewood, alcohol, home-made cigarettes, and other such merchandise in the filthy streets of the poorest slums of Mexico City:

Among the many people of previous good social, political and economic standing that I saw in this grievous situation among the insalubrious and ramshackle stalls in the unsightly and dusty Plaza de la Candelaria was a lawyer, no less, who for several years had filled an important office in General Díaz's judicatory system; wearing an old, flattened derby hat, and attired in a greasy butcher's apron, he was selling what he proudly affirmed to be calves' tripe, though to judge from its thinness and its repugnant aspect it seemed more like dogs' guts.[129]

The poor of Mexico City derived great consolation from their own suffering at this time on observing the members of the middle classes, formerly so haughty, now reduced to straits possibly even more desperate than their own (the lower classes were at least accustomed to such conditions and had no memory of anything much better). A special version of *La cucaracha*, making fun of the middle classes' recourse, in their dire need, to the lower-class fare that they deeply despised, was extremely popular in 1915:

> La cucaracha, la cucaracha,
> Ya no puede parrandear,
> Porque no tiene pa las gordas,
> Menos para vacilar.

> Hasta las bellas catrinas,
> De esas de chongo postizo,
> Las vemos comprar la masa,
> Formadas como chorizo.

[129] Op. cit., p. 398.

Hemos visto a catrincitos
Que del 'Buen Tono' fumaban,
Ahora compran del manojo,
Pues el hambre ya está brava.

Ahora hay unos catrincitos,
De esos que comían gallina,
Ahora los vemos hambrientos,
Espulgándose en la esquina.

Se han visto unos catrincitos
De bastón, levita y piocha
Que se van hasta Tepito
A comer pura escamocha.

También todas las rotitas,
De esas muy bien perfumadas,
Hoy le meten muy del duro
A las gordas enchiladas.

En fin, señores, termino,
Y les pido su clemencia,
El que compre este corrido
Tiene un año de indulgencia.

Compren estos nuevos versos,
Cántenlos hasta las cachas,
Todos los que no los compren
Se volverán cucarachas.

La cucaracha, la cucaracha,
Ya no quiere caminar,
Porque no puede y ya no quiere
Tantas pulgas aguantar.[130]

[130] These are selected verses of the original, which is much longer. It is reproduced in Ramírez Plancarte, op. cit., pp. 467–70.

The cockroach, the cockroach,
Can no more go out on the town:
He's no money for tortillas,
Let alone for having fun.

We see even classy women,
With their chignon wigs and all,
Go out to buy tortilla-dough,
All lined up like sausages.

We've seen smart young gentlemen
That smoked 'Buen Tono' cigarettes:
Now they get their baccy loose,
For hunger's really pressing hard.

We see smart young gentlemen,
Who used to feed on chicken meals,

For the bureaucrats and their families, then, the Revolution became by 1915 a desperate individual struggle for survival. This is the point at which Azuela portrays them in *Las moscas*, in full flight from the impossible conditions in Mexico City, following the Villistas in the hope that the latter will be victorious and give them jobs—or, in the event of a Carrancista victory, that an opportunity to change sides will present itself. Although Azuela paints the bureaucracy's situation as a grim one, however, he does not seem to believe that the Revolution finished with this sector of Porfirian society. *Las moscas* ends with his parasitical protagonists successfully changing sides and establishing some sort of a future for themselves. Their situation, indeed, improves considerably during the course of the novel; the only real loser at the end is the revolutionary Villa, the description of whose sad figure forms the novel's last chapter.

Azuela does not stop, in fact, at suggesting that many individual bureaucrats managed to wriggle through the Revolution and come out more or less intact at the other end: he explicitly attributes to them a decisive influence upon the Revolution. He summarizes his analysis of their revolutionary career through his mouthpiece in this novel, the Villista doctor, who states pessimistically that the Revolution has caused deep suffering and great bloodshed only to

> Sitting, hungry, at street corners,
> Picking at their lice and fleas.
>
> Some young blades have been observed,
> With morning coats and sticks and beards,
> Going over to Tepito,
> Just to eat left-overs stew.
>
> All the smart young ladies, too,
> Perfumed with the finest scents,
> Now really get their teeth into
> Tortillas with hot pepper sauce.
>
> Now, I finish, Gentlemen,
> Begging your forbearance, now;
> Anyone who buys this ballad,
> Gains a year's indulgences.
>
> Come and buy these new words from me,
> Go and sing them till you burst:
> All those here who do not buy them
> Will turn into cockroaches.
>
> The cockroach, the cockroach,
> Can walk not one step more;
> He cannot and he will not
> Put up with so many fleas.

become controlled in the end by the bureaucrats [p. 122]. This slightly unexpected idea is expanded elsewhere in the novel, when Señor Ríos explains happily to don Rodolfo why the revolutionaries need the bureaucracy:

There's more stupidity than evil about them. They know nothing about even the chapter headings of the financier's catechism. Revolution is a sure means of making a fortune; government is the only means of retaining it and making it accrue as it should: but just as the rifle is indispensable for the former, so the office worker is indispensable for the latter. They want to form a government by themselves; but they're like stones thrown up into the air, which wasn't made for stones: they are bound to fall, and since we represent an insurmountable force, the force of inertia, they will either fall into our hands or they will be annihilated in anarchy.[131]

This, too, is clearly Azuela's own analysis of the situation; his exaggeration of the effect of the bureaucracy upon the Revolution can possibly be explained by the strong hostility to them which he reveals in the novel and which he admitted to later.[132] It is worth noting, however, in support of Azuela's analysis, that another intelligent novelist of the Revolution, Antonio Ancona Albertos, came quite independently to a similar conclusion:

What, in the countryside, were tragedies of war were being turned into ridiculous farces in the cities, where the bureaucracy, with its refined hypocrisy, was letting the people kill each other so that names and words could be changed and so that it, unchanging, could turn the new names and new words to its own advantage. And the bureaucrats did not have to make any effort. Instead of crying 'Viva Díaz!' it was easy to cry 'Viva Madero!' and to write at the bottom of official communications 'Effective Suffrage; No Reelection' instead of 'Liberty and the Constitution'.[133]

Ancona is speaking only, however, of the Maderista stage of the Revolution.

The bureaucracy and the remainder of the lower-middle classes were on the periphery of the Revolution. We can accept that they may have exerted some marginal 'braking' effect upon it, that there is possibly some truth in the analyses of Azuela and Ancona; but it

[131] p. 881.
[132] *El novelista y su ambiente*, p. 1091: 'Now, on rereading *Las moscas* after many years, I realise that I was cruel and pitiless in my portrayal of that lot.'
[133] Op. cit., II, p. 12.

would seem that these two novelists, as a result of the repugnance that the parasitical and hypocritical bureaucrats caused them, considerably exaggerated their importance and influence. The state bureaucracy, 'a zone of friction between authority and society',[134] is a traditionally unpopular sector of society. The suspicion that the bureaucrat is by nature both parasitical, for he produces nothing tangible, and excessively powerful, for he makes decisions that are vitally important to the individual, is present in all societies in which there is a bureaucracy of any importance.[135] It is this general suspicion that Azuela and Ancona express. In Porfirian Mexico it is clear that the bureaucracy was kept firmly in its position of servant of authority, that there was no real danger of bureaucratization; this is reflected in the unusual pusillanimity of all the bureaucrats who appear in the novels of the Revolution (a pusillanimity which, though a personal defect, is a professional virtue). All the Mexican bureaucrats could aspire to do in the Revolution was individually to attempt to salvage something from their cruelly shattered world. Azuela illustrates how they went about doing so; it is revealing that, in spite of his conscious prejudices, he still chose to entitle his novel *Las moscas*.

The principal omission from this chapter is that of the non-belligerent rural poor, who were largely hostile to the Revolution both at the beginning in 1910 and 1911 [pp. 195–6] and at the end in 1914 and 1915 [pp. 167, 200, and 298], although they generally supported the revolutionaries during the fight against Huerta [pp. 297–8]. There is so little information about this large sector of the populace, passively enduring the dreadful sufferings of war, that nothing can be said about it in detail. Members of it appear as background figures in some of the novels, and as such they have been mentioned occasionally in the course of this study. The main influence of this sector was a negative one. Its ranks were so depleted and life was made so insecure for it that by 1915 food production in most parts of Mexico was very severely reduced. At this point the struggle virtually had to stop; there was no more fuel to generate fighting energy.

The point has already been made at the beginning of this chapter

---

[134] Lucio Mendieta y Núñez, *Sociología de la burocracia* (Mexico, 1961).

[135] *Ibid.*, pp. 53–4; S. N. Eisenstadt, 'Bureaucracy and bureaucratization', in *Current Sociology*, VII, 2 (1958), pp. 99–163.

that an analysis of the anti-revolutionaries is just as important as an analysis of the revolutionaries themselves for the proper understanding of a revolution; and also that in the Mexican case this principle—logical enough but often overlooked—applies especially strongly. The above study of Mexican anti-revolutionaries confirms that there were serious and far-reaching weaknesses in those sectors of society in whose interests it was to preserve the Porfirian world. The personal deterioration of Díaz himself and the consequent decline and decay of his political system were not the only deficiencies in this world, although some of the flaws in the social structure were, in part at least, consequences of this decline.

The élites of the Porfirian world showed acute symptoms of the estrangement from the rest of society that has been considered an important cause of revolution.[136] The exaggeratedly aristocratic mode of behaviour which characterized the old-established and the parvenu members of both the rural and the city élites, and which was so influential that it also permeated lower-middle-class *mores*, seemed calculated to set these élites apart from the rest of society and hence to alienate the non-élite. The degree of estrangement was, furthermore, increasing; the newest recruits to the élite were the ones who most assiduously cultivated the aristocratic style, and they added another element of their own which estranged them even more—the aping of foreign tastes and manners. Their children took things to still further extremes. All this, in turn, led to a potentially dangerous division within the ranks of the élite itself. In the wider framework of Porfirian society as a whole, the rift thus created between rich and poor was not yet so acute in 1910 as to polarize society into two opposite camps [pp. 22–3]; but the way was thus well laid for the full-scale class-war that developed after 1913. The serious implications for Mexico's economic development of the acceptance of the aristocratic ethos by the entrepreneurial sector have already been commented upon [pp. 39 and 264].

It is important, however, to place all this in perspective by noting that the tendency for the élites and the bureaucracy to adopt basically aristocratic value-systems, and hence to turn their backs on society's lower sectors, has been observed as a general phenomenon in Latin America. It has been suggested, with

[136] See especially Eckstein, pp. 145–8.

some conviction, that because of this the normal tripartite division of society is not applicable to Latin America—that there are only two valid categories, the upper sectors (status and prestige orientated) and the lower sectors (work and money orientated).[137] The social structure of late Porfirian Mexico was not, then, an original creation, but a development of the normal Latin-American model. The portrayal of mid-nineteenth-century Chilean society in the novels of Alberto Blest Gana, for example, shows élites similar in many ways to those of Porfirian Mexico. The behaviour of the Porfirian 'upper sector' should therefore be seen not as in any sense unique but as an exaggeration, caused by special factors, of tendencies all of which are normal in Latin-American upper sectors as a whole.

There were other weaknesses, though, in the Porfirian power-system. The Church, for example, acted less efficiently as an agent for the defence of the *status quo* than might have been expected. Its support of Díaz against Madero does not appear to have been altogether wholehearted; and after the latter's assumption of power it acted with so little finesse, sophistication, or intelligence in its defence of the interests of the wealthy that it soon attracted violent hostility, and lost the strong hold it had traditionally had on the thoughts and attitudes of the lower classes.

But above all, perhaps, it was the Army's weakness that was decisive, as has already been suggested above. Not only was it sadly inefficient, and increasingly so as the Revolution progressed; but the fact that it was inefficient was soon widely known, and the Army rapidly became an object of general scorn and derision. It would not be an exaggeration to say that the ineptitude of the Regular Army was the key to the whole Mexican Revolution.

---

[137] Richard N. Adams, 'Political Power and Social Structures', in *The Politics of Conformity in Latin America*, ed. Véliz (Oxford University Press, 1967). See also Véliz's 'Introduction' to *Obstacles to Change in Latin America*.

CONCLUSION

MANY of the detailed conclusions about the Mexican Revolution that this study leads to have emerged during the course of it. It is unnecessary, therefore, to repeat at length, for example, that the Revolution was an unusually haphazard and untidy one, lacking many of the features that have been considered general—and indeed indispensable—in revolutions by students of the subject; that this peculiarity can in large part be attributed to the weakness of the intellectuals at all levels; and that the Revolution would most probably never have happened at all but for a special circumstance, the extreme feebleness of the Army. It is tempting to suggest that the Mexican Revolution, unlike other great revolutions, was one which perhaps should not have happened, or at least which could with no great difficulty have been avoided. But then, of course, the ultimate proof that it was necessary was that it did happen.

To all of this the Zapatista revolution in Morelos was the important exception. The southern movement followed a path which at every stage was quite different from that of the revolution of the north. There clearly was genuine revolutionary unrest in Morelos in 1910, while in the rest of the country there equally clearly was not; among Zapatistas, unlike Villistas and Carrancistas, there existed widespread and genuine revolutionary idealism and a popular understanding of, and allegiance to, well-defined goals; the Zapatista intellectuals seem to have been somewhat more effective as such than their counterparts in other revolutionary camps; and the revolution of Zapata was more successful in achieving reforms which served immediate popular interests than was that of Carranza.

The Mexican Revolution as a whole, however, is distinguished from others by its failure to follow any of the general models proposed by theorists of revolutions. One of the most recent of such theorists has concluded that 'internal wars do not always have a clear aim, a tight organization, a distinct shape and tendency from the outset. Many seem to be characterized in their early stages by nothing so much as amorphousness. They are formless matter waiting to be shaped, and if there is an art of revolution, it involves, largely at least, not making or subduing it, but capitalizing on the unallocated political resources it provides.'[1] The Mexican Revolution was different—and deficient—in that, lacking the forces that could have shaped it, it never emerged from amorphousness. It had neither idealistic radical fervour nor adequate intellectual guidance to mould it and give it organization and purpose. Only because there were such palpable weaknesses in the forces working against it could it exist at all.

These general conclusions have been reached from a study which I have presented as a 'test case' of an unorthodox approach to social history. If these conclusions, and the detailed observations about human behaviour in the Mexican Revolution that have been made in the course of arriving at them, are acceptable as a contribution to the history of the Revolution, then the methodology outlined in the opening chapter of this book has stood the test of practice and is valid. The particular field of investigation which has here been chosen has its own peculiarities: the Mexico of 1910–17 is merely one of very many subjects to which the literary approach to social history could have been applied; but if the approach has been shown to be successful in this case, then it follows that it will be of use in the study of other societies which produced novelists. The approach would, however, have to be essayed in investigations of various other sorts of past societies before it could be established precisely to what extent it is generally valuable. Of the special, atypical features of the Mexican Revolution as a subject for socio-literary study—those features which tend to make it differ in important ways from other possible subjects for such study—some make it seem an exceptionally fertile field for this approach (and thus suggest that it would be rather less profitable in the study of other societies), while others indicate that, on the contrary, the approach might be even more valuable in other areas of socio-historical investigation.

Of the latter the most important is the failure of the novelists of the Revolution to produce any works of excellence, or even very many that are of any literary worth at all. A Balzac or even a Galdós would have been able to provide much more detail about the complexities and subtleties of attitudes and relationships during

[1] Eckstein, p. 142.

the Revolution than could even the best of the novelists of the period, Azuela and Ancona. If the idea of studying a society through its novels gives fruitful results in the case of the Mexican Revolution, it seems probable that it would prove even more profitable when applied to past societies which produced better novelists.

Against this important consideration there are factors which make it appear that in other ways the Mexican Revolution was a specially favourable example to have chosen as a test case for the literary approach to social history. There is the fact that other sources of information are inadequate, so that the novels become proportionally even more important than they would otherwise have been. But one of the central points of this book has been that the social information novels can provide is unique and cannot be provided by other sources, however plentiful they may be. Novels will contribute much original knowledge even about the most well-documented societies.

One of the reasons why other sources have been inadequate in this study is that we have been dealing with a society in revolution —a society, that is, which, under constant and acute stress, underwent rapid and drastic changes. In the short space of seven years a whole world was demolished and the embryo of a new one was created to take its place; and, in between, a temporary revolutionary society developed, structured according to the immediate needs of the moment. Into this transient society the old world dissolved, and out of it the new one developed, a synthesis of much that was new and revolutionary and much that was taken over from the old world (not even the most radical of revolutions can build entirely from scratch). This rapid dialectical process is what this study has attempted to trace. The sheer speed and complexity of the many different social and cultural changes which constituted this process was such that normal sources could hardly chart it adequately; it seems that the novel, with its full, integrated presentation of society as a continuum in both space and time, is more able to keep up with events. But there is no good reason for supposing that novels would not also be valuable in studies of societies at peace. All societies, in peace as well as in revolution, are dynamic; and the novelist's special ability to describe a society as a living, constantly changing whole, and to portray exactly the state of continuous flux which is produced in it by the interaction of its component parts, makes him an invaluable recorder.

A favourable factor in the above study has been the very small influence of literary sources upon the novels in question. In other studies of this sort that might be made, the literary affiliations of the novelists examined are likely to pose greater problems than they have here. On the other hand, of course, literary sources rarely exert so decisive an influence upon realistic novels as they do upon other forms of imaginative writing. The novelists studied here are also exceptional in their independence. They were writing in obscurity, most of them for their own private reasons, and without any real hope of achieving popular success or exerting any influence on society. Therefore extraneous considerations deriving from the need to please a certain public do not significantly interfere with the writing of the early novelists of the Revolution, as they do, for example, with the novels of the Revolution that were written during the 1930s.

Another advantage that the Mexican Revolution presents from the point of view of a socio-literary study is that there is a large enough number of sociologically-orientated novels written about it to ensure a reasonably wide and comprehensive coverage of social behaviour and developments during it. The coverage in novels of the various sectors of Mexican society could, however, have been better and less biased: as has been seen, the rural poor that formed the fighting masses of the Revolution receive scant attention from the novelists; and the Porfirian Army and the Church do not play as large a role in the novels as a whole as they might. Coverage is to some extent a question of luck: it just happened that none of the novelists had enough interest in, or knowledge of, the activities of the Roman Catholic Church in Mexico to present a close analysis of them in his work. Other gaps can, however, be explained by reference to the social history of the period, and they thus provide more evidence which is no less valuable for being negative. The principal example of this is the lack of direct information about the rural poor, a reflection of the massive class barrier which divided them from the middle-class novelists.

Altogether it seems probable that other societies of the recent past could be studied through their novels as profitably as that of revolutionary Mexico; and that the particular example chosen in this study—although, of course, it has special features—is reasonably representative and of general relevance. It is hoped, then, that what was claimed at the outset has now been confirmed:

that realistic novels, properly handled, can yield much information about society which no other sources can furnish. This is because of the novelist's special position in society and his unique approach to reality. The novel recaptures the intricacies of social and individual behaviour as no other source does; and it gives the reader access to sectors of society and to areas of private life to which there is normally no access. The novelist's licence to explore freely where other men would be considered impertinent intruders, and to say what others are not permitted to say, gives him a highly privileged position and gives his readers a special insight into the society he describes; and his artistic vision of reality enables him to present society from a viewpoint totally different from that of other observers. Only the novelist can tell us exactly what it felt like to live in past societies.

This is not, of course, to suggest that novels can be used as an exclusive source of social history. The historian should use all available sources, and it is the purpose of this book to demonstrate that the novel should not be overlooked as one more useful source among the many others. It is, furthermore, a particularly valuable source, because the information it offers is not to be found elsewhere. It is, however, a difficult source to handle. This particular difficulty can only be surmounted by, among other things, the constant and careful application of the techniques of literary criticism. This book also seeks to show, then, that a training in literary studies—the cultivation of the ability to identify and confront the problems involved in reading and understanding works of imaginative literature—is of value to the historian, not merely as a peripheral and decorative accessory to be acquired in the spirit of the dilettante, but as an integral part of historiographical method, of central, direct and concrete usefulness in important areas of historical investigation. This approach also ensures that a study of a past society takes into careful account the cultural traditions of that society. Historical and sociological studies are commonly at fault in failing to do so, or in doing so only in the most superficial and inadequate way. This book attempts to show that no society can be properly understood without a full knowledge of its cultural traditions and of the changes those traditions undergo, such as only a painstaking and systematic examination of its arts, and particularly of its literature, can give.

The point may perhaps tentatively be carried a little further.

The differences between the 'scientific', denominative approach and the 'artistic', connotative approach to reality have been outlined above [pp. 16–17 and 41]. There is a common tendency to accept the 'scientific' approach as the only one which is valid as a method of enquiry, not only in the physical sciences but also in such disciplines as sociology and history. The two separate meanings of the adjective 'scientific'—'accurate, knowledgeable and objective' and 'based on principles and methods of the physical sciences'—have become confused; so that it is often assumed that scientists have a monopoly of accuracy, and that those in other disciplines who aspire to accuracy must adapt the approach of the scientist as closely as possible. But the 'scientific' approach is, in fact, no more accurate than any other: reality is more than a series of isolated inanimate phenomena. The invisible affective properties of objects, and relationships between them—which the 'scientific' eye considers irrelevant—are a vital part of reality, and should be taken into account. The scientific attitude, in fact, when applied to human affairs, distorts reality by ignoring this important aspect of it; the 'artistic' attitude can claim to be more accurate because it is more comprehensive, and thus more able to cope with the complexity of human life (there is room in a novel for the presentation of, among others, 'scientific' viewpoints; but there appears to be no room in the work of modern 'social scientists' for the consideration of the 'artistic' viewpoint). Reality is composed of both 'facts' and 'connotations': a spade is both an object whose physical and chemical properties can be measured and a symbol of various human activities [p. 16]. The statement that it is exclusively one of these is false, and the argument whether 'scientific reality' or 'artistic reality' is the true reality is a false argument, which belongs more to the nineteenth than to the twentieth century. The ideal approach to social history, as to any other study of human activities, is the one which most fully combines the two approaches, which takes care of both qualitative and quantitative truth. The sources modern historians make most use of tend to make them show a quantitative bias in their work; the value of the literary approach is that it strengthens the qualitative side of historiography.

For the historian, then, the word 'literature' ought perhaps to signify rather more than just 'a collection of stories and legends about the past without meaning or significance' [p. xii]. No study of a past society can be complete without an informed and professional examination of its literature. This book will also, it is hoped, have shown that the converse is as true: that no study of a work of literature can be complete without a knowledge of the historical circumstances of its composition; and that the closer and more informed that knowledge can be made, the more fully will the work of literature be understood. The closer definition of the novel in terms of its exact relationship with society, which this book has attempted, provides new insight not only into society but also into the novel itself. The methodology of this study, although it was principally designed to elucidate problems of the social history of the Mexican Revolution, has also thrown new light upon the novels of the Revolution themselves. The historian is necessary to the literary critic, just as the literary critic is necessary to the historian. Their two separate disciplines complement each other fully. It is hoped that in this book their close interdependence will, in some measure at least, have been demonstrated.

BIBLIOGRAPHY

A. NOVELS

The novels of the Mexican Revolution that are used as sources in the above study are listed in Chapter 3, pp. 71–2. Others of importance are mentioned in the course of the book. A full list of novels of the Revolution will be found in my *Annotated Bibliography of Novels of the Mexican Revolution* (New York, 1971).

B. OTHER WORKS

ABC (Madrid daily), 1910–16.

ABREU GÓMEZ, ERMILO, 'La tragedia de la literatura revolucionaria', *El Nacional*, 4 Sept. 1937.

ACERETO, ALBINO, *El General Obregón a través de sus discursos*, Mexico, 1920.

ACEVEDO ESCOBEDO, ANTONIO, 'Alusiones a la literatura de la Revolución mexicana', *El Nacional*, 17 Nov. 1935.

ADAMS, RICHARD N., 'Political Power and Social Structures', in *The Politics of Conformity in Latin America*, ed. Véliz, Oxford University Press, 1967, 15–42.

AGUILAR, RAFAEL, *Madero sin máscara*, Mexico, 1911.

ALLOTT, MIRIAM, *Novelists on the Novel*, London, 1960.

ALVARADO, SALVADOR, *Mi actuación revolucionaria en Yucatán*, Paris and Mexico, 1918.

AMADO, ENRIQUE, *La revolución mexicana de 1913*, Madrid, 1914.

AMAYA C., LUIS FERNANDO, *La soberana convención revolucionaria, 1914–1916*, Mexico, 1966.

Apuntes para la historia. La cuestión religiosa en Jalisco, Mexico, 1918.

ARAQUISTAÍN, LUIS, *La revolución mejicana: sus orígenes, sus hombres, su obra*, Madrid, n.d.

ARENAS GUZMÁN, DIEGO (Genaro Saide), *El por qué del conflicto*, Mexico, 1912.

—, *Prensa y tribuna revolucionaria*, Mexico, 1916.

ARENDT, HANNAH, *On Revolution*, London, 1963.

AUB, MAX, *Guía de narradores de la Revolución Mexicana*, Mexico, 1969.

AZUELA, MARIANO, 'La novela de la Revolución mexicana', *El Universal Ilustrado*, 22 Jan. 1925.

—, *Obras completas*, 3 vols., Mexico, 1958.

322 BIBLIOGRAPHY

BAERLAIN, HENRY, *Mexico, the Land of Unrest*, Philadelphia, 1914.
BARRERA FUENTES, FEDERICO, 'Las novelas de la Revolución', *El Universal*, 8 Mar. 1934.
BENÍTEZ, JOSÉ MARÍA, 'Los escritores de la Revolución', *Crisol*, Aug. 1929, 109–10.
BLANQUET, AURELIANO, *Proclama a los miembros del antiguo ejército federal mexicano*, Veracruz, 1919.
BRINTON, CRANE, *The Anatomy of Revolution*, London, 1953.
BRUSHWOOD, JOHN S., *Mexico in its Novel*, Austin, Texas, 1966.
CABRERA, LUIS, *La cuestión religiosa en México*, New York, 1915.
—, *El pensamiento de Luis Cabrera*, ed. Eduardo Luquín, Mexico, 1960.
—, *Obras políticas de Blas Urrea*, Mexico, 1921.
CALOCA LARIOS, PEDRO, *La Revolución en Zacatecas*, Mexico, 1930.
CALVERT, PETER, *The Mexican Revolution, 1910–1914: the Diplomacy of Anglo-American Conflict*, Cambridge, 1968.
CAMMETT, JOHN M., *Antonio Gramsci and the Origins of Italian Communism*, Stanford, 1967.
CAMPA, DAVID L., 'The Mexican Revolution as Interpreted in the Mexican Novel', Ph.D. thesis, California, 1941.
CARDOZA Y ARAGON, L., *Orozco*, Mexico, 1959.
CARLETON MILLÁN, VERNA, 'The Literary Scene in Mexico', *Mexican Life*, Mar. 1938.
CARR, E. H., *What is History?*, 2nd edn., Harmondsworth, 1964.
CASASOLA, GUSTAVO, ed., *Historia gráfica de la Revolución mexicana, 1900–1960*, 4 volumes, Mexico, 1964.
CASTELLANOS, LUIS ARTURO, *La novela de la Revolución mexicana*, Rosario, Argentina, 1968.
CASTILLO, JOSÉ R. DEL, *Historia de la revolución social de México*, Mexico, 1915.
CASTILLO Y PIÑA, DR. JOSÉ, *Cuestiones sociales*, Mexico, 1934.
CASTRO LEAL, ANTONIO, ed., *La novela de la Revolución mexicana*, Madrid, Mexico, Buenos Aires, 1960.
CHEVALIER, FRANÇOIS, 'Un facteur décisif de la révolution agraire au Mexique: le soulèvement de Zapata, 1911–1919', *Annales*, XVI (1961), 66–82.
CLELAND, ROBERT GLASS, ed., *Mexican Year-Book 1920–21*, Los Angeles, 1922.
CLENENDEN, CLARENCE C., *The United States and Pancho Villa*, New York, 1961.
CLINE, HOWARD F., *The United States and Mexico*, Harvard, 1953.
COLLINGWOOD, R. G., *Speculum Mentis*, Oxford University Press, 1924.
COSÍO VILLEGAS, DANIEL, ed., *Historia moderna de México. El Porfiriato: la vida social*, Mexico, 1957.

—, *Historia moderna de Mexico. El Porfiriato: la vida económica*, 2 vols., Mexico, 1965.

CUMBERLAND, CHARLES CURTIS, *Mexican Revolution: Genesis under Madero*, Austin, Texas, 1952.

DÁVALOS, MARCELINO, *Carne de cañón*, Mexico, 1915.

DAVIES, JAMES C., 'Toward a Theory of Revolution', *American Sociological Review*, XXVII (1962), 5–19.

DELGADO, RAFAEL, *La calandria*, Mexico, 1891.

—, *Los parientas ricos*, Mexico, 1903.

El Diario (Mexico City daily), 1910–14.

Diario del Hogar (Mexico City daily), 1910–12.

DÍEZ CANEDO, E., 'Los de abajo', *El Sol* (Madrid), 3 Sept. 1926.

DI TELLA, TORCUATO S., 'Populism and Reform in Latin America', *Obstacles to Change in Latin America*, ed. Véliz, Oxford University Press, 1965, 47–74.

DRESEL, GUSTAVO, *Un nuevo sermón de la montaña*, Mexico, 1913.

ECKSTEIN, HARRY, 'On the Etiology of Internal Wars', *History and Theory*, IV, 2 (1965), 133–63.

EDWARDS, LYFORD P., *The Natural History of Revolution*, Chicago, 1927.

EISENSTADT, S. N., 'Bureaucracy and Bureaucratization', *Current Sociology*, VII, 2 (1958), 99–163.

FABELA, ISIDRO AND FABELA, JOSEFINA DE, eds., *Documentos históricos de la Revolución mexicana*, vols I–XIII, Mexico, 1960–8.

FERNÁNDEZ GÜELL, ROGELIO, *El moderno Juárez*, Mexico, 1911.

—, *Episodios de la revolución mexicana*, San José, Costa Rica, 1914.

FINER, S. E., *The Man on Horseback: the Role of the Military in Politics*, London, 1962.

FISCHER, ERNST, *The Necessity of Art*, Harmondsworth, 1963.

FLOWER, ELIZABETH, 'The Mexican Revolt against Positivism', in *Journal of the History of Ideas*, X (1949), 115–29.

FORSTER, E. M., *Aspects of the Novel*, 2nd edn., Harmondsworth, 1962.

FRANK, ANDREW GUNDER, 'Mexico: the Janus Faces of Twentieth-Century Bourgeois Revolution', *Whither Latin America?*, ed. Sweezy and Huberman, New York, 1963, 72–90.

FRÍAS, HERIBERTO, *Tomóchic*, Mexico, 1892.

FUENTES, CARLOS, *La muerte de Artemio Cruz*, Mexico, 1962.

GARIBAY K., ANGEL MARÍA (Director), *Diccionario Porrúa de Historia, Biografía y Geografía de México*, 2nd edn., Mexico, 1965.

Gil Blas (Mexico City daily), 1910–14.

GIMÉNEZ CABALLERO, E., 'Un gran romance mejicano', *Gaceta Literaria* (Madrid), Jan. 1927.

GONZÁLEZ, MANUEL PEDRO, *Trayectoria de la novela en México*, Mexico, 1951.

González Garza, Roque, Ramos Romero, P., and Pérez Rul, J., *La batalla de Torreón*, Mexico, n.d. (1914?).

González Navarro, Moisés, 'Mexico: the Lop-Sided Revolution', *Obstacles to Change in Latin America*, ed. Véliz, Oxford University Press, 1965, 206–29.

González Ramírez, Manuel, *La Revolución social de México. I: Las ideas, la violencia*, Mexico, 1960.

—, ed., *Fuentes para la historia de la Revolución mexicana. I: Planes políticos y otros documentos*, Mexico, 1954.

—, *Fuentes para la historia de la Revolución mexicana. II: La caricatura política*, Mexico, 1955.

Gramsci, Antonio, *Gli intellettuali e l'organizzazione della cultura*, 3rd edn., Turin, 1949.

—, *The Modern Prince and Other Writings*, London, 1957.

Grattan, C. H., ed., *The Critique of Humanism*, New York, 1930.

Greene, Graham, *The Lawless Roads*, London, New York, Toronto, 1939.

Gruening, Ernest, *Mexico and its Heritage*, London, 1928.

Guzmán, Daniel de, *México épico*, Mexico, 1962.

Guzmán, Martín Luis, *La querella de México*, Madrid, 1915.

Hauser, Arnold, *The Social History of Art*, London, 1962.

Hennessy, Alistair, 'University Students in National Politics', *The Politics of Conformity in Latin America*, ed. Véliz, Oxford University Press, 1967, 119–57.

Hernández, Julia, *Novelistas y cuentistas de la Revolución*, Mexico, 1960.

Herrerías, Ignacio, *En el campo revolucionario*, Chihuahua, 1911.

Hobsbawm, E. J., *Primitive Rebels*, Manchester University Press, 1959.

Hodges, H. A., *Wilhelm Dilthey, an Introduction*, London, 1944.

Hoggart, Richard, *Speaking to Each Other: II. About Literature*, London, 1970.

La Iberia (Mexico City daily), 1910–11.

Icaza y López Negrete, Xavier, *La Revolución mexicana y la literatura*, Mexico, 1934.

Iguíniz, Juan B., *Bibliografía de novelistas mexicanos*, Mexico, 1926.

—, *Bibliografía biográfica mexicana*, Mexico, 1930.

El Imparcial (Mexico City daily), 1910–14.

El Independiente (Mexico City daily), 1914.

Jiménez Rueda, Julio, 'El afeminamiento en la literatura mexicana', *El Universal*, 20 Dec. 1924.

—, 'El decaimiento de la literatura mexicana', *El Universal*, 17 Jan. 1925.

Johnson, Chalmers, *Revolution and the Social System*, Stanford, 1964.

Johnson, John J., *Political Change in Latin America: the Emergence of the Middle Sector*, Stanford, 1958.

—, *The Military and Society in Latin America*, Stanford, 1964.

KOHN-BRAMSTEDT, ERNST, *Aristocracy and the Middle Classes in Germany*, London, 1937.

LAWRENCE, D. H., *The Plumed Serpent*, Harmondsworth, 1961.

—, *Mornings in Mexico*, Harmondsworth, 1967.

LEAL, LUIS, *Azuela: vida y obra*, Mexico, 1961.

LEAVIS, F. R., *The Common Pursuit*, 2nd edn., Harmondsworth, 1962.

El Liberal (Madrid daily), 1910–16.

LEWIS, OSCAR, *Pedro Martínez. A Mexican Peasant and his Family*, New York, 1964.

LIEUWEN, EDWIN, *Arms and Politics in Latin America*, 3rd edn., London, 1963.

LIMANTOUR, JOSÉ YVES, *Apuntes sobre mi vida política*, Mexico, 1965.

LIND, JOHN, *La gente de México*, Veracruz, 1915.

LIST ARZUBIDE, ARMANDO, *Apuntes sobre la prehistoria de la Revolución*, Mexico, 1958.

LÓPEZ, ALFONSO E., *El interinato del General Victoriano Huerta: efemérides y sucesos sensacionales*, Mexico, 1913.

LÓPEZ ITUARTE, ALFONSO, *Las últimas revoluciones*, Mexico, 1911.

—, *Félix Díaz en Veracruz*, Mexico, 1912.

—, *La angustia nacional en 16 meses del gobierno de don Francisco I. Madero*, Mexico, n.d. (1913?).

LÓPEZ SALINAS, SAMUEL, *La batalla de Zacatecas*, Mexico, 1964.

LORIA, FRANCISCO, *Lo que significa nuestra revolución y manera de atender a las necesidades del pueblo*, Mexico, 1916.

LOYO, JORGE, '¿Con qué escriben nuestros autores?', *El Universal Ilustrado*, 11 Jan. 1925.

LUBBOCK, PERCY, *The Craft of Fiction*, 3rd edn, London, 1965.

LUKACS, GEORGE, *Studies in European Realism*, London, 1950.

—, *Sociología de la literatura*, Madrid, 1966.

'Un maderista decepcionado (léase avergonzado)', *El maderismo en cueros*, Havana, 1913.

MADERO, FRANCISCO I., *La sucesión presidencial en 1910*, Coahuila, 1908.

MAGAÑA ESQUIVEL, ANTONIO, *La novela de la Revolución mexicana*, 2 vols, Mexico, 1964–5.

El Mañana (Mexico City daily), 1911–12.

MARÍA Y CAMPOS, ARMANDO, *El teatro de género chico en la Revolución mexicana*, Mexico, 1956.

—, *El teatro de género dramático en la Revolución mexicana*, Mexico, 1957.

—, *Episodios de la Revolución: primera serie*, Mexico, 1958.

—, *Episodios de la Revolución: segunda serie*, Mexico, 1962.

—, *La Revolución mexicana a través de los corridos populares*, 2 vols, Mexico, 1962.

MARTÍNEZ, JOSÉ LUIS, *Literatura mexicana siglo veinte*, 2 vols, Mexico, 1949.

MARTÍNEZ LAVALLE, ARNULFO, 'La verdadera novela revolucionaria', *Crisol*, Feb. 1932, 111–15.

MARTÍNEZ VELADEZ, MANUEL, '¿Existe una literatura mexicana moderna?', *El Universal Ilustrado*, 2 Apr. 1925.

MECHAM, J. LLOYD, *Church and State in Latin America: a History of Politico-Ecclesiastical Relations*, 2nd edn, Chapel Hill, 1966.

MELGAREJO, ANTONIO N., *Crímenes del zapatismo*, Mexico, 1913.

MELLADO, GUILLERMO, *Crímenes del huertismo*, Mexico, n.d.

Memoria histórica de las labores de la asociación de damas católicas de Guadalajara, Guadalajara, 1920.

MENDIETA ALATORRE, ANGELES, *La mujer en la Revolución mexicana*, Mexico, 1961.

MENDIETA Y NÚÑEZ, LUCIO, *Teoría de la revolución*, Mexico, 1959.

—, *Sociología de la burocracia*, Mexico, 1961.

MENDOZA, VICENTE T., *Romance y corrido*, Mexico, 1939.

—, *El corrido de la Revolución mexicana*, Mexico, 1956.

—, *Lírica narrativa de México: el corrido*, Mexico, 1964.

'Un mexicano patriota', *Sangre mexicana—o—México para los mexicanos*, Mexico, n.d. (1913?).

Mexico, *Boletín de la Secretaría de Educación Pública*, Mexico, 1922–5.

—, *Diario de los debates del Congreso Constituyente*, 2 vols., Mexico, 1960.

—, *La educación pública en México*, Mexico, 1922.

—, *El Libro y el Pueblo*, Mexico, 1922–6.

The Mexican Herald (Mexico City daily), 1910–15.

MILLÁN, MARÍA DEL CARMEN, 'La generación del Ateneo y el ensayo mexicano', *Nueva Revista de Filología Hispánica*, XV (1961), 625–36.

MOLINA ENRÍQUEZ, ANDRÉS, *Los grandes problemas nacionales*, 2nd edn., Mexico, 1964.

—, *Esbozo de la historia de los primeros diez anos de la Revolución agraria de México (de 1910 a 1920)*, 5 vols., Mexico, 1932–6.

MONTERDE, FRANCISCO, 'Existe una literatura mexicana viril', *El Universal*, 25 Dec. 1924.

—, 'Críticos en receso y escritores desesperanzados', *El Universal*, 13 Jan. 1925.

—, 'Los de arriba y "Los de abajo"', *El Universal*, 2 Feb. 1925.

MOORE, ERNEST R., *Bibliografía de novelistas de la Revolución mexicana*, Mexico, 1941.

MORA Y DEL RÍO, JOSÉ, *Carta pastoral sobre la actual persecución religiosa*, Mexico, 1914.

MORTON, F. RAND, *Los novelistas de la Revolución mexicana*, Mexico, 1949.

MUIR, EDWIN, *The Structure of the Novel*, London, 1928.

MURILLO, GERARDO (DR. ATL), *Las artes populares en México*, 2 vols., 2nd edn., Mexico, 1922.

La Nación (Mexico City daily), 1912–13.

NARANJO, FRANCISCO, *Diccionario biográfico revolucionario*, Mexico, 1935.

NAVARRO, JOAQUINA, *La novela realista mexicana*, Mexico, 1955.

NORIEGA HOPE, CARLOS, 'Mariano Azuela', *El Universal Ilustrado*, 29 Jan. 1925

—, '*Los de abajo*, el doctor Mariano Azuela y la crítica del punto y coma', *El Universal*, 10 Feb. 1925.

NOVO, SALVADOR, 'Algunas verdades acerca de la literatura mexicana actual', *El Universal Ilustrado*, 19 Feb. 1925.

Nueva Era (Mexico City daily), 1911–13.

NUN, JOSÉ, 'The Middle-Class Military Coup', *The Politics of Conformity in Latin America*, ed. Véliz, Oxford University Press, 1967, 66–118.

OLSON, M., 'Rapid Growth as a Destabilizing Force', *Journal of Economic History*, XXIII (1963), 529–52.

La Opinión (Mexico City daily), 1914–15.

OROZCO Y JIMÉNEZ, FRANCISCO, *Carta pastoral*, Rome, 1916.

—, *Memorándum del Arzobispo de Guadalajara*, 1917.

ORTEGA, GREGORIO (JOSÉ CORRAL RIGAN), 'La influencia de la Revolución en nuestra literatura', *El Universal Ilustrado*, 20 Nov. 1924.

—, 'El protagonista de *Los de abajo*', *El Universal Ilustrado*, 15 Sept. 1927.

—, 'Azuela dijo . . .', *El Universal Ilustrado*, 27 Mar. 1930.

—, 'Recordando a Mariano Azuela', *El Universal Ilustrado*, 30 Nov. 1930.

—, 'Los que lucharon en la Revolución, los que la expresaron en el arte', *El Heraldo Dominical*, 18 Nov. 1934.

O'SHAUGHNESSY, EDITH, *A Diplomat's Wife in Mexico*, New York and London, 1916.

El País (Mexico City daily), 1910–14.

PALLARES, EDUARDO, *La inmoralidad de la prensa*, Mexico, 1913.

PARKES, H. B., *A History of Mexico*, 3rd edn., London, 1962.

PARRA, GONZALO DE LA, *De cómo se hizo revolucionario un hombre de buena fe*, Mexico, 1915.

PAZ, OCTAVIO, *El laberinto de la soledad*, 4th edn., Mexico, 1964.

PETTEE, GEORGE SAWYER, *The Process of Revolution*, New York, 1938.

El Pueblo (Mexico City daily), 1914–16.

PUIG CASAURANC, JOSÉ MANUEL, *El sentido social del proceso histórico de México*, Mexico, 1936.

QUIRK, ROBERT, *An Affair of Honor: Woodrow Wilson and the Occupation of Veracruz*, University of Kentucky Press, 1962.

QUIRK, ROBERT, *The Mexican Revolution, 1914–1915: The Convention of Aguascalientes*, New York, 1963.

RABASA, EMILIO, *La bola*, Mexico, 1887–8.

RAMÍREZ PLANCARTE, FRANCISCO, *La ciudad de México durante la Revolución constitucionalista*, 2nd edn., Mexico, 1941.

RAMOS, ROBERTO, *Bibliografía de la Revolución mexicana*, 2nd edn., 3 vols., Mexico, 1959–60.

RAMOS, RUTILIO, ALONSO, ISIDORO and GARRE, DOMINGO, *La iglesia en México*, Madrid, 1963.

RAMOS, SAMUEL, *El perfil del hombre y la cultura en México*, Mexico, 1934.

RAMOS PEDRUEZA, RAFAEL, *La lucha de clases a través de la historia de México*, Mexico, 1941.

REED, ALMA, *Orozco*, New York, 1956.

REED, JOHN, *Insurgent Mexico*, New York, 1914.

REED, NELSON, *The Caste War of Yucatan*, Stanford, 1964.

El reparto de tierra a los pobres no es pecado, Mexico, n.d. (1921?).

El resurgimiento mexicano, Mexico, 1913.

RIVERO, GONZALO G., *Hacia la verdad: episodios de la revolución*, Mexico, 1911.

ROJAS GONZÁLEZ, FRANCISCO, 'Sobre la literatura de la post-revolución', *Crisol*, May 1934.

ROSS, E. A., *The Social Revolution in Mexico*, New York and London, 1923.

ROSS, STANLEY R., *Francisco I. Madero, Apostle of Mexican Democracy*, New York, 1955.

SALADO ÁLVAREZ, VICTORIANO, '¿Existe una literatura mexicana moderna?', *El Excélsior*, 12 Jan. 1925

—, 'La literatura revolucionaria según Trotsky y la literatura revolucionaria mexicana', *El Excélsior*, 31 Jan. 1925.

—, 'Las obras del doctor Azuela', *El Excélsior*, 31 Jan. 1925.

SALAZAR, ROSENDO, *El balance social*, Mexico, 1918.

SÁNCHEZ, LUIS ALBERTO, *Proceso y contenido de la novela hispano-americana*, Madrid, 1953.

SÁNCHEZ AZCONA, JUAN, *La etapa maderista de la Revolución*, Mexico, 1960.

SÁNCHEZ ESCOBAR, RAFAEL, *Episodios de la Revolución mexicana en el sur*, Tlalpan, 1934.

SCHMECKEBIER, L. E., *Modern Mexican Art*, Minneapolis, 1939.

SERRANO, T. F., *Episodios de la revolución en México*, El Paso, Texas, 1911.

—, *¡El crimen del 22 de febrero!*, El Paso, Texas, 1913.

SESTO, JULIO, *El México de Porfirio Díaz*, Mexico, 1909.

SIERRA, CARLOS J., 'Zapata, señor de la tierra, capitán de los labriegos',

Boletín biobibliográfico de la Secretaría de Hacienda y Crédito Público, Suplemento al no. 361 (15 Feb. 1967).
SILVA HERZOG, JESÚS, *Breve historia de la Revolución mexicana*, 3rd edn., 2 vols., Mexico, 1964.
SIMMONS, MERLE E., *The Mexican Corrido as a Source for Interpretive Study of Modern Mexico (1870–1950)*, Indiana University Press, 1957.
SIMPSON, LESLEY BYRD, *Many Mexicos*, 3rd edn., University of California, 1962.
SMITH, RANDOLPH WELLFORD, *Benighted Mexico*, New York, 1916.
SOMMERS, JOSEPH, *After the Storm: Landmarks of the Modern Mexican Novel*, University of New Mexico, 1968.
SOREL, GEORGES, *Reflections on Violence*, New York, 1967.
SOROKIN, P. A., *The Sociology of Revolution*, Philadelphia and London, 1925.
—, *Social and Cultural Dynamics*, 4 vols., New York, 1937–41.
—, *Man and Society in Calamity*, New York, 1943.
—, *Society, Culture and Personality*, New York and London, 1947.
SOTO, JESÚS S., 'Arte y revolución', *Crisol*, Dec. 1929.
STABB, MARTIN T., 'Indigenism and Racism in Mexican Thought: 1857–1911', *Journal of Inter-American Studies*, I. 4 (1959), 405–23.
STANTON, ELLEN RUTH, 'La novela de la Revolución mexicana: estudio relacionado con el movimiento literario y social', Ph.D. thesis, S. California, 1943.
STONE, LAWRENCE, '*Theories of Revolution*', in World Politics, XVIII, 2 (1966), 159–76.
TANNENBAUM, FRANK, *Peace by Revolution*, Columbia University Press, 1933.
—, *Mexico: the Struggle for Peace and Bread*, 2nd edn., London, 1965.
El Tiempo (Mexican City daily), 1910–12.
TORRES RIOSECO, ARTHUR, *Bibliografía de la novela mejicana*, Harvard University Press, 1933.
La Tribuna (Mexico City daily), 1913–14.
TURNER, FREDERICK C., *The Dynamic of Mexican Nationalism*, University of North Carolina Press, 1968.
TURNER, JOHN KENNETH, *México bárbaro*, Mexico, 1964.
TURRENT ROZAS, ARTURO, *Hacia una literatura proletaria*, Jalapa, 1932.
TWEEDIE, MRS ALEC, *Mexico as I saw it*, 2nd edn., London 1911.
UNITED STATES DEPARTMENT OF STATE, *Papers Relating to the Foreign Relations of the United States, 1911–16*, Washington, 1918–25.
URÍA SANTOS, MARÍA ROSA, 'El Ateneo de la Juventud: su influencia en la vida intelectual de Mexico', Ph.D. thesis, University of Florida, 1965.

VALENZUELA RODARTE, ALBERTO, *Historia de la literatura en México*, Mexico, 1961.

VASCONCELOS, JOSÉ, *Obras completas*, 4 vols., Mexico, 1957.

VÉLIZ, CLAUDIO, 'Introduction', *Obstacles to Change in Latin America*, ed. Véliz, Oxford University Press, 1965.

Los verdaderos acontecimientos en las campañas del norte, Mexico, n.d. (1915?).

WARREN, AUSTIN and WELLEK, RENE, *Theory of Literature*, 3rd edn., Harmondsworth, 1966.

WILLIAMS, GWYN A., 'The Concept of "Egemonia" in the Thought of Gramsci: Some Notes on Interpretation', *Journal of the History of Ideas*, XXI (1960), 586–99.

WILLIAMS, RAYMOND, *Culture and Society 1780–1950*, London, 1958.

WOLFE, B. D., *Diego Rivera*, London, 1939.

WOMACK, JOHN, JR., *Zapata and the Mexican Revolution*, New York, 1969.

ZEA, LEOPOLDO, *El positivismo en México*, Mexico, 1942.

ZUM FELDE, ARTURO, *La narrativa en Hispano-América*, Madrid, 1964.

INDEX

YM